Moritz Busch

Bismarck

Some secret pages of his history; being a diary kept by Dr. Moritz Busch during twenty-five years' official and private intercourse with the great chancellor, with portraits. Vol. 3

Moritz Busch

Bismarck

Some secret pages of his history; being a diary kept by Dr. Moritz Busch during twenty-five years' official and private intercourse with the great chancellor, with portraits. Vol. 3

ISBN/EAN: 9783337383794

Printed in Europe, USA, Canada, Australia, Japan

Cover: Foto ©ninafisch / pixelio.de

More available books at **www.hansebooks.com**

BISMARCK

SOME SECRET PAGES OF HIS HISTORY

BEING A DIARY KEPT BY

Dr. MORITZ BUSCH

DURING TWENTY-FIVE YEARS' OFFICIAL AND PRIVATE
INTERCOURSE WITH THE GREAT CHANCELLOR

IN THREE VOLUMES
VOL. III

London
MACMILLAN AND CO., Limited
NEW YORK: THE MACMILLAN COMPANY
1898

CONTENTS

CHAPTER I

BUCHER, COBDEN, AND THE MANCHESTER SCHOOL—BÜLOW AND THE COMTE DE JOLIVAR—THE HOLY DRUJINA—KEUDELL IN THE PROGRESSIST PRESS—FOUR SECRETARIES OF STATE IN THE FOREIGN OFFICE—KEUDELL AND HIS ARREARS OF WORK—THE CHIEF AND THE PROGRESSIST ELECTIONEERING AGITATION—LIES IN LAUENBURG—INSTRUCTIONS RESPECTING UNRUH'S ARTICLE IN THE "DEUSTCHE REVUE"—WHY BENNIGSEN WAS NOT MADE MINISTER—THE CHANCELLOR ON THILE AND THE DIEST LIBEL—BUCHER ON HOLSTEIN—BUNSEN'S FRIENDS AND TRUTH—A MONUMENT FOR MY SON, WHO DIED AT SEA—THILE'S OPINION OF THE CHIEF—THE CHANCELLOR ON THE EGYPTIAN QUESTION, THE OPPOSITION TO THE TOBACCO MONOPOLY—THE EMPEROR, THE CROWN PRINCE, AND PRINCE WILLIAM—PHILOPATER AND ANTIPATER AT POTSDAM—BUCHER TENDERS HIS RESIGNATION—THE CROWN PRINCE AND THE PROGRESSISTS—THE VICE-CHANCELLORSHIP—ARTICLES AGAINST THE EMPRESS 1

CHAPTER II

BLEICHRÖDER AND GERMAN DIPLOMACY IN CONSTANTINOPLE—FURTHER INTERVIEWS WITH THE CHANCELLOR—RELATIONS WITH RUSSIA AND AUSTRIA—THE GABLENTZ MISSION—QUEEN VICTORIA—AN UNPLEASANT EPISTLE—A SEVERE REPRIMAND—BISMARCK COLLABORATES WITH ME—BUCHER'S JOURNEY WITH SALAZAR—A PRESS CAMPAIGN AGAINST ENGLAND—DOCUMENTS AND ARTICLES ON SOUTH AFRICAN QUESTIONS 70

CHAPTER III

THE CHANCELLOR ON BULGARIA AND SERVIA, AUSTRIA AND RUSSIA, THE BATTENBERGER AND THE TSAR—HIS VIEW OF THE TREATMENT OF THE RUSSIAN BALTIC PROVINCES—A COMPARISON BETWEEN ENGLISH PARTIES AND OUR OWN—GERMANY AND ENGLAND IN AFRICA—THE CHANCELLOR ON THE MILITARY QUESTION, AND THE THREATENED CONFLICT IN THE REICHSTAG—WHAT HE SAID THERE WAS ADDRESSED TO RUSSIA—THE TSAR'S CONFIDENCE IN THE CHANCELLOR—THE CROWN PRINCE AND HIS CONSORT—BISMARCK AND HIS WORK—WHAT IS GREATNESS?—THE CHIEF ON HIS OWN DEATH—INTERVIEW WITH THE CHIEF ON THE MARRIAGE OF THE BATTENBERGER, AND INSTRUCTIONS FOR THE "GRENZBOTEN" ARTICLE, "FOREIGN INFLUENCES IN THE EMPIRE"—BEWARE OF THE PRESS LAWS—NOT TOO VENOMOUS—A SURVEY OF BRITISH POLICY—THE CATALOGUE OF ENGLAND'S SINS—TWO EMPRESSES AGAINST THE CHANCELLOR—QUEEN VICTORIA AT CHARLOTTENBURG —DEATH OF THE "INCUBUS" 147

CHAPTER IV

THE EMPEROR FREDERICK'S DIARY—THE CHIEF ON THE DIARY AND ITS AUTHOR—THE GERMAN QUESTION DURING THE WAR OF 1870—THE EMPEROR FREDERICK AND HIS LEANING TOWARDS ENGLAND—THE CHIEF PRAISES THE YOUNG EMPEROR—"BETTER TOO MUCH THAN TOO LITTLE FIRE!"—I AM TO ARRANGE THE CHIEF'S PAPERS, AND DO SO—LETTERS FROM FREDERICK-WILLIAM IV. AND FROM WILLIAM I.—CORRESPONDENCE WITH AND CONCERNING THE CROWN PRINCE (FREDERICK)—LETTERS TO AND FROM ANDRASSY DURING THE NEGOTIATIONS FOR THE AUSTRO-GERMAN ALLIANCE—LETTERS FROM THE EMPEROR ON THE SAME SUBJECT—WILLIAM I.'S RELUCTANCE TO DESERT RUSSIA—CONVERSATION BETWEEN THE EMPEROR AND THE TSAR AT ALEXANDROWO—WILLIAM I.'S FINAL INSTRUCTIONS— BISMARCK'S ACCOUNT OF HIS RELATIONS WITH THE EMPEROR FREDERICK 190

CHAPTER V

SIGNS OF FRICTION BETWEEN THE CHANCELLOR AND THE YOUNG EMPEROR —WITH THE CHIEF DURING THE CRISIS—HIS ANXIETY ABOUT HIS PAPERS—HOW TO GET THEM AWAY—HIS RETIREMENT A FACT—THE EMPEROR WANTS TO BE RID OF HIM IN ORDER TO GOVERN ALONE WITH HIS OWN GENIUS—COURT FLUNKEYISM—HIS RETIREMENT IS NOT DUE TO HIS HEALTH, NOR IS IT IN ANY SENSE VOLUNTARY— LETTERS FROM BISMARCK TO WILLIAM I.—THE CHIEF ON THE

INITIATION OF PRINCE WILLIAM INTO PUBLIC AFFAIRS—THE GRAND DUKE OF BADEN'S ADVICE TO THE EMPEROR FREDERICK—THE CHIEF TALKS OF WRITING HIS OWN MEMOIRS—BUREAUCRATIC INGRATITUDE —FOREIGN OFFICE APOSTATES—ACCORDING TO BUCHER THE NOTES DICTATED FOR THE MEMOIRS ARE MERE FRAGMENTS, SOMETIMES ERRONEOUS — THE CHIEF'S LIFE AT FRIEDRICHSRUH — SCHWENINGER'S APPREHENSIONS 305

CHAPTER VI

AM INVITED TO FRIEDRICHSRUH—BUCHER AND THE PROPOSED "MEMOIRS"—HE DOUBTS WHETHER THE LATTER WILL BE COMPLETED—THE CHIEF—"BÜSCHLEIN" AS BEFORE—THE ANGLO-GERMAN AGREEMENT—THE EMPEROR AND RUSSIA—THREE KINGS IN THEIR NAKEDNESS—BÜSCHLEIN WILL WRITE THE SECRET HISTORY OF OUR TIMES—THE PRINCE GIVES ME IMPORTANT PAPERS TO EXAMINE IN MY ROOM : HIS RESIGNATION IN 1890, A DRAFT OF A CONFIDENTIAL STATEMENT OF THE MOTIVES OF HIS RETIREMENT AND NOTES ON THE ATTITUDE OF THE INDIVIDUAL MINISTERS ON THAT OCCASION—STILL ANOTHER BOOK ON BISMARCK IN VIEW ; CORRESPONDENCE ON THE SUBJECT WITH BUCHER AND THE CHIEF HIMSELF ; THE PLAN DROPPED—LAST VISIT TO BUCHER IN JANUARY, 1892—HIS DEATH—LAST STAY AT FRIEDRICHSRUH IN MAY, 1893— "GOOD BYE, DEAR OLD FRIEND." 350

BISMARCK
SOME SECRET PAGES OF HIS HISTORY

CHAPTER I

BUCHER, COBDEN, AND THE MANCHESTER SCHOOL—BÜLOW AND THE COMTE DE JOLIVAR—THE HOLY DRUJINA—KEUDELL IN THE PROGRESSIST PRESS—FOUR SECRETARIES OF STATE IN THE FOREIGN OFFICE—KEUDELL AND HIS ARREARS OF WORK—THE CHIEF AND THE PROGRESSIST ELECTIONEERING AGITATION — LIES IN LAUENBURG — INSTRUCTIONS RESPECTING UNRUH'S ARTICLE IN THE "DEUTSCHE REVUE"—WHY BENNIGSEN WAS NOT MADE MINISTER—THE CHANCELLOR ON THILE AND THE DIEST LIBEL—BUCHER ON HOLSTEIN—BUNSEN'S FRIENDS AND TRUTH—A MONUMENT FOR MY SON, WHO DIED AT SEA—THILE'S OPINION OF THE CHIEF—THE CHANCELLOR ON THE EGYPTIAN QUESTION AND THE OPPOSITION TO THE TOBACCO MONOPOLY—THE EMPEROR, THE CROWN PRINCE AND PRINCE WILLIAM—PHILOPATER AND ANTIPATER AT POTSDAM — BUCHER TENDERS HIS RESIGNATION—THE CROWN PRINCE AND THE PROGRESSISTS—THE VICE-CHANCELLORSHIP — ARTICLES AGAINST THE EMPRESS

On the 10th of July, 1881, Bucher wrote me the following note in pencil:—

"The Chief is having articles written on the played-out Liberals in the Vienna Parliament, from which a moral is drawn for our own people. It would certainly amuse him to see Glaser's letter, a precious production, which you will find in the enclosed book, reprinted. What do you think of the idea?

"In a few days I shall send you a pamphlet on the Cobden Club (written by me, of course secret). I would suggest that it should not be discussed until after the silly season, somewhere about the beginning of September, when we must again hammer away at the subject. I shall then supply you with plenty of material. In the meantime, it may be well to collect together the abusive language to which the pamphlet has given rise.

"In eight or ten days I shall send you an article on the origin of the Anglo-French Treaty of Commerce, which may be published immediately.

"BR."

Glaser's letter appeared in a small pamphlet, entitled, *An Austrian Minister and his Father*, published in Berlin, 1872, by Kerskes and Hohmann. It contained the following passage: "Another year, and the Chosen People shall have attained the object of the Holy Alliance,[1] which they concluded in Paris. We have no more ardent desire than to see the day arrive when we can bid him (Prince Adolph Auersberg) good-bye, and see his place taken by one from our midst" (the Jewish Liberals); and "then" (when the aristocratic party is suspected by the dynasty, and has fallen out of favour) "a really new and regenerated nobility, drawn from our people" (the Jews) "shall enter into power, and fulfil the mission to which God has called them." I had this

[1] The *Alliance Israelite* is here referred to. Glaser, the ex-Minister of Justice, was a baptised Jew from Bohemia.

letter reproduced in the *Grenzboten*, with a few introductory remarks.

On the morning of the 11th of July I called upon Bucher, from whom I ascertained that he had collected the material for his pamphlet on the Cobden Club in the British Museum, about a fortnight previously. He had gone to London, under instructions from the Chief, giving a false name, and holding no intercourse with anybody.

On the 21st I called on Bucher at the Foreign Office, to remind him about the pamphlet and the proposed *Grenzboten* article. He had been unable to write the latter, as he could not obtain a book which he required for the purpose. (This was the *Principles of Currency*, a work by the Oxford Professor, Bonamy Price, which appeared in 1869.) He gave me his pamphlet, and a quantity of material for the article upon it, to which he made some additions during the following days. He also sent me a number of English and French publications, to be used for the same purpose. In the meantime, Glaser's letter was emphatically declared to be a forgery by Glaser himself. Bucher, however, still held it to be "genuine in the main."

I now wrote a series of five articles, entitled "Characteristics of the Manchester School," based on Bucher's pamphlet, and the notes and books with which he supplied me. These appeared in Nos. 33 to 37 of the *Grenzboten*.

On the 27th of July Bucher related to me "an anecdote illustrating the way in which the Secretary of State von Bülow carried on business." Lasker called upon him one day to introduce a Frenchman, one Comte de Jolivar, who was going to Constantinople, and wished to have a letter of introduction to our Embassy there.

Bülow had this letter prepared, and added in his own hand a few words of warm recommendation to Werther, who was our representative at the Porte at that time. The Comte proceeded on his journey with this document in his pocket, and one of the first things he did on his arrival at the Golden Horn was to swindle a German artisan out of a respectable sum of money. This was soon followed by similar operations, which speedily came to Werther's ears, who probably had already felt surprised at the Frenchman having asked for and received recommendations from the Foreign Office in Berlin, instead of from that in Paris, or from the French Minister in Berlin. He reported these cases of swindling to the Wilhelmstrasse, and from there inquiries were addressed to the Foreign Office in Paris. The information received was to the following effect. Comte de Jolivar is not a Comte, but only a Chevalier, that is to say, *chevalier d'industrie*, who—as the police records show—has been condemned on several occasions for embezzlement and swindling, and was once prosecuted for forgery, but just managed to save his skin. "*Tableau*" in the office of our Secretary of State!

Bucher praised Hatzfeldt, who has entered upon the duties of his office in succession to Bülow, as a pleasant and easy chief. Speaking of Bunsen, Bucher said that he had written for the Secessionist *Tribune*. Bucher also referred to the controversy which he had recently fought out with Bunsen, in the columns of the *Norddeutsche Allgemeine Zeitung*.

On the 29th of July I received the following note from Bucher :—

"1. Can you get the enclosed inserted in the *Daily Telegraph*, or some other English newspaper, and send the Chief a copy ?

"2. Herewith the draft of an article on the commercial treaty, of which you must alter the introduction. The second edition of Bonamy Price which I have received from Baden (whence he also obtained the *Sophisms of Free Trade*, which he sent me for the 'Characteristics of the Manchester School') does not contain the letter from Chevalier. I have instructed Ascher to get the first edition at my expense, and to forward it to you. "Yours, BR."

The enclosure mentioned in paragraph 1 ran as follows :—

" It appears that a secret society has been formed in Russia, by a number of determined and loyal subjects of the Tsar, which is understood to be organised on the same lines as the associations founded for the purpose of assassinating him. This new society purposes to fight the Nihilists with their own weapons. Like the latter, who seek to terrorise the sovereign by attempts upon his life, the new society which has been constituted to oppose these criminals, will endeavour to keep them in check by hunting out and killing the chiefs of the band of assassins in Switzerland and England. It is a regrettable circumstance that honourable men in Russia should be obliged to resort to a kind of mediæval *Vehmgericht* as a means of protecting the monarch from these miserable cut-throats."

On the morning of the 30th I forwarded this paragraph to the *Daily Telegraph*, stating that it came from the "very best source," and adding that I should be thankful for its insertion. On the 31st, however, I received the following note from Bucher : " Herbert has just telegraphed to me to hold back the paragraph on the Anti-Nihilistic society for the present. Luckily

Sunday has intervened. Will you please countermand it by telegraph, and charge me with the costs?" I accordingly telegraphed to London, and the paragraph did not appear.

The second enclosure was worked up for the *Grenzboten*, and published in No. 32, under the title of "The Genesis of the Anglo-French Commercial Treaty." It was completed by an extract from Chevalier's letter, which was published by the *Pall Mall Gazette*.

In the meantime, on the 30th, I received the following note from Bucher: "As your articles on the Manchester School in the *Grenzboten* will one day form material for the historian, I would suggest that after the reference to Schlesinger and his association with the Treasury, you should insert the words: 'since the Macdonald affair at Bonn.' I will give you the particulars for your memoirs. They are very curious."

Bucher left for his holidays on the 1st of August.

On the 14th of September Bucher wrote to me that he was in Berlin, and on the 21st I called upon him. He told me that the Chief had again had "difficulties with the Emperor." The latter now reads no more newspapers. Recently, however, some courtier must have called his attention to a paragraph which he represented to come from the *Norddeutsche Allgemeine Zeitung*, to the effect that a Papal Nunciature was to be established in Berlin. The Emperor thereupon wrote the Chief a "snappish letter" which commenced somewhat in the style of Zwückanör (one of the comic figures in the *Kladderadatsch*) : "I am much surprised." The Chancellor first sent a short telegram, saying that he knew nothing of any such paragraph in the newspaper in question (which had contained nothing of the kind), and afterwards forwarded a memorandum on the subject, which filled three sheets of paper. "He was greatly incensed at the action of the Most Gracious." Tiedemann, who has now been definitively replaced by Rottenburg, goes in the first place to Bromberg, in the capacity of *Regierungspräsident*, and not, as he had desired, and expected, to Kassel as *Oberpräsident*. The mention of Keudell in the first *Grenzboten* article on the Manchester School, which has been described by the Progressist press as a "violent attack," has led that gentleman to state in the *Morning Post* that he had requested the President of the Cobden Club to remove his name from the list of members. He at the same time endeavoured to defend himself in Progressist journals, like the *Vossische Zeitung* and the *Berliner Tageblatt*, concluding, as usual, with self-praise. Bucher remarked: "These almost identic articles are written by himself. Only his signature at foot is wanting." These productions were forwarded to the Chancellor at Varzin, who thereupon had the following statement published in the *Norddeutsche Allgemeine Zeitung*:—

"The *Berliner Tageblatt*, the *Schlesische Zeitung* and the *Vossische Zeitung* publish articles respecting Herr von Keudell which are similar in effect, and which all conclude with the phrase that owing to his retirement from the Cobden Club the valuable services of the German Ambassador in Rome still remain secured to the State.

"It requires that complete ignorance of the customs prevailing in the service of the State, and particularly in diplomacy, and of the habits of the higher circles which distinguishes Progressist writers, for any one to imagine that an Ambassador's position could ever be endangered by a matter of such trifling importance as the circumstance that he had been nominated an honorary member of the Cobden Club six or more years ago. We are in a position to assure our readers that the matter has never been taken into consideration either officially or confidentially at the Foreign Office, nor has it ever called for any inquiry or exchange of views. The whole story as to the position of Herr von Keudell being in the least affected by that circumstance is simply an invention of Progressist writers, suffering from a dearth of 'copy.'

"We are not aware whether Herr von Keudell has resigned his honorary membership. If such be the case he will probably have been led to take that step by recent disclosures respecting the Cobden Club. So far as his relations to the Imperial service and the Imperial Chancellor are concerned, however, it is a matter of indifference whether this purely private step has been taken or not. That Progressist journalists believe the contrary is the consequence in part of their ignorance as to the relations existing between respectable people, and in part of their own sentiments, *i.e.*, of the furious rancour with which these partisan writers exaggerate and garble the most insignificant incidents. They assume that an equal degree of malice and violence prevails in circles to which they have no access. In short, they are partisans who are accustomed to treat with hatred and contempt every shade of difference from the party standard. In their eyes whoever is not a free-trader is either a knave or a fool. This is natural enough in those whose sole claim to honesty and intelligence is that they are free-traders. It is not so in higher circles, where there is more toleration, and less time for matters of secondary importance.

"The Imperial Ambassador, moreover, can hardly

care, we believe, to find unauthorised representatives and advocates in just such papers as the *Berliner Tageblatt* and the *Vossische Zeitung*. No one who does not belong to the political and social circles represented by these papers would willingly be credited with any connections with them, and this is doubtless sufficiently well-known in Rome for any such connection to be shunned, and for such damaging advocacy to be duly repudiated."

On the morning of the 25th of October I paid Bucher a visit at his lodgings. He complained that the Chief now occupied himself too much with press matters. Instructions of this description came from Varzin almost daily, and sometimes three or four together. No one in the office understood anything about them, neither the sons, nor Rantzau (who was paid for that purpose, but who, nevertheless, could only take down dictation from the Chief), nor Holstein, who was a mere " bungler," and least of all Rudolph Lindau, who " is quite incapable, has had no political or journalistic training, and can merely play the amiable, tell good stories and go out walking." He had been brought into the Office by family influence, which also kept him there. "In Japan he made the acquaintance of Brandt, our Chargé d'Affaires, through whom he obtained a connection with the Intelligence Department of the general staff. He afterwards (if I rightly understood) accompanied Brandt to St. Petersburg, where he was presented to the Grand Duchess Hélène, who recommended him to Bismarck. The latter sent him to Harry Arnim in Paris as a Press Attaché. He afterwards received an appointment at the Foreign Office—again on an exalted recommendation. The Prince knows that he is entirely unfit for the duties which he has to perform, but the Grand

Duchess protects him; and so, although he has been virtually shelved, it has been done in such a way that he appears to have control of press affairs."

Bucher said that Count Bill is on very intimate terms with Paul Lindau . . . with whom he had been in Hungary. Herbert had yesterday, on the instructions of his father, written Bucher a four-page letter, which he showed me, asking him, Bucher, to make a "journalistic onslaught" upon the Progressist candidate Klotz on account of his election speech. Rantzau, however, had been unable to obtain the most indispensable of essentials, namely Klotz's speech, and, in fact, knew nothing whatever about it. One of the Chancery attendants, however, was cleverer, and remembered that it had been printed in pamphlet form and distributed by the thousand. This man arranged to procure a copy.

"Sybel is another plague with which the Chancellor has afflicted me," continued Bucher. "It is not so long since Sybel was fighting against the Chief; but he has now been taken once more into favour, and is to write a history of Germany from 1860 to 1870." For this purpose the Chief had at first ordered that *all* diplomatic documents of this period should be laid before him. Bucher, however, pointed out that it would be necessary to make certain exceptions, some of which he mentioned, including those concerning the Hungarian Legion. The Prince agreed to this, and arranged that the documents mentioned by Bucher, as also the "Secreta," should not be shown to Sybel. The latter is now carrying on his researches at the Foreign Office, which Bucher does not regard as dangerous. He has come upon references to the documents that have been withheld from him, and has asked to see them, stating that he would anyhow have possession of them some day as Director of the State Archives. Bucher was, however, obliged to refuse his request. He complained of the responsibility imposed upon him in this matter.

He then went on to say that it was much the same with one Herr Poschinger, a Bavarian, who had taken it upon himself to describe Bismarck's work as Envoy to the Germanic Diet in Frankfurt. The Chief had given instructions that he was to see everything relating to this period in the first and second departments of the Foreign Office. Poschinger plunged into these, and then sent his *opus* to the Prince for revision. The Chief did not care to read it, and instructed Bucher to do so. "I then found that it was merely an endless string of extracts, and not a book but only materials for a book; and that while he dwelt discursively on insignificant details, he cursorily dismissed or overlooked altogether matters of real importance." That was pointed out to Poschinger, who revised his work in accordance with the suggestions made to him, abbreviating some parts and amplifying others, and then returned it to the Chief, who again forwarded it to Bucher. "It was now better material," continued the latter, "but it was still no book. I reported to the Chief in this sense, and he gave instructions to obtain Sybel's opinion on it. His agreed in the main with my own, but Poschinger discovered that Sybel had criticised him."

Bucher thought that the visit which the newspapers reported Gambetta to have paid to Varzin about ten days ago was possible, and indeed probable. He declared, on the other hand, that the discovery, made by the *National Zeitung*, that this visit took place at Friedrichsruh, was unfounded, because the Chief was at that time suffering from severe pain in the back, which made it impossible for him to travel. "I do not like to make inquiries on the subject," he said, "and I therefore know nothing positive about it. We should have reason to be thankful, however, if the visit took place, as it would make Gambetta impossible in France."

October 28*th*.—Met his Excellency von Thile to-day in the Potsdamer Platz. We first spoke about the elections. Thile had formerly abstained from voting, but this time—like Bucher and myself—had voted for Stöcker. He then asked what I thought of the report that Gambetta had visited the Chancellor. I replied that it appeared to me to be possible, and indeed probable. "I will tell you something," he said. "One of my acquaintances was recently at Frankfurt, where he put up at the 'Russischer Hof'—you know, 'Auf der Zeil.' In conversation with the landlord, with whom he was acquainted, he asked whether there was any news. 'Yes, and something of importance, Excellency,' replied the latter. Gambetta was here recently on his way home from Germany, and lodged with us. The head waiter asked his servant where they had been, and the man replied: '*Nous avons été à la campagne dans les environs de Danzig.*'"

November 9*th*.—Called this morning upon Bucher at his lodgings to inquire about the article in yesterday's *Post* stating that the Chancellor proposed to resign. I fancied the article came from Varzin, and was intended to prepare for a dissolution of the Reichstag, and to give the country an opportunity to choose at the elections between the Chief and the Liberals. According to Bucher, no one would believe that a general election would induce him to retire, and as to the dissolution of the Reichstag, that could only take place

if it perpetrated some piece of stupidity. The article was purposeless, merely an expression of ill-humour at Varzin, which Herbert, " with his usual ineptitude," had made public. " But they have been in the backwoods for half a year, and do not know what is going on in the world. The elections would have turned out better in many respects if the press campaign had not been so foolishly conducted. But these things are shockingly ill-managed at present. We have now no less than four Secretaries of State : Busch, the real one, who is good ; then Herbert at Varzin ; and Rantzau and Holstein here. These know nothing, and are incapable of doing anything properly. None of them reads the papers or knows what is going on, and if the Chief gives violent instructions they are carried out with still greater violence. It is sad that the Chief should think so much of providing for his family and finding places for them. Virchow was right when he brought that charge against him. And the other gentlemen are no better. In addition to the Secretaries of State we have the gentlemen who spend their time strolling about, and who are more often to be found out shooting than in their office." He then mentioned two, including Radolinski, ... and added : " After all it was just the same formerly, when, in addition to Thile, there were only two who really worked, yourself and Abeken. Hepke had hardly anything but trifles to deal with, and the aristocrats for the most part spent scarcely two hours in the office, just for a little gossip and a glance through the newspapers and despatches—Hatzfeldt, for instance, and Keudell, who was incapable to boot.'
. . . . " Hatzfeldt rarely came before two o'clock," said Bucher, " and often went away again at three. While they lived upstairs he usually came to play a

game of croquet. He would ask Wartensleben, 'Now what do you think of a little game of croquet to-day?' Wartensleben used then to say he would go up and see whether the Countess would care to join them, and when he came back with the message that the Countess begged to be excused as she had something else to do, Paul would remark, 'Well, then, one may as well say good bye,' and take himself off. . . . And Keudell could really do nothing. I suppose I have already told you the story about Taglioni and Keudell's thirty arrears of work? Well, at Versailles I was told by Wiehr—you remember him, the fat, bald deciphering clerk — it was simply frightful how little Keudell managed to do. When he sat down he wrote two or three lines, then pulled out his watch, took the rings off his finger and played with them, put them on again, wrote another few lines, stopped once more, and finally rose, leaving his work unfinished. On one occasion Taglioni took pity on him and offered to assist the Councillor. The latter was delighted with such an amiable fellow, and Taglioni actually disposed of some thirty items of work which were in arrear. But in spite of that a number of even sensible people had a high opinion of his power of work and his intelligence —people such as Gneist, for example, whom I know well, as we studied together. I always meant to enlighten him, but have not done so yet. It is necessary, however, that people should know Keudell if he is to be a Minister one day." Bucher then came to speak of Count Herbert again, and I said that the Prince had once observed to me that he had thought of promoting him to be Secretary of State, as he had worked for seven years under his own personal supervision, but that he was too young. "Yes," rejoined

Bucher, "and so he is still. Paul Hatzfeldt will not remain. Things will go on for the present in the same way. He comes at two o'clock and disappears again at five, attends to nothing beyond the interviews with foreign diplomatists, and troubles himself very little with the other business—which, for the matter of that, is no loss. But when the Prince comes back, and he is summoned to receive instructions two or three times a day, it will not be at all to his liking, and he will go back to Constantinople. He will be replaced by Herbert, that haughty and incapable fellow, and more than one of the officials will leave."

I asked, in conclusion, if he knew what the Chief had intended by the article on the Anti-Nihilistic society which I forwarded to the *Daily Telegraph*, and afterwards countermanded. "The Holy Drujina?" he said. "That was true. Such a society had been formed under the protection of the Emperor, who had subscribed a million and a half to its funds. Despatches have been exchanged between ourselves and St. Petersburg on the subject, and one of the members of the society has called upon Rantzau. But I cannot conceive what the Chief can have intended by the publication of the paragraph in England. If one of those gentlemen were to go there and murder a Nihilist leader, he would be hanged as a matter of course. The affair should have been treated as a profound secret, yet in a few weeks' time it appeared in full, with all manner of details and humorous comments, in the *Berliner Tageblatt*. When I mentioned this to Rantzau afterwards, he was simply terrified. Of course he had not read it, and wished to know where it had appeared. I told him the name of the paper, and let him hunt up the number himself. I used formerly to get him the paper on such occasions, but now leave that to him, so that he may have at least some occupation."

As I left, Bucher said: "If anything happens, I will let you know."

The Prince returned to Berlin in the afternoon of the 12th of November. At noon of the 15th a Chancery attendant brought me a letter from Sachse, saying that the Chief desired to see me at 1 o'clock on the following day, Wednesday. I arrived at the time appointed, and was shown in to the Prince at a quarter-past 1. He had been dictating to Count William before I went in. The Chancellor, who was in plain clothes, looked fresh and hearty, but began by complaining of his health. He had been ill, he said, during the whole five months of his holiday, even at Kissingen, but particularly at Varzin, where he had had to endure great pain. It was his old trouble.

He then spoke of the elections, and stated that in certain circumstances he would retire, as he had already intimated to the Emperor. "The centre of gravity has changed," he continued. "The Progressist and Secessionist Jews, with their money, now form the Centre. At first I was not in favour of this agitation (for Stöcker as an Anti-Semite). It was inconvenient to me, and they went too far. Now, however, I am glad that the Court Chaplain has been elected. He is an energetic, fearless, and resolute man, and he cannot be muzzled. The elections have shown that the German Philistine still lives, and allows himself to be frightened and led astray by fine speeches and lies. He will not hear of the protection of labour against the foreigner, nor of insurance against accident and old age, nor of any reduction of school and poor rates, but wants direct taxation to be increased. Well, he can have that, but not while I am Chancellor."

"Do you seriously mean that, Serene Highness?" I asked. "I believe they have only nibbled at the democratic bait just as they did formerly."

"It may be that they do not quite know what they want. But they have taken this course at the elections, their representatives vote against me, and, in order to govern I must have a majority—which I cannot find under these conditions. In case of necessity it might be possible to manage with a coalition of Conservatives and Clericals and such like, but the Centre Party has been against us all through the elections, and there is no trusting them. Folly and ingratitude on all sides! I am made the target for every party and group, and they do everything they can to harass me, and would like me to serve as a whipping-boy for them. But when I disappear they will not know which way to turn, as none of them has a majority or any positive views and aims. They can only criticise and find fault—always say No. You are right in saying that they have turned the people's heads with their fine phrases and lies. They make out that I am in favour of reaction, and want to restore the old *régime*. If I can get my monopoly, tobacco will cost three to five marks a pound, but cigars will be three times as dear as they are now. They have frightened the people by reviving the old stories of the past, Junker rule, the *corvée*, territorial jurisdiction, and even the *jus primæ noctis*, as, for instance, in Holstein and Lauenburg. There the Danish Kings had allowed all the ancient institutions to remain—unadulterated mediævalism. The Junkers ruled, and were decorated with the Order of the

Elephant. They took all the best posts as if they had inherited them. They held the most remunerative offices up to ten thousand thalers a year, or at least four to five thousand thalers; and yet they neither did nor could do anything except pocket fees and impose heavy fines. They farmed the domains among themselves, on the lowest valuations, and lived on the fat of the land. When I came there the people were obliged to drink the abominable beer which the Junkers brewed on their estates, and no one could purchase a piece of ground because they did not wish the population to exceed two thousand to the square (German) mile. There the people still remember all this misrule, and emissaries of the Progressists and Secessionists— who are just the same—threaten them with its revival, and warn them against me. I am represented as desiring to restore that state of things, yet the contrary is the case, and it was I alone who abolished it."

I reminded him of the homage of the Estates in Lauenburg, Bülow's anxiety respecting the maintenance of the Compact of the nobility, and the scene in the Ratzeburg Cathedral, asking if that was a correct account of the incident. He then related it to me once more, the narrative agreeing in all important particulars with that already given. Returning to the agitation that preceded the elections, he continued as follows: "They do not, however, even believe what they preach. They hate and slander me because I am a Junker and not a Professor, and because I have been a Minister for twenty years. That has lasted too long for them—hence their vexation. They would like to come to power themselves, and form a Government. But that is mere covetousness, and not ability, and if I were to make way for them they would be desperately embarrassed, and would recognise that they could do nothing. I was born a Junker, but my policy was not that of the Junkers. I am a Royalist in the first place, and then a Prussian and a German. I will defend my King and the monarchy against revolution, both overt and covert, and I will establish and leave behind me a strong and healthy Germany. To me the parties are a matter of indifference. I am also not a Conservative in the sense of the Conservative party. My entire past as a Minister is evidence of that. They saw that in 1873 in the question of the Inspection of Schools Bill, when they turned their backs upon me, attacked me in their papers, and wrote me absurd letters."

He took from the shelves near him a copy of a letter with which he had disposed of an old gentleman in Pomerania (Senft-Pilsach), who had at that time warned him to reflect and pray. This letter, which he read to me, directed attention, *inter alia*, to the Psalms, chapter 12, verses 3 and 4: "The Lord shall cut off all flattering lips, and the tongue that speaketh proud things: who have said, with our tongue will we prevail; our lips are our own: who is lord over us?" He then returned to the last elections, and observed: "The defectiveness of our institutions is shown by the credulity of the electors. It may come to this, that we shall some day have to say of the German Constitution, after all attempts at government and reform under it have failed, as Schwarzenberg said at Olmütz: 'This arrangement has not stood the test.' But that must not be printed now. It is only for yourself. . . . They have now invented another calumny. They take advantage of my attachment to the Emperor, and pretend that I am clinging to office, that I am devoured by the love of power. It may turn out differently, however, and I may say to them: 'Here you have it! Now let us see you govern!' That, however, can only be after a division on some important question, not on the electoral returns. The Emperor is half inclined to try it and let me go, if only for one session. Things cannot go on as they are much longer. Of course, I am not going to desert the Emperor; it would be unfair to leave the old man in the lurch. But I cannot renounce my convictions, and I will not have a return to the period of conflict. I demand more appreciation and better treatment."

Returning once more to the statement that the Liberal parties had been guilty of gross misrepresentation during the last election, he added that they had at the same time set the followers of the Government a good example by their excellent organisation, energy, and self-sacrifice. "Many people on our side, such as Herzog, for instance, have also given a great deal of money," he said; "but the Progressists have done more. They had all the treasure of the Hebrews at their disposal, and were at the same time thoroughly drilled and well organised."

"And now," he asked, "have I anything else for you? Unruh has published various things that should be refuted." He took up the October number of the sixth year's issue of the *Deutsche Revue*, which lay before him, and continued: "He maintains that he has written for historians, but he obviously intended to influence the elections. A great deal of it is erroneous, other portions are electioneering lies, and some parts require to be supplemented. Here, for instance, on page 9, he states that while I was still a member of Parliament I had a conversation with him which I concluded with the words: 'Now I tell you, if your party is victorious, you shall take me under your wing, and if my side gets the upper hand I will do as much for you. Shake hands on it!' This offer was actually made. And curiously enough, a similar proposal was made to me by d'Ester, the Radical member of Parliament. In this case, however, I declined, and said: 'If your party wins, life will no longer be worth living, and if we have the upper hand, then hanging shall be the order of the day—but with all politeness, up to the very foot of the gallows.'"

He turned over the leaves of the *Revue*, and continued: "There is no foundation whatever for the statement that the Opposition was not aware during the years 1862 to 1866 that I had a strong anti-Austrian policy in view. Besides, it is clear from Unruh's own 'Memoirs' that they were fully informed respecting this policy, and only offered opposition through hatred to me, the Junker, and in consequence of their own dogmatism. Here, on page 11, it is stated that shortly after the outbreak of the Franco-Austrian War in 1859, he had an interview with me at the Hotel Royal, when I said to him that for Prussia to come to the assistance of Austria would be an act of political suicide. I had entirely lost my sympathy for Austria. If we did not succeed in driving Austria out of Germany proper, and if she kept the upper hand here, then our Kings would once more be mere Electors and vassals of the Hapsburgs. There could be no doubt as to the attitude of the individual German Governments in case of a crisis. With the exception perhaps of a few of the minor States that fell within the sphere of Prussian influence, all of them, if forced to make a choice, would decide in favour of Austria. Prussia would, therefore, be isolated, but there were circumstances in which

she might have the entire German people as her
allies. . . . Surely that was plain speaking, and it
ought not to have been difficult afterwards to recognise
the connection between such language and the increase
of the army. They would not see it, however. . . .
On page 13 is another proof that they knew what I had
in view: 'When the King went to Baden-Baden,
accompanied by the Ministers Von Auerswald and Von
Schleinitz, Bismarck followed him, evidently with the
object of continuing his efforts to prevent assistance
being rendered to Austria.' And on the same page we
read: 'There is another circumstance which strikes one
as an important piece of evidence to show that
Bismarck's anti-Austrian policy, in so far as Austrian
influence in Germany was concerned, did not originate
in 1859, but was of older date. After 1866, speaking
in the House of Parliament to the former Landrath of
the Teltower district, I related to him my conversation
with Bismarck in 1859, whereupon he told me that
Bismarck had expressed the same anti-Austrian views
to him in 1854, and frankly confessed his anti-Austrian
policy. It was not until 1866, that is to say, twelve
years later, that it was practically applied. Bismarck
had therefore kept this plan of driving Austria out of
Germany before him all that time, and had resolutely
pursued it. This is of some importance in forming an
opinion upon the period of conflict.' That is certainly
correct. And is it possible that what that Landrath in
1854 and Unruh in 1859 ascertained from me personally had not also come to the knowledge of the others
and been present to their minds when they—the
Liberals—fought against me with the utmost violence
from 1862 to 1866?"

The Chancellor turned over a few further pages, and

then continued: "With regard to the situation in the autumn of 1862, Unruh was convinced (page 15) that 'if Bismarck desired to put an end to dualism in Germany, it was obviously impossible to do so without a war with Austria, and that for this purpose it was necessary to make the Prussian army as strong as possible.' That is therefore what I have already told you. In October (page 16), during a general meeting of the National Union at Coburg, he communicated the conversation of 1859 to a confidential circle. He writes: 'I told my old Prussian and my new German friends that they were quite mistaken in regarding Bismarck as a simple Reactionary or indeed as an instrument of reaction. He was certainly not a Liberal, but he had quite different ideas and plans in his head to those entertained by Manteuffel and his colleagues.' The gentlemen were in doubt, and wanted to wait and see how I acted. In 1863 they would appear to have acquired the conviction (page 18) that I had given up my schemes of foreign policy, and was now nothing more than a reactionary Minister—of foreign policy, because (as they inferred by a most extraordinary process of reasoning) in the interval there had been in domestic affairs political persecution, measures against Liberal officials, restrictions on the liberty of the press, and attacks upon the freedom of speech in Parliament. But what in the world had that to do with my foreign policy, and the belief in my anti-Austrian schemes? Moreover, on the next page, one ascertains that at this period Unruh & Co. had received an assurance from a trustworthy source that I had a struggle with the Austrians in view. The writer of the 'Memoirs' reports: 'Seidel, who was at that time Chief Burgomaster of Berlin, made me a communication which he said came from the Military Cabinet, of which General von Manteuffel was the head. According to this communication either Manteuffel or some one who was in intimate relations with him had said that Bismarck was exceptionally well fitted for the task of stamping out the Opposition in Parliament, and that when he had succeeded in doing that and the military organisation was secured, he must be set aside as he would otherwise bring about a war with Austria, and would use our increased military forces for that purpose. A conflict with Austria and a successful war against her would again drive the Conservative party from office. In order to keep the Conservatives in power it was necessary that Prussia should remain on good terms with Austria, and for that purpose they should even, if necessary, make concessions. This statement (Unruh goes on to say) looked highly probable. General Manteuffel was known as the head of the extreme Conservative or so-called Austrian party at the Prussian Court, and was much esteemed in Vienna. Bismarck had given frequent expression to his anti-Austrian plans even before he became Premier, and had indeed submitted them to the King himself. If Bismarck were to bring about a compromise with Parliament, and to conclude a peace with the popular representatives, his services, in the opinion of the Manteuffel party, would be of no further use, and he ought then to go. It would be quite different if in spite of the violent struggle with Parliament, he succeeded in carrying through the military organisation scheme. So long as the conflict with the popular representatives continued, he remained indispensable, his value increasing with the fierceness of the struggle.'

"This is a tissue of mistakes and contradictions.

In the first place there is no foundation whatever for the statement that Manteuffel wished to get rid of me, and that he was the head of the Austrian party. It was rather Schleinitz who held that position, and who afterwards was in frequent intercourse with the Austrians, his salon indeed being their rendezvous. Manteuffel was by no means a partisan of Austria, but on the contrary a Prussian officer of ardent Royalist patriotism. But in that case one would have thought that if the Opposition in the Diet had been imbued with Prussian patriotism, if they had desired to see the dualism in Germany put an end to and the German idea realised through Prussia, they ought to have supported me with all their might, knowing as they did that I had exactly the same object in view. And that would also have been wise from their Liberal standpoint, since it was of course known that a victory over Austria would drive the Conservatives from power. Finally, there was no reason to apprehend my overthrow by the Austrophil Conservatives, as, according to Unruh himself, it was known that I possessed the confidence of the King, who, it was indeed said, had himself called me his spiritual doctor. The Opposition, however, instead of acting on such considerations, adopted a diametrically opposite course. They acted in an unpractical, illogical, impolitic way, and against their own interests, blinded by their stupid animosity and pettyfogging dogmatism. It was necessary for the Liberals, if they desired to pursue a practical policy, to win for their cause—which could not be promoted without driving Austria out of the Confederation—the support of the King of Prussia, who had scruples as to a conflict with Austria, scruples which were encouraged by a section of his *entourage*. King William should have been gradually convinced of the necessity of breaking with the Vienna policy, and of attempting to give Prussia alone the leading position in Germany. I pursued this end, and Parliament should have done the same. Instead of doing so, however, they flew in the face of the King by refusing him the means for the reorganisation of the army, and they therefore lacked the necessary leverage for promoting their own views. There they were, floating in the air, with nothing to sustain them but the wind of their own speeches and self-conceit which deluded them into a belief in their own importance.

"Finally, Unruh says here (page 19) that I aggravated the struggle over the Military Bills into a constitutional conflict, that I assumed an aggressive attitude towards the Opposition, and endeavoured in almost every speech to incense them by jibes and sneers, all this for the sole purpose of maintaining myself in power and office against the Austrophil Court party; and, on page 20, he repeats the same charge in the following words: 'I am still of opinion that Bismarck used and took advantage of the conflict to maintain and strengthen his position.' Now that is a gross slander, such as would render a man liable to prosecution—a falsehood arising from the same blindness as another on page 16, according to which the great men of the National Union regarded me merely as the representative of reaction. I desired no reaction, then as little as now, when I am again charged with doing so. Had I desired it I could have had it. Unruh and his colleagues would not have been able to prevent it, and 'The People' who elected them, could have done nothing. But it was not the people. The determined attitude I adopted towards the Opposition in Parliament was just as little due to the love of power, or to the desire to strengthen my ministerial position. It was rather due to my innate Royalism, which has always been a leading feature in my character. It was this which made me hold fast to my position. In doing so I was guided by my sense of duty towards my King, who, in the circumstances then obtaining, could not have found another Minister. I remember saying to him, ' No one shall have it in his power to say that your Majesty cannot find a servant so long as there is one nobleman of the Altmark still surviving.' Otherwise, at that time, it was, honestly speaking, no pleasure to be a Minister. A Legation in Paris, or even in Frankfurt, would have been much pleasanter. There one had a good salary with little work, little responsibility, and little worry, and was not attacked and reviled on all hands. The provocation and the sarcastic speeches in Parliament, of which Unruh complains, were not intended to prolong or aggravate the conflict, but were an exercise of the *jus talionis*. I am stated on page 17 to have often been most offensive. There is no denying that. But even when my expressions were offensive, they were not nearly so offensive as the language used against me and other members of the Government by speakers in the House. They were much coarser and more malicious than I ever was, indeed actually abusive and threatening, speaking of 'a Ministry of tight-rope dancers,' of ' the reactionary brand of Cain,' and other unflattering epithets. I was not the man to submit to that sort of thing. It was not in my nature to turn the left cheek to the smiter. On the contrary, I defended myself and paid them back in their own coin. Then, in addition to that, there was my contempt for the doctrine of popular sovereignty, and my disgust at the Byzantine veneration paid to it by the Opposition. That was an abomination to me, and revolted me even more than their venom.

"The passage here on page 22, as to the motives of my attitude on the question of the payment of members in the North German Diet is amusing, and indeed ludicrous. Unruh says: 'At that time I was still in favour of payment, but said to Bennigsen I did not believe that Bismarck would give way; perhaps it was entirely out of his power to do so. It seemed to me as if he had entered into binding engagements with the Upper House, which he expected later on to swallow universal suffrage, when the several States had given their necessary approval to the North German Constitution.' With the Upper House! A body which always stood apart from active politics, and had no influence of any importance. An absurd idea!

"On page 24 he recalls a remark made by Loewe, that one of the chief defects of the German Constitution is that it was made after my own heart. Now, that is a mere phrase which no amount of reiteration in party newspapers and speeches during the last few years has brought any nearer to truth.

"On page 25 he says: 'As far back as 1867 it must have become clear to every person of insight that there was no possibility of Parliamentary government under Bismarck. An essential condition of such government is that in certain circumstances there should be a change of ministers and parties capable of furnishing and supporting a Cabinet.' This is quite true. 'Parties capable of furnishing and supporting a Cabinet'—where were they to be found during the past two decades? I have seen none, neither one with a majority nor one with a positive programme. And, least of all, in the Liberal camp. All their manifestoes and speeches have consisted merely of fault-finding criticism and negation. They have never brought forward anything positive. They have only a thirst for office, ambition and envy, but not the power which is essential to productive government.

"On the same page he says : ' Almost all parties, in so far as they are not hostile to German unity, consider the Imperial Chancellor to be absolutely indispensable.' And yet from 1877 onwards I have been subjected to the most bitter hostility even from the National Liberals, and before and during the last elections the Progressist party gave out the watchword ' Away with Bismarck ! '

"The statement which immediately follows is also a mere hackneyed phrase : ' A party which has no principles of its own, but only aims at securing a majority for the Government, affords no reliable support in critical and dangerous times.' One would like to know why. Does the Opposition with its Liberalism perhaps offer such support, with its untrustworthiness, its suspiciousness, and vacillation, its huckstering and knuckling down, and its petty criticism and dogmatism ?

"On page 29 it is represented as a matter of indifference whether the idea of a Zollverein Parliament was originated by me or by Delbrück. I take it that this ought not to be a matter of indifference to Unruh, who claims to provide materials for future historians. The idea did not come from Delbrück, but from me. As can be seen from Hesekiel's book, I mooted it as far back as the time when I was in St. Petersburg, and embodied it in the treaties of 1866, which secured its fulfilment.[1]

---

[1] As far back as the 2nd of April, 1858, he wrote from Frankfurt to a friend (see Hesekiel, page 183) : "I believe that the Zollverein, which must be reorganised after 1865 . . . will provide an opportunity of securing the exercise of the right of federal consent in customs matters on the lines of the Union scheme of 1849, and establishing a kind of

But he, as a Liberal and a member of the learned classes, must of course get the credit of having first originated it, not a Junker. I do not wish to say anything against Delbrück's ability and merit, but it would never have occurred to him that the Zollverein could be turned to account in that way, for although he had a great deal of talent, he had no political instinct.

"On page 30 Unruh states: 'During the debate on the Tobacco Taxation Bill, when Bismarck had declared a monopoly to be his ideal, Bennigsen informed me that he had broken off the negotiations into which he had entered with Bismarck in the autumn for joining the Ministry, and had told him that he could not commit himself to the monopoly.' That is not true, or at least only half true. This is how the matter stood. In 1877 Eulenburg wished to retire. I offered his post to Bennigsen. He demanded that Forckenbeck and Stauffenberg should also be appointed Ministers, but there were no posts vacant for them. In the meantime Eulenburg hit upon another idea. He went to the King and incited him against me for having had anything to do with Bennigsen. His Most Gracious was offended, and in a brutal letter forbade me to treat any further with Bennigsen. Several months passed, during which time it transpired in the press that Lasker also counted upon a seat in the Cabinet. Bennigsen

customs parliament." On the 18th of September, 1861, in a letter to a friend, which was written at Stolpmunde on the way from St. Petersburg to Berlin (same work, page 189), he said: "I do not see why we should be so coy and reserved with regard to the idea of popular representation, whether in the form of a confederation or of a customs parliament. An institution which enjoys legitimate authority in every German State, and which even the Conservatives in Prussia would not willingly dispense with, cannot be opposed as revolutionary. . . . In that way one might create a thoroughly Conservative national representation, and at the same time secure the gratitude of even the Liberals."

came to me subsequently in the Reichstag, an unusual thing for him to do, and inquired about the tobacco monopoly. I replied that I was in favour of it and would try to carry it, whereupon Bennigsen declared that he could not support the measure, and withdrew from the negotiations. Out of politeness I forebore to tell him that he was no longer in my mind, as I had been forbidden to think of him.

"Further on Unruh says : 'From that time forward there was an obvious change in the attitude of the Imperial Chancellor towards the National Liberals.' That is incorrect. The contrary is the case. From that time forward the National Liberals treated me with mingled coolness and hostility, withdrawing their support in the Diet and attacking me in their newspapers—chiefly in the *National Zeitung*, which is the most mendacious of them all, full of hypocrisy and trickery.

"On page 31 Delbrück's free-trade system is spoken of as having been for a long time in force. The question here is what is meant by 'a long time.' The system which is here named after Delbrück has only been in existence since 1865, and we first began to entertain serious doubts respecting it in 1875. Up to the latter date I had had no time to think of its advantages or disadvantages, as I was obliged to devote my whole mind to watching and averting the serious danger of coalition which then existed.

"On page 32 there is a falsehood obviously calculated to influence the elections. I am made to say that I wished to 'drive the National Liberals to the wall,' while people heard at the same time that I intended to make a complete change in the previous customs and commercial policy. This is impossible. I

first thought of the latter in November last; and to
'drive to the wall' is an expression which I have never
used, either in this connection or in any other. It is
not to be found in my lexicon. Every one knows
whether he is apt to use a certain phrase or not, and I
am quite satisfied that I have never used that phrase.

"The dissolution of the Reichstag after the Nobling
outrage is represented as a measure directed against the
Liberals. It was in reality the very opposite, an act of
complaisance on the part of the Government towards
the Liberals. I wished to make the change of opinion
with regard to the Anti-Socialist laws easy for them by
means of a dissolution and new elections. But that is
the way with these gentlemen and their excessive
amour-propre. If one does not always stand hat in
hand before them, they regard one as their enemy, and
full of arrogance. But I cannot do that. I do not set
much store by criticisms and speeches intended for the
newspapers. Indeed, I lack altogether the bump of
veneration for my fellow man."

At this moment Theiss announced the Minister
Mayback. I rose, and putting under my arm the
number of the *Revue* which he had given me with his
grey, red, and blue pencil marks and comments, was
about to leave. Before going, however, I said: "Might
I venture to ask whether Gambetta has called upon you,
Serene Highness?" "No," he replied. "He has said
so himself, and it is the fact. Of course it is evident
from his journey to Dantzig that he had thought of
paying a visit to Varzin. He doubtless reconsidered
the matter there, or they may have written to him from
Paris that it would not make a good impression." On
Maybach coming in at this point the Chancellor said:
"We were just speaking of Gambetta. It was
not my business to deny the report of his visit to

me. People might have thought that I had some grudge against him—that I wished to hold aloof from him, which was not at all the case."

I took my leave and immediately wrote down what I had heard. The first part respecting the results of the elections was worked up into an article entitled "The Chancellor Crisis," which appeared in No. 48 of the *Grenzboten* ; the crticism of the Unruh Memoirs being utilised for an article in No. 49.

After I had received copies of these and of a third article, "The Imperial Chancellor and the Reichstag," I handed over all three at the palace at noon on the 2nd of December for delivery to the Prince. An hour later I received the following letter from the Imperial Chancellerie, signed by Sachse :—

"Under instructions from the Imperial Chancellor I have the honour to request you to call upon his Serene Highness to-day at any time up to 5 o'clock. The Imperial Chancellor mentioned at the same time that the articles which you have submitted to him cannot possibly be published in their present form."

I presented myself at the palace at 3 o'clock, but could not see the Chancellor, as Prince William was with him, and Mittnacht, the Minister, was announced to follow. On my returning again at 4 o'clock Mittnacht was with the Chief, but left in about ten minutes. Immediately afterwards the Chancellor sent me word that he was waiting for me in the garden. On my passing through the door of the large antechamber, I found him standing outside with his dog. He shook hands in a friendly way, saying immediately afterwards, however : "But what have you been doing, Doctor ? Why, that is all wrong, the very opposite of what I wanted. Surely the article is not yet printed ?" I regretted that it was already published. "That is most unfortunate," he rejoined. I asked which of the articles he meant. "Why, that about Unruh," he answered. "You have said exactly what Bennigsen asserted. It might have been written by one of my worst enemies. And the other is also not correct—often pure nonsense. I remember it was just the same three years ago with the things you sent on to me to Kissingen and Gastein— in many places the direct contrary was the truth." I replied that that was only the case in one instance, in the story about Rechberg, which was then left out. He would not agree to that, however, and continued: "You must submit these articles to me before they are printed. You now trust too much to your memory, which is not so good as it was formerly, or you have not listened attentively. I related it all to you quite differently."

At this point we were interrupted by Count Bill, who brought a message. When he had gone the Chief took the article out of his pocket, and as it had grown dark we passed through another door into his study, where he looked through the passage once more. At the first, on page 395, where I—following Unruh's statement—made the Chief say that in the year 1859 the German Governments "with the exception of a few minor States which fall within the sphere of influence of Prussia, would all join Austria. The former would, therefore, be completely isolated, yet she would have allies if she knew how to win and to treat them, namely the German people," he said: "That's pure nonsense. Directly contrary to history. Why, you should have known that . . . But, no, I misunderstood the sentence. I read it wrongly in my hurry. The 'former' and 'she' referred to Prussia. There I have done little Busch (Büschchen an injustice. . . . But further on, here (the passage on 398) where I say that the people could have done nothing against a reactionary policy during the period of conflict. That is unfounded. I cannot say that. It should have been 'would have done nothing.' No doubt they would have desired to do it. Well, on page 401, that is again an oversight on my part. Here I overlooked the first 'not.' (He referred to the passage : "The expression 'drive them to the wall' has not only not been used by me in this connection, but was never used by me at all.") But all this about Bennigsen is quite wrong—the second part of it. There you have written in his interest. If that were a correct account I should have told a lie. My main object in the article was to explain that point, and you ought to have known from the *Norddeutsche* how the matter really stood. You should know that the article in that paper was written at my instance. But I suppose you do not read the official journals. No further negotiations took place with him after the interview at Varzin, that is with Bennigsen respecting the ministerial post, although I did not break with him otherwise. It is true that my son wrote to him once more, but I knew nothing of this. And Eulenburg did not decide to remain. He had had enough of it. He went to the King, however, told him of my negotiations with Bennigsen, and incited him against me. I had been in treaty with these Liberals behind his back, &c. The King did not inform me that Eulenburg did not wish to retire, but wrote me an exceedingly rude and snappish letter somewhat to this effect : How dare I enter into negotiations with this rabid Radical, this archdemagogue, and expressly forbade me to treat with him any further. That did not take place 'several months, but only three or four days after the Varzin interview. The statement that Lasker reckoned on obtaining a portfolio is correct. On the other hand it is quite incorrect to say that *out of politeness* I abstained from telling Bennigsen that I did not think of him any more, as the post was no longer open. It was still open, as you might have seen in any calendar. Surely you know that Friedenthal only held it provisionally. The truth is I could not explain to Bennigsen that his Most Gracious had forbidden me to negotiate with him any further."

While speaking thus the Chancellor underlined the passage referred to, page 400, lines 19 to 28, in so far as he had corrected them, adding notes of exclamation and remarks such as "No," and "three days." I expressed my regret at the harm that had been done and observed that it could be put right in the next number of the *Grenzboten*. He agreed to this and wished to see the correction before it appeared. I promised to submit it to him. Finding in the course of his examination that the misfortune did not extend to more than some five lines in an article of nine pages, his excitement gradually subsided. Indeed, the "Büschchen" at the beginning had already sounded less severe, and at the close he said "I must have a breath of fresh air before dinner. Come along!"

We strolled up and down in the park for about an hour longer, and spoke of other matters. I congratulated the Prince on the success with which he had repelled the attacks of his opponents in the Reichstag three or four days previously. "Yes, successfully," he rejoined. "That's very fine, but what good has it done? They have, all the same, refused the 80,000 marks for an adviser on political economy; and the Government has now no means of keeping itself informed." I remarked that they had obviously been influenced by their own ignorance of pratical affairs, and particularly with industrial matters, as well as by jealousy and fear. Bamberger's assertion that they knew enough themselves was no proof of the contrary. They wished to appear before the public as the only infallible wiseacres, and also being doctrinarians, they could afford to ignore economic facts.

We then spoke about Windthorst, of whom the Chief said: "His vote against the Government has destroyed the slight degree of confidence I was beginning to feel in him." The conversation then turned upon Bennigsen's Parliamentary activity, and I remarked on the striking circumstance that up to the present he had taken no part in any of the debates. The Prince rejoined: "It is very sensible on his part to keep silent, although he is a good speaker. He sent the others to the front—Benda, and he also voted against it—a further proof that he and his party are quite untrustworthy. He has no decided views, he is not frank, and he is afraid of Lasker. With him it is always vacillation and half measures. Do you play cards?" I replied in the negative. "But you know the cards?" "Yes." "Now, at whist he always keeps three aces in his hand, and gives no indication that he holds them. He can no longer be counted upon, and besides his followers have been greatly reduced owing to their vague and vacillating policy. Nevertheless, he still sits there with the same high opinion of himself and the same dignified air as formerly when he commanded hundreds; and he will continue to do so even if they should be reduced to thirteen, like George Vincke's Old Liberals. There is nothing to be done with the others either. It has now come to pass, through the absurdities of the Liberals, that the tag, rag and bobtail, the Guelphs, Poles, and Alsacians, the Social Democrats, and the People's Party, turn the scale, putting those they support in the majority. Mittnacht, who was with me before you came, is of the same opinion. In future we shall have to count upon the Governments rather than upon the Reichstag, and, indeed, we may ultimately have to reckon upon the Governments alone."

I said that the whole Parliamentary system would in time lose all credit, even with the public, through such senseless attacks and votes. It brought everything to a standstill, but was itself unable to produce anything better. "The effect of the recent debates," I went on, "is already here and there observable. This morning I met Thile, who stopped me and asked what I thought of the Parliamentary struggle. He was immensely pleased with the attitude you had adopted. A friend of his, whom he did not wish to name, but who was an admirer of the new era, though up to the present by no means favourable to you, had said that the manner in which you spoke and repelled the attacks of the Opposition was simply magnificent, and excited universal admiration. And women speak with disgust of the way in which you were hounded down and personally insulted by the Progressists and Lasker. A Hanoverian lady, of Guelph sympathies, spoke to my wife yesterday in this sense. This disgust and this pity for you will gradually affect the men, and help to bring about a change in the present tendency. I myself feel no pity, I only foresee your triumph. Pray excuse me for comparing you to an animal, but you remind me of the picture of a noble stag, which time after time shakes off the snarling pack, and then, proud and unhurt, regains the shelter of his forest, crowned by his branching antlers." "Yes," he said, "one might take another animal, the wild boar, which gores the hounds and tosses them away from him."

He was silent for a time, and as we walked up and down he hummed the tune "Wir hatten gebauet ein stattliches Haus." He then remarked suddenly: "But if they go on in that style they will ultimately meet the fate to which I alluded—the Luck of Edenhall. You know Uhland's poem? It will be a case of Bang! and snap goes the German Constitution! You spoke of Thile. Do you mean the former Secretary of State?" I said "Yes, I meet him sometimes as he lives in my neighbourhood." "He is a dangerous man," he observed. "He was quite incapable. He could do nothing, and wrote nothing, because he was afraid it would be corrected; and yet I kept him for ten years, although he conspired against me with Savigny. He is to blame for the Diest libels, which led to the prosecution. I heard the whole story and how it began from Rothschild. Savigny went to him about the promotion of the company in question, and asked him if he could not let him have a share in it. Rothschild said no, he had already been obliged to part with a large share, a million and a half—meaning to his branches, the houses with which he is associated. Savigny, however, thought he was alluding to me, and would appear to have hinted something of the kind, but Rothschild seems either not to have understood him, or not to have answered with sufficient clearness. Savigny then carried the tale further, telling it first to Thile, who mentioned it to his brother, the general, instead of speaking to me, his chief, and in this way Diest ultimately came to hear of it. But, as Minister, I have never done any business with Rothschild, and even as envoy at Frankfurt very little. I drew my salary through him, and on one occasion I exchanged some stock for Austrian securities. I have not found it necessary. My profession as Minister has brought me in something, and through the grants and the gift of the Lauenburg estates I have become a rich man. It is true that if I had gone into a business, or carried on a trade, and devoted to it the same amount of labour and intelligence, I should doubtless have made more money."

We then returned once more to the recent debates in the Reichstag, and I again expressed in strong terms the contempt I felt for the Opposition. "You were always a gentleman pitted against vain and vulgar creatures," I said, "and in saying that I am not thinking of your rank as a Prince." "No, I understand—a gentleman in my way of thinking," he rejoined. "Lasker's Jewish forwardness and presumption," I continued, "the Professors with their priggish airs of superiority, and their empty pathos; Hänel, the self-complacent and pathetic doctrinaire—it is impossible to imagine anything more repulsive. He wanted to be Minister of Justice in 'sea-surrounded Schleswig-Holstein.'" "Yes," said the Chancellor, interrupting me, "they had divided the parts among themselves before the piece had been secured, and they probably have done the same thing now. Nothing came of it, however, after the interview which our Most Gracious had with me upstairs in the yellow chamber, where he remained with me from 9 o'clock until near midnight." "And where he heard the simile of the chickens in Low German," I added. "And then that impudent, lying, clown Richter, and the whole tearing, snarling, sprawling pack face to face with simple, solid, positive greatness. It was as if you belonged to an entirely different species." "Yes," he said, "when I lie down in bed after such debates, I feel ashamed of ever having bandied words with them. You know the way one feels after a night's drinking, if one has had a row and perhaps come to blows with vulgar people—when one begins to realise it next morning, one wonders how and why it all came about." Then after I had promised to make the corrections immediately and send them to him, he took leave of me with the words "Good evening, Busch. Auf Wiedersehen." Busch! Not "Herr Doctor" as usual.

In two hours I sent him the corrections, which I received back through a Chancery attendant before 10 P.M. There were only a few alterations in the second half.

On the 2nd of January, 1882, I again visited Bucher. He complained in general of the incapable *entourage* of the Prince, including his sons, and of Rudolf Lindau, whom they favoured because he gave card parties and made himself useful to them in other ways. (. . .) He was a mere tradesman without education or political knowledge. The Prince wished to make things comfortable for himself, and no blame to him, but he was mistaken if he thought the machine would still go on working as it ought to. In that respect the choice of the *personnel* was of importance, and those who were now engaged, particularly in the press department, were almost constantly blundering. The stuff which Paul Lindau wrote for the *Kölnische Zeitung* was also of little value.

We then spoke about the negotiations with the Curia, which were making satisfactory progress; of Held's contribution to the social history of England; of Taine's account of the Jacobins, in whom Bucher discovered some characteristics of the Progressist party; of Stirum, who had also left because he was not disposed to put up with the intrigues of the clique that surrounded the Prince, and who had told him, Bucher, that he "preferred in future to admire the Chancellor at a distance"; and of the Chief's recent criticism of my article. I said that the Chief must be mistaken in asserting that after the visit to Varzin he had had no further negotiations with Benigsen respecting his joining the Ministry, as he had himself told me that at that time Herbert had written to Bennigsen, which he would scarcely have ventured to do without his father's knowledge. Bucher agreed with me, and added that some one had expressed the opinion that Bennigsen had acted like a gentleman with regard to the statements published by the semi-official press. Bucher arranged to send me Taine's book when he had finished reading it, in order that I might write an article upon it. He is extracting passages which point to the similarity between the Jacobins and the Progressist party.

On the evening of the 8th of January, Count William Bismarck sent me an article for the *Grenzboten* on "Agricultural Credit in Prussia."[1]

On Monday, the 16th of January, I took back the third volume of Taine's *History of the Revolution, La Conquête des Jacobins*, to Bucher. He told me that according to a conversation with the Chief, a campaign would presently be opened in the press in order to clear up some points respecting Stockmar and Bunsen. He was to write a pamphlet on the latter in which various documents, of which only portions were given in Frau von Bunsen's book, would be published *in extenso*. I could then make myself useful by utilising this information, in addition to which he would give me further material. We then spoke of the Coburg clique, of Abeken, who had been described on one occasion by Bunsen as the "magnificent Abeken," of Max Müller of

[1] This article was published in the *Grenzboten* without delay. Articles in the same sense appeared later in No. 33 of the *Deutsches Tageblatt* (Feb. 2) and a few days previously in the *Norddeutsche Allgemeine Zeitung*.

Oxford, with whom he had spent some pleasant hours, of Geffcken, and finally of Hepke. On my asking how it was that the latter had fallen into disfavour with the Prince, Bucher said that in 1862, shortly after the Chief had come into office, Hepke, who had charge of the German reports, reproduced, almost literally, in a brochure which he published under the title of "A Word from a Prussian," a memorandum which Bismarck had submitted to the King. Although this pamphlet was anonymous, the Chief came to hear of it, and forbade Metzler to mention it in our papers. Then, again, shortly before the war of 1866, Hepke, "through vanity, in order to show how well informed he was," communicated some scheme that was in hand against Austria to the Austrian Envoy, probably at dinner, and this came to the knowledge of the Chief later on, after our reconciliation with Austria, most likely through Rechberg.

I then turned the conversation on Thile, mentioning what the Prince recently said to me. Bucher still maintained that Thile is a gentleman and very good-hearted, and questioned whether he were as incapable as Bismarck had described him to me.

On the 26th of January, Bucher sent me the first and third volumes of Nippold's edition of Bunsen's biography, the proof sheets of a refutation by him of a letter from Prince Albert to Stockmar, explaining Bunsen's "fall" (which was published first in the *Münchener Nachrichten*, and afterwards in the *National Zeitung*), and finally some rough notes for a *Grenzboten* article, which I prepared and published by the 2nd of February in No. 8, under the title "Bunsen's Friends and the Truth." Bucher's refutation was to appear in the February number of the *Deutsche Revue für das gesammte National-Leben der Gegenwart.* In the rough notes he spoke as follows of Bunsen :—

"He took away with him copies of official documents, (just like Arnim), which his family published in a mutilated and therefore falsified shape. You may indeed without hesitation throw out the suggestion whether he did not perhaps take the originals. He did, as a matter of fact, take away at least three. This whole section of the book (*i.e.*, of the biography, so far as it relates to Bunsen's retirement) is a fable, written in despite of the author's better knowledge. That the King afterwards wrote him a friendly letter, &c. is explained by the distinction which Frederick William IV. was in the habit of drawing between the official and the friend, as in the case of Radowitz. The Memorandum is a schoolboy's exercise. Austria to extend her borders as far as the Sea of Azof, Poland to be restored—a terrible suggestion to be so coolly uttered—Prussia to get Austrian Silesia, one of the Provinces most devoted to the Imperial House, and Moravia!

"Vol. II. p. 557. His views concerning the proper preparatory education for the diplomatic service. That did not succeed in the case of Theodore (one of Bunsen's sons). He must have achieved something out of the common at Lima and Alexandria, since after a short stay at these places he was on each occasion superseded, and had ultimately to resign. If he had had the preliminary training which he scoffed at, instead of a mere professorial education, he would probably not have been guilty of the follies and insubordination of the 1st and 4th of March 1854.

"You will find particulars as to the æsthetic International in the index at the end of the third volume.

You are better versed in the religious type of humanity than I am. Every third word is God. Bunsen seems to have considered that the *lieber Gott* took quite a special interest in him.

"A *bon mot* which circulated in London : The learned regarded him as a diplomat while the diplomatists believed him to be a *savant*. The self-flattery in the account of the conversation with Clarendon, Part III. Bunsen and Pourtales certify to each other's excellences. The source of Albert's letter, Part III. page 356. Bunsen complains of his Government to Albert.

"A popular explanation of the political side of the book will doubtless be also necessary for the dull-witted Philistine. Prussia should involve herself in war with Russia, and what was to be the compensation ? 1. That the English fleet should enter the Baltic. This would mean at least, that the Prussian coasts would be protected against the Russian fleet. 2. That the four Plenipotentiaries (of the Vienna Conference) should announce Prussia's community of interest in the overthrow of Russian predominance. Much good that would have done us ! How often has the integrity of Turkey been declared to be a European interest ? And the idea of an Anglo-Prussian alliance (the Old Liberal dogma) which so frequently crops up in the book is equally absurd, and shows a complete ignorance of English policy, which never enters into permanent alliances without positive and limited aims. Part III. 201 and 207."

On the 2nd of February I again called upon Bucher. He gave me various further particulars respecting the "great patriot and meritorious diplomatist," Bunsen, and his sons. The old gentleman's chief reason for tendering his resignation so hastily was that when about to take his holiday after the catastrophe, he was not paid his full salary as an envoy for six months, as he had demanded, but only for six weeks, as provided by the regulations. Theodore, whom Bunsen described to Thile as the most gifted of his sons, had made himself impossible at Lima, by his tactlessness in holding intercourse with the Opposition party, and using his influence on their behalf. He afterwards held the post of envoy at Stockholm, which he resigned when the Government refused him leave to marry a very wealthy German-Russian lady from the Baltic Provinces. He now enjoys possession of this lady. Another son has a fat benefice in England. "Frau Schwabe," the "Elpi's Melena" of the newspapers, who is frequently mentioned in the Nippold edition of the biography, is an enormously rich German Jewess, widow of a manufacturer, and a friend, not only of Bunsen, but also of Garibaldi, to whom she sent, after he was wounded at Aspromonte, an artistic armchair in "letter form," that is to say, pasted all over with postage stamps. Bucher expects that George von Bunsen will reply to our articles. He, Bucher, will then write an answer from further official documents, for publication in the *Norddeutsche Allgemeine Zeitung*.

On the 17th of February I left a proof of my *Grenzboten* article on Bunsen at the Imperial Chancellor's palace for submission to the Prince. It was in an envelope and signed "Moritz Busch," but was accompanied by no letter. I ascertained at the same time from the porter that the Chancellor had not been quite well for some time past. On my way back through the Leipzigerstrasse I met Bucher, who was delighted with "the fine goings-on in England now." I asked what he meant, and he replied: "Why, the

Standing Orders in Parliament, the Closure. Our people may well ask themselves whether they are equally pleased with this new feature in their ideal."

The extracts from Taine, properly grouped and spiced with references to the German connections of the Jacobins, namely the Progressists, appeared in Nos. 7 and 9 of the *Grenzboten* under the title "The True Story of the Jacobins." I also wrote an article on Gladstone's measure referred to by Bucher. This was published in No. 10 of the *Grenzboten* under the title, "Gladstone, and Liberty of Speech in Parliament."

On the 10th of March I received the news of the death of our son John, from Captain Alm of the *Dora Ahrens* at Falmouth. He had died at sea on the 19th of December last, on the return voyage from Corinto, in Nicaragua. Falling overboard during a violent storm in the vicinity of the Falkland Islands, he was unable to hold on to the rope which was thrown to him, and was swallowed up in the waves. With him, our only son, disappeared my best love, my energy and pleasure in work, my pride and my hope. Henceforth my life is overshadowed by this grief. He was only thirty-one years of age, had lived the hard life of the sailor, and passed two severe examinations, so that we had reason to hope that we should soon see him the captain of a handsome craft. Now he lies at the bottom of a distant sea, and all that remains of him is the memory of his dear face and his brave, high-minded nature. Fearless, truthful, and devoted to his duty, he died as he had lived in the service of his ship, as the soldier dies for his flag, his king and his country. He was a man, a character, and death has no power over such! God has further use of them. But we shall never see him again with mortal eyes, and can only wreathe his portrait with laurels and forget-me-nots on his birthday, the 13th of April.

> "Lass mich im düstern Reich,
> Mutter, mich nicht allein!"
> "Nicht allein! Wo Du auch weilest.
> Ach! Wenn Du dem Tag enteilest,
> Wird kein Herz von Dir sich trennen."[1]

All our friends manifested the greatest sympathy for us, in which the Imperial Chancellor also did not fail to join. He wrote me on the 16th of March:—

"MY DEAR SIR,—I have heard with sincere regret of the heavy loss which you have suffered, and although I have no consolation to offer in such circumstances, I cannot refrain from expressing to you my heartfelt sympathy.

"BISMARCK."

With this these notes may be concluded. Evening has set in.

The sense of duty as a chronicler awoke again before the pain of our loss had subsided. I again felt an interest in other things besides the portrait of our dear departed son, and so returned to my diary. The lines dedicated to his memory shall remain, however, as a monument to him, and a reminiscence of days full of sorrow, and weeks of deep prostration and melancholy.

On the morning of the 29th of March I called upon Bucher. He declared that the anti-German party in Russia was growing dangerous, and though the Emperor

---

[1] "*Euphorion.*—Leave me not in the gloomy realm, mother, not alone!
Chorus.—Not alone, wherever thou biddest. ... Ah, if from the day thou hastenest, still each heart will cling to thee!"
—*Faust*, Part II. These lines are from the lament on the death of Byron which Goethe incorporated in his poem.—TRANSLATOR.

appeared to be our sincere well-wisher, he would perhaps be unable to withstand it. It was true that he had spoken very sharply to Skobeleff who told Schweinitz, as he was returning with him from Gatshina, that the Emperor had severely reprimanded him (il m'a donné un savon). The General actually looked depressed. A Russian diplomatist (Nesselrode, if I understood rightly) once said of Holstein when the latter was with Bismarck in Petersburg years ago: "Ce jeune homme sait une foule de choses, mais il n'est pas capable d'en faire une seule."

Pope Leo has shown great readiness to meet us half way in personal questions. Among other things, he had originally desired to appoint to the bishopric of Osnabrück a former Jesuit and pupil of the Collegium Germanicum, who had been recommended to him by Tarnassi. But when our Government pointed out that the candidate referred to had taken part in various forms of anti-German agitation, the Pope unhesitatingly dropped him.

On the 12th of May I met Thile in the Linkstrasse, and accompanied him part of the way to his house. He expressed his regret at our loss and his pleasure that the Chief had likewise done so. The conversation then turned on Hatzfeldt, and he said that Bismarck had always favoured him, "pitying him for having such a mother," which, after all, was very nice on his part. He had also dispensed with the diplomatic examination in his case. Besides Hatzfeldt had talent and was good-hearted in addition. As evidence of the latter he mentioned that he frequently visited Goltz, who was suffering from cancer of the tongue, although it was scarcely possible to stand the atmosphere of the sick room. He, Thile, had also repeatedly visited the sufferer. Bismarck, on the other hand, had never gone to see him, although they had been on very friendly terms formerly. "It was enough to turn one's stomach," he said. It was true that subsequently, just before Goltz had moved, the Chief called at the old lodgings, and then gave as an excuse: "I was at his place but he had left." Thile then added the following characteristic anecdote: "Of course you too are an old student of Goethe, and remember the poem 'Füllest wieder Busch and Thal, still mit Nebelglanz.' This was being recited on one occasion, and when the reader came to the passage—

> 'Selig wer sich vor der Welt
> Ohne Hass verschliesst,
> Einen Freund am Busen hält
> Und mit dem geniesst.'

(Blessed is he who retires, without hatred, from the world, and enjoys his retreat in communion with a single friend.) Bismarck exclaimed: 'What! Without hatred? What a tailor's soul he must have!" In reply to my inquiry whether this story was absolutely authentic, he mentioned Keudell as his authority.

At 6 P.M. on the 8th of June, three days after the Chancellor's return from Freidrichsruh, I left a note for him at the palace in the Wilhelmstrasse, requesting him if he had anything for me to do to name a day and hour on which I should call for the necessary information. At 8.30 P.M. I had a letter from Sachse stating that the Prince "wished to speak to me for a few moments," and requested me to call upon him next day at 12.30 P.M. I called at the time appointed, and after waiting for about half an hour, while the Chief was dictating to one of his deciphering clerks who wrote shorthand, I was admitted to see him, and the "few minutes" extended to a full hour. The Prince was in plain clothes, with the exception of military trousers. He had grown thinner, so that his coat hung in folds over his shoulders. Otherwise, however, he looked well, and was evidently in good humour. He greeted me with a shake hands and " Good day, Büschlein." Then, inviting me to sit down, he said : " You want fodder, but I have none. There is nothing going on either in domestic or foreign affairs. You recollect that little bit of a Herzegovina, and now we have that little bit of an Egypt. It is not of much concern to us, although it certainly is to the English and also to the French. They set about the affair in an awkward way, and have got on a wrong track by sending their iron-clads to Alexandria, and now, finding that there is nothing to be done they want the rest of Europe to help them out of their difficulty by means of a conference. Nothing can be done with the fleet without a landing force, and this is not at hand, so that it will be merely a repetition of the demonstration before Dulcigno. In that case it was the rocks, here it is the European warehouses, otherwise they would in all probability have already bombarded the place. It is also a question whether they would not have come off second best, as the Egyptians have very heavy guns, and their artillery is not bad. But so far as a conference is concerned, it is like an inquiry round a board of green cloth, the interests of the Powers are not the same, and therefore it will not be easy to come to any practical conclusion. The Sultan too will not co-operate. He is not without justification in declining to do so. If he can put things right by writing letters and sending plenipotentiaries—which we shall know one of these days—the Western Powers will have reason to be

thankful. If not there will be no alternative left but
for the Padishah to send his Nizams to restore order
there. That is due to the absurd policy which
Professor Gladstone has pursued from the beginning.
He tries to come to an understanding with France and
Russia, forgetting the fact that their interests in the
Levant are quite different to those of the English. He
surrendered all the valuable results which English
policy had tried to secure during the past eighty years
in its dealings with the Porte and with Austria, and
thought he could work miracles when he had offended
them both. And in France they have also taken a
wrong course out of consideration for public opinion.
Egypt is of the utmost importance to England on
account of the Suez Canal, the shortest line of communication between the eastern and western halves of
the Empire. That is like the spinal cord which connects
the backbone with the brain. Any increase of Turkish
power does not affect England injuriously in this, or
indeed in any other respect. France thinks more of
the prestige to be gained by the Porte if it exercises a
mediating and controlling influence in the Egyptian
question, and fears that her own prestige in Africa
might suffer. Nevertheless, France has also very important material interests there, since there are 14,000
Frenchmen in Egypt and only 3,000 English. It was
in vain for me to point out to them that an Arabian
Empire, such as Arabi may have in view, would be far
more dangerous to their position in Africa than any
strengthening of Turkish influence on the Nile. The
Porte is an old European landowner who is deeply in
debt, and who can always be reached and subjected to
pressure if he becomes too exacting. It is impossible
to foresee what effect an independent Egypt would have

upon the French position in Africa. That is doubtless recognised by Freycinet, but he is afraid of the traditions, prejudices and vanity of the French, and of Gambetta, who manipulates them. It is true the division in the Chamber turned out favourably, indeed very much so, but even assuming that Gambetta cannot return to power shortly, the wind may soon blow from another quarter, and the understanding with England come to an end. A campaign in co-operation with the French, a military occupation, would be a hazardous undertaking for the English, as the French could always send more men than they, who require their soldiers in Ireland, and who have altogether none too many. If France had the larger force there she would of course exercise more influence and play the leading part, and it would perhaps be difficult to get her out of the country again. The rest of us would not co-operate in a military sense, as for the present the question is one of comparative indifference to us, and it is no business of ours to pull the chestnuts out of the fire for other people, particularly for the English. So there they are, with their ships, in a blind alley, and now they want a conference to put the matter right. Here also we are expected to come to their assistance, and bring pressure to bear on the Porte, thus embroiling ourselves with the Sultan—a suggestion which, of course, we must politely decline."

"Much in the same way," I said, "as the English before the last Russo-Turkish conflict wished you to forbid the Russians entering upon hostilities, merely because that did not suit England's policy, and when Queen Victoria wrote to you and the Emperor to that effect." "Yes," he rejoined, "and it was the same before the Crimean war, when Bunsen pleaded their cause. They must manage to get out of the difficulties into which they have plunged by themselves—having made their bed they must lie on it."

The dog, which had been standing behind me and occasionally made his presence known by snarling, now began to bark. "He notices that there is a stranger outside," said the Prince, who rang the bell and ordered the attendant to keep the dog in the outer room. He then continued: "In home affairs there is also nothing of importance that you are not weary of. They will reject the tobacco monopoly. There is no other course open to them now." "But, Serene Highness," I said, "you will submit it to them again, and carry it through in three or four years' time?" "That depends upon circumstances," he replied, "upon the future elections. I have no intention of pressing the tobacco monopoly out of a mere liking for this particular method of fiscal reform. The monopoly is an evil, but it is still the best of all available means of reform. . . . I first want to get from them my certificate that I have done everything in my power to do away with an unfair form of taxation, but that they would not hear of it. Then they may settle the matter with their electors and justify their conduct, should it perhaps result in an increase of the class tax (a form of direct taxation), while other burdens cannot possibly be reduced."

"Then one might as well emigrate," I said.

"Certainly," he rejoined. "The class tax, which at present is retained only in this country, is one of the chief causes of emigration. If you only knew for how many evictions it is responsible among the poorer and indeed even among the middle classes! It is like the Russian poll tax, and does not permit of any equitable distribution of the burden in accordance with the condition of those who have to bear it, while indirect taxation distributes itself automatically. My object was to provide a remedy for this and to lighten the burden of the poorer citizens. That ought also to have been the object of the Diet. But you have seen from the discussion on the Appropriation Bill how little disposed they are to do so; and Lingen's motion, which was adopted by the Commission, will not even admit the necessity of a reserve."

I observed: "The emphasis laid upon economy in his motion is quite after the manner of the pedagogue, and of the narrow-minded Philistine. It does not sound as if it came from the Parliament of a great empire, but rather as if the vestry of Little Peddlington were casting the light of its wisdom upon the subject. This petty huckstering spirit is characteristic of all Liberalism. The majority of them are 'snobs' with a sprinkling of 'swells.'" [1]

"That is true," he said. "They certainly have not much amplitude or breadth of view, and they are bent on obstinate resistance to the Emperor's message, in which a far higher standpoint is adopted. But that is their nature. They only think of their joint stock companies, *i.e.*, their Parliamentary parties, and whether their shares will rise or fall if this or that is done or left undone. They trouble their heads very little with anything beyond that. Besides they hope that the old Emperor will soon die and that his successor will give them a free hand. The Emperor, however, does not at all look as if he were going to oblige them. He may live for a long time yet and indeed reach a hundred. You should see how robust he is now, and how straight

---

[1] The author is responsible for this use of the words "snob" and "swell."—TRANSLATOR.

he holds himself! From what——(I understood, Lauer) says, the Nobiling phlebotomy has been of benefit to him, both physically and mentally, the old blood has been drawn off, and he looks much less flabby than formerly. We are now on good terms, better than we have been for years." "And the Successor will have to follow the same course," I said. "He cannot govern differently without doing mischief." "Oh, yes," he rejoined. "He also would like to retain me, but he is too indolent, too much devoted to his own comfort and thinks it would be easier to govern with majorities. I said to him : ' Try it, but I will not join in the experiment!' Perhaps they are out in their reckoning however, and a long-lived sovereign may be followed by a short-lived one. It seems to me as if this might be the case. He who would then ascend the throne is quite different. He wishes to take the government into his own hands ; he is energetic and determined, not at all disposed to put up with Parliamentary co-regents, a regular guardsman !—Philopater and Antipater at Potsdam ! He is not at all pleased at his father taking up with Professors, with Mommsen, Virchow and Forckenbeck. Perhaps he may one day develop into the *rocher de bronze* of which we stand in need."

He then came to speak of his other schemes of reform, and observed : "The so-called Socialistic Bills are in a tolerably fair way. They will force themselves through, and develop further, even without me. The most pressing and necessary measures will in the main be soon carried. But it is unsatisfactory that they should want to bring the funds for the relief of the sick into too close connection with the insurance scheme. In this case it is not advisable that the payments in kind should be transformed into money payments."

He then gave a technical explanation, the details of which I was unable to understand, and was therefore unable to remember fully. I said: "But it is intended to drop the State subsidy, through which you hoped to reconcile the labouring classes, by getting them to recognise that the State not only makes demands upon them, but also comes to their assistance, procuring relief for them in case of need, and providing for their future as far as possible."

"No, not dropped," he replied, "but it is not immediately necessary in the new form which the Bill has taken. In about five or ten years it will be seen how far the contributions go, and in fifteen years' time it may be asked whether, and to what extent, the State should contribute. It is sufficient for the present that all sums falling due are immediately paid, the State guaranteeing the amount."

He again explained this in detail, and then said: "I am tired and ill, and should prefer to go, once I got my release from the Reichstag, but I do not like to leave the old Emperor alone. When he lay on his back after the outrage, I vowed to myself that I would not. Otherwise, I would rather be in the country at Friedrichsruh. I always felt better there; while here I get excited and angry, and become so weak that I can scarcely work for a couple of hours without losing hold of my ideas. How beautiful and fresh it was there in the country. I enjoyed every day, driving out and seeing how fine the rye looked, and how healthy the potatoes!"

This led him on to speak of the hope which he had of a good harvest, and that again to the price of corn in Germany and England. In this connection he observed, *inter alia*: "The opinion that low prices for corn mean happiness, welfare and content is a superstition. In that case the inhabitants of Lithuania and Rumania ought to be the most prosperous of all, while prosperity should decrease in proportion as you come west towards Aix la Chapelle. In England, the price of corn is now lower than here, and yet discontent prevails among the poorer classes, Radicalism is spreading, a revolution is approaching, and that democratic republic for which Gladstone and his friends and associates, Chamberlain and Dilke, have helped to pave the way, will come. It is just the same in Spain and Italy, where the dynasties, it is true, will offer resistance, but probably to no purpose. In France it remains to be seen whether the Republic will maintain itself, and if it does a condition of things will arise similar to that in America, where respectable people consider it disgraceful to have anything to do with practical politics, or to become a Senator, Congress man, or Minister."

On my rising he walked about the room for a while, continuing to speak, but sat down again soon as if he felt tired. He mentioned Herbert, who is still in London, and from this I turned the conversation on to Hatzfeldt, remarking that his appointment as Secretary of State had not yet taken place. He rejoined : "That is due solely to the fact that he himself has not yet declared in favour of remaining. He has still to complete his arrangements, and settle with his brother about a mortgage. Moreover, I cannot blame him if he prefers to draw—(I did not catch the amount) in Constantinople, where things are cheaper, than 15,000 thalers here. He has a fortune of about 100,000 thalers. I wanted more for him, 60,000 marks, but the Federal Council rejected the proposal, as they could not give the Secretary of State more than the Imperial Chancellor, who receives only 54,000, but who has become wealthy thanks to public grants. You cannot expect everybody to be prepared to make sacrifices. Every one is not disposed to lead a simple life, cutting his coat according to his cloth, and to forego great entertainments and other expensive habits; and then it is a case of five into four won't go, so I borrow one. He must, however, decide between this and July. Otherwise we shall have to ask Dr. Busch."

"No, thank you," I replied. He said: "There are two doctors of that name, and I mean the other, not Büschlein. But Busch has as poor health as Hatzfeldt, who is effeminate to boot, wraps himself up like a Frenchman, and goes to bed when he has a headache or cold, so that I have already been obliged to do their work instead of their taking over mine."

"From these invalids he passed on to the Empress. "She lives on and is again in good health, but a great deal of my illness comes from her intrigues. Schleinitz is also on his legs again, although he was very ill. Doubtless he thinks: 'Perhaps there may be some more Jewish *pourboires*, so I must keep alive!'"

I asked if he would speak in the debate in the Reichstag on the monopoly. "Yes," he said, "if my health permits it. Not for the purpose of convincing them, but to bear witness before the country, and then to demand my release." I inquired whether he intended to go to Kissingen again this summer. "No," he replied. "Although the waters have usually been very beneficial, they did me no good the last time. For nearly four months afterwards I was tormented with hæmorrhoids that were fearfully painful, burning like hell fire." He then added a description of the symptoms.

Before leaving I also asked: "How do you like the

Chevalier Poschinger,[1] Serene Highness? There is a great deal of interesting matter in the collection, but it seems to me that he might have made a better choice. But I suppose all the documents did not come into his hands?" He replied: "That, too, had something to do with it. But there is a great deal that has not got into the archives, such as my letters to the late King, which were retained by Gerlach and which his heirs will not easily part with. But even as it is, the book is very instructive, as it contains a great deal which was not known so accurately before; and it is perhaps well that those letters and other things should remain unpublished for the present."

He had in the meantime shaken hands several times by way of taking leave of me, but each time started some new subject which caused me to remain. He now reached me his hand for the last time, and thanking him for giving me the pleasure of seeing him after such a long interval I took my leave. As usual after such interviews, I went straight home in order to write down what I had heard without delay, before anything else should chance to blur the impression.

On the 15th of July I again visited Bucher. He complained once more of the indifferent way in which business was done at the Foreign Office and in the Imperial Chancellerie. Herbert sent his father, Holstein or Rantzau private reports of what he picked up in London society, the clubs, &c.—mostly gossip—which was then forwarded to the Emperor and occasionally made use of in the press. The correct thing for him to do would be to communicate what he had heard to his Chief, the Ambassador, who could then forward it

---

[1] The editor of a collection of Bismarckian documents of the Frankfurt period.

separately, or include it in his own despatches. Herbert reported recently that after the murder of Cavendish and Burke, Gladstone, when sitting in his place in Parliament, covered his face with his hands in order to show the depth of his affliction, although the event was in every way opportune for him. That evening, however, he was . . . . Rantzau then came to him, Bucher, to say that the Chief would like to see that mentioned in one of the papers, but not in the *Norddeutsche Allgemeine Zeitung*, and to ask whether he, Bucher, would see to it. Bucher replied that his instructions were to write only for the *Post* and the *Norddeutsche*. He would, however, prepare it for the press and Rantzau could then give it to Lindau, who might get it into the *Kölnische Zeitung*, or into one of the Hamburg papers. After a while Rantzau returned and said that in Lindau's opinion one of the phrases would be better if translated into the *oratio obliqua*. "But," said Bucher, smiling, "it was a quotation, yet neither of them recognised it, although it was taken from Schiller. I said to him they could do what they liked with it, and since then they have not pestered me with such matters." Bucher confirmed what the Chancellor had told me respecting Prince William's attitude and way of thinking in political matters. He added that the Prince had told some of his acquaintances how much he disapproved of his mother reading the *Volkszeitung*, and identifying herself with the views of the Progressist party. Bucher then mentioned that a member of the Crown Prince's *entourage* had informed him that one of the leaders of the National Liberals had recently stated that they were not so very much opposed to the tobacco monopoly, but wished to "keep their consent to it as a gift for the next emperor." He added

"I was about to write that to the Chancellor, whom I now rarely see; but I saw from his speech on the monopoly that he had already been informed of it." In Bucher's opinion the most important feature in the Egyptian question is "that we may expect it to lead to a breach between France and England. . . . . Our relations with Austria are excellent. What he was not able to tell you at the time is a fact. We have a formal alliance with the Austrians, and the Chief has also done something more, so that we are quite safe from war for several years to come."

With regard to Hatzfeldt, Bucher said : " He wants to have the Secretaryship of State offered to him so that he may make his acceptance conditional upon exorbitant terms for himself. But the Chief, in order to avoid placing himself under any obligations, means to leave it to the Emperor to settle matters with him."

We finally spoke about Eckardt, whom it was intended at first to employ in the Literary Bureau, but who has now a prospect of an appointment in the Ministry of the Interior. Bucher thinks the affair is a demonstration of the Chief's against the Russians, who "always fancied until now that we must run to answer the bell whenever they ring." Eckardt, by the way, no longer makes the extracts from the newspapers for the Foreign Office. . . . .

On the 19th of July, Bucher sent me an article from the *Deutsches Tageblatt* of the 16th of July, entitled "Hirsch-Bleichröder-Rothschild and Germany in Constantinople." It disclosed the financial intrigues of this group of bankers, "choice members of the Chosen People," who exploit Turkey under the pretence that they are protected by the German Government in the persons of its representatives. It energetically protests against this trio, and particularly against "Bleichröder, who knows how to take advantage of the credit which Germany enjoys at the Golden Horn in association with persons who only manifest their national sentiments and their patriotism when these can be turned to account for their own transactions." Bucher wrote: "I send you this article for your Memorabilia. It will be frequently mentioned hereafter. *Justizrath* Primker of Berlin, is the agent of Bleichröder here referred to."

On the 2nd of August I received a card from Bucher, in which he said: "I have to-day taken leave of absence, and at the same time tendered my resignation. I will tell you why at some future time. Auf Wiedersehen."

I therefore called upon him (Bucher) on the 2nd of October, and at once inquired whether he decided to retire or to remain on. He replied that he would remain for the present. On the 1st of August he begged the Chief to obtain the Emperor's consent to his retirement. In this letter the only motive which he gave was consideration for his health (growing nervousness), although, as I knew, he had other and stronger reasons. He then proceeded to Bormio, whither the Prince's answer followed him. The Chief wrote that before regarding his request as final, he would like Bucher to come to Varzin to talk over the matter—he would doubtless also be pleased to see the place once more. He (Bucher) arranged to go there on his return from his holiday, and accordingly proceeded to Varzin on Tuesday last. There the Chancellor explained to him that he still required the services of his knowledge and ability, and although he could quite conceive that he was ailing and tired, he believed he could get over that difficulty by giving him as much holiday as he liked at all times, summer and winter. In future, also, he should be immediately under him. To this Bucher replied that he did not wish to retire altogether, but he had had a mind to take up some work of importance which he could have done at home in connection with documents in the Archives that had not yet been used. He believed he could do that work as well as the officials of the Archives (Poschinger and Sybel). That might also be done, the Chief said, but he must remain in the service; he was indispensable to him. Bucher then begged to be allowed two days to think the matter over, after the lapse of which time he acceded to the Prince's wishes. He does not expect any good to come of the arrangement, however, as in his opinion there will be no change in the condition of affairs.

I then inquired how the Chief was getting on. Bucher replied: "Not very well. He suffers from face-ache, which occurs constantly and is often very bad, but passes away again after a while. The doctor thinks it comes from a bad tooth, and has advised him to have it out or let the nerve be killed. But the Chief will not agree to this, as he does not believe in the doctor's opinion. When this is not tormenting him he is still the same old amiable *causeur*, and he often has moments of inspiration too, when he speaks on political affairs with astounding far-sightedness. I shall hardly enjoy much more of it, however. During recent years I have seen him more seldom than yourself, sometimes not for two months at a time. But perhaps that may improve again later or indeed very soon. A few days ago when I was speaking to Rantzau about my resignation, he said that was surely not necessary. It was true that the Emperor might live to a great age, but he would probably not govern much longer and then it would be the turn of the Crown Prince, who had not altered since the conflict he had had with his father twenty years ago. (Freytag's account of this conflict was handed over by me for publication to the *Süddeutsche Zeitung* in Frankfurt-on-the-Main somewhere about the summer of 1862. It made a great sensation at the time and caused no little anxiety.) He was a regular Progressist and already he made no secret of it. While I was away he had accepted Ludwig Löwe's invitation to inspect his revolver manufactory, and even deigned to take breakfast there. Recently, on entering a Court gathering at which Puttkamer and also three Progressists, including Mommsen and Virchow, were present he passed the Minister by and joined the Liberal trio, with whom he then conversed in a demonstrative fashion. It must be remembered that this took place at a time when an action was being brought against Mommsen for insulting the Chancellor. The Chief was quite aware of this and speaking of the future Emperor, he had said: "He will wish to retain me, but I shall lay down my conditions, which he will agree to, but he will not keep his promise." Bucher continued as follows: "Then the Chief will resign and proceed to Varzin, which he even now does not wish to leave, and a sort of colony will be founded there in connection with which they doubtless have me also in view. It is then intended to write memoirs. Speaking to me about them in 1877, he said: 'I have still a great deal to say to the world.'—The Progressists are aware of the Crown Prince's views and they will then want to form a Ministry taken from their own ranks. Virchow has hinted as much in public speeches, adding that the entire policy of the country including foreign affairs would be different.—Bismarck was a gifted politician who represented a system of diplomacy which, except by himself, had long since been regarded as played out. That would lead to a pretty state of affairs, but would not last long. In the meantime, however, many blunders and an immense deal of harm might be done."

I then asked what he thought of Bismarck's religious sentiments, giving him my reasons for thinking that his wife had influenced him in this respect. He agreed with me and said that the views of the Moravian Brethren prevailed in her family. For the rest it was very difficult to form an opinion on those matters. He then observed that Bismarck also believed in ghosts. There is a castle in East Prussia which no one will inhabit as it is said to be haunted by the ghost of a lady who committed some crime. She is visible in broad daylight. On one occasion, when this story was told in Bismarck's presence and some of the company spoke of it as folly, the Chief said there might very well be something in it, and that one ought not to laugh and jeer at such things, as he himself had had a similar experience.[1]

Bucher also considers such things possible. He said: "A very remarkable incident of that kind once occurred to myself. When I lived on the Lutzow Embankment—it was during the first years of my appointment when I had a great deal to do and was so tired in the evening that I used to fall asleep as soon as I lay down—one night I saw my mother stoop down over my bed and smile contentedly, as if she were pleased that I had now begun a regular life. I am quite certain that it was not a dream."

---

[1] Probably at Schönhausen. See Hesekiel's *Buch vom Grafen Bismarck*, p. 19.

Finally I told him I intended to leave Berlin and return to Leipzig, as I had too little opportunity of seeing and being of use to the Chief, and found little society for my wife and myself. I would remain until February, in order to take leave of the Prince in person, and then proposed to come to Berlin a couple of times every year to visit him. In the meantime, I would now and then take the liberty of requesting him (Bucher) to furnish me with advice, explanations and materials in political affairs, while, on the other hand, I also should be at his disposal, as before 1878, whenever he wished to secure the insertion of anything in the press. Should the Chancellor retire at any time I would write him immediately, that he might count upon my services. Bucher approved of these suggestions.

On the 2nd and 3rd of November Bucher sent me a number of newspaper extracts referring to Bleichröder and his relations with Hatzfeldt, and Augusta's intrigues against Bismarck, with which the latter in a pencil note had associated the Jesuit, Father Beckx. Bucher intends to write me further on the subject.

On the morning of the 6th of November I called on Bucher at his lodgings, and reminded him of this promise. He gave me the following information. "Hatzfeldt intends to become Vice-Chancellor. For that reason he has had himself made Minister of State, a measure which was unwelcome to the Chief, and which was managed with difficulty owing to the opposition of his colleagues. Hatzfeldt has had that represented in the press as necessary, supporting the contention by precedent. Hohenlohe was once Vice-Chancellor. I will cut out some of the newspaper articles and send them to you. He had a *démenti* of the article on the Hatzfeldt-Schapira affair (reproduced by the *Volks-*

zeitung from the *Süddeutsche Post*) published in the *Deutsches Tageblatt*, which the Chief reads. This article was written by Viereck, a Social Democrat, while the *démenti* was probably by Holstein or Fuchs. Hatzfeldt is gradually disclosing his Catholic sympathies, using his influence, for example, with the Minister of Public Worship for the appointment of certain Catholic clergymen. Bleichröder, senior, applied to the Parisian Rothschild and the *Discontogesellschaft* to co-operate in his great Turkish railway and tobacco monopoly scheme, as his own funds were not sufficient; without success, however, as the latter did not wish to have any dealings with such a corpse as Turkey. He had also been to Busch, the Under-Secretary of State, and had hoped to obtain his support for the scheme, as in the Rumanian affair, which was a disgrace to us. The support was given in that case owing to the pressing appeals of the old Hohenzollern, Prince Charles' father."

On one occasion in the sixties Corvin (Wiersbycki) [1] had at Bucher's instance written in an English newspaper against the Empress Augusta. The Chief had instructed Bucher to get this done, as such attacks influenced the Court, which was afraid of the press. Corvin then borrowed a hundred thalers from Bucher, and only paid him back twenty-five. "He probably forgot the remainder. But the article was very well done." Finally Bucher mentioned that Lindau was now ill. The Prince's son had formerly begged in writing not to let it be noticed that Lindau was incapable, and he had retained the letter. "Heyking has now for a considerable time past been looking after the press; but,

---

[1] Formerly a lieutenant in the Prussian army, then an officer of the revolutionary forces in Baden, and finally a democratic writer.

while you and I managed that alone, he has taken on a Count Henckel as an assistant. The latter, who reads the newspapers for him, has again appointed one of the men in the office to act as amanuensis, and do 'the scissors and paste.' They are fond of their ease, these aristocratic gentlemen!"

CHAPTER II

BLEICHRÖDER AND GERMAN DIPLOMACY IN CONSTANTINOPLE—FURTHER INTERVIEWS WITH THE CHANCELLOR—RELATIONS WITH RUSSIA AND AUSTRIA—THE GABLENTZ MISSION—QUEEN VICTORIA—AN UNPLEASANT EPISTLE—A SEVERE REPRIMAND—BISMARCK COLLABORATES WITH ME—BUCHER'S JOURNEY WITH SALAZAR—A PRESS CAMPAIGN AGAINST ENGLAND—DOCUMENTS AND ARTICLES ON SOUTH AFRICAN QUESTIONS.

On the morning of Monday, the 27th of November, 1882, I called upon Bucher to hand him a packet with two articles and a letter to be forwarded to the Prince at Varzin, which he promised to do. The latter ran as follows :—

"HOCHVEREHRTER HERR REICHSKANZLER,

"Every man has his own ambition. Mine consists in studying and giving as true as possible a picture of your Serene Highness. I am accordingly about to write a new book respecting you in which the more important material scattered through my previous book will be brought together and supplemented from my own observation, and such sources as the letters in Hesekiel's work, and the despatches published by

Poschinger and in Hahn's collection. It will not be a biography, but only a detailed character sketch, in a number of chapters, such as Bismarck and Parliamentarism, Bismarck and the German Question, Bismarck and Religion, the Legend of Junker Bismarck, Bismarck and the Diplomatists, Bismarck and the Social Problem Bismarck as Public Speaker and Humorist, Bismarck and Austria, France, Russia and the Poles, and, finally, Bismarck in Private Life. The way in which I propose to treat the subject will appear from the two articles herewith enclosed, which I would beg you to regard as mere preliminary studies. The first of these, 'Bismarck as a Junker,' being a harmless sketch, has already been published in the monthly periodical, *Aus Allen Zeiten und Landen*, and the second, 'Bismarck and Religion,' is to appear in the *Grenzboten*. In case of new material coming into my possession both shall be re-written for the book, the object of which is to assist the future historian, and at the same time to be useful to yourself. Everything calculated to interfere with the latter purpose shall be omitted. It is highly desirable that I should receive your Serene Highness's help in the course of the work. I therefore venture most respectfully to recall the fact that Hesekiel was greatly assisted in this way, and that your Serene Highness in 1873 held out hopes to me of similar assistance. Moreover, as many parts of the book will certainly produce the impression that the author is well informed, it is to be feared that should it at the same time contain errors, the public may also accept them as true.

"I therefore beg in the first place that the two specimen articles may be kindly revised and returned to me, supplemented with as much new material as possible, and, where needful, corrected. I would afterwards, with your permission, send in from time to time legibly written copies of other chapters, and crave the same consideration for them.

"It may be said that such books should not be written during the lifetime of the person described. I take the liberty of rejoining that they can be best done at that time, if confidence is reposed in the writer, as he can then obtain fuller information than can be found in archives, the contents of which are not always, later on, rightly understood by every one.

"Should your Serene Highness desire to communicate verbally with me on the matter, I am ready at all times to obey your commands without delay.

"Your Serene Highness's most respectful and devoted
"DR. MORITZ BUSCH.

"BERLIN, *November 26th*, 1882."

At 11.30 A.M. on the 1st of December, Bucher called upon me to return the two articles that had been sent to Varzin, namely, "Bismarck as a Junker" and Bismarck and Religion." He at the same time communicated to me the contents of a letter from Count Herbert, to the effect that the Prince had read the articles through, and had said with regard to the second that he could communicate nothing on a matter of so personal a character; and that he could not remember having made the statement on page 2 that he had "brought about three great wars." It might be possible to insert the word "perhaps" in that sentence. His (Herbert's) personal opinion was that nothing more ought to be written about his father, and if he had any influence with me he would use it in this direction. I explained to Bucher that if the Prince himself had asked me not to publish anything more about him, I should most *probably* forbear to do so, but that Herbert had no claim to any influence upon me. " What is Hecuba to me ? " I concluded.

December 19*th.*—Received the following letter from Bucher :—

"A horrible cough has deprived me of my night's rest for the past fortnight, but I am a little better since yesterday. As you do not read many of the newspapers, I send you two extracts which will furnish material for the history of the morals of our time.

" 1. *Norddeutsche Allgemeine Zeitung,* of the 15th instant.—The following in print :—' *Herr Justizrath* Primker is returning to Constantinople in order to join the Council for the administration of the Turkish State Debt in connection with the establishment of the tobacco monopoly and the unification of the Debt. The reports received from various correspondents respecting that gentleman's failure or success in connection with any other financial mission are all erroneous. How far the investigations made by *Herr Justizrath* Primker respecting matters of commerce and means of communication in the East may be utilised in the interest of German capital remains a question for the future.'" Bucher then goes on to say : " Unquestionably prepared by Bleichröder, and intended to serve as a kind of official credentials for his agent. You are sufficiently acquainted with the position of that newspaper to know that such an article would not have been accepted unless some one in the Foreign Office (Hatzfeldt) had had the matter in hand."

" 2. *Deutsches Tageblatt* of the 19th instant.—The following also in print :—' We are pleased to learn from an incidental paragraph in the *Norddeutsche Allgemeine Zeitung* that *Justizrath* Primker, one of Messrs.

Bleichröder's agents for international transactions, has had and has no other financial mission in Constantinople than to represent their firm. We are glad to see this statement in the *Norddeutsche Allgemeine Zeitung*, because—as one of our well-informed Vienna correspondents has shown—*Justizrath* Primker has contrived in Constantinople to make it appear as if he were on the staff of the German Embassy, and as if the German Government were backing him up with all its influence and approval, a circumstance which we should deeply regret, as Primker's efforts are directed to promoting the interests of Bleichröder and of the notorious Baron Hirsch, and do not tend to the furtherance of the general interests of the German Empire on the Bosphorus. Herr Primker is again going to Constantinople, ostensibly to take part in the work of the Council of the Turkish Public Debt in introducing the tobacco monopoly administration and unifying the State Debt. The Council, as is well known, has charge of the interests of the European creditors of Turkey, and with this object supervises the administration of the Turkish Public Debt. It protects, however, only the interests of the larger creditors, as is shown by the attitude adopted by Herr Primker, who knew how to secure all the advantages for Herr Bleichröder and his partners, while entirely neglecting the claims of the poorer holders of Turkish securities in Germany, so that they actually came off worst of all in the arrangements ultimately made. And yet it was these who ought to have been considered in the very first place, as the net receipts of the Turkish railways amounted to about four million francs, a sum which was sufficient to provide for a fair interest on the securities. It is well known, however, that Baron Hirsch is still able to withhold these receipts from the Turkish

Administration, and is assisted in doing so by his business friend, Herr Bleichröder, who is quite indifferent as to whether the interests of others and particularly of German creditors suffer thereby. One hawk does not peck out another hawk's eyes. Even if we can do nothing to remedy this state of affairs, we can at least help people to recognise the bird by its feathers.' (Bucher's letter now follows once more.) I am sufficiently acquainted with the management of this paper to know that such an article must at least have been sanctioned in a higher quarter (Bismarck)."

December 20*th*.—The day before yesterday I wrote to the Imperial Chancellor begging for an interview, and in case there were anything to mention in the press to supply me with the necessary information. At 1.30 P.M. to-day a Chancery attendant brought me a letter from *Hofrath* Sachse, marked "Urgent," in which Bismarck "requested me to be good enough to visit him this afternoon at 4 o'clock." I went to the palace at the time appointed. Theiss showed me in to the Prince, with whom I remained for three-quarters of an hour. He had a white beard, and was sitting at his writing-table. After reaching me his hand he said : "You have doubtless come with great expectations, and think I shall have something to say to you about the article in the *Kölnische Zeitung*—the one on Russian armaments.' I asked : "Did that come from here?"

He: "No, not from me; but from the military authorities."

I : "And the statements are correct?"

He : "Certainly. They are constructing many more railways than they require for trade and traffic, and the garrisons in the western towns and fortresses have been placed almost upon a war footing. I should not be surprised if there were a war with them next year. The Bourse has also shown itself much concerned, but I believe that the fall in quotations arises rather from anxiety respecting France. But (he continued) you have been indiscreet in the *Grenzboten* in your reference to the alliance with Austria. It has been very awkward for them (in Austria), for the Hungarian Diet can now come and demand information on the subject."

I replied: "I thought that the matter had gradually leaked out. Three or four months ago some one, I forget now who it was, said to me that everybody now knew that a formal alliance existed, and not a mere memorandum. Perhaps my informant had it from Vienna. I was therefore of opinion that it could do no harm, and might possibly be of use if I mentioned it incidentally, as I did in the *Grenzboten* article, and I was quite astounded when all the newspapers wrote leading articles upon it. I must be very much mistaken if I have not seen something similar elsewhere."

"Yes," he said; "but it was a State secret, and if you had only remembered from whom you had it, an inquiry might well be instituted. It is quite possible that something of the kind had already been said elsewhere; and if what you wrote had appeared in another paper, perhaps no one would have taken any notice of it. But you have given the *Grenzboten* such a nimbus that it is placed on a level with the Official Gazette. That is not good for you as a writer. You are regarded as, in the highest degree, inspired."

I: "That is a matter of indifference to me. It only excites hatred and envy; and I have never associated with the local journalists."

"Well," he said, smiling, "you can destroy this nimbus if you will only write something thoroughly silly."

I: "And if you then have a vigorous *démenti* inflicted upon me."

He: "But, seriously, you can to a certain extent correct the statement which you blurted out inadvertently, by saying that in doing so you believed you were only repeating what was already known; and you might go on to add a number of useful observations, as, for instance, that, if the alliance did not actually exist, it ought to be brought about, as it would be of great advantage and would fulfil the requirements of two peace-loving Powers—and, further, that we should very much regret the truth of the assertion made by the *Kölnische Zeitung* that it had only been concluded for five years; in that case it should be extended over a longer period. Finally, it would be in accordance with the interests of both Empires to strengthen and consolidate the good political relations existing between them by closer commercial relations on a treaty basis."

He then returned to the question of the Russian armaments, and said, *inter alia* : " Now I am to assist ! But they can settle the matter themselves. Three years ago I made proposals to them which they would not accept. Now let *them* settle it ! "

He reflected for a while, and then suddenly exclaimed : " Can you find us money, and rid us of the bailiff? . . . Parliament will not agree to the licensing tax, not even the Conservatives, each one of whom is cleverer than the other, while they are all of them wiser than the Government. Here there is nothing but discord, and the majority are blockheads. What is the use of their Conservatism when they will not support us? A progressive income tax is unjust, and would not be of much assistance, but an equitable income tax would be good and useful. That can be obtained by self-assessment, and it would in a short time cover the deficit in the four classes. The higher classes—14,000—pay about seven million marks, and to double that amount would be oppressive, it would mean a tax of 26 per cent. The capitalist is either a mortgagee, and if his taxes are raised, he turns upon his debtor and raises his interest to 5 or $5\frac{1}{2}$ per cent. interest, instead of 4 ; or a loan and debenture company, and then its securities would lose as much in value as the tax amounts to ; or a holder of industrial shares, and then the tax might reduce or indeed destroy the export trade in the manufactured article. The State cannot tax its own securities, and therefore there only remain foreign securities and railway shares. People are not afraid of the capitalist, but only of the tobacconist, the wine merchant, and the brewer. Of the capitalist one may say :—

> " 'I prithee take thy fingers from my throat ;
> For though I am not splenetive and rash,
> Yet have I in me something dangerous,
> Which let thy wisdom fear !' "

If the Conservatives were at one with the Government all would be well. As it is, however, we shall doubtless be obliged to dissolve again in February, and then there will not be so many Conservatives returned. The King has so far committed himself that he can no longer govern with the bailiff. His position is most painful, and he will ultimately ask the country again and again whether the bailiff is to be retained."

He then spoke about Wedell-Malchoff's motion for taxing time bargains on the Bourse. In his opinion it was not a bad idea, but the phrase " time bargains " should be defined, and in such a way as not to include genuine transactions in rye and spirits or cash transactions. Furthermore, it should start, not with two per mille, but, as the Government had proposed, with one per mille. The latter would be feasible, and of course once a beginning had been made it could be raised. The mistake here was that they were trying to get at dishonest transactions, and thus to introduce a moral tax, whilst such transactions could not possibly be defined or reached. The Chancellor's statements were somewhat to the foregoing effect. More I cannot say, as I did not understand all these financial explanations, in which he doubtless credited me with more technical knowledge and capacity than I possess to supplement their purport.

In the course of his remarks he mentioned Bleichröder's name, and I asked whether he had noticed certain hints that Bleichröder's schemes with regard to the Turkish tobacco monopoly and railways were being promoted by German diplomacy. He denied the fact. It was true, indeed, that in the Rumanian affair Bleichröder had been supported, because, in that instance, in addition to some distinguished gentlemen, a great number of small investors were concerned. Of the former he mentioned Ujest, and, if I am not mistaken, Lehndorff. There Bleichröder had really done good service, "gallantly risking his money, and it was for that reason that he had been ennobled by the King." Primker, on the other hand, he described as "clever but unscrupulous." As to the Austrian Government, he observed that they had committed themselves too far with Hirsch.

We finally came to speak about his neuralgia, which caused him a great deal of pain. I suggested that it probably came from a bad tooth.

He: "Others have thought the same, but the doctor has hammered at all my teeth, and says they are sound.

No, it is a nervous affection, muscular pain, particularly when I am worried and excited. That is why I do not attend the Parliamentary sittings; for what a delight it would be to certain people if, in the middle of a speech, I suddenly made a wry face, and were unable to proceed!" He dismissed me with the words: "Adieu, Büschlein, auf Wiedersehen! But take care to avoid further indiscretions."

January 14th, 1883.—Called this morning on Bucher to give him my new address.

Bucher then expressed a hope that the Bleichröder swindle, which was becoming more and more widely known, would ultimately be mentioned in the Reichstag. I told him that, in speaking to the Chief recently, I had referred to certain newspaper articles on the subjects, and that he declared he knew nothing of diplomatic influence having been exercised in that way at Constantinople, and had, moreover, praised Bleichröder's action in the Rumanian affair. Bucher exclaimed angrily: "Well then, he lied to you in that matter. . . . It is true, indeed, that Bleichröder and the Disconto Bank plunged into the affair gallantly, but it was not for the sake of the poor tailors, cobblers and cooks that had blundered into it, but because the Prince of Hohenzollern was also involved."

Bucher also denounced as "a lie" the Prince's statement that the article in the *Kölnische Zeitung* which followed the paragraph in *Grenzboten* on the Austro-German Alliance, and emphasised, first its five years' duration, and then the warlike preparations of the Russians, did not come from the Foreign Office, but from the military authorities. (Perhaps this assertion was intended to lead me into some "blunder" which would have deprived the *Grenzboten* of its "nimbus.") . . .

"The article is by Kruse, who as you are aware is here. I know also who corrected it." (Probably Bismarck, or possibly Bucher himself under his instructions.) The fact that the Chief told me to advocate the renewal or prolongation of the treaty, with additional commercial provisions, (this was done subsequently in the *Grenzboten* and was noted and emphasised by the *Post*) tallies according to Bucher with a proposal which the Chancellor made in Vienna. He was, however, informed in reply that that would not do, as Austria-Hungary consisted of an industrial and an agricultural country, with different interests. Bucher condemned the proposal, saying : " He is in too great a hurry, because he thinks he has only a few more years to live." I shall now take care to get away from Berlin as soon as I can, and thus avoid further risk of hearing and circulating untruths from the Chief's mouth.

January 28th.—Wrote to the Chief yesterday, informing him that the editor of *Harper's Monthly* (published in London) had asked me to write an article upon him, and if possible, also to send a photograph of the Prince with his new full beard. At the same time I added a request for an interview. On the same evening I received an answer from the Imperial Chancellerie that the Prince begged me to do him the honour of calling upon him to-morrow, Sunday, at two o'clock. I went accordingly to-day, and had to wait for a while, as the Minister of Justice was with the Chancellor, and Hatzfeldt was already waiting in the ante-chamber with Möller, the Under Secretary of State. When Hatzfeldt was called in Möller dropped into conversation with me, and asked me whether I was the author of *Count Bismarck and his People*. He then turned out to be an admirer of my former books also. He had read, among others, the *Pilgrimage to Jerusalem* and even the *Wanderings between the Hudson and the Mississippi*. When Hatzfeldt came out, the attendant immediately called me in. The Chief, who gave me a very friendly reception, had a particularly bright colour in the face. He asked: " Now then, what is it you want me to tell you for the article? All the principal facts are known." I replied that I had come less on that account than for the photograph. They had written to me that thousands of Germans in America would be much interested in seeing his portrait with the new beard. " Yes," he observed, " they now show their interest in the old country by overloading me with contributions for those who have suffered by the inundations on the Rhine. I have not the least idea what I am to do with them. I have talked over the matter with the people in the Reichstag, they must distribute the money. As to the photograph, however, the man suggested in your letter (Brasch, in the Wilhelmstrasse) cannot do it, as I have promised Löscher and Petsch, with whom I have always been satisfied. But I cannot go to them at present as I should catch cold in this weather, and also because I do not go to the Emperor, and he would be surprised if I were to be seen going to the photographer. But I should myself like to see a portrait with the beard, as I do not know how long I shall keep it." I suggested that he should let Brasch take two photographs only, as he lived close by and would bring his camera here, one of them being for *Harper* and one for me. He could be forbidden to sell any copies. But the Chief considered that that would be a breach of his word, and showed a disposition to lose his temper, so I let the matter drop.

He spoke of the way in which they "hated him in Parliament," although " he had done them no harm." " I cannot understand it," he continued. " It is not so with other Ministers, even with those who have done nothing but commit blunder after blunder, while I, at least, have maintained peace for them. Surely the present Ministry in France is a wretched concern, English policy has been an unbroken series of blunders for the last three years, and Gortschakoff, with his vanity, also makes all sorts of mistakes; yet no one in their own countries worries and hampers them in every direction. Nor in other respects have I ever given them ground for dissatisfaction. Other Ministers speculate on the Stock Exchange, and take advantage of their office and information to make money. It is asserted that several French Ministers do so, and such cases also occur in Austria, and particularly in Hungary, where the Zichys have made millions in railway shares. Manteuffel and Schleinitz took advantage of their position in the same way. No one can say anything of the kind against me. The Diest-Daber statements were slanders. I have never held speculative securities, but only regular dividend-bearing stock. It is only the national grants that have given me my competency. I have made nothing, but was, on the contrary, much better off formerly than I am now, in consequence of the low prices of corn and timber and unwise purchases of land. . . . Nor have I led a loose life, but have, on the contrary, been always a respectable father of a family. And nothing of the kind can be said of my sons either. (Really ?) No charge can be brought against me, and nevertheless I am hated. But I am tired. I have lost my old passion for shooting and riding, and I fear I shall soon lose my liking for politics. I am sacrificing my health. I ought to live in the country, and the doctors say that if I were free from business, and could spend three or four hours a day in the open air, I should be well again. But I do not like to desert the Emperor, who will soon be eighty-seven, when he begs me with tears in his eyes to remain. Nor can I expect him to accustom himself to others."

I inquired how he now stood with the Crown Prince, and he replied, "Latterly he has been very amiable to me, particularly at the various festivities." Then returning, without any transition, to the subject of Parliament and its opposition to himself, he said: "I have maintained peace for them with a great deal of trouble. After 1870 everybody expected war in a couple of years; but so far it has not come, and perhaps, indeed, it may never come again. We are now on a better footing with Russia than we have ever been before, and with Austria we have concluded an alliance." I asked him if he was still negotiating for an improvement of the treaty in a commercial direction. He rejoined: "I will not tell you that, as you have been indiscreet enough to let it be known that it was only concluded for a period of five years. The *Kölnische Zeitung* has reproduced that from the *Grenzboten*."

I: "I beg your pardon, Serene Highness, but the converse was the case. I could not have said it before the *Kölnische Zeitung*, because I was not aware of the fact until I read it in that paper." He maintained his opinion until I offered to prove to him that he was in error, by sending him the *Grenzboten* article. He then went on to relate: "They (the Austrians) thought they might satisfy their greed in that way. I imagine that I am doing them a good turn and making them a present, and then they come with their conditions. I have rejected them. A commercial treaty is possible in which we might grant them more favourable terms than to the others, and in which the tariff would not be raised, indeed perhaps reduced. The high duties which we have imposed upon Russia and America need not be applied to Austrian maize and barley. The importation of cattle may also be allowed, although that is scarcely feasible in view of the certificates given in Galicia and Hungary, where everything can be bought and everybody can be bribed. But commercial union and a common customs frontier are out of the question, for Germany takes plenty of imported goods, and superior foreign wines are consumed here in Germany, while even a groschen would be too much for a Slovak or a Raizen (*i.e.*, a Servian of Slavonia or Lower Hungary), who uses nothing of the kind. Even here there is a great difference between the Elbe Duchies or the Rhenish provinces and East Prussia or Upper Silesia."

He then came once more to speak of the peaceful times in which we are now living, and said: "You have only to look at the newspapers and see how empty they are, and how they fish out the ancient sea-serpent in order to have something to fill their columns. The feuilleton is spreading more and more, and if anything sensational occurs they rush at it furiously and write it to death for whole weeks. This low water in political affairs, this distress in the journalistic world, is the highest testimonial for a Minister of Foreign Affairs.

After a moment's silence he went on: "Then you propose to return to Leipzig?"

"Yes," I replied, "since the death of my son, my wife requires amusement and society, which are not to be had here, but which she may find in her own native town."

He: "Well, but surely any one who writes on politics ought to live in Berlin, where politics are now made."

I: "But Leipzig is only three hours from here, and during the months when you are in town I can easily reside here."

He: "That is not necessary, but you might come

every fortnight, or when anything occurs, and ask me."

He again complained of the neuralgic pains, at the same time dipping his finger, as he had already done frequently, in a wine glass containing some strong-smelling yellow liquid, with which he rubbed his right cheek bone. "That relieves me for a short time," he said. He then continued: "But I am very tired. I have now been engaged in politics practically since 1847, nearly forty years, and that is exhausting. At first in Parliament, then at Frankfurt, where I was very busy, having work thrown upon me from Berlin also."

I: "That can be seen from Poschinger's book, which I am now reading and making extracts from."

He: "Yes, but he does not say that I also wrote numerous letters to the King from Frankfurt,[1] and that I came no less than thirteen times in one year to Berlin to see him."

I: "It looks almost as if already at Frankfurt you had been his Minister for Foreign Affairs—at least Manteuffel drew his inspiration from you in the principal questions."

He: "Yes, the late King discussed all great questions with me, and Manteuffel put up with it."

I mentioned that the extracts which I was making from the documents contained in Poschinger's book were intended in the main for the chapter on "Bismarck and Austria," in which I proposed to embody what I had personally gathered in 1870, as, for instance, Prince Luitpold's abortive letter to the Emperor Francis Joseph.

He: "Certainly! But as long ago as 1866 I made an attempt to come to an understanding with them.

---

[1] These, doubtless, included those contained in the fourth volume of *Preussen im Bundestage*, which had not been published at that time.

I suppose I have already told you the Gablentz story?"

I: "No, but you have told me others from that period, as, for instance, how the King wanted to annex portions of Saxony, Bavaria and Bohemia, and how you persuaded him not to do so."

He: "Well, it occurred in this way. Just after the first shot had been fired (in reality it must have been about a fortnight before) I sent Gablentz, the brother of the general, to the Emperor at Vienna with proposals for peace on a dualistic basis. I instructed him to point out that we had seven or eight hundred thousand men under arms, while they also had a great number. It would therefore be better for us both to come to an agreement, and making a change of front towards the West, unite our forces in attacking France, recapture Alsace, and turn Strassburg into a federal fortress. The French were weak as compared with us. There might be no just cause for war, but we could plead with the other Powers that France had also acted unjustly in taking Alsace and Strassburg, whence she had continually menaced South Germany ever since. If we were to bring these as a gift to the Germans they would accept our dualism. They, the Austrians, should rule in the South and have command of the seventh and eighth army corps, while we should have command of the ninth and tenth and the federal command in chief in the North. . . . Dualism is a very ancient institution, as old as the Ingævones and Istævones, Guelphs and Ghibellines."

I observed: "Already under the Othos, indeed as long ago as Charlemagne with his Franks, and the Saxons." "High German and Low German," I said. "With a Celtic fringe below and a Slavonic fringe above."

"Well," he continued, "Gablentz submitted his proposal to the Emperor, who seemed not disinclined to entertain it, but declared he must first hear the views of the Minister for Foreign Affairs, Mensdorff, you know. He, however, was a weak-minded mediocrity, unequal to ideas of that calibre, and he said he must first take counsel with the Ministers. They were in favour of war with us. The Minister of Finance said he believed they would beat us—and he must first of all get a war indemnity of five hundred millions out of us, or a good opportunity for declaring the insolvency of the State. The Minister of War was not displeased with my suggestion, but in his opinion we ought to have our own fight out first, and then we could come to an understanding and fall upon the French together. So Gablentz returned without having effected his purpose, and a day or two afterwards the King and myself started for the seat of war."

I thanked him warmly for this important and startling communication, and asked him if I might use it in my book. He replied: "Yes, it is for that purpose that I have related it to you. But not in detail, merely the main features. Proposal for peace on the dualistic basis, united attack upon France, and the reconquest of Alsace."

I then asked once more whether he wished to read the book before it went to press, and he said: "Yes, in order that you may not include anything false in my epitaph."

I: "That would certainly not be done intentionally. You know that I worship you, and would let myself be cut into a thousand pieces for you."

He: "Ah, no; not into so many! It is not necessary."

I: "Well then, only into two pieces, so that one

might see half a Büschlein (little Büsch) fall to the right and half to the left!"

On my then begging him as soon as his health permitted to let Löscher and Petsch come to take his portrait, he promised to do so, adding: "If they do not care to come, then the other man can—what's his name?"

I: "Brasch, here in the Wilhelmstrasse, at the corner of the Leipzigerstrasse."

He: "But I must first keep my word."

I: "I did not ask you to do anything contrary to it. I only thought of Brasch because he took a very good photograph of my late son."

He: "How did the thing happen?" I then related shortly the circumstances of my son's death.

He: "That is a sad case, and there are many to share your misfortune, all who had relatives on board the *Cimbria*."

I: "But my son was engaged in his profession, in the fulfilment of his duty, and died bravely and conscientiously for his ship like a soldier for his flag."

He reached me his hand, and said, "Auf Wiedersehen!" I had been with him fully three-quarters of an hour, and all this time good old Möller had to wait in the antechamber.

On returning home on the evening of the 3rd of February, I found lying on my table a letter from Count Bill, in which, at his father's request, he enclosed a new photograph of the latter with a full white beard.

On the 24th of February I wrote to the Chancellor begging to be allowed to take leave of him personally, as I proposed to start for Leipzig on the following Thursday. I handed the letter to the porter at the palace at 11 A.M., and in about an hour and a half I received an invitation through Sachse to call upon the

Prince at 3 o'clock. He was in the room behind his study, which opens on the garden. He was in an armchair, half sitting, half lying, and had beside him a small table covered with documents. After he had asked me how I was, he complained that he still felt very poorly. When one trouble left him another set in. The neuralgic faceache often prevented him from sleeping. If he could only go to the country, away from business, things might improve; but the King would not grant him leave, and " pestered him with all sorts of unimportant orders," &c., as, for instance, with the question as to who should go to St. Petersburg to attend the coronation. " He thinks," he continued, " that if I can manage to keep on my legs I shall live to be old,—and if not, why then I must die in the fulfilment of my duty. . . . And here in the Foreign Office I have no proper assistance. Look at that pile of documents which I must read through myself!" I said: " Of course there is not much to be done with Hatzfeldt. He has little ability, and still less inclination, to work. He only wants to amuse himself, and to draw a big salary for doing so." "Yes," he replied, "Hatzfeldt does little for his money, and has neither a good memory nor a taste for business." He then continued: "The Crown Prince is also inconsiderate, and torments me with matters of no importance; and, in addition to that, the people in the Diet are committing all sorts of blunders. How abusive they have been during the past few days! But it is the same everywhere with Parliaments and Ministers." I remarked: "Quite so, for instance in France." "It is no better in England," he rejoined. "The European is no longer making progress. There is nothing more to be done with him." He repeated that he was sick of politics, and wanted quiet. He then spoke of the

Kulturkampf, observing: "The Pope is really well disposed, but he is not so powerful and independent as one may think; he is dependent upon people who will have no peace. For some time it appeared as if a *modus vivendi* could be arrived at, but now that is at an end. On the signs of approaching fine weather Windthorst threatened to strike and resign the leadership of the Centre party. He wants a stormy sky for other purposes, for stirring up discontent and strife, and they on the other hand need him, or think they do. They accordingly became frightened in Rome, and now they are once more making themselves unpleasant." I said: "Catholicism has always been a secondary consideration for Windthorst. He is, above everything else, the well-paid advocate of the Guelphs."

He rejoined: "Ah, he believes in nothing whatever. He has absolutely no religion."

He caught sight of an envelope which I had brought with me and laid on the table beside us containing an enlargement by Brasch of his photograph by Löscher. He asked: "What have you there?" I answered: "It usually happens that granting one request brings on another, and that is the case now. I have had your last portrait enlarged and mounted, and I would now beg your Serene Highness to write your name under it as a souvenir. Of course it can be done in pencil." "No," he said, "in ink." He rang for the attendant and asked for "a pen to write my signature," and then wrote under the photograph: "v. Bismarck, Berlin, 24 February, 1883."

I thanked him and said: "It is then arranged, Serene Highness, that I may come here and address myself to you occasionally when anything of importance arises, particularly when there would seem to be anything on foot in which you might wish to have

some one near you in whom you could repose special
confidence? And as to the book, I may send you the
proofs in a few months? We shall probably not begin
printing before August." He agreed to all this, and
then said: "Well, good-bye, Busch. Auf Wiedersehen!
Enjoy yourself in Leipzig 'an der Pleisse.'" He
pronounced these words with a true Saxon accent.

On the 13th of May I came from Leipzig to Berlin,
and reported myself to the Chancellor by letter. . . . .
On the 15th Sachse sent me word that the Chancellor
expected me at 3 o'clock. I presented myself punctually
at the time appointed, and had to wait while the Chancellor had a short interview with Rottenburg. . . . . The
latter referred to Colonel Vogt's *Grenzboten* article on
Thibaudin, and mentioned that the Imperial Chancellor
had remarked that it was no business of ours to point
out to the French that their army was in bad hands.
Count Rantzau also came across to shake hands with
me. The Chief's youngest grandchild, Heinrich, some
five months old, was also in the antechamber, and he
also gave me his little hand to shake.

I was then with the Prince from 3.5 to 4 P.M. He
was in plain clothes, and sat at his ordinary double
writing-table. He did not look ill, but complained as
usual of his neuralgia. He said: "It now extends
over the whole body, the chest and abdomen, and I can
no longer exert myself to think or work for any length
of time—two hours at the outside; then I must give up,
or drink champagne or something of that kind to keep
myself going for a while longer. I ought to get out of
harness altogether, but the Emperor will not consent to
this, and even when I go to the country, business and
worry now follow at my heels." I asked: "Worry
with the gentlemen in Parliament?" "Ah, no," he
replied; "I no longer read their speeches and brawling.

It is the Ministers. Scholz is all right, as also Bötticher and Maybach, although the latter is somewhat blunt,—but the others, and particularly those in the Foreign Office!" I said: "But surely Bucher and Busch are able and diligent." "That is so," he rejoined; "but Bucher is cross-tempered and soured, and Busch is sinking under his load of work. I was mistaken in Hatzfeldt. He is very good for negotiating with the King and the Crown Prince, but he thinks only of his own interest, and would like to be my successor; but he has no sense of duty and no love of work." I added: "One or at most two hours' work in the day, as formerly—and then to play a game of croquet or lawn tennis with Mrs. or Madame So-and-so." "Yes," he said, "that's his way. Like Lucca. *Unser Paulchen ist sehr faulchen* (Our little Paul is very lazy). "His Excellency Herr von Keudell also wanted to become Imperial Chancellor one day, and absurd as the notion was, he worked it through his friends in the press, who had to praise him up to the skies and represent him as your intimate adviser. But I always regarded him as quite insignificant in politics, and in addition to that he could never do any work. He found a difficulty in managing the most ordinary affairs. I was often obliged to do things for him, and once at Versailles Taglioni, the deciphering clerk, finished off no less than thirty documents for him with which he was in arrears. It is true that he was very clever in looking after his own interests."

He: "Yes, and he also knew how to get himself a rich wife, and to take advantage of the position which he acquired through the friendship of my wife and his own musical talent. Moreover, he knew how to impress people with his importance—through his silence. But there was nothing behind it. He is stupid, empty and incapable. He was unable even to manage the Pay Department properly."

I: "On going to Constantinople it is said that he left a deficit of 80,000 thalers."

The Chief then spoke of Hohenlohe, and appeared to think more highly of him than he did of Hatzfeldt. He also referred to Radowitz and afterwards to Radowitz's father, alleging that the "Jesuitic attitude of the latter was responsible for Olmütz." "You know what sort of a man the late King was," he continued. "For years, during which something might have been done, Radowitz kept him occupied with all sorts of tailoring and ornamental matters, with mediæval questions of costumes, uniforms and coats of arms. He acted as Keeper of the Wardrobe to his fancies: whether such and such counts were or were not received, and the Knights of St. John, and the Wetterau bench of Counts, and the absurd question whether Saxony and Hanover should retain the right to appoint envoys,—as if a barber could not have intrigued successfully against our policy so long as they had the power. He amused the King with such trifles as these until it was too late."

He then came to speak of Lady Bloomfield's Memoirs, the Tauchnitz edition of which he brought in from the next room, and asked me to review it in the *Grenzboten*. He said I should find "the genuine English arrogance in the lady," who was "much pleased at the opposition of the Crown Princess (the present Empress Augusta); and full of the profoundest aversion to everything Prussian and German." In 1866 she "had been anti-Prussian to the backbone," and had "libelled our officers as the French did in 1870 with their story of the clock." In this connection he referred to the merino goats which the Prussians were alleged to have driven away with them from Bohemia. This led him to speak of the Crown Princess and her " English self-conceit," whereupon I reminded him of the story of the silver plate of the English shopkeepers and of the Prussian nobility which he then repeated to me as before. On my remarking that the Queen, her mother, was also unfriendly to us Germans, and had always sided with the Belgian-Coburg clique, &c., he denied that this was the case, and said that, on the contrary, she had " on the whole been favourable to us."

He then continued : " I wish you would some time or other refute the charge that I have acted inconsistently in the struggle with the Curia, and that I have changed my opinions and aims in the ecclesiastical question, and in others. That is the sort of criticism which can only proceed from some one who has never occupied the position of a leading Minister. Whoever has held such a post for any considerable time can never absolutely unalterably maintain and carry out his original opinions. He finds himself in presence of situations that are not always the same—of life and growth—in connection with which he must take one course one day, and then perhaps on the next another. I could not always run straight ahead like a cannon ball. (Doubtless a reminiscence of Schiller, "Piccolomini," I., 4.) Had I done so I should have knocked my head against a wall. When the situation changed I was obliged to alter my plans. Such changes in the situation were, moreover, chiefly due to the fickleness of parties, and, therefore, if any one is to blame they are. Their action, on the other hand, was in great part influenced by their envy. That is the national vice of the Germans. They cannot bear to see any one hold a high and leading position for any length of time. One of the most important changes was produced by the formation of the Catholic party, the founders of which might at the beginning have been expected to support the Government. Savigny, you know. It, however, weakened my position. The entire struggle with the Centre party would have taken another form, and have had a different issue, if I could have fought it out at the head of the Conservatives. I had risen from their ranks, but if I was to do justice to the requirements of the time it was impossible for me to continue in agreement with them on all points. This, and the long-suppressed hatred and envy of old comrades of my own class and faith, which very soon broke out, drove me over to the Liberal side. An understanding had to be come to with the latter if the Empire was to strike firm root, and so I was obliged to come to an agreement with the strongest party, a thing which I had tried in vain to do in 1866, when it was also desirable. It was particularly necessary in those years when Germany was threatened with a Triple Alliance like that of the Kaunitz period. The latest achievement of German diplomacy is to have prevented the formation of such a coalition against us for thirteen years. The Government was forced to appear at the head of the Liberals, at the head of the majority, in order to avert this coalition. The Conservatives fell away from me on that account. I would remind you of the Inspection of Schools Bill, and of the attitude of the *Kreuzzeitung*, and of the libels published in the *Reichsglocke*. And just as the situation was thus altered at that time, so it was again changed in 1878, through the defection of the Liberals. Here, too, it was envy and self-importance, and the desire to rule. I was no longer supported, or only in a lukewarm fashion. They were not sorry to see me weakened by the opposition of the Centre party, so that I should be forced to negotiate with them. The Progressists combined with the Centre against me. The Secessionists acted in very much the same way. From this time forward the National Liberals were silent in the struggle with Rome. They were pleased at the embarrassments to which it gave rise, and wished to have a weaker Government in order that they might appear stronger. When the Government had to strike the Liberals out of its reckoning, it naturally followed that I had to slacken my opposition to Rome. I cannot speak any longer now, or the faceache will return."

He then rose, but continued to speak of his illness for a while as he walked up and down, describing it as very painful, "like shingles." I further asked if I might in a few months send him the proofs of my book. "What book?" he said. I answered: "That which your Serene Highness has already twice promised me to read through." He then thought for a moment, and promised once more to do so, whereupon I took my leave, with wishes for his speedy recovery. He said he had no longer any hope, and only expected to grow worse. (. . . .)

On the 11th of July, after the Chancellor had left Berlin for Friedrichsruh, Grunow sent him the first sheets of my book, *Unser Reichskanzler*, to read through before they were sent to press. On the 16th of July, Count Bill returned me these proofs, with the following lines:—

"FRIEDRICHSRUH, 16/7, 1883.

"DEAR SIR,

"I enclose the proofs herewith. All that has been struck out is a passage in a private conversation. It would be better to omit altogether expressions of a similar character made in conversations of a confidential nature. (Of course, here and in what follows it is not the writer, but the Chancellor who speaks.) Many things may be said that are not suitable for publication; among these are animadversions upon Imperial institutions, such as the Constitution, for example.

"With much esteem,
"Count W. Bismarck."

The portion struck out appeared in the third sheet, (page 31, in the first volume of the work as afterwards printed, following the words "einmal zu Grunde gehen,") and ran: "Then it will be Bang! and snap goes the German Constitution. There might be a repetition of Schwarzenberg's saying, 'This arrangement has not stood the test.'" The Prince has also corrected an oversight (Vol. I., p. 12, line 24), striking out the syllable "*un*," where I had written "*unmöglich*" by mistake—evidence of the care with which he had read it through.

On the 18th of July, Count Bill returned more proofs which were accompanied with the following letter:—

"Dear Sir,

"Although my father cannot act as collaborator but must confine himself to a more negative part, suggesting to you the suppression of incorrect or unsuitable passages, he nevertheless requests you to replace the portion within brackets on page 6, by the enclosed, as the latter is more in harmony with the facts.

"With much esteem,
"Count W. Bismarck.

The enclosure here referred to was dictated to Count Bill, and appears in the book *Unser Reichskanzler*, Vol. I., pp. 54 and 55.

On the 20th of July further proofs, up to the end of the first chapter, arrived from Friedrichsruh. These again included alterations that had been dictated to Count Bill by his father.

When the Prince shortly afterwards proceeded to Kissingen, Grunow continued to send him the proofs, as he had received no orders to the contrary. They were not returned, and the printers had therefore to stop work. I, however, received the following long letter from the Chancellor, which was written by an amanuensis on official foolscap, like a State document, the two sheets being tied together with silk thread in the Imperial colours.

"KISSINGEN, *August 3rd*, 1883.

"DEAR SIR,

"You probably have no adequate conception of the state of my health and of my need of rest or you would doubtless not be the only person who begrudges me the latter, while the Emperor and the Empire and all their officials respect it. Possibly you have also no notion of the difficulties of the work which you expect me to do. On former occasions of a similar kind I have corrected all errors of fact which had arisen through mistakes on your part or on that of others. Now, however, you wish to submit to the public with regard to my way of thinking and my inner man inferences drawn from observations made by yourself and others, which in great part are actually incorrect. (He had then in his hands Chapters II. and III., and a considerable portion of Chapter IV.) It is, therefore, not surprising that your conclusions do not correspond with the facts, so that if you

were to publish them I should be forced to controvert
and refute them. There are a number of gross errors of
fact, and confusions of jest and earnest, in the expressions and incidents upon which you base your view of
my supposed way of thinking. You assume that in
everything that I have ever said in your presence for
the entertainment of my guests at table, or in my own
home, or in what you have gathered from the unreliable
accounts of third persons, I have invariably given serious
expression to my inmost feelings with the conscientiousness of a witness giving evidence on oath before a Court.

"In view of the pedantry with which you utilise
scattered fragments of conversation, a man in my position
would be obliged never to depart for a moment from a
formal mode of expressing himself or step down from his
official stilts. Everything you say in particular respecting my attitude towards Christianity and the question
of the Jews is not only monstrously indiscreet, but
thoroughly false. (Everything?) The jokes about my
superstition have already appeared in print, and in so far
as there is any truth in them are just mere jokes or
consideration for the feelings of other people. I will
make one of a dinner party of thirteen as often as you
like, and am ready to undertake the most important and
delicate business on a Friday.

"At the present moment I am particularly interested
in setting public opinion right as to my share in the
Catholic question. What you give on the subject is
incomplete and superficial, and as soon as my health has
improved I should like to supply you with better
material. For that purpose it would be necessary that
I should see you personally as soon as I have finished
my cure. If I were to correct this and other points by
correspondence I should have to myself rewrite your

book. But I must be left absolutely in peace for the duration of my Kissingen cure, and cannot occupy myself editorially with such difficult and delicate questions as those you touch upon.

"I would suggest to you to recast your book altogether, as in its present form I do not believe it will be favourably received. The work is far too lengthy, and, in particular, it contains too much material published long since by yourself and others. What is new in it is in part of little interest, while other portions are incorrect, so that I should be obliged publicly to dispute their accuracy.

"I shall be very pleased to read the further proofs in order to form an idea of the whole. When I have done that, I can afterwards give you my opinion in Berlin or Friedrichsruh, but while I remain here I must decline every description of critical or editorial work.

"(Signed)   v. BISMARCK."

In reply to this communication, I excused myself for having sent the proofs, through my ignorance of his absolute need of rest, and by recalling the fact that, in 1878, I had been permitted to send him such proofs to Kissingen and Gastein. The printing was then postponed for about eight weeks, until the beginning of October. On the 5th of that month I wrote to Friedrichsruh to ask whether it was now agreeable to him to receive me for the purpose of the interview which he had mentioned as desirable in his letter of the 3rd of August. On the 6th of October Count Herbert wrote that his father would be glad to see me as soon as he had read the proofs sent to him in the summer. Owing to his journey and the state of his health he had not been able to do so up to the present.

The work remained at a standstill for four weeks more. This was very disagreeable to Grunow, who repeatedly requested me to press the matter at Friedrichsruh. I declined to do so, as *I* could wait. He then wished to write to the Prince himself, describing his embarrassment. I tried to dissuade him, but as he nevertheless repeated the suggestion, I told him he might do so at his own risk, and also gave him a few ideas for his letter. Next day he told me that he had written. On the 9th of November I received the following letter from Friedrichsruh :—

"FRIEDRICHSRUH, *November 8th*, 1883.

"DEAR SIR,

"The Imperial Chancellor has received a letter dated the 5th instant from Johannes Grunow, publisher, of Leipzig, in which he urges despatch in the supervision of the proofs of your work. The letter contains the following sentence :—

"'The manuscript was ready and in my hands eight weeks ago, and I do not know what excuses to make without prejudice to the truth unless I can communicate to those who are pressing me the real cause of the delay. This has not been done up to the present, but if the delay should continue for any length of time it will, to my great regret, be scarcely possible to avoid it, unless I receive some other explanation.'

"It is obvious that the Imperial Chancellor cannot continue a correspondence with a person who even now threatens him with disclosures. On the contrary, he is disposed to leave this gentleman to publish your work, if he should think proper so to do, reserving to himself the right of criticising it afterwards. Before he comes to any decision on this point, however, he desires to discuss the matter with you verbally, and requests you to visit him at Friedrichsruh, bringing with you your copy of the proofs of your work.

"I beg of you to be good enough to let me know shortly beforehand the day and hour of your arrival.

"I am, honoured Sir, with profound esteem,
"Your most obedient,
"F. RANTZAU."

I thereupon announced that I should arrive at Friedrichsruh on the 12th of November. I started on the 11th, and, travelling *viâ* Berlin, reached Friedrichsruh shortly after 12 o'clock on the following day. I was met at the station by a servant, who accompanied me to the Prince's house and showed me to my room. Shortly afterwards I was called downstairs, where I had a friendly reception from the Chancellor and his wife. We then took lunch, Rantzau being also present, and immediately afterwards the Prince went with me into his study in order to discuss the matter that had brought me hither. He first gave expression to his indignation at Grunow's letter, in which connection I also came in for my share. Among other things which he said was: "You have turned me into a bookseller's hack; I am to be exploited like a Christmas speculation, and harnessed to his cart, the impudent fellow! He should have known nothing whatever of my assistance!" I explained to him that I had to inform Grunow owing to the possibility of a considerable delay in the return of my proofs, that I had previously mentioned this to him, the Chancellor, and that he had agreed, and that the same course had been adopted in the case of the first book. In his excitement he appeared to have overlooked what I had said, as he went on as follows:

"That must remain between ourselves. I can trust you. You may write to me. But he! What right has a bookseller got to correspond with me, to warn and threaten me?" I tried in vain to appease him, endeavouring to show that the passage quoted by Rantzau when read in connection with the remainder of the letter was perhaps not a threat, but only a strong and not particularly felicitous expression of Grunow's difficulty and embarrassment. The latter was a man of straightforward character, who knew how to keep his own counsel, and who was incapable of wishing to bring pressure of a threatening character to bear upon the Chancellor, for whom he entertained the highest regard. He then rang for Rantzau, and asked him to bring Grunow's letter, which he handed to me to read. I could not see that it contained anything more than a cry of distress on the part of the publisher, who had promised the booksellers that a certain book would appear at a fixed date, and who feared he could not keep his word nor find any sufficient excuse to give them. I was as little affected by this embarrassment as I was by any loss which Grunow might suffer in case the book was not published at Christmas. I could have waited for a long time, and even if that were not the case it would never have occurred to me to press him. He said: "You acted in a perfectly proper way when the matter was postponed, and I had not expected anything different from you. But all the same that remains a threat on his part, and a piece of presumption, and I hesitated whether I should not decline to have anything further to do with the book, and afterwards publicly contradict erroneous passages in it. But then I thought of you, although I altogether object to having books written about me and to people trading with me and my affairs. Poschinger has done so, and sold my despatches and letters, forgetting even to send me any remuneration." (Sometimes his humour does not desert him even in his anger.) "Besides, this new book is not so good as the preceding one. It does not contain much that is new, and what it does is false. You are not such a good observer as you were; you have grown older; and you want to divine and picture my inner man from fragmentary observations, which were mainly misconceptions. You draw conclusions from occasional utterances which you jotted down under the table-cloth. According to you I am always in deadly earnest, as if I were on oath, &c."

I abstained from urging what could be said on the other side, and his excitement gradually subsided. Taking some of the proofs he sat down at his writing-table and invited me to take a place opposite, in order that I might note down his corrections and additions. He was rather impatient over it, said my hearing was not so good as formerly, and complained that I did not take down dictation as rapidly as his sons, and so on. On this occasion we went through the greater part of the third chapter, and he had very much less to object to and alter than I had apprehended from his letter of the 3rd of August. By far the greater part of these pages he turned over without any remarks. With respect to the others he made observations that had no reference to the book, as for instance: "Thadden, a narrow-minded fellow, who has no brains." After about three-quarters of an hour he stood up and said: "I must now get some fresh air." He strode up and down the room, however, for a while, as before, and began again to vent his anger at the presumption and threats of "this bookseller who wanted to harness me to his Christmas cart."

Ultimately, however, he quieted down, grew more friendly, and showed me over the apartments, including his bedroom. In one of the first of these was hung a portrait in oils of a Roman prelate of high rank. In reply to my inquiry he informed me that it was Cardinal Hohenlohe.

He then went out for a walk or drive, while I proceeded to my room and wrote out his observations and the corrections which he had dictated to me. This room, which contains pictures of Grant, Washington and Hamilton, looks out on the park. After 3 p.m. I paid a visit to the Head Forester, Lange, with whom I took a drive.

At a quarter past six I was called to dinner. Among those present, in addition to the Prince and Princess, were the Rantzaus, Dr. Schweninger, of Munich, who was in attendance on the Chancellor, and Herr von Ohlen, another of the doctor's patients. The Prince, as I now observed for the first time, suffered from a slight attack of jaundice. Schweninger (a man of lively temperament, with dark hair and beard, who seems to be very much at home here) diagnosed the Prince's ailment as chronic catarrh of the stomach, and has been successful in his treatment. (. . . .) While taking our coffee, which was served in the Princess's room, the conversation was at first of little significance. It turned on Becker's portrait of the Prince during the Frankfurt period, and on two groups of his male and female ancestors, who from their costumes would appear to have flourished in the time between the death of Luther and the Thirty Years' War, and on the portrait of his sporting grandfather with the shot-gun, which was formerly in Berlin, but has now found a place here too. The conversation gradually grew more lively and interesting; and the Chancellor, who had remarked in the *tête-à-tête* with me at midday that he would henceforth be careful of what he said in my presence, had probably forgotten his intention. On my stating, among other things, that the war of 1870 appeared to have had an excellent effect upon the national feeling in Saxony, he added, "and still more so in Bavaria. I once said jestingly to Fabrice[1] that we should live to see order restored in Saxony one day by Bavarian troops." Speaking of Court circles in Berlin, he complained: "Whenever I performed on the political tight-rope they hit me on the shins, and, if I had only fallen, how delighted they would have been! Particularly the eternal feminine (das ewig Weibliche)."

It was only after lunch on Tuesday, the 13th, and again before dinner, that the work with the Prince was resumed, when Chapter II., the remainder of Chapter III., and about half of Chapter IV. were weeded out, the weeds again proving much less abundant than I had anticipated. He maintained that in the second chapter I made him out to be a "hypocrite" in religious matters, an idea which he had no difficulty in entirely disproving, inasmuch as he justified his belief in God among other things by a reference to facts which could only be accounted for by the existence of a Deity.

In the second section he began to dictate to me an account of his attitude towards the Kulturkampf, which he broke off on our being called to dinner. Before that he again suddenly renewed his grumbling at Grunow, I, too, coming in for a small share. He was also displeased with my long full beard. "My wife asked me," he said, "if you were older than I. 'No,' I said, 'I thought you were four or five years younger.' But she was right.

[1] The Saxon General and Minister of War.

It's your beard. It should be cut shorter. As it is it makes you look fearfully ancient."

On Wednesday, the 14th, the Chief set to work on the proofs with me after breakfast. At Chapter IV. he exclaimed: "Look here, you must have a thoroughly wicked heart. You are delighted every time you hear and can jot down a disagreeable remark about somebody." I rejoined: "I cannot trust myself to give any opinion upon my own heart. But one thing I do know, it has always been devoted to you. I only hate your enemies." He afterwards reflected for a moment, looked at the clock, and said: "I must now go out to receive Giers, who is coming from Berlin to discuss important matters with me. We shall introduce you and Schweninger to him as doctors of medicine, for if he ascertained that Dr. Busch belonged to another variety he would be afraid that he was being watched and that it would get into the newspapers. By the way, you have included him among the Jews in your diplomatic chapter, and that must be struck out. (I had referred to his name, Giers, as a russified form of Hirsch.) He may be a Jew, although he asserts that he is the son of a Finnish officer. But we must not write that, as he is well disposed, desires peace, and does what he can to secure it. He is quite indispensable to us."

The Russian Minister arrived between 2 and 3 P.M. The Chancellor received him at the station, drove with him to the house, and then conferred with him until nearly 6 o'clock, when Giers dined with us, the company remaining together over their coffee until about 9 P.M. Giers is a man of medium height, and would seem to be well advanced in the fifties. He has somewhat of a stoop as he walks. His features are of a slightly Jewish cast, a characteristic which is also evident in his gestures and movements, there being something in the hands in particular which recalled our Semites. On this occasion he spoke only in French.

On Thursday, the 15th, I wrote in my diary: Giers went off again last night about 10 o'clock, and Schweninger and Ohlen left at noon to-day. I took lunch with the Prince's family, Count William being also present. The Prince, who, by the way, now observes great moderation in diet and drinks only the lightest wines, read despatches, and gave Rantzau instructions for replying to them. The subjects were Bulgarian affairs, and the North Sea and Baltic Canal. I then retired to my room to work, and afterwards made an excursion to the Aumühl. As I was about to return I saw the Chief coming towards me in a carriage. When he recognised me he reached out both hands towards me from a distance, left the carriage, and walked back with me to the mill. (I therefore fancy that he cannot have been so very angry with me.) He described to me a pretty pathway through the woods on the other side of the streamlet, saying: "I know you are also a lover of lonely country walks." Yesterday evening over our coffee, after Giers had left, he also said: "I always feel happiest in my top-boots, striding through the heart of the forest, where I hear nothing but the knocking and hammering of the woodpecker, far away from your civilisation."

Again at work with the Chancellor from 4 o'clock onwards. He told me his wife had said: "The doctor may be very clever and amiable, but all the same you should be on your guard at table when he is present. He always sits there with his ears cocked, writes everything down, and then spreads it abroad." She herself, however, in her simple way, forgot to keep on her guard to-day. While seated on her right at dinner my napkin accidentally dropped, and, lo and behold! her Serene Highness, the lady of the house, bent down for it before I could prevent her! I felt that I had been fearfully awkward.

On Friday, the 16th, the Chief dictated to me the conclusion of the long passage respecting his attitude towards the ecclesiastical struggle. He then gave me, for insertion in the fourth chapter, the following statement with regard to Bunsen :—" During the Crimean War, when he was Minister in London, he reported to Berlin that England offered us Schleswig-Holstein in return for our joining in the war against Russia, whilst he stated in London that Prussia would join if she received the Duchies. Both statements were false, and when the affair became known, he was dismissed. I had something to say in the matter. The King exclaimed : ' Why, he has been my friend for twenty years, and now he acts in this way!' Old General Rauch observed : 'Yes, he has also lied and betrayed your Majesty for twenty years.' 'One cannot allow that to be said of a friend,' rejoined the King." He then proceeded to other matters, and on my asking whether there was any subject which I could deal with in the press, he at first replied in the negative, but then said : " Giers found the Emperor very frail, and perhaps he will not last much longer. Well, when he dies, I shall go too. He is a gallant old gentleman, who has always meant well, and whom I must not desert. But I will make no experiments with the Crown Prince. I am too old and weak for that. Things will not go on particularly well, and on the whole I am convinced that what we have built up since 1866 has no stability." In the course of his further remarks he mentioned the

Crown Princess, "a Liberal Englishwoman," "a follower of Gladstone," and maintained that she "has more influence upon her consort than is desirable." He then spoke once more of his need of repose and a country life, referring to Berlin in very disparaging terms, and scarcely allowing it even to be a handsome city. He insisted that owing to the drainage there was already a bad smell in every house, and that in a short time, the place would become utterly intolerable. He said in conclusion: "I have always longed to get away from large cities and the stink of civilisation. Every time I return I feel that more and more, and I have earned my leisure." I remarked that I could fully understand that feeling, and also his reluctance to serve the coming King, on account of his opinions; but surely he would not abandon a work which was so entirely his own, and retire altogether from the political stage. He would at least take his seat in the Upper Chamber and be elected to the Reichstag, where he could offer advice and admonition. He replied: "Yes, but not like the others in perpetual and uncompromising opposition." I said, "Then please remember this little fellow when you want anything done in the press. I shall always be at your service." "All right," he replied, and reached me his hand. "You can then come to me and arrange my papers. (With a significant smile.) There is still a great deal of good stuff there." I begged leave to remain the following day, as it was such a pleasure to me to be near him. "Oh, certainly!" he said; "but you must not ask me to play cards with you or otherwise entertain you."

I remained over the 17th, made several excursions on foot through the woods to the east and west, and was present in the evening after dinner when Lange made his report as to the administration of the estate. I started for Berlin at noon on the 18th, and returned to Leipzig on the 19th. There I received in instalments from Rantzau the bulk of the remaining proofs. The Chief sent two more to Bucher in Berlin, whence I had to fetch them.

I immediately noted down the following particulars of the conversation I had with Bucher on this occasion. I praised the Countess Rantzau as being good-natured and unaffected. " Well," he rejoined, "she is cleverer and more prudent than her mother. The Princess, for instance, is not fortunate in the selection of her acquaintances. First she had the little hunchback Obernitz. Then Babette, Meyer was her friend and confidant—an intelligent body, but . . . . . She was often with her in Berlin and elsewhere, and as the Princess heard a great deal about political affairs and spoke of them to others, Babette, while she was with her, certainly overheard many things and then repeated them to others. . . . . It was afterwards Frau von Wallenberg's turn. She was the worst, and she it was who had most opportunity for eavesdropping and keeping other people informed. You know that the Prince generally goes through his official papers at lunch time, and gives instruction to his sons or to Rantzau as to the answers to be returned. She could hear all that, and take note of it for Holstein, who has recently developed, owing to his ambition, into a very dangerous intriguer. He is accustomed to communicate to Paulchen (Hatzfeldt, the Secretary of State), everything he ascertains in this and other ways."

I turned the conversation on Bucher's share in the negotiations respecting the candidature of the Prince of Hohenzollern for the Spanish throne. He gave me a detailed account of this. The first time he was in

Madrid in connection with that affair was in Easter and then in June, 1870.[1] He gave the following particulars of his second journey: "It was a rush hither and thither in zigzag, accident playing a large part in delaying and hindering as well as in promoting my purpose. Salazar came to me on the Saturday, and wanted to have the final decision of the Prince by Monday. I replied that that would not be possible in such a short time, particularly as I did not know where the Prince was staying at the moment, and of course he would have to be consulted first. Nor was it an easy matter for me to get away at the time. He said he knew the Prince was in Reichenhall, and added, '*Selon ce que vous me dites je renonce.*' I replied: 'I assume that you will write a statement of what has passed between us, which will find its way into the Spanish archives; and as they will some day be open to historians, I should not wish to take this responsibility upon myself. I will travel with you, first to Madrid, (improbable, but so I heard it,) and then to the Prince of Hohenzollern. He said he would take one of his liegemen with him, a man who would fling himself out of the window without hesitation if he told him to do so. A curious condition of things still prevails there, the obedience of feudal vassals, the devotion of the age of chivalry. Well, we started for Reichenhall, travelling first in separate compartments so as to avoid notice in Paris, and afterwards together, as he did not understand German and his companion spoke only Spanish. On my making inquiries at the office of the baths, I found that the director was at a neighbouring village, and the others could give me no information

[1] On the 13th of September, 1883, Bucher's brother, Bruno, who is settled in Vienna, told us at Helbig's in Leipzig, that Lothar Bucher had also been at Sigmaringen with Prince Leopold of Hohenzollern in the spring of 1870. Grunow was present on this occasion.

respecting the Prince. They believed he was not there. I drove out to the village they mentioned and found that the director had left. On returning to Reichenhall I proceeded to the police station. As I was going up the steps I was met by a rather shabbily-dressed man, who stopped and said he supposed I wanted to go to the police office, but it was now closed. He, however, belonged to it, and would go back with me. I told him I was looking for the Prince of Hohenzollern, to whom I had a communication to make. He replied that the Prince was here, and lived at such-and-such a place, but under another name. I therefore proceeded thither with Salazar, but only found the Princess, who told us that her consort was now with his father at Sigmaringen. We packed up once more and made off for Sigmaringen, where we found them, and they agreed. They could, however, decide nothing without the consent of the King, who was at Ems. We then started for that place, and were received by the old gentleman, who was very gracious to me and agreed to what I submitted to him. I then went to Varzin to report to the Chief. It was a regular zigzag journey with obstacles." Bucher added that he had taken shorthand notes of his conversation with Salazar, which he "still possessed." At least, so I understood him.

On the whole the Prince in his collaboration with me struck out a little over seventeen pages out of a total of nearly 900, while he contributed some twenty-two pages to the two volumes. The first edition of 10,000 copies was issued at the end of February 1884, and by the autumn of 1885, 6,500 copies had been disposed of, although the Liberal press did its worst to run the book down. An English translation was published by Macmillan in April, and some months later arrangements were made for an Italian edition. (This translation, by Brandi, was only published at Milan in the spring of 1888.)

On the 14th of March, 1884, I again took up my residence in Berlin; and on the 16th I called upon Bucher, to present him with a handsomely bound copy of my book, *Unser Reichskanzler*. He had already got it, however, and had read it through without coming across any inaccuracies. He made three suggestions for some supplementary material on the issue of a new edition.

According to Bucher, the Chancellor had returned this time from Friedrichsruh in excellent condition, had already been twice out riding in the Thiergarten, and once for a walk there. He had drawn up a memorandum for the Emperor, showing that the home policy of Gladstone, the extension of the franchise, must lower the position of the English aristocracy and with it that of the Crown, which was of course only its head. The Emperor's minute said that he was much struck with this statement, and suggested that it should be laid before the Crown Prince—a suggestion to which the Chief agreed. In Bucher's opinion the Chancellor would on certain conditions consent to remain in office when the Crown Prince came to the throne, but the latter would not keep his promises, and then Bismarck would retire. A further communication of Bucher's was also interesting, namely, that the "refutation of the absurd attack of the *National Zeitung*" (on my account of Gablentz's mission), which was contained in the *Norddeutsche Allgemeine Zeitung* was written by the Prince himself.

A few days after this visit to Bucher I wrote to the Imperial Chancellor, informing him that I was again a resident of Berlin, and begging him in case there was anything I could do for him in the press to kindly let me know when I might call upon him to take his instructions. I received no answer to this letter. My intercourse with Bucher continued. On the 3rd of July, he sent me a card informing me of his departure for Laubbach, near Coblenz.

On the 27th of July, I received the following letter which had been returned owing to an incorrect address and then re-despatched :—

"KISSINGEN, *June 30th*, 1884.

"DEAR SIR,

"Rarely has a book excited my interest to such a degree as your *Unser Reichskanzler*, which I have perused whilst taking the waters here. As it will have produced a like impression upon others a new edition will soon be required. I therefore consider it my duty to call your attention to an error which I have also noticed in the French and English newspapers. The letter of the Minister President of the 26th of December, 1865, which was made public entirely against my will and in consequence of a gross indiscretion which has not yet been quite cleared up, was not addressed to the clergyman, Roman von André, but to the *Rittergutsbesitzer*, Andrae-Roman. In addition to this you will allow me to correct a few of the following observations, as, for instance, that on page 158. I have always spoken and written to Prince Bismarck not from a clergyman's standpoint, but with the consciousness that in matters of faith our views were identical, and with a feeling of hearty affection for his powerful individuality, having fully recognised his greatness long before he became a public character.

"Allow me to add one further remark. The somewhat cool attitude adopted by Bismarck towards the clergy as such did not originate in the conflict with the *Kreuzzeitung*. It existed long before that date, and was closely connected with a similar attitude towards the Church, and arises from entirely different causes, which I need not enter into here. That clergymen, or, indeed, laymen, in signing 'the Declaration' made themselves sponsors for any of the vile and malicious calumnies, which—I regret to say—were at that time heaped upon the great man, I must dispute until that charge has been proved in some specific case. I speak only of those Conservatives who hold the same religious belief as Bismarck. I was pained and surprised to find for the first time in a letter addressed by the Prince to my friend von Holtz during the General Synod, that he entertained this view. I immediately put myself in communication with a considerable number of my co-signatories to the declaration who were present in Berlin at that time, and *all* those with whom I spoke on the subject agreed with me that the public declaration by Bismarck (I have neither this nor the text of the declaration itself with me at the present moment) —his declaration, namely, that 'after the unfortunate articles in question no *respectable* person *could* continue to read the *Kreuzzeitung*,' was the sole cause of the counter-declaration, that we considered ourselves to be respectable persons, although we continued to read the *Kreuzzeitung*. It does not contain a word of approval of any 'vile and malicious calumnies.' I have never read nor approved of the *Reichsglocke*. The statements respecting the death of my relative, Herr von Wedemeyer, are also very hazardous, and would be difficult to prove. It was at that time decided to send to the Prince a joint statement, which was to be drawn up by me. At the desire, however, of a person closely connected with the Prince this decision was altered, and it was arranged that each should write separately to him in the sense indicated above. This was done in a great number of cases. There are, however, different kinds of Conservatives. The most reliable, if not always the most pliant, those who hold the same religious belief as the Prince, have always been and will ever remain on his side.

"With the most profound respect,
A. ANDRAE-ROMAN."

On the 23rd September I called upon Bucher, who had undergone a course of massage and hygienic gymnastics at Laubbach, and had been back in Berlin for about five weeks. He again complained of the "shocking way in which business was conducted in the Foreign Office"; and in particular of Hatzfeldt and Holstein. For a long time past he had given up saluting the latter. He would "like best of all to leave the place, if that were only possible." He praised Count Herbert as "very diligent and not unskilful," and was of opinion that the Prince intended to make him Secretary of State at some future time. Münster, "who is more English than German, and does very little," having allowed some question to hang fire, the Chief sent Herbert to London, where he at once took it into his own hands, pressed it through, and finally settled it satisfactorily. "Another person placed in the position of the Ambassador would have resigned in such circumstances." I suggested: "Angra Pequena, and the long delay in answering the Chancellor's inquiries?" Bucher replied in the affirmative. He then said: "It will not be pleasant to work under the young man, but work will be done, and things will not be allowed to drag on in such a slow and slovenly way. Herbert has also a good memory, and has been a great deal with his father. He was often present at interviews with important personages, at which matters of great moment were discussed that do not appear in the official documents, and in that way he has had splendid opportunities for learning." Bucher agreed with me regarding the meeting at Skiernevice as a "spectacle intended to show Europe the good understanding which exists between the three Emperors." He added, however, that "the relations between Austria and Russia leave much to be desired in many respects." He furthermore confirmed the fact that the Chief, "in view of the cool and repellent attitude of Gladstone, has for a long time past been working towards a better understanding with France, and not without success." After speaking of the Balkan Peninsula, and hinting at an understanding respecting it, Bucher said he had a mind to write something on the despatch of an English Commission to Sarakhs for the purpose of settling the question of the frontier between Afghanistan and Russia, but he had not yet been able to collect the geographical materials. These remarks showed that he had been busy with this question recently. I offered to publish something of the kind in the *Grenzboten*, and he promised the necessary materials from the library of the Foreign Office, and in particular the account of O'Donovan's travels. He saw the Prince (who has now returned to Fredrichsruh) a short time ago; he thinks that the journey to Skiernevice has done him good, as he is much less stout, feels thoroughly well and also works hard.

Bucher called at my house at 8.45 A.M. on the following morning with a collection of newspaper extracts on various subjects for my use. I had, however, gone out. On my returning the bundle of papers given to me on the 28th of September he gave me some further particulars of the way in which Herbert had dealt with the English. On Lord Granville asking him in the course of the negotiations respecting Angra Pequena whether we were not contemplating an ultimate expansion of territory towards the interior (Query, towards the East, in the direction of Bechuanaland and the Boer Republic), he retorted, not over politely, that that was " a question of mere curiosity," and indeed finally, " a matter that does not concern you." The Chief showed him the letter in which that was reported, and was pleased with his son's sturdiness. The English have now so far yielded in the matter that the Ministry has not confirmed the resolution of the Cape Government to annex the country around Angra Pequena. " Münster," he said, " must leave London, but I doubt whether there is any truth in the report that Herbert has been selected as his successor." He afterwards said : " When the Germans, a short time before the conclusion of the Preliminary Peace at Versailles, sank some English coal ships on the Lower Seine and the English made a row on the subject, the Chief asked me, ' What can we say in reply ? ' Well, I had brought with me some old fogies on the Law of Nations and such matters. I hunted up what the old writers called the *jus angariæ*, that is to say, the right to destroy the property of neutrals on payment of full compensation, and showed it to the Chief. He sent me with it to Russell, who allowed himself to be convinced by this ' good authority.' Shortly afterwards the whole affair with the *jus angariæ* appeared in *The Times*. We wrote in the same sense to London, and the matter was settled. A short time ago, when I had to look up something in the documents of the war period, I found that the two papers which I had written in this matter were gone. They had been removed by our mutual friend Abeken through jealousy of me." I reminded him of O'Donovan's work, but he said that just now the *Grenzboten* article would be premature. In this connection he gave me a short survey of the relations of the English and the Russians in Afghanistan, which showed that he was fully informed on that subject. I finally suggested that I should now give a description in the *Grenzboten* of the scandalous treatment of Ireland by England, based upon Lecky's book, which he promised to get for me from the Foreign Office library, but which I already had. I wrote the article which appeared shortly afterwards.

The Prince having returned from Friedrichsruh, I wrote to him (on the 27th of October), requesting him, in case he wished anything said in the press respecting the Brunswick question or any other topic of the day, to let me know when I might have the honour of receiving information as to his intentions in the matter.

This letter also remained unanswered. It would therefore appear that the Chancellor will have no further intercourse with me, having apparently taken offence at something or other. His will be done! And so we bring the diary to a close.

Supplementary.

Bucher frequently mentioned to me that South African affairs were also of importance to us. On my expressing my readiness to deal with the subject in the *Grenzboten*, he promised me material for the purpose, and twice I reminded him of his promise.

On the 3rd of November, 1884, he wrote me : " I cannot yet spare the documents on South Africa, as they may be required for use any day. You will doubtless have noticed this from the articles in the *Norddeutsche Allgemeine Zeitung*. Besides, this is not the right moment. You must first know what the Boers have to say in reply to the accusations of the English.

"In the meantime another article would be desirable in No. 47 on the debate in *The Times* of the 1st instant. I have done some of the preparatory work for you in this matter, and send you herewith for perusal a bundle of papers in which you will find a variety of material. The subject of Protection in England must, it is true, be dealt with very cautiously, as it is in our interest that England should maintain her present tariff, and we must bear that in mind.

"It is absurd to believe that the tariff question is governed by any absolute principle which applies to all peoples and all times. Every nation must know or must learn from experience what is best for itself. We therefore do not dream of teaching the English, although they are so generously anxious to teach us, and although the change from the system of natural forces (by which, since 1815, the preceding generation of Prussian statesmen raised the country to prosperity) to the free-trade doctrines that have been accepted by the official world and the majority of the legislative bodies since 1850, must be ascribed in great part to English writers, and German journalists paid by England. Now of the complaints that are being raised in England, one has an obvious application to the condition of affairs in Germany, namely, that which relates to foreign competition in agricultural produce and cattle breeding. Then you can deal with the arguments of the other side that a return to Protection is impossible in England, recognising at the same time that there are sound reasons for this contention. Conclusion: we also can suggest no remedy ; probably this extraordinary state of affairs must be a consequence of the peculiar development of England—on the Continent the Thirty Years' War, the Spanish War of Succession and the Napoleonic Wars (1870 was also a 'wonderful year for England' in consequence of our war). The peoples of the Continent rend each other to pieces in wars and revolutions. England, which, with the exception of the unimportant French landing in Ireland, has seen no enemy on her soil since 1066, is 'making money' and helping herself to the best colonies. If, as there is every reason to believe, we are now on the eve of a long era of peace in Europe, those conditions will no longer exist under which the wealth of England has, as Gladstone says, increased by leaps and bounds." I wrote this article immediately, on the lines laid down by Bucher, and basing it on his material. It appeared in No. 47 of the *Grenzboten*.

On the 16th of November Bucher again sent me material for an attack upon England. This I worked up into an article entitled "England and the Cholera," which was published in No. 49 of the *Grenzboten*. This article argued that England had destoyed hand weaving in the East Indies by its customs legislation of 1817, thus depriving large numbers of people of their livelihood. This, together with the bad harvests, resulted in famine, which in turn weakened the population and made it less capable of resisting the cholera which arose through malaria, heat and overcrowding at the places of pilgrimage, and which accordingly assumed an epidemic form! England was also responsible for the extension of the scourge to West Africa and Europe, as, in order not to disturb her trade and shipping, she exercised no proper supervision.

On the 24th of November I again called upon Bucher to remind him of the promised documents from the Foreign Office respecting the struggle between the English and the Boers. He said that just now in particular it was impossible to spare them, or at least those of a later date than 1879, as the Chief and Hatzfeldt might want them for reference any day. He would, however, send me the earlier papers, though he really ought not to let any of them leave his hands. He is of opinion that England is afraid of a war with the Dutch element in South Africa, and that Warren would certainly not be able to recruit his volunteers except among the English settlers there. He then said: "Just keep a sharp look out on the news from Afghanistan. Something will happen there soon." I said: "I suppose the English expedition which left Quetta to take part in the settlement of the frontier has arrived?" He replied: "No, it has only got as far as Herat. But General Lumsden, who has gone by way of Teheran, is already on the frontier, and has discovered that an important point, Puli Khatun (the women's bridge—the men ride through the stream beside it) a place as to which a decision had yet to be arrived at, was already in the possession of the Russians. The *Daily News*, the organ of the Government, is surprised at this, and complains of the action of the Russians. The Chief will probably have something on the subject written for the *Grenzboten*. Of course it cannot go into the *Norddeutsche*."

I then asked if there was any truth in the report that Busch, who, by the way, is married to a Jewess, would shortly leave and be given a Legation. Bucher replied in the affirmative.

I: "Herbert will then be his successor?"

He: "Yes, certainly."

I: "In that case Hatzfeldt's position will be rather shaky."

He: "Certainly, he will then be superfluous, and that is doubtless the Chief's intention. Herbert will then read through the despatches with him at breakfast, and the Chief will explain what is to be done with them, so that Herbert will bring everything ready prepared for us to deal with."

On the 28th of November Bucher's servant brought me three thick bundles of Foreign Office documents on the Transvaal question. I made extracts from these, and returned them to him personally five days later. They consisted of English blue books, and of despatches from Münster, Count Herbert Bismarck, Alvensleben at the Hague, and the German Consul in Cape Town. They extended over the periods from the 16th July, 1881, to the 31st of March, 1882; from the 1st of April, 1882, to November of the same year; and from December, 1882, to the 15th of March, 1884. These I worked up into three articles, under the title of "England and the Boers," which appeared in the first three numbers of the *Grenzboten* for the year 1885. These were followed immediately afterwards by an article on "Santa Lucia Bay," in No. 4, which concluded with a statement by Bucher; and one on "England and Russia in Asia," which was also suggested by him, and for which he had sent me extracts from the English newspapers, together with O'Donovan's book on Merv. The latter article appeared in No. 6 of the *Grenzboten*. Together with the documents there was also a very violent appeal (in English, and printed on red paper) to the nations of Europe to help the Boers, on which Bucher had written, " You may keep this."

(Here follow some letters exchanged between Dr. Busch and Herr A. Andrae-Roman, which led to the interview of the 18th of February.—THE TRANSLATOR.)

On the morning of the 18th of February I called upon Andrae, who was staying with Knack, the pastor of the Bohemian Lutheran community, at his residence, No. 29 Wilhelmstrasse. He introduced the pastor to me as his son-in-law. My visit lasted from 8·45 to 10 A.M. Andrae is a tall stately man, with a white full beard, apparently well on in the sixties. From his accent a Hanoverian, he himself said that he came from East Friesland. He first repeated that, owing to the unfortunate experience he had had he must be cautious in what he said, and that he doubted whether we could understand each other, as from my book I appeared to have a different religious standpoint to his. With regard to the first point, he referred to Bismarck's letter to him, published by Hesekiel, of which he said : " I really do not know how it came to be published. I read and showed it to some intimate friends, but I never allowed it to go out of my own hands. But it impresses itself strongly on the memory, so that a Schleswig-Holstein ecclesiastic of high rank actually knew it by heart. It was moreover printed, not in the first place by Hesekiel, but by a democratic newspaper." He likewise referred to Diest-Daber, who also went very thoroughly into things, and immediately noted down everything he ascertained ; describing him as " clever and in reality honourable." He had attacked Bismarck owing to a communication from Moritz von Blankenburg, which was based upon a misunderstanding. I endeavoured to dissipate Andrae's mistrust, observing that anything he might now tell me on the subject in question was not intended for immediate use in the press, and should not be published at all without his permission, at least certainly not before Bismarck's death. I was only collecting for history, which would ultimately claim its rights. As to the difference of our religious views, I told him that I had studied theology, and had adopted theosophical ideas, and in this connection mentioned Jacob Böhmen. Andrae was intimately acquainted with Bismarck many years ago, had visited him at Frankfurt-on-the-Main, and afterwards on several occasions in Berlin. He added: "Indeed I may go so far as to say that I was for a long time on terms of close friendship with him. Formerly he listened with pleasure and with great patience to the views of others. Of course whether he was guided by them was a different matter. Probably that is now no longer the case, which would be natural enough with one who has achieved such great things—and at the same time has had so much good fortune." He then went on to speak with the greatest admiration of Bismarck's extraordinary political genius, was convinced that he was a "sincere Christian," and assured me that he "made no secret of the fact even as long since as the Frankfurt period. But then, and even before that time, he showed coolness towards the clergy and the Church."

I: "I beg your pardon, but how do you mean that? What do you understand by the Church? The entire Christian community, the faithful, the community of saints; or the institution with certain observances and means of salvation, sacraments, public forms of divine service, sermons, &c. ?"

He replied that the latter conception was what he had in mind. He then continued: "It is an old story with him, and connected with the manner of his conversion. At that time the clergy in Pomerania were not what they are at the present day. The majority of them were Rationalists, and when the change took place it did not originate with them, but with a few laymen, like Below, (not Below-Hohendorf, as I interrupted him to suggest,) Senfft-Pilsach, and Thadden. They came forward to a certain extent as preachers, and as the clergy held and preached rationalistic views, often in opposition to them—in sectarian opposition. Blankenburg, and Bismarck's father-in-law in Reinfeld, an excellent old gentleman, were also of the number. Their views somewhat approached those of Gichtel. Others inclined to the old Lutheran doctrines. (Therefore not to those of the Moravian Brethren, as I had supposed.) Bismarck came under their influence and joined them. Hence his coolness towards the clergy and the Church. (Gichtel's 'Gott in uns,' and Bismarck's 'Nicht durch Predigermund sich erbauen'—'Seek not edification from the mouth of the preacher.') It was not due to the clerical signatures at foot of the Declaration."

He then went on to say that Bismarck misunderstood "the Declaration." According to him, Holtz wrote to the Prince that he regretted having had a hand in it. Bismarck was greatly pleased at this, and wrote Holtz a long letter expressing his satisfaction. Andrae disapproved of the step taken by his friend Holtz, "as an individual demonstration," and suggested that the signers of "the Declaration" should send a joint explanation of its real meaning to the Chancellor, and reject the false construction put upon it, namely, that they wished to express their approval of the articles in the *Kreuzzeitung*. They wanted to adopt this course, but Bismarck informed them, through Limburg Stirum, that he did not wish them to do so, and would prefer that they should write to him separately. In that way the idea of a collective explanation was dropped. Andrae is of opinion that the intercourse between Moritz von Blankenburg and the Prince still continues, although they only see each other on rare occasions. "There was never an absolute breach between them, as their wives continued to meet as they still do."

We then spoke about the Kulturkampf, and Andrae expressed his surprise that Bismarck should have entered upon it, as he must have known that a struggle with a spiritual power had no prospect of success. His action was doubtless determined by the creation of the Centre party. I defended him on the lines of the statement dictated to me at Friedrichsruh.

The conversation then turned upon the relations between the Chief and the Emperor. Andrae said of the latter: "His merit lies in the creation of the new army, and in the fact that he recognised the right men and held firmly to them." He added the following anecdote: "A Minister who could no longer endure his position by the side of Bismarck tendered his resignation to the Emperor. The latter urged him to remain. 'We must all learn to be patient,' he said. The Minister nevertheless resigned. The Emperor, on the other hand, did not part with Bismarck, considering it his duty to retain him." I observed: "It was a case of necessity; it would have been impossible to get on without him." Andrae replied: "Yes, but the Emperor's merit was in recognising that fact."

Andrae then talked a great deal about Hanover, saying that the clergy there "were willing to yield obedience to the authorities who had power over them." He proceeded: "Before the war of 1866, we, the Conservatives, were divided into two parties—Gerlach and Marquart, and, on the other hand, those who considered a war with Austria inevitable. Ultimately an effort was made to bring about an understanding, and we invited Gerlach to attend a meeting, accompanied by a few others of his way of thinking, in order that he should not be alone. He agreed and came, when he made the following prophecy: 'There are only two possible results: either we are defeated, and then it is all over with us, and there will be a partition of Prussia; or we are victorious, and then we must have a Liberal *régime*, as that is the only way in which, unification of Germany under Prussia can be brought about.' And so it has come to pass. Bismarck demanded an indemnity, and then for many years worked in harmony with the Liberals, so far as that was possible."

As I was leaving Andrae promised to give me further information later on in case I asked for it. "But not in writing. I frequently come to Berlin, and shall be glad to meet you again."

I continued in regular communication with Bucher during the year 1885. I visited him on New Year's Day; called at his house on the 11th of February to return O'Donovan's *Oasis of Merv*, but could not see him, as he lay ill in bed; a few days later we had a short talk on the Lucia Bay question; and again on the 25th of February I had a long conversation with him at his lodgings. At first we spoke about the Chief, whose health, he said, was now thoroughly restored. He was "quite young and rosy," and was "working fearfully hard." The conversation then turned on Hatzfeldt, who "got sick with fear at the thought that he might have to take part in the West African Conference, and that the Chief might appoint him to represent the Foreign Office in the Reichstag, and so took a holiday. . . . There is really nothing the matter with him, but he has managed to obtain a long leave of absence. As Herbert is now there, it is a question whether he will return any more. And we shall not miss him, either. Business will be done as well, or better, in his absence. He would certainly have been removed from his post as Secretary of State before this if they only knew where to put him." I said: "Keudell is probably not disposed to give up his sinecure in Rome to him." Bucher replied: "Keudell really takes things too easy. We thought he would send in a report on the Italian expedition to the Red Sea, and he, in fact, promised one. But what was it when it came? A description of the ball recently given by him, how he danced a quadrille with the Queen, how the knights of the Order of the Annunziata danced *vis-à-vis* to him, and other fine and important matters of the kind, all in the fullest detail. The Princess is to blame for this. The other members of the family, including the Chief, have long since been convinced of his incapacity. At the beginning, during the first few months, I myself thought there was something in him. He played the part of the mysterious, reticent thinker, occasionally speaking very well, and with far-reaching and brilliant ideas. But one soon recognised that they were not his own, but were borrowed from the Chief."

The inhuman pair of us then rejoiced at England's misfortunes in the Soudan, and I expressed a hope that Wolseley's head would soon arrive in Cairo, nicely pickled and packed. This led the conversation to Central Asia. Bucher was of opinion that although the Russians would not now occupy Herat, they would take up such a position that at the next opportunity they could annex it as they had done Merv. He then referred to the intention of the English to disband the native contingents of the Indian Princes, amounting in all to 300,000 men and 1,200 field guns, and to the "demonstrative review of the Rajah of Scinde." I then mentioned the rising of the blacks at Kitteh against their English friends, and he said: "They are threatened by a conflict with the French in Burmah." In reply to my question: "Have we given up South Africa, or is the Lucia Bay affair still open?" he said that the matter was still under consideration. (....)

At 1.30 P.M on the 30th of March a Chancery attendant brought me the following pencil note from Bucher:—

"His Highness would like to have an article which appeared in the *Daily Telegraph* of the 15th of January (or a few days earlier) dealing with the question of the different aspect things would assume if an English Princess were Empress of Germany. Perhaps you have this number?

"Yours, BR."

Unfortunately I had not kept the number, as I told Bucher in a note which I sent back by the same messenger. This doubtless explains the Chief's recent speech in answer to Richter's allusion to the dynastic connection between England and ourselves.

On the morning of the 19th of April paid Bucher another visit. He wished me to draw a comparison between the bellicose attitude of *The Times*, and that which it observed previous to the outbreak of the Crimean War, particulars of which were to be found in Kinglake's *Invasion of the Crimea*, Vol. III., p. 31. He believes that it is now inspired by Lord Dufferin. There can be no question of war, as England has not the necessary means at present, and Russia has for the moment no idea of seizing Herat, or even the mountain line beyond it. In the Afghan campaign of 1839 the English required for a force of 38,000 men no less than 100,000 camp followers and innumerable pack animals. Nothing of this kind is now ready. It was said that 20,000 men passed in review before Abdurrahman and Lord Dufferin at Rawal Pindi, but in reality they had only 11,000 men there altogether. The commissariat department was badly managed. Graham's troops at Suakim had only one pair of boots each, and when an Irish regiment knelt down at mass one could see that the soles were all torn and were patched with pieces of the tin cans which had contained their preserved meats. The soldiers they have at home are for the most part too young to be employed in the tropics. The English would require four months to get from Quetta to Herat. The Russians could reach it much sooner. The ideas as to the prospects of the two parties which Münster had been hoaxed into believing were mere nonsense. Bucher put all these facts together for the Prince, who submitted them to the Emperor in the shape of a direct report. "The Crown Prince's people," said Bucher, "are very cross and very angry with the Chief because he will not act as mediator in St. Petersburg and help England out of her embarrassment, and because he opposes her schemes at Constantinople. The English have offered the Turks the occupation of Egypt in return for permission to pass through the Dardanelles and the Bosphorus. The Sultan was, however, informed from Berlin and Vienna that we too had a word to say in the matter, and our officers in Stamboul would take care that the passage was stopped by torpedoes."

On the 20th, Bucher sent me the third volume of Kinglake's book, and I wrote the article desired by him, which appeared in No. 18 of *Grenzboten*, under the title "Prospects of Peace and *The Times*."

On the 22nd of April I called upon Secretary of State von Thile, whom I had met on the way home a few nights before, when I announced my visit. He was very friendly and communicative, and we conversed together from 11 to 1 o'clock. (. . . .)

Thile gave me the following particulars of the agreement with Russia in 1863: "Bismarck risked a great deal thereby. We might have got ourselves into a war with France, who would have begun by attacking us. Napoleon was furious, because he had heard nothing beforehand. Goltz wrote that he might be pacified if the treaty were communicated to him. This was done. Bismarck sent the treaty to Goltz, with instructions to read it to the Emperor alone. Even the Ministers were to know nothing of it. Napoleon was astounded at its contents, and exclaimed, 'Why, this is worse than I had anticipated!' It had no further consequences however."

On Sunday, the 31st of May, I found in the *Daily Telegraph* of the 29th a leading article on the Emperor's indisposition, in which the alteration in the policy of Prussia which would result from the approaching change in the occupation of the throne was regarded as full of hope for England. It was asserted among other things that Prince Bismarck would no longer exercise the influence which he now did upon the Sovereign. I immediately called upon Bucher with the paper, which I handed to him in order that he might communicate the article to the Chief. He cast a glance at the principal passages underlined by me, and promised to cut out the article and send it to the Chancellor without delay, mentioning at the same time that I had brought it. He would doubtless deal with it in some way—probably get me to write an article on the subject in the *Grenzboten*. But he was going to leave Berlin on Tuesday (the 2nd of June). Bucher went on to say that it would really seem as if the Emperor were not at all well just now. I asked him what was the meaning of Lord Rosebery's visit. He replied: "It is in the main as the newspapers represent it. He has been instructed to find out what the Chief's views are on various questions. No negotiations have taken place. I was invited by the Prince to dine with them one day, and the conversation turned on indifferent matters, such as dogs, &c. Rosebery said nothing on the main question, namely, Afghanistan. It was the Chief who first turned the conversation on to it." I suggested: "But the present understanding will doubtless be merely provisional?" He: "I believe the matter will come up again in about five years, when the railways are finished. The Russians expect to have the line from Kisil-Arwat to Askabad ready by 1886, and it will then be carried on to Merv and to the Oxus in the direction of Samarcand. The English are building their line from the Indus to Candahar, by a détour *viâ* Pishin, and not through the Bolan Pass, which is the shortest route, but where it would run for twelve (German) miles through defiles which the natives would be able to block by simply rolling rocks down. But on the Pishin route also they will meet with great difficulties, and will not be ready for a long time. . . . . Rosebery's visit was brought about by Herbert, who, by the way, has not shown particular skill in the recent African negotiations. He can be very offensive at times, which is useful, but he has not sufficiently mastered these colonial questions. He does not understand, for instance, that colonies require a coast if they are to prosper, and so he made concessions which we are now trying to alter. He allows himself to be won over too easily. Rosebery had been particularly successful in that, and has quite mesmerised him."

Speaking of the Emperor once more, he said : " His death will be a bad thing for us. Rottenburg believes that the Chief will not retain office under the new Emperor, and in that case it is not impossible that Keudell may become Chancellor. He is in high favour at the Crown Prince's. They stay with him in Rome, and people believe him far more capable than he really is. He has provided for that in the press; as, for instance, through Meding, at considerable cost to his own or the Embassy funds. (. . . .)

At 12 o'clock (I had called on Bucher with the *Daily Telegraph* article at 9 A.M.) a servant from the Chancellor's palace came to my lodgings to inquire whether I could call upon the Prince at 3 o'clock. At a quarter past 3 I was shown into the Chancellor's study, and did not leave until ten minutes past 4.

He was dressed in black with a military stock, and, as usual, sat at his writing table. He first quieted Tiras, who sprang out and wanted to fly at me, shook hands with his accustomed friendliness, and after I had taken a seat opposite him, asked me how I was, observing : " You still look exactly the same, not a bit changed." He mentioned that during the time he had not seen me he had been overloaded with work. " Even to-day I have been sitting here since 8 o'clock in the morning," he continued; "and it is the same from week's end to week's end. The only break is at lunch time, and, as you know, I also work then, reading despatches and telegrams and giving instructions, &c. I must do almost everything myself. Hatzfeldt is an excellent ambassador, and he is also very good here at receiving the diplomatists,—clever and intelligent, but ailing and incapable of serious continuous work, impatient of routine, and in addition to that he is frivolous and has a poor memory. Busch is no longer of any use either, and must get out of harness. Bojanowski is ruined, and his Councillors are intriguing against him. My son is not yet sufficiently trained, and has much to learn." I said: "But Busch was an excellent worker and knew the business!" "Yes," he replied, "but that is no longer the case. The clock will no longer work. Latterly he has been constantly unwell. . . . . Herbert is getting on very well in many things, but he must yet, as the French say, *faire ses caravanes*, or, as it is better expressed in English, 'sow his wild oats.' *Faire ses caravanes*, you know, originally meant to join one of the campaigns against the infidels, in which one had to take part before becoming a knight of Malta. It therefore signifies to get through one's blundering as a beginner and to grow wise by experience."

He then took up the *Daily Telegraph* article which Bucher had pasted on a sheet of paper and enclosed in a letter, which also lay on the table. He said: "You have sent me this. I thank you for it."

I: "I thought it would interest you, particularly one passage, as Bucher asked me a few weeks ago for a leader of the same kind for you, as he knows I receive the paper. I had not kept that number, but I afterwards came across it elsewhere, and the article was translated for the Emperor. I therefore thought you would be glad to see this one immediately."

He: "Yes, and it is of interest. But it would hardly do to write anything against or upon it just now. It would have to be done very cautiously, and at the present moment in particular it would not look at all well. The old gentleman is in a very critical state, and you know it seems to me almost like the case of a woman whose husband is dangerously ill, and who talks to people about what she will do afterwards; or, more correctly, as if my wife were dying and I were to say how I should act after her death, and whether I should marry again or not. We must wait until the hour has come for a decision to be taken. It appears that the Crown Prince wishes to retain me, but I must carefully consider whether I ought to remain with him. There are many arguments against it, and many also in favour of it; but at present I am more disposed to go and have no share in his experiments. But I might look at it as Götz von Berlichingen did when he joined the peasants—it will not be so bad; and if I remain many things can be prevented or rendered less harmful. But what if I were then not to have a free hand?—to have colleagues like Forckenbeck and George Bunsen, and ceaseless worries with them; while latterly the old gentleman allowed me to do what I thought proper, and even to select Ministers and replace them by others? Besides, there is the co-regency of the Crown Princess, who influences and completely governs him. Yet what will the result be if I leave them to themselves? The entire position of the Empire depends upon the confidence which I have acquired abroad. In France, for instance, where their attitude is based exclusively upon the faith they place in my word. The King of the Belgians said recently that a written and signed contract would do less to put his mind at ease than a verbal assurance from me that such and such a course would be followed. It is the same with Russia, where the Emperor trusts entirely to me. I still remember at the Dantzig meeting how he conversed with me for a long time in his cabin and listened to my opinion. The Emperor (William) was not over pleased at his taking no notice of the parade and the various celebrations; but he left us alone all the same. And the Empress—the Danish Princess—said to me: 'Our whole confidence rests upon you. We know that you tell the plain truth, and perform what you promise.' .... Of course I could retire and see how they got on without me, and then when they called me back after their experiment had failed, I could bring things back into the old course. It would then have been proved that affairs could not be conducted in that way. He doubtless would not venture upon such experiments if he had not got me in reserve. It was just the same with the new era when the King gave Liberalism a trial, because he had me to turn to eventually. But I am an old man, over seventy, and for twenty-nine years I have exhausted my strength in the service of the State, and can no longer do what I once did. I can no longer accompany the King wherever he goes—on journeys, shooting parties and to watering places. I can no longer ride to manœuvres and parades, so as to prevent his being alone with others, and to take immediate measures against the intrigues and influence of opponents. If I were to persist in that sort of work my illness would return, and I should soon be dead."

He drew out from among the books on his right a letter from Dr. Schweninger, who had written to him that he had escaped a dangerous illness through regular diet and the greatest possible abstinence from mental exertion; but that if a recurrence of it were to be averted he must continue to follow the same course. He then said: "The Crown Princess is an Englishwoman.

That is always the case with us. When our Princesses marry abroad they doff the Prussian, and identify themselves with their new country,—as for example the Queen of Bavaria, who ultimately went so far as to become a Catholic; and the lady in Darmstadt (it is obvious that this was a slip of the tongue, and that he meant Karlsruh), as well as the consort of the Emperor Nicholas. Here, however, they bring their nationality with them, and retain it, preserving their foreign interests. . . . . Our policy must not necessarily be anti-English, but if it were to be English it might prove to be very much against our interest, as we have always to reckon with the Continental Powers." He further observed that the Crown Prince would be influenced in his liking for England by consideration for Queen Victoria, and (here he mimicked the act of counting money) her generosity." He has but a slight knowledge of State affairs, and little interest in them, and he lacks courage. I reminded the Chief that he, too, had had to infuse courage into his father on the railway journey from Jueterbogk to Berlin during the period of conflict. He then related that incident once more, and added: "He said that I should first come to the scaffold—at that time I was called the Prussian Strafford; but I replied: 'What finer death could a man have than to die for his King and his right?'"

He then came to speak of the Emperor's illness, for which—as he asserted—"the women were to blame, with their desire to give themselves importance. He was already ill, hoarse, when they talked him over into driving with them to church. And then the Grand Duchess wants to play the loving daughter before people, and so she accompanies him when he, like every one who works a great deal, would prefer to drive out alone; and at the same time she argues with him, even when the wind is in their faces, so that he catches cold if he answers her. It was only his daughter's persuasion that induced him to go to Hatzfeldt's dinner. He ought not to have done that. (Probably according to Lauer's opinion.) As he sits at work, Augusta sticks her head into the room and asks in a caressing voice, 'Do I disturb you?' When he, always gallant in his treatment of ladies, and particularly of Princesses, replies 'No,' she comes in and pours out all sorts of insignificant gossip to him, and scarcely has she at last gone away than she is back again knocking at the door with her, 'I am again disturbing you'; and so she again wastes his time chattering. Now that he is ill—you know what his complaint is—she is a real embarrassment and plague to him. She sits there with him, and when he wants to be left alone he does not venture to tell her, so that in the end he gets quite red from pain and restraint; and she notices it. That is not love, however, but pure play-acting, conventional care and affection. There is nothing natural about her—everything is artificial, inwardly as well as outwardly."

The conversation then turned upon Brunswick, and I said: "Surely we shall soon have that now? It will shortly be Prussian?" He replied in the negative, saying: "It must remain independent, because without the two votes of the Duchy the Federal Council would no longer be of the slightest importance—Prussia would always have a safe majority. The Brunswickers, too, are anxious to retain their independence. In order to maintain the present balance of voting power in the Federal Council, I have always rejected the overtures of the small fry such as Waldeck, &c., that wanted to be absorbed in Prussia. Things can be managed as they are, and we must give the larger States no reason to mistrust us. *Their* confidence also is part of my policy, and during recent years they have always trusted me."

He was silent for a while and looked at me. I rose to go, and thanked him for this day's invitation and the confidence in me which it manifested, adding that I was all the more pleased as I had been under the impression that he had been angry with me for my last book, and that I should not see him again. He clapped me on the shoulder in a friendly way and said: "No, Büschchen, everything remains as of old between us two. It is true that you contributed to my illness with your book, as it gave me a great deal of work." I replied that nothing of the kind should occur again, and gave him my hand upon it.

On Tuesday, the 2nd of June, I went to Bucher to tell him that I had been with the Chief, and to read him my notes of the interview. He already knew that I had been called to see him. In connection with what I told him respecting the Chancellor's resignation or retention of office under the future Sovereign, he said: "He has also given the French to understand . . . . that possibly the next Emperor may not continue his policy, so that in future it would be well for them in Egyptian affairs to keep their demands and actions within such limits as they thought they could, if left to themselves alone, assert and maintain against the English." (. . . .)

Bucher smiled at the apprehension which I now expressed that the Chief had been offended at my book. That, he said, was a mistake. With regard to the Prince's remark that it had given him a great deal of work (he doubtless alluded chiefly to the revising of the proofs) Bucher observed : " Yes, I have had a good deal to write on the subject to Reuss, for Andrassy complained of various passages. But what he imagined he had read was not in the book at all ; he had read it superficially, and we convinced him of that fact." Finally Bucher thanked me for the account of my interview with the Chancellor, which he described as very interesting.

During the first half of June I made an excursion on foot from Dresden to North Bohemia, to Lausitz, then back to Dresden, and from there to Moritzburg and Meissen, in order to finally rid myself of a determination of blood to the head which had seriously troubled me all the winter. After my return to Berlin, I called upon Bucher on the 16th June to ask him, in the first place, what attitude should be adopted in the press towards the new Ministry in England. I observed that Gladstone had defended English interests although in an unskilful and feeble way, and that Salisbury would not suit our purposes any better, indeed, perhaps less, because they would be more energetic. He replied that Salisbury is blunt in manner, as he had himself experienced when he was in Berlin. He might, however, for the moment be more welcome to the Chief than Gladstone, who had been seeking a *rapprochement* with Russia in favour of which there seemed to be a party in that country. Salisbury, on the other hand, had spoken too strongly against Russia to leave much prospect of an understanding at the present time between the Tories and St. Petersburg. True, one could not say what might happen in this respect later on, and the new English Ministry would also seek an understanding with France.

He then mentioned Count Herbert's second mission

to London, which had not turned out so well as the first one respecting Angra Pequena and the Fiji Islands, in which he had taken up a very strong position with good results. The second mission should have appeared, as far as the public was concerned, merely a visit to Rosebery, with whom Herbert stayed. Its object, however, was to negotiate respecting Lucia Bay and the Benue district; and Herbert, who was not sufficiently well acquainted with the maps, &c., conceded too much to Rosebery, who was very sharp, so that the result was disadvantageous to us. We lost Lucia Bay. The English Minister argued that they could not abandon it to us, as it was impossible to allow the Cape Colony to be hemmed in on both sides. On the Benue, however, they have annexed a large piece of land, well situated for their purposes.

Bucher then complained of the "gross ineptitude" displayed by Gerhard Rohlfs in his mission to Zanzibar. "He got it," he said, "through the 'paidocracy,' as Busch calls it,—through the influence of the Chancellor's sons upon their father, and he has spoilt everything. Contrary to the regulations, which require an examination to be passed first, he was appointed Consul-General without any examination, although he is not particularly well informed. . . . . The trap had been very cleverly prepared for Sultan Burgasch. He has a sister who is married to a German, a Hamburg merchant named Reute, and lives now in Germany. Burgasch had robbed her of her inheritance, and this was to be the starting point of the scheme. She was to go out to Zanzibar and press her claim, and an accident might possibly occur to the lady,—her brother might have her strangled. In the meantime Rohlfs was also to go out, quite quietly, by way of the Red Sea, and not on board a man-of-war.

He, however, induced the Chief to let him travel *viâ* London and the Cape; and at Cape Town he talked imprudently about his mission and position to some officers of Warren's expedition (to Bechuanaland), so that the English got wind of the matter, and were able to take their measures accordingly (this was under Gladstone's Government, through their Consul, Kirk). And in Zanzibar itself he committed one blunder after another. When this came to the knowledge of the Chief he said in his own family circle that he would recall him. Paul Lindau, who constantly haunts the Chancellerie, got it into the newspapers, whereupon a *démenti* was issued. Later on, however, the Prince returned to his former intention, as Rohlfs proved quite useless." .... Bucher further related that Herbert had provided himself with a deputy Under Secretary of State in the person of Darenthall, who was to act for himself when he was absent. Darenthall is an admirer of Keudell, with whom he spent nine years in Rome, where there is nothing to do, as everything is sent there ready prepared. He cannot have gained much experience of the world there, while others sent to various posts became acquainted with different countries and conditions of life. He did not, however, turn out badly as Consul-General in Egypt. When he comes to the office I shall take a long leave of absence in order not to lose the last trace of my self-respect." .... Bill, who will shortly get married and who is going to Hanau, has also "picked out a successor, von Rheinbaben. It is true that he belongs to the old nobility, but he is quite incapable,"—a statement in support of which Bucher produced sundry evidence. Finally we rejoiced that the Emperor was quite well again, and Bucher added: "Yes, and in very good humour, as may be seen from the remarks which he makes on the matters submitted to him." (. . . .)

On the 16th of October Bucher called at my lodgings to inform me that on Hatzfeldt's departure as Ambassador for London, Herbert Bismarck is to be appointed Secretary of State, and that the latter has selected Holstein as Under Secretary. The Chief had some one else in view, apparently Berghen, but Herbert would probably be able to carry out his views with regard to Holstein. He had already made up the differences between the latter and the Princess. In these circumstances he, Bucher, meant to retire. He had already asked the Prince on several occasions to arrange for his retirement on the score of ill-health. Although the Chief had, through Herbert, declined to do this, and only granted him a six months' leave of absence, he would probably on the conclusion of that period renew his request. He intends to leave on the 1st of November, and to spend his holiday on the Lake of Geneva. On parting he said : " Adieu ! I must now return to the treadmill."

CHAPTER III

THE CHANCELLOR ON BULGARIA AND SERVIA, AUSTRIA AND RUSSIA, THE BATTENBERGER AND THE TSAR—HIS VIEW OF THE TREATMENT OF THE RUSSIAN BALTIC PROVINCES — A COMPARISON BETWEEN ENGLISH PARTIES AND OUR OWN—GERMANY AND ENGLAND IN AFRICA—THE CHANCELLOR ON THE MILITARY QUESTION, AND THE THREATENED CONFLICT IN THE REICHSTAG—WHAT HE SAID THERE WAS ADDRESSED TO RUSSIA—THE TSAR'S CONFIDENCE IN THE CHANCELLOR—THE CROWN PRINCE AND HIS CONSORT—BISMARCK AND HIS WORK—WHAT IS GREATNESS?—THE CHIEF ON HIS OWN DEATH—INTERVIEW WITH THE CHIEF ON THE MARRIAGE OF THE BATTENBERGER, AND INSTRUCTIONS FOR THE "GRENZBOTEN" ARTICLE, "FOREIGN INFLUENCES IN THE EMPIRE"—BEWARE OF THE PRESS LAWS—NOT TOO VENOMOUS—A SURVEY OF BRITISH POLICY—THE CATALOGUE OF ENGLAND'S SINS—TWO EMPRESSES AGAINST THE CHANCELLOR—QUEEN VICTORIA AT CHARLOTTENBURG—DEATH OF THE 'INCUBUS.'

AT 11 A.M., on the morning of the 5th of January, 1886, I handed in at the Imperial Chancellor's residence in the Wilhelmstrasse a letter offering, as usual, my services and requesting an interview. Having received a favourable reply, I was at the palace punctually at 3 P.M., and was at once shown in to the Prince. He shook hands saying: "How do you do, Büschlein?" I sat down at the writing table opposite to him. On my remarking that he looked exceptionally well, he complained of the continuance of his faceache, which did not arise from a bad tooth, as I had supposed, and for which Schweninger could do nothing. His cure had only prevented him from getting stouter and relieved his biliousness. He then said: "There is nothing going on in politics just now."

I: "One sees that from the newspapers. You take care that they shall have nothing of importance to write about. You have again preserved the peace for us."

He: "In Bulgaria, where the Austrian policy was inconceivably bad. It was as if they had no agents whatever there, no one to observe and report. They were of opinion that the Rumelian business was instigated by the Russians and in their interest, and so they thought 'If you let your Bulgarians loose we will march out our Servians.' They obviously promised the latter more than they could perform, and when the war went against Milan made enemies of both sides. Khevenhüller acted too roughly. He threatened the Prince that if he did not call a halt within twenty-four hours the Austrians would march against him. And the Servians were also obliged to stop and their action crippled. Now the Bulgarians complain, 'If you had not crossed our path we should be in Belgrade by this time,' and the Servians, on the other hand, assert that if they had not been ordered to keep the peace they would have renewed the struggle with fresh forces, and wiped out their defeat. The policy which they are carrying on in Vienna is that of the father confessor and the banker. The Länderbank, which advanced the Servians the money for the war, is acting like the Caisse d'Escompte in Paris, and exercises similar influence. It is as if Cohn, the banker at Dresden, wanted to influence our policy. They ought to know in Vienna that the events in Rumelia are the result of English wire-pulling, and that it is England who supports the Prince. He has been on bad terms with the Emperor Alexander for years past. He is a man of intelligence, but false and untrustworthy, and that is known in St. Petersburg. At the present moment the Battenberger is the main hindrance in the way of a satisfactory settlement of the Bulgarian question. The Emperor does not trust him even after his recent praise of the Russian officers. Order must be re-established from the outside, through an occupation by foreign troops—but who is to supply them? It would not do for the Russians to undertake the job, and just as little for the Austrians."

I: "Might I ask what is your opinion of the character of the Emperor Alexander?"

He: "He is better than his reputation in our newspapers, more sensible, a simpler nature, and above all more honourable. Quite different to his father, more manly, and neither imaginative nor sentimental. He is a respectable father of a family, has no *liaisons* and makes no debts. Having nothing to conceal, it is not necessary for him to trouble his head with vain imaginings and tricky deceptions. But he is subject to ecclesiastical influences."

I: "Pobedonoszeff?"

He: "Yes, and others." He then related: "He was in Copenhagen during the complications with the English respecting Afghanistan, and Giers telegraphed to him repeatedly begging him to return. He remained, however, saying, 'Giers has his hands full (hat die Hosen voll) but he must see for himself how he is going to put the matter straight.'"

I: "He has been described to me as stupid, exceedingly stupid; but that was from a Baltic source."

He: "In a general way that is saying too much, but of course allowance must be made for the inhabitants of the Baltic Provinces. Poor people! But we cannot help them. History furnishes many instances in which Divine Providence has permitted such nobler communities and peoples to be swallowed up by a larger but less noble nation. In this case it is unwise on the part of the Government, and it does more harm to Russia than to us, when they allow such a breeding establishment for good generals, like Todtleben, and for capable diplomatists as they possess in the nobility of the Baltic Provinces to be ruined. They have in view the unity of the Empire and not without reason, as is shown in the case of the Poles, but that they should carry it so far and go to work in such a crude way, and in particular that they should incite the populace against the upper classes! I have often wondered why more of them do not sell out and emigrate. But this oppression is more damaging to the Russians than to us, and, moreover, the Baltic Germans never formed part of the German Empire, although they have always been closely associated with the popular life of Germany."

I asked: "Might I inquire on what footing your Serene Highness now stands with the Crown Prince? You have recently been dining with him."

He: "Oh, quite satisfactory, and for several months past, as also with *her*. When the Emperor seemed to be drawing near his latter end, he approached me, as he saw that the time was at hand when he must plunge into the water and swim on his own account. Ever since we have been on good terms. He wishes to retain me, and when he commands as King I must remain, although I am ill and require rest—but we must come to an understanding first. The main point for him is to get some one to conduct the foreign policy. Domestic affairs would go on all right under Bötticher, who manages them quite well, except that he is rather too vehement, so that water must sometimes be poured into his wine." He then spoke against the "collegial system"[1] and in favour of a homogeneous administration.

I mentioned the Emperor and the jubilee of his reign, observing that a good text for a sermon on that occasion would be found in Ecclesiasticus, where it is said "The work praiseth the master, and his hands do honour to a wise prince"; and in particular the further passage "the prosperity of a ruler resteth with God; he giveth him a worthy Chancellor;" and again, "A wise servant shall be ministered unto by his master, and a master that hath understanding murmureth not thereat." (I had already directed attention to these passages[2] in the *Grenzboten* of the 31st of December of the previous year.) He smiled; after remarking that the Emperor had acted conscientiously in State affairs and knew

---

[1] In this system the Ministers are on a footing of equality with each other.

[2] These passages would seem to come from the tenth chapter of Ecclesiasticus, but the English version does not appear to contain any reference to the "löblichen Kanzler." The version given above is, of course, translated from Dr. Busch's quotation.—THE TRANSLATOR.

how to subordinate his *amour propre* to the interests of the country, he said: "He always gave me to a great extent a free hand, although he had been accustomed previously to command, while his brother, on the other hand, could never have got on with any independent Minister."

I then referred to the Irish crisis and the English parties, observing that there one saw plainly what Parliamentarism resulted in, and whither it led a State. Our Liberals would have had a similar experience in Posen and in Polish affairs generally, but, happily, they had not the same influence here as they have in England. He said: "Parliamentarism only works where there are merely two rival parties that come to power alternately, and where the members of the Legislature are well off and unselfish, and do not find it necessary to struggle for their personal advancement. I am no advocate of absolutism. Parliamentarism is good even here, as a veto upon the resolutions of unwise Governments and bad monarchs—for purposes of criticism. In England, up to the present, there have been two great parties, whose principles have latterly not differed very widely, and both desired the welfare of the country and nothing for themselves. They were the representatives of a few hundred families who were well enough off not to want more, and who could therefore study exclusively the welfare of the whole community—a remark which at bottom also applies to Kings, who should be under no necessity to think of their own interests. The Irish are now coming in as a third party, together with the Radicals, who are still more dangerous. It is worse here in Germany. We have eight or ten parties and the leaders are place hunters, who want to improve their own positions and become Ministers, and who also put themselves at the service of the capitalists—not without a consideration."

He then spoke about the Kulturkampf, and mentioned that the Pope was now thoroughly well disposed. I said: "Of course you have done him a great pleasure in asking for his mediation in the difference with Spain, and given him an importance for which he has every reason to be grateful." He smiled and said: "Well, he has invested me with his highest Order, and has at the same time written me a very flattering letter." We then spoke of other Orders and I asked him how many he had now. In 1872 he had, I believed, already sixty-four.

He: "There can hardly have been so many. Since then, however, the Siamese and other Asiatics have added theirs."

I: "Japan was also included with the two great razors, the case containing the swords with which you were raised to the rank of Daimio."

He: "Even the Emperor of China has made me a present, a great elephant tusk with carved figures, flowers, houses and birds, all so deeply cut out that you almost see through the carving. It is believed that th carving took eight years. You ought to have a look at it some time. It stands in the corner on the black chimney piece in the second room upstairs, near the large *salon*." He rang the bell and instructed the servant to show me upstairs when I was leaving.

"Why have we not been able to secure the Santa Lucia Bay?" I asked. "Ah!" he replied, "it is not so valuable as it seemed to be at first. People who were pursuing their own interests on the spot represented it to be of greater importance than it really was. And then the Boers were not disposed to take any proper action in the matter. The bay would have been valuable to us if the distance from the Transvaal were not so great. And the English attached so much importance to it that they declared it was impossible for them to give it up, and they ultimately conceded a great deal to us in New Guinea and Zanzibar. In colonial matters we must not take too much in hand at a time, and we already have enough for a beginning. We must now hold rather with the English, while, as you know, we were formerly more on the French side. But, as the last elections in France show, every one of any importance there had to make a show of hostility to us."

I inquired as to the spirit monopoly, and he replied: "They will scarcely pass it, but we shall introduce it. They will look upon us as people who have evil intentions against the country, and in particular against themselves, their rights and powers, and who must, therefore, be kept in check and taught to entertain proper respect towards the representatives of the people, to which category, of course, we do not belong. But after all we are only fulfilling the duties of our office, part of which is to promote the interests of the State to the best of our ability."

On my saying," Well, Münster is now in Paris," he observed: "A change has taken place in him. He is now less phlegmatic, more diligent, and sends fuller reports, which, moreover, have something in them." (. . . .)

"Bucher is also away," I observed, "on a long leave of absence, for the present."

He: "Yes, because he has begged me, I should say ten times, to allow him to retire on account of his health. I have at length given him leave for six months on full pay. He was an excellent book of reference for all occasions, as his good memory had enabled him to read and collect a great deal of information. In addition to that he is a good and worthy man "—a statement in which I heartily concurred.

By this time it was nearly 4 o'clock, and on his pausing for a moment I rose to go. Before leaving I begged him to let me know when he thought I could be of any active use in the press, and he promised to do this. The servant then showed me upstairs through the large *salon* (in which a Christmas tree was still standing, as well as a table covered with presents), and from this into a room opening on the garden. Here were large full length portraits in oils of the Emperor William, in ermine robes, and the Emperors of Austria and Russia, an oil painting of the proclamation of the German Empire at Versailles (at that time only the frame, the picture having been removed to be varnished), and on the black chimney piece the Chinese elephant tusk, almost two metres in length. In another room I saw an excellent new portrait of the Chancellor (painted by Angeli, according to the servant), and, leaning against a sofa, a half length portrait of Pope Leo XIII., by Lenbach. (. . . .)

May 29*th*.—I called on Bucher . . . . who told me he had received the Emperor's order placing him on the retired list, together with the instructions of the Imperial Chancellor, by which it was accompanied. In conclusion the Chancellor thanked him for his long service, and added " hearty " good wishes for his future. . . .

We remained good friends, and Bucher frequently joined Hehn and myself at our Wednesday evening meetings at Trarbach's. I visited him repeatedly in the autumn and winter of 1886 and in January, 1887, on his return from the visit to Stirum. On the 13th of January I took him the payment for an article which he had written for the *Grenzboten* and which was published in No. 41 of that paper, on "Two Diminishers of the Realm." (These were Gladstone and Windthorst, the comparison having been drawn at the suggestion of Bismarck.) On this occasion Bucher told me that he prepared the draft of the Constitution of the North German Confederation. At that time (after the return from Nikolsburg in the autumn of 1866) Bismarck lay seriously ill at Putbus. Savigny, who as Secretary of State should have attended to the matter, took Keudell into his counsels and they thought the thing could be done by introducing a few alterations into the old Constitution of the German Bund. Bucher had to draft the preamble for it. On his return he was summoned to the Chief, who declared Savigny's performance to be worthless, and dictated to him, Bucher, with the assistance of "a little book," probably Pölitz's work on the various Constitutions, the main lines of a Constitution for the new Federal State, which he then wrote out with the help of a clerk, and—when the latter was unable to write any longer—in his own hand. He began work in the afternoon and went on with it all night through and until next morning. After the Chief had made a few alterations he immediately had twelve copies of the Constitution written out in the Foreign Office. Bucher also gave me some particulars of Keudell's stupidity. When he was going to Rome the Chief, for his personal information, explained to him his views about Italy, saying that we should not tolerate a move towards France. Keudell thought he should mention this to Visconti-Venosti, and did so. The Chief disapproved, and instructed him to take the first opportunity of stating to the Italian Minister that what he had said was merely the expression of his personal views. He has, however, omitted to report whether he had carried out these instructions.

On the 15th I wrote to the Prince asking for an appointment, and in accordance with the reply, called at the palace in the Wilhelmstrasse on the 27th of January, 1887. While I was waiting, first Rottenburg and then three little Rantzaus with their nurserymaid passed through the antechamber. (. . . .) At 2.15 P.M. Theiss called me in to the Prince. He came towards me, reached out his hand and asked how I was. I replied: "Well, and as one sees from the newspapers it is the same with yourself."

He: "Not during the last few days. I have an oppression and pains here (he passed his hand over his chest), I fancy something like inflammation of the lungs"—a statement which was open to grave doubt, as he looked quite healthy and rosy.

When Tiras had been driven away and I had taken a seat opposite him at the writing table, he asked: "Now then, what have you been doing in the press recently?"

I replied: "A variety of things in the *Grenzboten* on the situation. But you yourself have said the last word on the subject in the Reichstag, fully and convincingly—for sensible people. But I fear it will not last long. The stupid people will not die out in the land, and no sooner have you enlightened them, than somebody will take pains to put the light out again. The clerical press continues to pile up misrepresentations and lies, and the large and small sheets of the Progressist party do the same to the best of their ability; while the judicial luminaries of the provinces help to stir up discontent."

He: "Yes, and all the pettifogging attorneys. I

fancy, too, from the creduility of the public there is little improvement to be hoped for from the new elections."

I: "It is a pity that the representatives of the people, as they call themselves—the representatives of the cliques—were not excluded by the Constitution from all interference in military and foreign affairs. It should only have been allowed in exceptional cases, and on the special invitation of the Government. Such a provision had been unfortunately omitted from the North German Constitution." He said that was not quite the case, but it was true that at that time mistakes had been made, as he was ill at the beginning, and the "Ministry of War," which was jealous of the "Military Cabinet," introduced various unpractical provisions. He then explained to me the present legal position, much as he had already done in the Reichstag, reading and commenting upon the paragraphs in the Constitution which affected this question, beginning with § 60. He concluded with the words: "Things may again develop into a conflict, if the three Powers which have equal authority cannot come to an understanding in the hour of danger. Our first and greatest necessity is a strong and steadfast army, as that secures our external freedom, our existence, our possessions against the foes that threaten us from without. Of course we could defend these without the present Constitution, and could certainly do so more successfully without a Reichstag like the last one, which was much less an expression of our unity than of our divisions and Particularism and which was little else than a hindrance in the defence of our most important interests. I could immediately secure the sanction of the Emperor to a change in this respect, and that of the Federal

Governments also. But that must wait yet awhile—until we see how these and perhaps the next elections turn out. If no better Reichstag is elected, when the compromise, *i.e.*, the septennate, has run out, the first thing will be to put into force the provision which allows the Emperor to call out contingents proportionate to the population, the only restriction arising from financial considerations. He has always the right to raise as many soldiers as he considers necessary, and of course the expense thus incurred must be voted.—But what I wanted to say to you is this. I have used reassuring language in the Reichstag with regard to the present attitude of Russia towards us. But many considerations had to be passed over in silence to which it would not have served my purpose to give utterance, but which may be indicated in the press—cautiously. There, I was speaking not only to the members of the Reichstag and the German public, but also to foreign countries, and to a particular quarter where I wished to let it be seen that I trusted to their insight, good will and love of peace, and where such confidence is appreciated—the Emperor Alexander—especially when it comes from a quarter in which he himself may and really does repose unlimited confidence. That is quite true. The Emperor and Giers now anticipate no danger for Russia from Germany, and consequently do not think of attacking us; and so far as the immediate future is concerned they will in all probability not adopt a hostile attitude towards us, if things remain as they now are in Germany and Russia. At the same time a change may occur in the situation. There is, in addition to the Emperor, a kind of public opinion, parties that must be reckoned with even now, and which in a war between Germany and France would exercise all the greater influence on the decisions of the Crown, in that their views and demands would appear to coincide with the real interests of Russia. There you have the Panslavists, with their hatred of the Germans and their leaning towards France. And then there are the Poles and the Liberal Russians, who desire a war with us in the hope that it would result in the defeat of Russia and secure their ultimate aim, namely, independence for the Poles and a Constitution for the others. In case of a conflict between Germany and France, these parties would exert a stronger pressure in exalted regions than they have ever been able to do up to the present, through their newspapers, and their allies in the army, in the Ministries, and in Court circles. Even the possibility of their efforts ultimately affecting the judgment and love of peace prevailing there—as did actually occur under the late Emperor, before the last Russo-Turkish war—would force us to send an army of observation of at least 100,000 men to our eastern frontier to watch the 200,000 soldiers stationed by Russia in her western provinces, thus considerably weakening our available forces against France. Moreover, supposing that, in spite of this, we were victorious, public opinion in St. Petersburg and Moscow, and ultimately the Government under its pressure, would scarcely suffer us to turn our victory to sufficiently good account in order to thoroughly weaken France for the next thirty or forty years, as that would be a strengthening of the German Empire which might arouse serious apprehension in Russia. Finally, it may be regarded as well-nigh certain that while we were engaged in the west the Russians would attack Austria, as her armaments, even more than ours, require strengthening—a duty which she has hitherto with culpable levity neglected—and in the long run we should doubtless be obliged to come to her assistance. Of course I could not say all that, and even in the press it must be very cautiously dealt with."

I observed: "I do not know whether I am right, but I fear a war with Russia less from any apprehension of defeat, than because, in case of victory, I do not see what we could take to compensate us for the great sacrifices incurred."

He: "Certainly, and for the great number of troops we should lose. That keeps me from a war with France also. In that case, too, it is a question of 'Was kannst Du, armer Teufel, geben?' (Thou, poor devil, what canst thou give?)"

I: "In the long run the milliards were also no blessing, at least not for our manufacturers, as they led to over-production. It was merely the bankers who benefited, and of these only the big ones." From this we came to speak of the Stock Exchange and the present fall of prices, whereupon he remarked: "Bleichröder told me recently that he too has mobilised his forces, and at the right moment, some time ago."

I mentioned having read in the *Boersenzeitung* that, according to a small South German newspaper, the Emperor had been much incensed at the rejection of the Army Bill, and had spoken in the presence of Bismarck and the Crown Prince of a step which, if carried into effect, would have aroused the deepest regret. People thought that this referred to his abdication. But who could have circulated and made public the account of such an incident? He said: "The only element of truth in the story is that he was very angry with the Opposition. There was no question of abdicating. But he might very well be induced to agree to a step which would put an end to all the difficulties that the Reichstag can raise in military matters." He then spoke once more of the Opposition parties, and their mendacity and fictions ; as that he (Bismarck) wants to abolish or to restrict universal suffrage, and with the assistance of an accommodating Parliament, to introduce tobacco and spirit monopolies, and what not besides, even to the revival of serfdom. "That is only credited by the stupid voters. They themselves, Richter and his apostles, do not for a moment imagine that anything of the kind is intended. It is a mere electioneering dodge of a gross and audacious description, according to Goethe's recipe : '*Willst Du sie betrügen, so mach es nur nicht fein.*' And it is the same with that lying rascal Windthorst, and his priestly followers. At one moment liberty is threatened, and then the Church, and all this merely to hide the fact that he will not let the Empire have peace, and wants to pave the way for the return of the Guelphs to Hanover. The whole crowd are hypocrites, and wear masks, and in all this Parliamentary mummery I am the only one who shows his face. They are Particularists one and all, in spite of their professions. The German Liberals are Particularists for their party, and the others are territorial Particularists. They are all striving for disintegration and dissolution. But when all is said and done, a Prussian King of to-day can, if they don't want him, renounce the Empire and exist for himself alone."

I asked : "How do you stand with the old gentleman at present ?"

He : "With the Pope? Excellently, and in this question, too. He also trusts me and has reason to believe in my fair play. I told him I was prepared to go still further, meaning that I should even be pleased to see a Papal Nuncio in Berlin. But the King will not have it. He thinks in that case he would have to become a Catholic in his old age. The Ministers are also against it, but without reason. I am not afraid of it. On the contrary, things would go better. At present, Windthorst is the Nuncio, the Father of Lies. We know now exactly how he carries on with Rome. We have letters of his in our hands. A real Nuncio could not lie in that fashion to us and to the Pope, who is well disposed and reasonable. He would be an ecclesiastical diplomatist, whose aims would be purely ecclesiastical, and who would not wish to lose credit with the Government and render himself impossible. He would have to carry out the instructions of his superiors in Rome—not at Gmunden —and those instructions would be imbued with a peace-loving spirit and would be favourable to the maintenance of the Empire—as may now be seen from the desire expressed by the Pope that the Centre party should vote for the Army Bill."

I: "What I was really thinking of was the Emperor and your relations to him."

He: "I have also been on the best of terms with him for a long time past. Apart from the question of the Nunciature we are in perfect agreement upon all points. The Crown Prince, too, is at present everything I could wish him to be, *she* is likewise thoroughly well-disposed towards me."

I: "Mr. Gladstone's admirer? Why, that is most satisfactory."

He: "They are now quite reasonable. They have no intention of introducing any change when the old gentleman goes, and they have repeatedly told me so. They are still afraid that I may not remain. And really I often wish it were otherwise, as I would rather go and spend my last days at Friedrichsruh, as a mere spectator."

I: "And have Dr. Busch to arrange your papers, as your Serene Highness suggested three years ago."

He: "Yes, that too. But I must remain as long as a Prussian King wants my services and wishes to retain me."

I: "And after all you would not like to desert your work and let it fall into the hands of people like Virchow and Forckenbeck. You once spoke to me about Götz von Berlichingen and Metzler, the ringleader of the peasants."

He: "That by remaining I could at least prevent the worst from happening. Such an eventuality is no longer to be apprehended. People deceive themselves greatly if they imagine there will be any considerable difference under the new King. But my position is difficult enough now that I no longer have the strength to work continuously at all manner of things, although there is always so much to be done. All the Ministers come to consult me upon subjects which, properly speaking, do not concern me, and make me responsible for them. That is the case even with the Ministry of the Household, where Schleinitz, the lazy fellow, neglected everything, and Stolberg is often away. But one must do his duty. As to what you say about my work, it looks great, but after all it is of the earth and transient. Besides, what is the meaning of 'great?' Germany is great, but the earth is greater, and how small the earth is in comparison with the solar system, to say nothing of the whole universe. And how long will it last?"

I: "Hegel maintained that the earth was the sole planet with intellectual life, thought and history."

He: "Yes, because it was upon the earth he philosophised. Certainly there are worlds where things of much greater importance are thought and done. But that is the way of these professors (he mentioned Virchow, Du Bois Reymond, and then asked what was the name of the third natural philosopher—I suggested 'Helmholtz'), they speak as if they knew everything; while they undoubtedly know a great deal in their own science, even there they are ignorant of the real root of things, to say nothing of other matters. They go as far as the cell, but what causes the cell?"

I: "I picture the world to myself as a point, that may be termed the first cause of God, which then extends itself to a ball, filling the void."

He: "And yet permits it to exist for ever." I rose to take leave. He gave me his hand and said: "I am glad to see you look so well and not in the least changed. And such a lot of hair still. Let me see." I bent down in order that he might see the crown of my head, and he said: "Yes, it's your own. I thought you wore a wig. But the beard is growing white. You should get it cut off and have your moustache dyed. Then you would be quite young."

The most important part of this interview, which finished at 3 o'clock, was worked up into the article, "War Clouds in the West," which appeared in No. 6 of the *Grenzboten*, and was forwarded to the Prince.

March 25th—For about a week past various newspapers have published a statement to the effect that Keudell has tendered his resignation on the ground that the alliance between Germany and Italy which was concluded a short time since was not drawn up through him but through the Italian Ambassador in Berlin. A diplomatic negotiation of the highest importance had therefore been carried on over his head, and he had been merely instructed quite at the end to hand over to Robilant the reward for his good offices in the shape of the Black Eagle. In other words, Bismarck had looked upon him as fit only to fulfil representative functions of a formal order, and had acted accordingly. At last! How often does the pitcher go to the well before it is broken, said I to myself, as I read a *démenti* in the *Kreuzzeitung*. So not yet awhile? (. . . .)

At 10 A.M. on the 28th of April one of the Chancery attendants brought me the following note: "The Imperial Chancellor would feel obliged if Dr. Busch would do him the honour to call upon him to-day at 2.30 P.M. Berlin, April 28th, 1887." (No signature.) I went at the hour appointed and was told by the porter that Rottenburg wished to see me first. The latter said that the Prince had two commissions for me: one a description of the League of Patriots, and the other an article on the Hammerstein motion (respecting the Evangelical Church). At 3 o'clock Theiss showed me into the Prince, with whom I remained until 3.45 P.M. He again complained a great deal about his ailments and insomnia, as well as of being overburdened with work by all the Ministries. "Nevertheless," I remarked, "on your last birthday you outlived the year in which you prophesied you were to die," and I reminded him of what he had said at Versailles and at Varzin, adding that I now took the liberty for the first time of congratulating him on his birthday, because the last one marked an important division of his life. He smiled and said: "Yes, a division. I had observed that there were certain divisions in my life, with changes and alterations physical and mental, a certain recurrent cycle of years (I believe he said eleven) and from that and some cabalistic figures I had reckoned that I should reach the age of seventy-one years and die in 1886. As that has not happened I shall now probably live to the age of eighty-three or eighty-four." He then came to speak of the subject which had led him to send for me. It appeared that he was not thinking so much of Hammerstein and Co., as of the embarrassment of the Ultramontanes in dealing with their "priestocracy," the demagogues of the middle and lower clergy, whom they had summoned to their assistance against the Government, and who had now cast off discipline and were disinclined to follow the Pope's instructions. He compared their embarrassment to that of the wizard's apprentice in Goethe, and spoke of the "Anti-Papal Catholics." He concluded: "I should not like to have that said in one of our papers. We still want the Centre party for the sugar and spirit taxes."

I then mentioned the League of Patriots, and afterwards turned the conversation on to Alsace-Lorraine. On my observing that it might, perhaps, be possible to annex it to Prussia, or divide it between Bavaria and Baden, he replied: "To unite it to Prussia would strengthen by thirty votes the Opposition in the Lower House of the Prussian Diet, where things are now very tolerable. The Bavarians will not hear of it either, and still less the people in Baden, who are in absolute terror of such a change. If we were only living in the time of Charlemagne we could remove the Alsacians to Posen, and place the inhabitants of the latter country between the Rhine and the Vosges, or form an uninhabited desert between ourselves and the French. As it is, however, we must try some other method." We then spoke about the Crown Prince, who, he said, was understood to have a polypus in the throat. It would be no wonder if he did not recover, as "she" never allowed him to have more than eleven degrees (Réaumur) of warmth in his room, and obliged him at Ems to go into the cold and windy mountain districts, and to cross the Rhine in storm and rain, &c.

I said: "It appears that Diest-Daber wishes to proceed with his action once more."

He: "But how can he do that?" He then gave me an account of the affair, which originated in an action against Diest for libel. This was afterwards transformed by Klotz into a prosecution against him, Bismarck, which resulted in his vindication. He concluded: "Diest is suffering from the mania of persecution, that is to say, in its active form—he must persecute somebody. It would now seem to have turned into megalomania." On our coming to speak of his fortune, I said: "To show what superstitions prevail on this subject, a tradesman, who is otherwise a sensible man, told me recently that you possess a fortune of at least a hundred millions." He thereupon gave me a detailed account of his circumstances, and spoke of the value of his various estates, adding that he was not thinking—"as his sons wished him to do"—of increasing his capital, but rather of rounding off and improving his property. He mentioned Chorow and Sedlitz, and the purchases of land in the Sachsenwald, and similar matters. "I cannot help it," he said. "When a neighbour's property wedges itself into mine, and I see a fine clump of trees on it that are going to be cut down, I must buy that piece of ground." In making such purchases he often paid too much, and frequently the estates were not well managed by those to whom they were entrusted. Thus, although in good years, when high prices were to be had for timber, &c., his profits might amount to about 100,000 thalers, he had, on several occasions, had no surplus whatever over his expenses.

"Moreover," he continued, "it costs me more to live in the country than in Berlin; and in Varzin my horses, with their fodder, cost me more than here. If I could sell my estates at what is probably their real value, I might doubtless get four millions for them." He referred me to Rottenburg for the material for the articles. The latter handed me for use in the article on the League of Patriots the indictment drawn up by Tessendorf of Leipzig, the Imperial Chief Prosecutor (21st April, 1887), against ten inhabitants of the Reichsland (beginning with Köchlin-Claudon of Mülhausen, and winding up with Humbert of Metz), giving the history and description of the association. For the second article on the "Anti-Papal Catholics," he sent me a few days later, by a Chancery messenger, a report of the Ober-Präsident of Westphalia to the Minister of Public Worship, together with about a dozen newspaper extracts. The article on Deroulede's horde appeared in No. 19 of the *Grenzboten* under the title of "The League of Patriots," and the other, "Embarrassments of the Centre Party," in No. 20 (of the 12th of May). I personally left both at the palace for the Chancellor.

During May and June Bucher met Hehn and myself regularly every Wednesday evening, sometimes at Huth's and sometimes at Trarbach's. He wrote for me the *Grenzboten* article on "Maharajah Dhuleep Singh," which appeared in No. 26. He also promised a further article for that paper, drawing a comparison between the reigns of Queen Victoria and Queen Bess, of course not to the advantage or credit of the former, as, according to. him, the Chief, with whom he had recently dined, and who had invited him to pay him shortly a visit at Friedrichsruh, wished to see something of the kind done in connection with the Queen's jubilee. On the 28th of June Bucher started for the dragon's lair in the Sachsenwald, having sent me a card on the previous day to let me know. He was back in Berlin in about ten days. Five of these were spent at Friedrichsruh, and the remainder of the time with Kusseroff in Hamburg. He told me that the Chief was not disposed to let him fire off the articles on the two English Queens. He would think over the matter, but in any case it should not appear in the *Grenzboten*, as that paper's connection with him was suspected.

On the 1st of March, 1888, I received a letter from Rottenburg requesting me to call upon him, as the Imperial Chancellor had instructed him to discuss a certain matter with me. I went to him on the morning of the 2nd of March, and he told me that the Prince wished to have a portion of Beust's book, *Aus drei Viertel jahrhunderte*, beginning on page 346 of the second volume, dealt with in the press, and for that purpose he would give me verbal instructions. I should first, however, read up the book in order to inform myself on the subject. When I had done so I was to send him, Rottenburg, a few lines, and he would then report to the Chancellor and let me know the day and hour on which the latter would receive me. I borrowed Beust's book from Hehn on the same day, and carefully read over the part in question several times. This referred to the attitude of Austria before and during our last war with France, together with the differences it produced between Beust and Grammont. On the 5th I wrote to Rottenburg that I now believed myself to be sufficiently acquainted with the subject to understand and turn to good account any further information which the Imperial Chancellor might give me. I received no answer, however, inviting me to see the Chief. He was occupied with more important matters than Beust's former policy, the illness and death of the Emperor William, and the accession of his son to the throne.

On the evening of the 28th of March at Knoop's Bucher related the following particulars to myself and Hehn. (Casually foreseeing what was generally known a few days later, or informed of and prepared for it.)

"Princess Victoria, the daughter of our new Emperor and Empress, now about twenty-two years of age, was to have been married some time since to the Battenberger, who at that time was still Prince of Bulgaria, but already a tool of English policy. He made the acquaintance of the Queen of England's granddaughter during his European tour. The thought of a marriage was probably suggested by the grandmother in London, who wished to see the position of her servant secured against Russia by an alliance with our Court. The scheme leaked out, and came to the ears of the Chief Of course he was anything but pleased, and did not conceal his objections from the Emperor, but on the contrary expressed them both verbally and in a statement which I had to prepare. It would show us in a bad light at St. Petersburg, and it was not right to subject a Prussian Princess to the eventuality of a compulsory departure from Sofia. The Emperor recognised this and issued his veto, which must have been very unpleasant for the Crown Princess." (. . . .)

April 6th.—On the Chief's birthday Prince William, now the Crown Prince, while offering his congratulations in person, invited himself to dine with the Chancellor. During dinner, according to the newspapers, he proposed a toast to the following effect: "The Empire is like an army corps that has lost its commander-in-chief in the field, while the officer who stands next to him in rank lies severely wounded. At this critical moment forty-six million loyal German hearts turn with solicitude and hope towards the standard and the standard bearer in whom all their expectations are centred. The standard bearer is our illustrious Prince, our great Chancellor. Let him lead us. We will follow him. Long may he live!" Coming from a member of the reigning house such language should mean a great deal. "Our great Chancellor"—words already used a short time ago by his Imperial and Royal Highness—"let him lead us; we will follow him!" What high appreciation and what modest self-suppression and honourable subordination on the part of the future Emperor! May God reward him for it, and grant him victory under that standard! But what does his mother think of it? Yesterday a Vienna telegram in the *Kölnische Zeitung*, which was greeted with scarcely concealed satisfaction by the Progressist newspapers, reported that Bismarck intended to retire. This leads one to think of the "Englishwoman" on the throne of the Hohenzollerns, and of "Friedrich der Britte" (Frederick the Briton) who is to govern according to her views. Has the toast of the 1st instant given offence to Guelphish self-conceit? Or has the Chief again advised against the suitor with the Bulgarian kalpak, who may have pressed his suit again and with a better prospect of success after the death of the Emperor William? At 10.45 A.M. this morning I handed the following letter to the porter at the palace to be immediately forwarded to the Chief: "In presence of the extraordinary report of the *Kölnische Zeitung*, which is now being circulated in the newspapers, I would beg your Serene Highness kindly to remember that in the future as in the past I hold myself absolutely and unconditionally at your disposal, and shall always continue to do so."

April 7th.—At 11 A.M. a Chancery attendant brought me a letter of this day's date from the Imperial Chancellerie, with an appointment to call upon the Prince at 2 o'clock. I was punctually in attendance; but on entering the antechamber, Friedberg, the Minister of Justice, arrived and was shown in to the Chief before me, remaining for about three-quarters of an hour. During this time Minister von Puttkamer also came in, and went away again after a conversation with Rottenburg. Thereupon the latter came to me and said it was doubtful if the Prince could receive me to-day, as he was very much exhausted. He had, however, informed him that I should be there at 2 o'clock. When he called me in, would I " make short work of it ?" I replied that that depended upon the Chancellor and not upon me, but I would offer to come on another day if he were not disposed for the interview at present. At 2.45 P.M. Theiss showed me in to him. He was in undress uniform, and looked quite well, although, after he had shaken hands and asked how I was, he complained of his nervous excitement and insomnia. " I can only get a little sleep with the help of opium and morphia. I am over-worked, and, in addition to that, as you have read in the newspapers, I have latterly been worried by the people at Charlottenburg—by the women. The doctors insist that I should go to the country. Schweninger prophesies that otherwise I shall suffer from all possible forms of nervous diseases, together with typhoid. Besides, I ought to go to Varzin, to see after the damage done by the inundations. The Wipper has carried away all my mills, and to rebuild them may cost hundreds of thousands; but I cannot leave, for who knows what they would do when my back is turned—the women who want to have a share in the government—the Englishwomen? You have seen in the papers that I am thinking of retiring on account of conflicts and Court influence—not with the Emperor, who is much more reasonable and shares my views. The question now is as to the marriage of the Battenberger to Princess Victoria, which the Queen of England has in view. Three years and more ago, under the old master, it was actively promoted by her daughter, the present Empress, at first in secret. As soon as I then heard of it, I made representations to the Emperor, verbally and in writing. He allowed himself to be convinced by the reasons I adduced, and refused to give his consent, although she said the Princess loved him. Of course, he is a handsome man, with a fine presence; but I believe her nature is such that she would accept any other suitor, providing he were manly. Moreover, that is entirely beside the question. We must look at the political objections and dangers. The old Queen is fond of match-making, like all old women, and she may have selected Prince Alexander for her granddaughter, because he is a brother of her son-in-law, the husband of her favourite daughter, Beatrice. But obviously her main objects are political—a permanent estrangement between ourselves and Russia—and if she were to come here for the Princess's birthday, there would be the greatest danger that she would get her way. In family matters she is not accustomed to contradiction, and would immediately bring the parson with her in her travelling bag and the bridegroom in her trunk, and the marriage would come off at once. Probably the Battenberger, too, would have been here by this time if I had not stepped in, for they are in a mighty hurry over there in London."

I asked: "What is the actual condition of his Majesty at Charlottenburg? Is it really cancer, and how long is it likely to last?" He: "Cancer, and Bergmann has already given his opinion, some time ago: it is a question of three weeks or three months. Externally it is not very noticeable. He holds himself upright, and walks with a quick step. But his face (he pointed with his fingers between the cheekbones and the nose) has during the last few days become thinner, and he looks tired and depressed from the excitement. They actually ill-treated, abused and martyred him when he declined. He is glad that I have come to his assistance, as she is too much for him in argument. It is true that so far only a postponement has been secured. If the marriage nevertheless takes place, I can no longer remain in office, for I should then have lost all confidence in the future. That young and impetuous woman's will would prevail more or less in other things too, while I should lose at St. Petersburg that reliance on my straightforwardness which I have so laboriously regained with the Emperor Alexander in spite of all sorts of incitements against me. It is true that in Charlottenburg they are most anxious to retain me—she also. They wrap me up in cotton wool and velvet. That also found expression in the rescript; but as the recognition was of too generous a character it aroused in my mind less pleasure and hope than doubt as to its sincerity, and as to whether something was not concealed behind it. If I can merely postpone and not entirely prevent these English influences upon our policy, if my remonstrances are no longer successful, and my voice not listened to, why should I continue to torment and overwork myself? I will not be a mere cloak for the follies of other people. If it were still the old Emperor with whom I was called upon to blunder along in this way—but to allow myself to be made use of by this Englishwoman, for her whims, for foreign interests, with danger and detriment to ourselves!"

I said: "The Emperor was after all a splendid old gentleman, a real King, with a high sense of duty and well-intentioned, and who knew how to appreciate you."

He: "A trustworthy comrade, who would not leave one in the lurch."

I: "It is true that he sometimes made your life a burden, and did not always treat you well."

He: "Yes, but that was not done through illwill, but through misunderstandings and insufficient knowledge of the matter in hand. When anything of importance was going on he usually began by taking the wrong road, but in the end he always allowed himself to be put straight again. Thus during the period of conflict when he could no longer get any Ministers, he wished to abdicate. When I was summoned to him at Babelsberg he had the act of abdication ready signed. He said: 'If I cannot find any Ministers who will govern as I think right then my son had better try his hand.' I assured him that I was prepared to be the Minister he wanted. 'Even against the majority?' he asked. 'Yes, even against the majority,' I replied. 'Well then, that's all right,' he said, and tore up the document, and with it a whole sheet of concessions to the Liberals, which he had previously read to me."

I: "Then afterwards when you travelled to Juterbogk to meet him. The ladies at Baden had filled him with apprehensions as to an impending revolution, and he already saw the scaffold awaiting him, and you—you infused courage into him by appealing to his honour and grasping his sword knot, as you once expressed it to me?"

He: "Yes, and on other occasions he had too much courage, and wished to move too rapidly and take too much. Thus in 1864 he wished to march into Jutland without Austria, and at Nikolsburg to continue the war as far as Vienna." I recalled the attack of hysterical weeping there. "Then at first he wanted to have half of Saxony, half of Hanover, Ansbach and Bayreuth, and a piece of Bohemia from Austria, until I persuaded him how unpractical that was."

"And in 1870 the military conspiracy at Mayence before the march into France, and afterwards at Versailles his attitude towards the claims of the Bavarians?" I added.

He: "Certainly, when they actually proposed to proceed to violence against Bavaria and afterwards intended to deny her rights which she was entitled to claim."

I said: "The expression 'cloak' reminds me of its converse. Monarchs are often adorned with other people's feathers. If a battle is won at which one of them happens to be present as a spectator, he is said to have won it, although of course the staff has really won it; and so it is in your case in the field of politics."

"Why, yes," he replied; "but if the work is done and succeeds that is the main point. It is a matter of indifference who did it."

He reflected for a moment, and then continued: "The new Empress has always been an Englishwoman, a channel for English influence here, an instrument for the furtherance of English interests. In her present position she is more than ever so, and the Battenberger is to be another tool of the same kind. In England they do not tolerate any foreign influence—you know how Palmerston and the others accused, opposed and persecuted the Prince Consort for his alleged or real influence over the Queen. We however are expected to submit to that sort of thing, and regard it as a matter of course. We are an inferior race, ordained to serve them. So the Queen thinks too, and her daughter is of exactly the same opinion. They are working in partnership. I would suggest to you to take the present opportunity of treating this subject fully, dealing with it from a diplomatic and historical standpoint, showing how England has at all times sought and still seeks to influence us for her own ends, and often against our interest, to use us for promoting her own security and the extension of her power, lately through women, daughters and friends of Queen Victoria. In doing so, please to make use of a small work that was published a few years ago in Switzerland under the title of *Co-Regents and Foreign Influence in Germany (Mitregenten und fremde Hände in Deutschland)*. The anonymous author is not unknown to me. It is Duke Ernst of Coburg, and his account is on the whole correct."

I said: "Doubtless it must be, since he belongs to the clique: Leopold of Belgium, Victoria in London, Victoria in Berlin, Stockmar, and also Josias Bunsen in the heyday of his career."

He: "Yes, but that is no longer the case, as you will see when you read the pamphlet. You can go further back, however. Give a survey of English policy during the last couple of centuries."

I: "Something of the kind must have existed even previously. An Englishman was once even German Emperor, Richard of Cornwall, before Rudolf of Hapsburg."

He: "Yes, but confine yourself to modern history, going back as far as the beginning of the last century. Throughout that period the policy of England has constantly been to sow dissensions between the Continental Powers or to maintain existing discord, on the principle of *Duobus litigantibus tertius gaudens*, and to use the one against the other so that they should be weakened and damaged for the benefit of England. These efforts were first directed against France, then against Russia. First it was the Emperor in Vienna who had to wage war on their behalf, and then we were to take up the cudgels for them. Remember the Spanish War of Succession and the Battle of Dettingen. At that time it is true every State in Europe was threatened in its liberty and existence by the universal monarchy which was then in course of development in France, but none so much as England herself. And then think of the Seven Years' War in which the English took the lion's share of the booty, although they had ventured and accomplished comparatively little, while we conquered the French colonies for them. Latterly they have tried to play us off against the Russians who have become a danger for them on the Bosphorus, and still more on their Indian frontier. We are expected to make good the deficiencies of their military forces, threaten the Russian flank, and hold them back when they propose to march. First, during the Crimean War, in which by the way the French had little reason to join, we were urged, quite against our own interests, to co-operate with the Western Powers in opposing the Emperor Nicholas. I assisted in preventing that. Later on, in 1863, England wanted to see the Polish insurrection supported, as a means of weakening Russia, a course whereby we should have forfeited an old friend who might prove a still better friend to us in the future, and have gained no trustworthy friendship in the West by way of compensation; while in the Poles we should have strengthened an ancient foe, and created a natural ally for France. In 1877, when it was seen that a Russo-Turkish war was imminent, we were expected to exert our influence at St. Petersburg to prevent it—in the interest of humanity—as *The Times* demonstrated. Queen Victoria urged us to do so in a letter to the Emperor, which was handed to him by Augusta, who added her own intercession, and in two letters to myself. Humanity, peace and liberty,—those are always their pretexts when they cannot by way of a change invoke Christianity and the extension of the blessings of civilisation to savage and semi-barbarous peoples. In reality, however, *The Times* and the Queen wrote in the interests of England, which had nothing in common with ours. It is in the interest of England that the German Empire should be on bad terms with Russia. Our interest is that we should be on as good terms with Russia as the situation allows. Latterly I have directed my endeavours towards this end, and I have succeeded, in spite of various opposing influences;—and now the Battenberger is to be called in to nullify my success, to inspire the Emperor Alexander with fresh suspicions, and to supply the Moscow press with plausible grounds, which would have at least appearances in their favour, for asserting that we entertain secret designs. Prince Alexander, who has been selected as bridegroom for the daughter of the German Emperor, would, if that marriage were to take place, not only appear but actually be a permanent channel for English influence with us—that is the essence of the scheme—emphasise and repeat that—so far as this influence is directed against Russia. He is really a Pole, through his mother, who married, as a Fräulein

Hauke, a member of a family which is neither old nor illustrious. (. . . .) Such a relationship is decidedly not suitable for the Prussian Royal House and a daughter of the German Emperor. The Emperor Frederick sees and feels that too, perhaps even more than we do, for he has a very high opinion of his family and its dignity. But apart from that the more important point is that the Emperor Alexander hates the Battenberger with his whole heart, indeed there is perhaps no one else whom he knows and hates so thoroughly."

I said: "The unheard of rudeness of the letter striking his name off the Army List, a communication well nigh unparalleled in the intercourse of Princes."

He rejoined: "Yes, and other things too. But he richly deserved it through his falsehood and treachery. As a nephew of the deceased Empress he was regarded in St. Petersburg as a fitting instrument for advancing Russian interests as Prince of Bulgaria; and that was quite legitimate in view of the gratitude which the Bulgarians owed to Russia for their liberation, while it was also the ultimate and real object of the war of 1877. At first he governed in this sense, but he afterwards took up with the English, who wished to create a Greater Bulgaria to serve their purposes, and like Rumania be under obligations to them. It was to be developed into a new kingdom, which should stand in the way of Russia. That had been planned long beforehand, and the way had been prepared by various measures; but the Prince always tried to dispel any uneasiness by beautifully reassuring speeches and categorical promises. Finally he pledged himself to Giers not to make any kind of change in Eastern Rumelia; and yet shortly afterwards the revolution broke out in Philippopolis, with his previous knowledge and co-operation. It would be a miracle, and utterly opposed to human nature, if the Emperor Alexander did not hate him with a deadly hatred for this dishonourable conduct, this breach of faith. He will never forgive him, and will always look upon him as a sworn enemy, embittered moreover by having been driven out. If he were accepted as a member of the German Imperial House, it would fill the Emperor with a suspicion which nothing could dissipate. It would be a permanent threat to peace. He would not on that account declare war upon us immediately and without more ado, as Napoleon did in similar circumstances in 1870; but he would hold it to be a confirmation of all the old doubts as to our sincerity which we had proved to be unfounded, and the Russian press would renew its agitation with the same violence and malice as formerly, and with more success. It is not yet certain that Russia would take up arms against us if we were to be again attacked by the French; but if the Russians were to declare war upon us the French would certainly join them immediately. And after all in such a war we should not be so very certain to win, while it would be a great misfortune even if we were victorious, as in any case we should lose a great deal of blood and treasure, and also suffer considerable indirect damage through the interruption of work and trade, and we should never be able to take anything from the French or Russians that would compensate us for our losses. It is only the English who would benefit by it. It would be an English war if the Battenberg marriage led Russia to join the French attack on us. We are well armed, but at all events large masses of troops would be put into the field against us, and Austria has not yet developed her defensive forces as she could and should do; and no real confidence could be placed in Italy. It is possible that the French may regain their footing there and win back the Italian friendship, if other parties came into power. Indeed even a Republic is possible, and Italy may resume her irredentist schemes and claims against Austria."

I said: "I shall keep all that in mind, and write the article as well as I can. Perhaps I may be allowed to mention the influence brought to bear by the English ladies against the bombardment of Paris. You remember: 'Schurze und Schürzen'" (aprons and petticoats; that is to say, freemasons and women).

"Yes, do that," he replied; "but at the same time remember the press laws. Be very cautious, diplomatic, and not too venomous; and always emphasise the fact that it is foreign influences that are working against me; not the Emperor, but the reigning lady and her mother." .... "But," I said, "will it not throw an unfavourable light on the Emperor, making him appear weak and pitiable, if one says that he is opposed to the Battenberg project, but may be brought to give in to the demands of the ladies?" He replied: "It is not necessary to say that in so many words; but it is nevertheless a fact—and it was much the same with the late Emperor, who had also to struggle against feminine influence, and was thankful to me when I stiffened him against it. In these cases he used to say to me: 'Do it in such a manner that they may fancy they have had their way, while we really manage as it should be.' On the whole, I got on well with him."

After I had been with him somewhat over three-quarters of an hour, he called my attention to a very curious little work of art which stood on his writing table. It consisted of a large grey pearl mounted with diamonds and rubies, representing the head of a greyhound with a golden tobacco pipe in its mouth. This, he explained, was "a present from Mexico." I then took my leave, and he was about to lie down to sleep. In the antechamber Theiss told me that while I had been with the Chancellor the Grand Duke of Baden called to see him. He had told him, however, that the Prince "had a conference," and he accordingly went away. I proceeded direct to Bucher's in order to repeat to him as literally as possible my conversation with the Chief, and thus to impress it more firmly on my mind. He had the Duke of Coburg's pamphlet, which he lent me. He also gave me the following example of the manner in which the feminine half of the present Imperial family have been anglicised. "Princess Victoria, the Battenbergerin *in spe*, had a difference with her brother on one occasion respecting some household arrangement. 'After all, that is much better managed at home,' she said. 'At home? What do you mean?' he asked. 'Why, at home in England,' she replied. The particular epithet which Prince William applied to her is not known for certain, but it was either 'goose' or 'sheep'" (. . . .)

On my return home at 6 o'clock I found the following note, enclosing an extract from the *Deutsches Tageblatt*, lying on my table:—"Dear Sir,—Prince Bismarck begs you to kindly introduce the article discussed to-day by a reference to the enclosed statements of *The Times*, in order that it should not appear to be written without any immediate occasion.—Yours truly, ROTTENBURG."

On the 8th of April, having again been summoned to the Chief, I called at the Chancellor's palace, and was shown in without much delay. The Prince, who was reclining in a *chaise longue* near the window, was reading the *Kölnische Zeitung*. I had to draw up an armchair close to him. He said: "Here is the *Kölnische Zeitung* writing against *The Times*, and also the *Frankfurter Zeitung*. You might also mention this in the article of which we were speaking yesterday, and correct them where necessary. The main point is that the Emperor is on my side. A syllable must be added here" (he pointed to the word "Kaiser," which was underlined in red)—"Kaiser*in*. It is a struggle between the Emperor and Empress. She, as an Englishwoman, is in favour of the Battenberger; he will not have him, first for political reasons, like myself, and then because he actually hates him, for he dislikes the idea of a *mésalliance*, as he is very proud of his dynasty and position. Two Empresses are fighting against his opinion and mine,—those of India and Germany; and Victoria the daughter simply talks him down. She can make much better use of her tongue than he can. It has always been so, and now more than ever, owing to his illness and the way in which worry affects him. Besides, he is deeply devoted to his family. I was present on one occasion when she set at him so violently with her feminine logic and volubility that at last he sat there quite silent and depressed. He is delighted every time that I come to his assistance against his combative wife." I related Bucher's story about Victoria No. 3 and her brother. "Yes," he said, "that is quite credible. At home with her daughters, she, the German Empress, only speaks English, the language of the Chosen People, and the Princesses write English letters to their father."

He continued: "Look here! There they talk of my attachment to the dynasty. Well, that is quite correct, but it was more so under the father, the old master. I had all along wanted to retire at his death, and if I remain it may be taken as certain that I do so only on an understanding that I continue the old policy I have followed hitherto, and am protected from foreign influence and from the interference and misgovernment of women, which was never carried to such lengths as it is at present. I would therefore beg of you to call attention to the Progressist journals, to these Court Jacobins—use that word—who receive their orders from Charlottenburg, through the women whose names figure at the head of the Address, Frau Helmholtz, Schrader, and Stockmar, whose late husband was Secretary to the Englishwoman when she was Crown Princess. These Byzantine hypocrites, these democrats who wag their tails and crawl more abjectly than the most extravagant absolutist, would like to degrade me from being a servant of the State and of its head into a Court menial, although of course it is both my right and my duty to form my own opinion and maintain it like anybody else, all the more as I bear the responsibility for the mistakes, or, as in the present instance, the obvious follies that are committed in important matters." He continued to dilate on this theme for a few minutes; and then again suggested that I should make use of the pamphlet of Duke Ernst of Coburg. He sent for Rottenburg, and told him that in using it elsewhere the passages which I should quote were not to be employed. When Rottenburg had gone I asked: "Are you quite sure that it was he who wrote it? It is very strong for him, although from the style, which is rather vulgar and careless, it might well be his work, besides which he is acquainted with the facts through being closely connected with the Queen." He replied, smiling: "He himself told me so" (in English). I then spoke of his autobiography, which I described as badly arranged and prolix. "Yes," he said, "he has somewhat the same failing as Beust. He can suppress nothing—not the most trifling circumstance respecting what he has done or tried to do, and collected." I inquired as to the instructions respecting Beust's book. He replied: "That must wait. We have now more important matters to deal with. Later on, perhaps. For the present you might get them to give you the book. I have underlined a few things which appear to me to be incorrect. But now I must try to get some sleep. At present my pulse goes on an average fifteen beats in the minute faster than it did during the preceding reign." I took my leave, with good wishes for his speedy improvement. I had been with him about twenty minutes. In the following three days I wrote the desired article, and sent it to the *Grenzboten*, where it appeared in No. 17, under the title, "Foreign Influences in the Empire."

April 25*th*.—This evening at Knoop's, Bucher described the candidature of the Prince of Hohenzollern, in which he himself had taken a part, as a "trap for Napoleon." He added that neither the Emperor William nor the Crown Prince had the least idea of this feature of Bismarck's manœuvre, of which he, Bucher, also gave particulars to the Crown Prince after his journey. They both regarded the candidature as a means of exalting the glory of their House.

April 28*th*.—This afternoon met Bucher in the Königin Augusta Strasse. . . . . He said, smiling: "I have just heard a surprising piece of news. Grandmamma behaved quite sensibly at Charlottenburg. She declared the attitude of the Chief in the Battenberg marriage scheme to be quite correct, and urged her daughter to change her ways. Of course it was very niece of her not to forget her own country and to wish to benefit it where it was possible for her to do so, but she needed the attachment of the Germans, and should endeavour to secure it; and finally she brought about a reconciliation between Prince William and his mother." I asked, "Have you that on good authority?" "On very good authority," he replied. "Well," I said, "that is highly satisfactory, and we shall act accordingly in the immediate future, for, of course, we do not hate Victoria II. on account of her extraction, but because she feels as an Englishwoman and wishes to promote English interests at our expense, and because she despises us Germans. The question is whether in the long run she will heed this maternal admonition. It is not easy to rid one's self of a habit of thought of such long standing." He agreed with me in this.

April 29th.—I read this morning in the *Berliner Boersen Zeitung*: "We are in a position to state that the Imperial Chancellor, as was indeed to be expected, is most indignant at the notorious article in the *Grenzboten* slandering the Empress Victoria, and that he has given expression to his condemnation in very strong terms. In this connection exceptional importance is to be attached to the sympathetic article in the *Norddeutsche Allgemeine Zeitung* on the Queen of England's visit." Doubtless as that paper is in the Bleichröder's service, this utterance has been inspired by that firm, over which floats the flag of the British Consulate General. Well informed? Possibly, indeed probably. A disclaimer? Why not! Quite in order! *Tempora mutantur*? But I shall never change towards him, nor he doubtless towards me. He will once more call for his little archer when he again wants an arrow shot into the face of this or that sun, and "Büschlein's" bow shall never fail him. My "libellous article" was, I see, indignantly denounced in the *Daily Telegraph* and the *Neue Freie Presse*. In doing so the former described the *Grenzboten* as "a publication which, for well-known reasons, is read with attention throughout Germany." The *Neue Freie Presse* spoke of a want of tact which would be regarded as impossible if it were not in evidence in black on white. Excellent! In this manner what I had written secured a wide circulation, particularly as other journalistic hacks will probably without wishing it have recommended the article in a similar way. (. . . .)

After the death of the Emperor Frederick, I wrote to Bucher a few lines expressing the satisfaction I felt that we were relieved of that incubus, and that his place was now to be taken by a disciple and admirer of the Chief.

CHAPTER IV

THE EMPEROR FREDERICK'S DIARY—THE CHIEF ON THE DIARY AND ITS AUTHOR—THE GERMAN QUESTION DURING THE WAR OF 1870—THE EMPEROR FREDERICK AND HIS LEANING TOWARDS ENGLAND—THE CHIEF PRAISES THE YOUNG EMPEROR—"BETTER TOO MUCH THAN TOO LITTLE FIRE!"—I AM TO ARRANGE THE CHIEF'S PAPERS, AND DO SO—LETTERS FROM FREDERICK WILLIAM IV. AND FROM WILLIAM I.—CORRESPONDENCE WITH AND CONCERNING THE CROWN PRINCE (FREDERICK)—LETTERS TO AND FROM ANDRASSY DURING THE NEGOTIATIONS FOR THE AUSTRO-GERMAN ALLIANCE—LETTERS FROM THE EMPEROR ON THE SAME SUBJECT—WILLIAM I.'S RELUCTANCE TO DESERT RUSSIA—CONVERSATION BETWEEN THE EMPEROR AND THE TSAR AT ALEXANDROVO—WILLIAM I.'S FINAL INSTRUCTIONS—BISMARCK'S ACCOUNT OF HIS RELATIONS WITH THE EMPEROR FREDERICK.

July 16th.—After it had been whispered in the press for some time that the Emperor Frederick had left a diary which did not throw a very favourable light upon Bismarck, and that this was at present in the hands of the Queen of England, a second version of the story (*Berliner Boersenzeitung*, evening edition of the 13th) is now reproduced from the *Matin* and other French papers. This is to the following effect. During the lifetime of the Emperor William I. Prince Bismarck prepared a frank statement respecting the European situation and his own political views, which he handed to the Emperor, believing that the latter would survive his son, and that the document would thus pass direct, without any intermediary, from the grandfather to the grandson. Frederick ascended the throne, and found the Bismarck memorandum. All the efforts made by the Chancellor to recover possession of it were in vain, and on Frederick's death it was found that the document, which contained the most secret ideas and schemes of the Chancellor, had come into the possession of Queen Victoria, who declined to give it up. In this form the story is doubtless akin to that of the sea-serpent, and yet it is perhaps not entirely without foundation. Anyhow, it is possible that a diary by the late Emperor may be in existence, and may have been put into a place of safety by his consort or her mother.

On the 20th of September I received from Grunow the October number of the *Deutsche Rundschau*, containing the diary of the Emperor Frederick during the war. I reviewed it in No. 40 of the *Grenzboten* without having any doubt as to its being in the main genuine. On the 24th Hedwig announced the arrival of one of the Chancery attendants who had been sent by Rottenburg to request me to call upon him at 2.30 P.M. I went, and he showed me a letter from the Imperial Chancellor (written by an amanuensis) desiring him to request me to come to Friedrichsruh, and to bring with me my notes taken during the war, as the diary of the Emperor Frederick appeared to contain inaccuracies. I promised to start next morning, whereupon Rottenburg arranged to telegraph to Rantzau to stop the 8.30 A.M. train at Friedrichsruh where it does not usually stop. Nothing was to be said in the newspapers about my visit. I replied that that went without saying so far as it depended upon me. I had always felt disgusted at the merest mention of my name by that pack. On the same evening Rottenburg sent me a letter requesting me not to leave Berlin, but to come to the Imperial Chancellerie at 10 A.M. on the following morning, as other arrangements had been made.

I appeared punctually at 10 A.M. in the Chancellor's ante-chamber, where I met the Secretary of State, Von Schelling (medium height, red face, white hair and small white moustache) who was shown in to the Prince before me. As Rottenburg informed me while I was waiting, the Chancellor had arrived and wished to see me. He added, however, that he might not be able to see me now, in which case I should return at 2.30 P.M. Rottenburg also inquired if I had already found any inaccuracies in the diary published in the *Rundschau*. I replied that so far I had only noticed some trifling errors, and that on the whole I considered it to be genuine, but not complete. Schelling remained for half an hour. On his leaving, Rantzau came out and spoke to Rottenburg, whereupon the latter again requested me to return at 2.30 P.M., as the Chief was too much occupied to be able to speak to me now. On my return at the hour named he said that the Chancellor had still no time to receive me and was going back to Friedrichsruh that evening. There was, therefore, no alternative but for me to go there likewise. It would be well if I were to start next morning and telegraph to him shortly before my departure in order that he might arrange for the train to stop at Friedrichsruh. I promised to leave by the 8.30 train from the Lehrter station, which arrives at Friedrichsruh about 1 P.M., and also to take with me my notes, of which he again reminded me.

September 26th.—About one o'clock I arrived at Friedrichsruh station, where Rottenburg was waiting with a carriage for Count Solms, our Ambassador in Rome—who travelled by the same train—and myself. On our way to the house, the Privy Councillor told us that the Prince had gone out for a walk in order to freshen himself up, as he had done a great deal of work last night. At 2.15 P.M. I met him at lunch, at which the Princess, Rantzau and his wife, his Excellency von Solms, and a Prioress, whose name I have forgotten, were also present. The Chief, as was his custom formerly at Varzin and here, read through, signed and otherwise disposed of various documents. After lunch Rottenburg, on his instructions, handed me a memorandum on the diary published in the *Rundschau*. This was directed to the Emperor and was to appear next day in the *Reichsanzeiger*. While I was reading this through in his study, the Chief came in, asked me to give it to him, and made a few corrections and additions in it. I then read it through in my own room upstairs, after which the Chancery attendant, Kleist, took it away. I then chatted with the three little Rantzaus, who were trying their skill at archery at an improvised target near the coach-house; advised them in the matter, and in that way, apparently, won the good will of the still very childlike and unaffected boys. Then a short walk with Solms in the park on the banks of the Aue. On my return, I found a carriage standing before the door of the house; and the Chief sent word to say that he was going out for a drive, and would I like to come with him. Of course I would. We then drove for about two hours, first to Silt, afterwards to Schönau and finally to the Billenbrück, and then home through the beech wood on the right bank of the Aue. On the way, the Prince spoke to two gamekeepers about the scarcity of partridges and the fish poachers; while he discussed the state of the crops, and the condition of the cattle with a cowherd whose charges were feeding in a field of vetches. Further on, he entered into conversation with overseers who were looking after the potato digging and with labourers who were ploughing with oxen. In the intervals he had a long conversation with me on the manner in which the Crown Prince's diary should be dealt with. He introduced the subject by the remark (in English): "I am afraid you have forgotten your English." On my answering, "No, sir, by no means," he continued the conversation in that language on account of the coachman. He began: "As you will have seen from what you read, we must first treat it as a forgery, a point of view from which a great deal may be said. Then, when it is proved to be genuine by the production of the original it can be dealt with further in another way." I said that on the whole it appeared to me to be genuine, but incomplete, on the one hand, while, on the other, there were interpolations, probably by Victoria No. 2, in support of which opinion I quoted examples. I also told him that, in ignorance of his plans, I had already dealt with the matter in the *Grenzboten* a week before, according to my own views, and in certain flagrant instances condemned it cautiously.

Another course was, however, still open to me. I then repeated to him, from memory, the commencement of the article in question. He rejoined: "You were quite right. I myself consider the diary even more genuine than you do. It is quite insignificant, superficial stuff, without any true conception of the situation, a medley of sentimental politics, self-conceit and phrase-mongering. He was far from being as clever as his father, and the latter was certainly not a first-rate politician. It is just that which proves its genuineness to me. But at first we must treat it as doubtful." The conversation then turned on the details of the diary. I asked if he had spoken to the Emperor on the subject, and he replied in the affirmative, saying: "He was quite in a rage and wishes to have strong measures taken against the publication." He then came to speak of the demand for Imperial Ministers. We have them, of course, only without the title and name. The Imperial Chancellor is their permanent President,—permanent, because with us the the power of the Emperor is greater under the Constitution than in other countries which are ruled by alternating Parliamentary majorities. I suggested that Gustav Freytag might perhaps at the instance of the Empress Victoria have edited the diary and arranged for its publication. I tried to show the probability of this suggestion by a reference to his political views, to the confidential position which he occupied towards the two Victorias, and in particular to an instruction to Brater's paper in Frankfurt in the summer of 1863, during the conflict between the King and the Crown Prince respecting the "Press Ordinances." He considered, however, that the trick would prove to have been done by Hengst, a writer who serves the Court, and particularly its ladies, in the press. He then repeated the main points of the memorandum which I had previously read. I now ascertained for certain that this was a report on the diary in the *Deutsche Rundschau* which the Chancellor, by the Emperor's command, had submitted to the sovereign a few days ago. He added various details: " In 1870 the Crown Prince was only partially initiated into the negotiations, as the King feared that he would write about them either to his consort, or direct to Queen Victoria and her Court, whose sympathies were with the French. In the second place, he might also have done harm, as his views with regard to the demands upon our German allies went too far, and he was thinking of coercive measures which were urged upon him by his good friends at Baden and Coburg—as, for instance, Roggenbach, who always was a fool. He had therefore only a superficial knowledge of the course of affairs. It is, nevertheless, suprising that these notes, which are supposed to have been written down day by day, contain so many misconceptions, confusions and chronological errors. A great deal of it cannot possibly have been written by the Crown Prince, and must have come from his *entourage* or the publisher. Here it is said that, in the middle of July, I wanted to return to Varzin because peace was no longer in danger, while he, of course, knew that I considered war to be inevitable, and had declared my intention to retire when the King showed a disposition to yield. It is also inconceivable that the Crown Prince endeavoured at an early date to secure the Iron Cross for non-Prussians, in view of the fact that at Versailles he was opposed to it, and it was I who first suggested it. He represents this as the beginning of the struggle between him and me as to the future of Germany, although he must surely have remembered former differences of opinion between us, that led to some very lively discussions which one would not be likely to forget. It was before or immediately after Sedan, at Beaumont or Donchery, and the conversation took place in a long avenue through which we rode side by side. We came to high words over our respective views as to what was expedient and morally permissible, and when he spoke of force and of coercive measures against the Bavarians I reminded him of the Margrave Gero and the thirty Wendish Princes, and also of the Sendling massacre. When he held to his opinion, however, and suggested that I should carry it into execution, I said to him (scarcely in so blunt and plain a fashion) that there were things which a Prince, perhaps, might do, but no gentleman would attempt. Such conduct would be an act of perfidy, and an outrage upon allies who had fulfilled their obligations, quite apart from the folly of such an attempt at a time when we had further use for them. The statements in the alleged diary as to my position in the Emperor question in 1866, on my intentions in connection with the dogma of infallibility, my idea of an Upper House and the Imperial Ministries, can hardly have been written by the Crown Prince either. In 1870 he could no longer doubt that the Empire, in the form which he had in his mind in 1866, would have been neither useful nor feasible—in fact it would not have been an Empire at all. What he desired in 1866 was not an Emperor but a King of Germany—the other Kings and Grand Dukes being reduced to their former rank, merely Dukes—as if that were an easy matter to bring about. We had already put an end to the Upper House at Beaumont or Donchery, and had dealt with the Imperial Ministers in like fashion. He, too, must have finally recognised that the dogma of infallibility was of slight importance for us, and that I regarded it as a blunder on the part of the Pope and advised the King to let it rest during the continuance of the war. Even a hasty thinker like the Crown Prince could scarcely have concluded from that that I intended to oppose it after the war, and therefore this passage was doubtless not written by him. At least for the present we must continue to doubt the genuineness of this and other statements." He then spoke of Bray, who, as an Austrian sympathiser, delayed the mobilisation of the Bavarian troops in 1870; and of King Lewis, who—at that time of sound German principles—was "our sole influential friend in Bavaria." Returning to the Crown Prince's idea of 1866 and to his Upper Chamber, the Chancellor observed: "An Emperor or King of North Germany would have created a division between North and South Germany such as did not exist under the Customs Union; and an Upper House with Princes and elected members was impossible." I then reminded him of the importunity of Baden and Coburg, who at Versailles worried him with memorials and verbal counsels, questions, &c., to that effect, and of his indignation at the unexpected visit of the Grand Duke Frederick during dinner. I then mentioned to him what Bucher had told me about the sensible attitude adopted by the Queen of England at Charlottenburg, which he confirmed, adding that at the interview which he had had with her he had in part prompted the admonitions which she addressed to her daughter. In this connection I asked whether the statement in Bleichröder's *Boersenzeitung* as to his strong condemnation of my article, "Foreign Influences in the Empire," were true. I added that, *rebus mutatis*, I should have considered it quite conceivable, and had indeed said as much. He replied, smiling: "Nonsense! quite the contrary. I have several times expressed my high appreciation of it. The article was really quite first rate, and the Coburg pamphlet was also very aptly applied." Driving along in the dusk on the right bank of the Aue, we passed a boarding school, and were greeted with cheers three times repeated by a crowd of children (doubtless the pupils and their teacher). "They will," he said, "have taken the grey-bearded gentleman seated by me for a Rumanian or Bulgarian Minister on a visit." "Then I too have had a share in the ovation," I rejoined, "and shall take it with me to Berlin as a souvenir." He afterwards requested me to look through my diary to-morrow, to see if there were any further chronological or other mistakes in the publication of the *Deutsche Rundschau* and to report to him on the subject.

After dinner, which began at 7 o'clock and lasted for about an hour, coffee and cognac were served in the next room, while the Prince seated himself on a sofa in the corner, behind a table with a lamp. There he read the newspapers and smoked a long pipe. We followed suit with cigars. I had some conversation with Rantzau, who is now about to leave for his post at Munich, concerning "Friedrich der Sachte," and my intercourse with him and his "Ministers," as well as on the old Schleswig-Holstein agitation. The Princess then brought me a book kept by her, in which I had to write my name and the date. I was preceded in this by various distinguished and eminent people, celebrities of the day, Ministers, Ambassadors, Envoys, &c. It will one day be an interesting collection. Afterwards met Solms upstairs in the corridor leading to his and my room, and hastily gave him a little (well deserved) praise for his sharp diplomatic scent in the months preceding the French war. This moved him to invite me to his room, where he gave me detailed particulars of his experiences and achievements at that time, but unfortunately in French, whereby some points were lost to me. (. . . .)

On the morning of the 27th I again spoke to the Ambassador as he was on the point of starting for Berlin and Rome. "Adieu, old friend, and if you ever come to the Eternal City be sure to visit me. But what I said to you last night about the Paris affairs must not appear in your memoirs." "No, Excellency, a mere reference to the conversation without any details. I know how to respect your confidence as well as that of other people." "Yes, I am convinced that you have gathered a great deal about our affairs which does not appear in your books."

During the forenoon, in accordance with the Chief's desire, I went through my diary up to our stay at Ferrières. At lunch the Prince observed, after first recommending me to take some herring: "They are wholesome, and I always have some since Schweninger advised me to take fish. Moreover, it is a very fine and good fish, and is only looked down upon because it is so plentiful and cheap. Since I began in 1883 I must have disposed of over a thousand of them." In the evening, after dinner, the Prince, while looking through the newspapers, suddenly said: "Yes, since 1840 the Princes have begun to degenerate. I will give you an example or two (looking towards me). In 1858, before Prince William, afterwards Emperor, acted as Regent for his brother, there was a reactionary intrigue on foot with which Manteuffel was not unconnected, and in which they also wanted me to join. Its object was to induce the sick King to withdraw his authority, and to let Queen Elizabeth govern through the Ministers. I did not join in that scheme, but on the contrary started for Baden—or was it somewhere else in South Germany? —and told the whole story to him (the Prince of Prussia). He was not at all disconcerted by the plan, however, and declared himself ready to retire immediately. It was therefore a matter of perfect indifference to him. But I argued it out with him. What will be the result of such a move? It is surely your duty to hold on! Send for Manteuffel at once. And Manteuffel actually came, after having hesitated for some little time, excusing himself on the ground of illness, and so the affair went no further. Then at Babelsberg, when I was called thither in order to be made Minister. In his despair he had the act of abdication ready signed, and it was only when I offered to stand by him in spite of Parliament and in spite of the majority that he tore it up. This restored his courage and confidence and his sense of royal duty, which in his unfortunate position had, until then, been a matter of utter indifference to him. He afterwards held to it firmly enough." The Chancellor added that of late years the deceased monarch through this sense of duty had sometimes caused him considerable difficulties, as his knowledge of affairs was limited and he was slow in comprehending anything new. Of the present Emperor he said: "He has more understanding, more courage and greater independence of Court influences, but in his leaning towards me he goes far. How considerate he was the last time he came here! He was surprised that I had waited for him till 11 o'clock, a thing which his grandfather was incapable of saying. And in the morning he waited for me, and although he is accustomed to rise much earlier he did not get up until 9 o'clock, thinking that I slept till that hour. I was just washing and only half dressed when he put his hand on my shoulder, and I hurriedly pulled on my dressing gown in order to be to some extent in a proper condition to receive him." I said: "Yes, Serene Highness, you now appear to have everything one could wish for you. A docile and grateful pupil and warm admirer stands by your side as ruler and chief authority in the State, and we, your people, rejoice with all our hearts, and hope that it may long remain so."

"It is only in trifles and matters of secondary importance that one had occasionally some little reason to find fault with him, as for instance in the form of his pronouncements. After all, that was a little too much of a good thing when he said: 'Forty-two millions and eighteen army corps on the field.' 'If at last the whole nation lies hushed in the silence of death.' If every German soldier and civilian is dead, what significance can the independence and inviolability of Germany still have? And new-fangled words from the newspapers, such as '*unentwegt*,' '*voll und ganz*,' to say nothing of '*diesbezüglich*,' do not look well in his proclamation." The Prince rejoined: "In his reference to the battlefield it would certainly have been enough had he said: 'And if I were to be the last man upon the field of battle nothing that we have conquered shall be lost!' But that is youthful vivacity, which time will correct. Better too much than too little fire!" I then conversed with Countess Rantzau, and recommended to her a climatic cure, deep breathing in the open air. He looked up from his paper and said: "Pulmonary gymnastics? I too have tried that, and still do occasionally."

Up to lunch time on the morning of the 28th I read through my diary, and came upon a number of passages that seemed likely to be of use to the Chief. On being called down to lunch I met a gentleman who was paying a private visit. He was introduced to me as Privy Councillor of Embassy Brauer, a portly man of about thirty-six, who has a slight touch of the South-west German accent. The conversation turned on the Crown Prince, and the shallowness and poverty of thought which characterised his diary. From this the Chief again concluded that the publication in the *Deutsche Rundschau*, or at least a great part of it, might be genuine. He again spoke in English on account of the servants. I took the liberty to remark that according to page 138 of my diary it appeared after all that he had had a conversation on the German question with his Royal Highness at Versailles on the 16th. He rejoined: "Yes, but then he has mixed it up with a former one, and moreover I cannot have advised him to propose to the King that the Bavarians should be disarmed." I added that that must have been said ironically—a suggestion of such a monstrous description that no one could take it seriously.

On his rising from table to go to his study, I followed him outside in order to tell him privately that I had found some passages in my diary which might be of interest to him, mentioning in particular Fleming's despatch on Mohl's report. He said he would like to see them in the afternoon, and would send for me for the purpose. "I must now answer Augusta, who has once more administered to me one of her gracious Model Letter-Writer epistles." Later on, when I brought him the diary with the passages of interest marked, he praised Mohl's description of the relations of parties in Bavaria as apt and accurate. On my saying that it would doubtless have been in the hands of the Grand Duke of Baden three months before the differences at Versailles, and that he would certainly have communicated its contents to the Crown Prince, he answered in a tone of contempt: "Ah, that is mere talk on his part. He never took anything seriously, or studied it thoroughly. Do you really think that they were seriously concerned, to read despatches, and to think over and note the contents of reports? They just met in order to smoke and exchange ill-natured gossip." He then related once more: "It was before the conference at Donchery when he spoke of using force against the Bavarians, and of eventually shooting down the two army corps if necessary. I said to him that would be an act of unheard-of treachery, which a Prince might decide upon, but which no gentleman could perform. That would be a course similar to Gero's, in his treatment of the thirty Wendish Princes, a perfidy which had such fatal consequences for the whole Ostmark." On this occasion he also repeated his plan of campaign with regard to the publication in the *Rundschau*: "First assert it to be a forgery, and express indignation at such a calumny upon the noble dead. Then, when they prove it to be genuine, refute the errors and foolish ideas which it contains, but cautiously, and bearing in mind that he was Emperor and father to the present Emperor." He then exclaimed suddenly: "Well, he is gone! Made off with himself, with the Public Prosecutor at his heels. Geffcken, I mean, who published it, and who for the matter of that is no Democrat, but a Particularist." I mentioned to him that, during the latter half of the fifties, Geffcken, under the *nom de plume* of "Victor," had, as a friend of Freytag's and a petty diplomat of the sniffing and spying order, supplied the *Grenzboten* with Opposition gossip inspired by the Crown Prince and the Coburg clique; that he was afterwards a diligent promoter of the Augustenburger's cause, but that in 1877, as pointed out in the "Friction" articles, his place-hunting propensities had been recognised at Karlsruhe. I then asked whether he had read *Hofrath* Schneider's posthumous work on the Emperor William, and added, "he did not appear to be well-disposed towards you." "Certainly not," he rejoined; "and he had good reason for it. He hated me because I had spoilt a fine business for him. A cousin of mine, a Bismarck-Bohlen, wanted to marry one of his daughters, his senior by eleven years, who had driven him crazy by her coquetry. I pulled him away from her by his coat-tails. She might have captured a big estate with him." I further expressed the opinion that the death of the Emperor Frederick had saved us from an evil future, and in particular from English influence on the foreign policy of Prussia and of the Empire, and from an estrangement with Russia. "Yes," he rejoined; "he was in favour of the Orleans, used his influence for a daughter of Nemours, was on the side of Poland, of Denmark, and against the war of 1866,—always in favour of what fell in with the views of the English."

Before lunch on the 29th I begged Rottenburg to ask the Chief whether our business was now at an end, and I might consider myself at liberty to return home. I received no answer, however, although I reminded Rottenburg of the matter. I spent the day in my room, in a bad temper, having nothing to do and feeling bored, and could not go for a walk, as it rained up to dusk. After dinner reference was again made to the Crown

Prince's incapacity, of which the Chief treated us to an exquisite example. He related: "We had at that time a secret treaty with the St. Petersburg people which now no longer exists. Under it we were to remain neutral in case of war breaking out between England and Russia. On my mentioning the treaty to the Crown Prince he remarked: 'Of course England has been informed and has agreed to it.'" Great laughter, in which the ladies also joined. The deceased sovereign evidently stood badly in need of a wax candle to light up his head—more so, indeed, than even a certain uncle in Thuringia. (. . . .)

On Sunday, the 30th of September, Rottenburg came up to my room about noon, and said: "I have asked the Chief as to your going home, and he wishes you to stay at least for a few days longer, so that it may look like a visit, and not as if you had been specially summoned here for a purpose. How do you spell *Commercy*?" I replied: "With two 'm's' and a 'y.'" "He will probably question you about their stay there." I looked it up, and found that we had arrived at that place at 2 P.M. on the 23rd of August, 1870, and left it at noon on the 24th; that the Chief had had a conference with the King there, and that Waldersee and Alvensleben dined with us. Mentioned that to the Chief at lunch, when by the way, as on the previous day, he returned my greeting with a "Guten Morgen, Büschlein"; and when, among the other good things provided, a basin of peasoup with bacon was served up to me by the Princess's orders. This is a favourite dish of mine, as I happened to let out on Friday in the course of conversation on various delicacies. The Prince spoke of the Crown Prince's inadequate acquaintance with modern history, as shown by his reference in his diary to the Emperor and Empire as new ideas emanating from himself and his party. "That was the aspiration of many a German long before he was born. The *Burschenschaft* sang and drank to it immediately after the War of Liberation, and when I went to Göttingen those were the ideals I carried with me, and if those students had not fought so shy of duelling and beer drinking I might have joined them and got myself involved with them in the subsequent inquiry." He then related as further evidence of his political views at that time his bet with Coffin, whom he, by the way, knew to be still alive. "As far back as 1848 the idea of an Emperor was well to the front, but it was unworkable, principally because people were thinking of other things at the same time. The beginning of the Empire already existed in the North German Confederation, only Bavaria did not want to come in yet, as was indeed the case in 1870 also, when I had a great deal of trouble to secure her adhesion. On the other hand, I had a hard fight with our Most Gracious Master, who for a long time would not hear of being Emperor. 'But does your Majesty wish to remain a neuter for ever?' I said to him one day. 'What do you mean by that?' he said. 'Why, that hitherto you have been the Presidency (das Sie bis jetzt *das* Präsidium sind.')" If I rightly understood the Chief at lunch the reason of his question as to Commercy was that it was there he recommended the King to confer the Iron Cross upon the South Germans. "Moltke," he said, "was entirely against it, asking whether he himself had any Bavarian Order."

At dinner in the evening the guests included General Leczinsky, who was in uniform, as was also the Chief. In conversation on a variety of subjects both at the table and afterwards, L. showed himself to be a well-informed man of sound views. He was engaged in the campaigns in Baden, Schleswig-Holstein, Bohemia and France, and has in addition travelled a great deal. He is now stationed in Hamburg, whither he returns to-day. Brauer leaves for home to-night, starting for Berlin at 11 o'clock.

Monday, October 1st.—At 9 A.M. Rottenburg came to my room, and asked me once more the date of our stay at Commercy. I told him. It actually turns out that the point in question is, that it was here the Chief first spoke to the King about giving the Iron Cross to non-Prussians and to the Bavarians in particular. In the evening, Rottenburg and I took a long walk past the Aumühl into Holstein, and arranged to make similar excursions in other directions, principally through the Sachsenwald, where there are a number of good roads, and which is now beginning to take on autumn tints. Rottenburg is a frank and amiable man, with whom one is soon on good terms. He is intelligent and well-informed, particularly in social questions. He has an extensive knowledge of public men, and would appear in addition to be an excellent worker. He comes from Danzig, and spent five years in London for the purpose of study.

After dinner something in the conversation led me to inform the Prince of Andrae's letter to me, and of my meeting with him. He observed that Andrae was a vain intriguer, and that the story about Stirum was not true. Moreover, not only Holtz, but the majority of the others who signed the "Declaration" wrote to him, Bismarck, separate letters of excuse. The Princess remarked that Andrae was one of the worst of the "Deklaranten." I ascertained at the same time that her mother was a Gichtelite, and that Below-Hohendorf was their Grand Lama—an epithet which the lady did not use, however. The Chief then read a little of the book, *Bismarck unter drei Kaisern*, but after looking through it for a while he soon laid it aside. In reply to my question whether there was anything in it, he said: "Oh, no; a mere hack's work! Put together with scissors and paste from the newspapers and such sources, without much knowledge of the subject or real coherence."

During our walk I had mentioned to Rottenburg my longing for some work to do, and had sought refuge from my boredom in three volumes of Hallberger's *Ueber Land und Meer*, which I found in my room. He promised to send me Schmidt's work on the French Revolution, but did not do so. In my despair I plucked up courage and applied to the Chief himself, asking him if he could not give me something to do, if it were only ciphering, deciphering or copying, perhaps some matter of no importance,—"for my part it may be making out lists or adding up accounts." He smiled, and, after reflecting for a moment, said: "Perhaps I can find some more interesting occupation for you to-morrow. I will see."

On Tuesday, October 2nd, took a walk through the wood to Dassendorf and back, which occupied from 11 to 1 o'clock. The weather was very fine. At lunch I ascertained from Rottenburg that the Prince wished to give me a number of letters to look through. When the Chief got up from table he whispered something to Rottenburg at the door, whereupon the latter came back to me and said the Prince was now going upstairs to look out the papers. In about a quarter of an hour I was summoned to his study, where he had several large packets of documents lying before him. He began: "I once

VOL. III   P

promised you that you should arrange my papers. Here are some of them—letters and other things from the Frankfurt and St. Petersburg period. Here for instance is the Gerlach correspondence, and there are letters from Frederick William IV. to me." He read over one of the latter to me, and then said : " I think you will find other matters of interest among them. I myself can no longer remember exactly all they contain. Take these upstairs with you, and settle how you are going to arrange them. I think the chronological order will be the best." Was I not delighted ? Such confidence ! and such a prospect of fresh information ! the fulfilment of a hope that had almost died. Pleased beyond measure I hurried off with my burden and immediately set to work on them, first glancing through the various papers at hazard. The sifting of this treasure was to commence next morning, and to be continued on the following days with as little interruption as possible.

On the 3rd of October we were joined at dinner by the Head Forester, Lange, one of the Prince's managers and an expert who was engaged in laying down meadows. On the 4th the technical controller of one of the Customs division at Hamburg dined with us. Schweninger arrived on the 5th. He behaved very nicely, and was, indeed, almost tender in his manner on my expressing my admiration of the unquestionable service he had rendered in restoring the Chancellor's health. He wished to visit a patient of his in Mecklenburg, a lady of the nobility, but on the 6th he was still at Friedrichsruh, where he was treated by all the members of the family as a friend of the house. On the 8th we again had the Head Forester at dinner, as well as a prosperous timber merchant and coal-mine owner from Westphalia. In two hours Minister von Bötticher was expected to arrive from Berlin. At table the Prince related that formerly, and even since he became Minister, he was sometimes obliged to dance with Princesses at Court entertainments until the old gentleman (King William) expressed his displeasure. He excused himself by saying: "What is one to do, your Majesty, when Princesses command?" The Princesses were accordingly informed of the prohibition. Keudell was also passionately fond of dancing formerly, and Radowitz too, but the King also broke the latter of this habit.

ADDENDUM.—Yesterday the Chancellor once more returned to the subject of King William's anxiety in 1866 to utilise his victories in a different way to what he (Bismarck) advised. "His mind was set on Northern Bohemia, half of Saxony, half of Hanover, Ansbach and Bayreuth, &c., and it was difficult to get the idea out of his head." At lunch to-day I told the Chief (in English on account of the servants) that I expected to finish my work in two or three days, and to return the papers to him in linen envelopes, arranged according to the years. He replied (also in English): "Then you have lost no time, seeing what a quantity of them there were. But I have also a number of others for you. The work is not yet over, as there is a lot more there, more recent and perhaps more interesting for you. Have you found anything of importance among the first batch?" I said I had. He called attention to the contrast between Gerlach and Manteuffel, the Minister, which was evident from their letters. He also mentioned Niebuhr, of whom he remarked: "It is with him as with many pious people of his sort: he has no tact, regards himself as the envoy of an anointed King, and as his representative considers himself to be also anointed."

On the 9th of October I had been a fortnight at

Friedrichsruh, and on the 10th the last envelope would be filled, but other important work intervened unexpectedly. Two documents arrived from the Ministry of the Household, a short and a long war diary of the Crown Prince, afterwards Emperor Frederick, both written in his own hand, the first presumably an extract, or perhaps the original of the harmless part of the latter, the second obviously written for the most part after the war, and with many additions. Both are to be speedily examined, and, as Rottenburg informed me on bringing me the documents, I was to do part of the work, examining the latter portion of the first of the two manuscripts, while the Chief dealt with the earlier portion and he (Rottenburg) with the second. I also assisted Rottenburg afterwards, as the papers had to be sent back to Berlin in two days. The diary in the *Deutsche Rundschau* is not from the shorter version, but from the far more comprehensive one of the Ministry of the Household, the interpolations of which are in great part of a political nature, and are often highly characteristic, although deficient in real statesmanship. The writer is in every respect mediocre and superficial, no talent and no character, although he is thoroughly at home in fault-finding and abuse. We collected and noted down in our section some particularly fine specimens of his manner of thought, and of these a small selection may be here given. They do not include the finest of all, which I had to leave to Rottenburg or for the Chief, who came into our bureau (at 11 o'clock at night) while we were making the extracts, and was pleased to find that I was so diligent in my efforts to be of use. On the 4th of January the author of the interpolated diary had read " with great satisfaction " the reflections upon the new year published by the *Volkszeitung*, and was "horrified" that the Minister of War had forbidden the circulation of the paper. On the 2nd of January an eulogy of the Queen of England, "who stands up for us Germans at every opportunity, knows very well what are the issues involved, and understands German affairs." On the 8th of January he notes Odo Russell's satisfaction at Bismarck's having yielded in the matter of the English coal ships (a matter which H.R.H. had much at heart). —On the 11th of January Prince Luitpold's "unworthy" proposal respecting the military oath of allegiance of the Bavarians, had, like Bismarck's irritability, greatly worried his Majesty.—January 17th. Bismarck, speaking to Schleinitz in the antechamber, had "peevishly" exclaimed that he could not conceive why there should be a joint conference of the Chancellor of the Confederation and the Minister of the Household in presence of the King. Then a very detailed account of the interview respecting the Emperor and Empire at the Prefecture. On that occasion the King was very excited and vehement, and the Crown Prince was afterwards so unwell that he had to take medicine.—February 1st. Interesting addition respecting Frederick of Schleswig-Holstein, "who, like myself (the Crown Prince) regrets the manner in which the Empire has been brought into existence, &c."—February 14th. A somewhat lengthy account (an addition) of an interview between the Crown Prince and Bonnechose.—16th. Conversation with Russell on the consequences of English neutrality. (In another passage apprehensions for beloved England, owing to Bismarck's leaning towards Russia and the United States). 22nd. Doubtless an interpolation of a much later date. That "after the peace our next task must be the solution of the social question." It is certain that the good gentleman with his narrow views and small brain never thought of that subject until Bismarck found time to take the matter in hand, and discovered ways and means for dealing with the evil which would never have occurred to his Royal Highness and his *Volkszeitung.*—26th. Conversation with Père Hyacinthe on the Catholic Church (and also on Döllinger). As was to be expected, the Crown Prince has high praise for that superficial and sentimental individual, and feels that his words have actually given him a sense of exaltation and a feeling of deep peace.— March 10th (pp. 351, 352 of the MS.). Lengthy statement of political views, of which extracts have appeared in the *Deutsche Rundschau.* The interpolated diary goes as far as the 17th of July, 1871, at Munich, and then a few pages follow respecting his stay in England and at Wilhelmshöhe.

On the 10th of October his Excellency von Bötticher appeared at lunch. Intelligent, practical looking face, tall figure, and a moustache with a tuft trimmed after the fashion of Napoleon. On going to the chimney piece for a light for his cigar brings me one also. The Chief, who as usual occupied himself at lunch with reading through and signing official documents, looking up from a paper, suddenly remarked: "'*Unentwegt,*' Busch can't bear that word." The Minister looked at me and smiled. "That is so," I said, "and I consider '*diesbezüglich*' still more abominable. The former has come to us from Switzerland, and the latter from Vienna." The Chief then sang the praises of the herring to Bötticher also, mentioning that he eats it regularly, and adding some remarks on other means of promoting health, as, for instance, that here when the weather is favourable he rides or walks for two or even three hours daily, his quantum in the latter case being five thousand paces, and not infrequently more.

On the 12th of October the documents which the Chief had handed over to me to arrange had all been read through, put into chronological order, and numbered consecutively in red pencil from 1 to 308. These were packed in eight large envelopes, each docketed with the year and the dates and numbers of the first and last documents contained in them. Further particulars of the contents, which I offered to give, were declined by the Prince as superfluous. These papers consisted for the most part of letters, the remainder being reports, memoranda, drafts, and telegrams. The following is a survey of the contents.

First Envelope. The year 1851. (Also includes a letter from Prince Charles, dated March 21st, 1848.) Nos. 1 to 29. They begin with the 5th of June and end with the 24th of December, and consist in great part of letters from the Minister and General Manteuffel, from R. Quehl, from Bismarck to Manteuffel, and from General L. von Gerlach. Contents of the latter: That of the 23rd of November, against the new Hamburg Constitution, Senator Hudtwalker's mission, a scheme for giving the Estates a position side by side with Constitutionalism. That of the 4th of December, again on the Hamburg Constitution. That of the 20th of December, considerations on Bonapartism, after the *coup d'état*, request for an expression of opinion on the situation, with the hope that their views coincide.

Second Envelope. 1852. Nos. 30 to 85. Begins with the 5th of January and ends with the 30th of December. Principally letters from General Gerlach and Minister Manteuffel, R. Quehl, King Frederick William, a rescript by that sovereign, four almost illegible notes from the Prince of Prussia, and, finally, a communication from Bismarck to Gerlach, dated the 5th of January, reporting on the change of Ministers in Nassau, the question of the fleet, the relations of Austria to France, and possible anti-Prussian schemes of Schwarzenberg, the views of the English Chargé d'Affaires, Edwardes, on Bonapartism. The first letter from the King begins with the words: "I would remind you, dearest Bismarck (theuerster Bismarck), that I reckon upon you and your assistance in the approaching debates in the Second Chamber respecting the shape to be given to the First Chamber." Further on there is a reference to "the low intrigues of the conscious or unconscious coalition of scabby sheep on the Right and stinking goats on the Left to defeat the Royal intentions." "A sad sight, and in any circumstances sufficient to make one tear his hair, but on the field of the dearly-purchased, lie-producing machine of French Constitutionalism! (Ein trauriger Anblick, unter allen Verhältnissen zum Haare Ausraufen, aber auf dem Felde der theuer angeschafften Lügenmaschine des französische Constitutionalismus)." The rescript (of the 3rd of June) appoints Bismarck Chargé d'Affaires in Vienna, and summons him to Berlin to receive instructions. The second royal letter (of the 5th of June) introduces him to the Emperor Francis Joseph and says, *inter alia*: "I am pleased that your Majesty will be able to make the acquaintance of a man who is here honoured by many and hated by others, on account of his chivalrous loyalty and his irreconcilable opposition to revolution in every form. He is my friend and loyal servant, and comes to your Majesty with the fresh and lively impress of my principles, of my line of action, of my will, and, I may add, of my love for Austria. If it be deemed worth while, he can inform your Majesty, and your Majesty's advisers on various matters as I believe few are capable of doing, and if misunderstandings of an old date have not struck too deep a root, which God in His mercy forbid, his brief official sojourn in Vienna will truly be rich in blessings. Herr von Bismarck comes from Frankfurt, where what the middle States, with their leaning towards a Rhenish Confederation (die rheinbundschwangeren Mittelstaaten) call the weak P. of P. (Query—the weak points of Prussia) has always elicited a powerful echo and has frequently made recruits. He has watched all this and whatever was going on there with a sharp and penetrating eye. I have commanded him to answer every question that may be addressed to him by your Majesty and your Ministers as if I myself had addressed them to him. If your Majesty should be pleased to ask for an explanation of my views and my action in the matter of the Hessian Constitution, I feel sure that the course taken by me, even if it should not perhaps have the good fortune to meet with your approval, will at least secure your respect. The presence of the beloved and glorious Emperor Nicholas has been to me a real encouragement, and a certain confirmation of the strong hope that your Majesty and myself are at one in the truth that our triple, unswervingly loyal and active union can alone save Europe and the froward, yet so beloved, German Fatherland from the present crisis, fills me with gratitude to God, and increases my old and faithful affection for your Majesty. Do you also, my dearest Emperor, preserve for me your love from the days at Tegernsee, and confirm your confidence and your weighty and powerful friendship to me which are so indispensable to the common Fatherland. From the bottom of my heart I commend myself to this friendship as your Imperial Majesty's true and most cordially devoted Uncle, Brother and Friend." Gerlach's letter to Bismarck of the 9th of March condemns the language used by B. in an interview with the King respecting the First Chamber, and in particular that he had not pointed out how his Majesty, "through the attitude which he had adopted, had estranged the nobility, disorganised the parties, and shaken the position of the Ministry."—15th April. An inquiry at the instance of the King concerning the truth of the rumour that Prince Frederick of Baden was thinking of becoming a Catholic. Then an announcement that Nesselrode was coming to Berlin and that Bismarck was to be introduced to him. G. praises the excellent report on the situation in Bismarck's letter to Manteuffel on the representation of the Confederacy in the Danish negotiations. He laments the death of Schwarzenberg, and expects nothing better from Bach and Buol. Reports that Rochow has arrived with very good news; regrets that England and Austria should fraternise with Bonapartism and that the Emperor Nicholas should have also allowed himself to be taken in by its anti-Constitutionalism. According to an enclosure of the 21st of April, the rumour respecting Prince Frederick was unfounded.—12th April. Telegram: "There is no hurry with the answer in the (Baden) religious affair."—18th April. Bismarck was to come to the debate on the First Chamber. The King counted upon his doing so. "We have now assembled the publicans and sinners, . . . and the speeches in the Chamber will soon begin again." —9th May. Gerlach agrees with what Bismarck had said on the debates in the Chamber; reports that the King was greatly incensed at Arnim's speech, and that he doubtless recognises that "his whole salvation lies in the hands of the Junker party." He does not anticipate that all will go well in Berlin, although the Emperor of Russia remains there for twelve days, and Francis Joseph has ordered a Prussian Grenadier uniform.—17th May. Gerlach shares Bismarck's indignation at a newspaper article which was probably inspired by Manteuffel; considers M. to be an honest man, but he has had a singular political past, and cannot come to a good end, unless he sends Quehl about his business. Examples of his inconsistency. "M. has a yearning towards Bonapartism," "which, after all, has no future." All is going well with the Emperor and Empress of Russia, "but when they see these things one cannot expect them to entertain much respect for our policy." Alludes further on to the Zollverein and the opening of direct negotiations for a commercial treaty with Austria; and concludes with a suggestion that Bismarck should come to Berlin, remaining there while the Chamber was sitting and until the departure of the Russians, "in order that one might consider what should and what could be done."—May 19th. Gerlach reports that Manteuffel, in speaking to him, had defended Quehl, and declared that he would rather resign than part with him. Quehl asserts that he has received a very reassuring letter from Bismarck. Manteuffel is considered indispensable, and so the only course would be to take Westphalen, who deserves it "for sticking to a principle and for his high-mindedness." His fall would signify a renunciation of the principle of restoring vitality to the Estates as against Constitutionalism. A marked opposition was now developing between Absolutism and the liberty of the Estates, between the atheistic and the Christian State, and the Manteuffels inclined towards Absolutism and political atheism.—May 29th. Under instructions from the King Gerlach calls attention to the circulation of Dulong's pamphlet, "Der Tag ist angebrochen," and observes that his Majesty wishes action to be taken against this state of things in the press.—July 21st. Gerlach censures Wagner's attitude towards Manteuffel, whose position, it is true, is scarcely tenable "unless he decides to enter into alliances with respectable people." G. regards the future with apprehension, "not that a revolutionary Parliament is now probable, but owing to fear of the rising bureaucracy with its measures of police and its weakness in the days of trial," days which must come, as Bonaparte will be driven into action abroad by the failure of his internal policy. Bismarck ought to "carry on a positive federal policy" in order that the others should not take the wind out of Prussia's sails. After the probable victory in the matter of the Zollverein, our dull-witted opponents will presumably lack material for fresh attacks. We should then assume the offensive.—July 23rd. Gerlach begs Bismarck to take up the question of the Hamburg Constitution (against the proposed reform of the new Constitution). Further on, the news that Gerlach has written to Manteuffel that he should not allow himself to be governed by the Conservative party but that he should show himself their master, "and once under the yoke, govern with them."—July 26th. The Conservatives of Hamburg have begun to move and are anxiously awaiting the note of the Federal Diet; and Bismarck should meet this desire. "The position of affairs in Berlin is an extraordinary one." Gerlach spoke very strongly to the Premier but without any hope of success. Manteuffel "must be retained at all costs, as his probable successors are simply a terror." Gerlach's brother in Magdeburg wishes to visit Bismarck at

Frankfurt.—July 29th. Gerlach was highly pleased at Bismarck's letter of justification, and communicated its contents to the King, who has not entertained the suspicion therein mentioned. The Zollverein business promises to go well. In dealing with it Austria has "behaved in a miserably intriguing fashion. What a pitiful policy in presence of the revolution, and of the sovereignty of the people, of which Bonaparte is the incarnation! On a smaller scale, however, our own policy is just the same." In connection with the Hamburg affair, Bismarck should publish the Notes and Rescripts of the Confederacy to the Senate by an indiscretion. This, which has hitherto been a mild request on my part, is now a strong expression of the King's desire."—August 3rd. Renewed request that Bismarck should take up the cause of the Hamburg Conservatives. It has now come to such a pass with Manteuffel that no one trusts him, and he trusts nobody. If this mistrust is to be removed, the Ministry must be supported in every possible way.—October 8th. Gerlach complains of Manteuffel and Wagner, and at the instance of the King urges intervention in the Hamburg affair. Hübbe, the leader of the Conservative party there, has been to see him and the King.—November 13th. Gerlach is of opinion that the internal situation is good, if Bismarck "will remain at his post as sentinel on the Rhine (not become Minister?) and keep a sharp eye on the inception and development of the Rhenish Confederation." If he comes to the Chambers he should get elected to the First "where there is a lack of talent." G. thinks him better off with Rechberg as a colleague rather than Hübener, because the former is opposed to Bonapartism, while the latter is in favour of it. There is nothing to be done in Hamburg except to procrastinate. The idea of revising the draft prepared by the nine deputies, instead of the old existing Constitution, is absurd.

Third Envelope. 1853. Begins with the 2nd of January and ends with the 14th of December. The first is a letter from Frederick William to Manteuffel on the Danish detachment in the Holstein federal contingent. It says : " In my opinion this should not be tolerated by the German Confederacy if it still retains a spark of honour. We must speak at Frankfurt like honourable Germans, even if they through their ingrained dishonesty will not listen to us. Germany, however, shall and will hear us. If the particulars given by the newspapers should be confirmed, I authorise you to send this little note, in the original, to Bismarck, and to consult details with him." The following letters are chiefly from Gerlach, Minister Manteuffel, and the Prince of Prussia, and include a further communication from King Frederick William to Bismarck, dated the 12th of September : " My dearest Bismarck, a misunderstanding prevails in my brother William's circles, a solution of which is necessary to the satisfaction of everybody concerned. At Doberan I received a letter from him, in which he loudly laments Manteuffel's now certain retirement, which he rightly characterises as a calamity. I asked William for a solution of this riddle, as, of course, everything had been settled three weeks ago, and my perseverance had been crowned with success. He wrote to me in reply about a week since, that he was glad of this, but you, my good Bismarck, had received a letter from Putbus, from the contents of which you, like himself, could draw no other conclusion. From Sans-souci I asked him who was the writer of this letter. He told me Gerlach (Polte) ; to-day I questioned Gerlach, and he assures me most positively that he has written nothing of the kind to you from Putbus. Here you have the puzzle Schlemassl, in the German-Jewish dialect Unravel it for me and William as soon as possible. Let your pen be guided by the purest truth." Bismarck replied to this that Gerlach had written him that he wished to induce Manteuffel to remain, as it appeared impossible to replace him. He had only received this letter however on the 17th or 18th of August, at Ostend. The following letters from Gerlach are worth mentioning. January 8th. (Report of a conversation which Gerlach has had with Ex-Minister v. d. Decken on constitutional changes in Hanover, in which the King of Prussia should assist. The letter desires Bismarck to take up this matter, but first of all to write and give his opinion.) Another of the 28th of January. (For the present Bismarck is not to trouble himself about the Hanoverian affair. Opinion of Prokesch. Gerlach would like to have Bismarck in Berlin, as he fears grave crises, and, according to him, the people should be given clearly to understand that Bonapartism is our worst foe. . . . . Bonaparte will direct his lust of conquest against Spain.) Finally, Gerlach's letters on his conflict with Manteuffel. This conflict was clearly indicated in the letter of the 23rd of February, in which it is stated, *inter alia*, that Manteuffel had through Quehl taken a turn downwards, because he doubted the truth of what came to him from above; he wants to see the Conservative party destroyed, and he allows himself to be tempted by Quehl into secret opposition to Westphalen's measures.

Fourth Envelope. First half of the year 1854. Begins with an undated letter from Gerlach, probably written in January; it is followed by one from Manteuffel dated the 4th of January, while the remainder are mostly letters from the latter to Gerlach, together with reports by Bismarck, and finally, two letters of Seckendorff's from Stuttgart, the second of which is dated the 27th of June. The following are of special interest. A note of the 17th of March, from the Prince of Prussia, asking Bismarck for information on the Eastern Question, and the reply thereto, a rather lengthy draft by Bismarck; then his report as to an interview which he had with the Prince at Baden, with the result that the latter yields to the royal will, though opposed to his own convictions; a letter from Bismarck to Gerlach on the Bamberg results; an exhaustive report by Bismarck on Buol's view of the Eastern Question, which the former considers to be correct—doubtless addressed to Manteuffel; another report to the latter on the Bamberg Governments, Bismarck wanting apparently to keep them in check, and also respecting Bunsen and Gagern.

Fifth Envelope. Second half of the year 1854. Begins with a letter of the 1st of July from Gerlach (who finds that Manteuffel is now taking a proper course) and ends with a letter of the 31st of December. The intervening papers include among other things a confidential report by Bismarck to Manteuffel on the abstention of Würtemburg from the existing agreement between the other Governments in favour of the alliance of April 20th; letters from Manteuffel and Gerlach; an (autograph) memorandum by Bismarck on the attitude of the Bamberg people, and of Buol towards Prussia. It says: "We cannot consent to an aggrandisement of Austria, because the importance of Prussia in respect of physical force would be approximated thereby to that of Bavaria. The Western Powers will want to restore Poland, which would be less against the interests of Austria than against those of Prussia and Russia." The remaining papers include letters from Alvensleben, Bunsen, Pückler, Wolzogen and Schulenburg.

Sixth Envelope. The year 1855, but only from the 2nd of January to the 14th of August. Then come breaks in the correspondence up to November 1858. Chiefly letters from Gerlach and Manteuffel. Also a letter from Frederick William to King John of Saxony (dated 18th January); five or six from Savigny (in one of which he laments that Prussia has missed an excellent opportunity of placing herself at the head of Germany) and from Schulenburg, &c. There is a characteristic letter from Gerlach, dated the 4th of January, in which he writes : " I believe that we should be in agreement if you were here, that is to say, as to the measures to be taken, if not also as to principles— for I hold to the Holy Scriptures, which teach that we must not do evil in order that good may come of it, because those who act in that way are very properly damned. Now to coquet with Bonapartism and Liberalism is to do evil, and moreover, to my thinking, it is unwise in the present case. This you forget (a mistake into which every one falls who has been away from here for some time). . . . How can you go on finessing indirectly with such an utterly unprincipled and untrustworthy Minister, who is involuntarily lured into the wrong path, and with a master whose peculiarities, to put it mildly, defy calculation ? Just remember that F. D. (Fra Diavolo, pseudonym for Manteuffel) is a Bonapartist on principle ; think of his behaviour in connection with the *coup d'état*, and of what Quehl wrote under his patronage—and if you want to know something new I can tell you that he has now written to Werther expressing the foolish opinion that if one wanted to be useful to Russia the way would be to adhere to the treaty of the 2nd of December in order to have a voice in the negotiations; indeed I believe that F. D. has actually advised the King to adhere to the treaty of the 2nd of December, that is to say, with modifications, these, according to the way in which things are done here, being of the nature of reservations which our adversaries would afterwards ignore, without paying any attention to us in the event of their non-observance. Our policy moves along a very narrow path, upon a tight rope, and so far one may say that it has maintained its equilibrium, *i.e.*, it has not fallen into the abyss on either side, yet its course remains anything but secure. . . . The King, and you also, appear to attribute an exaggerated importance to our participation in the conferences. What good is this gloriole to us, as we can turn it to no account so long as Austria (as is clear from Gortschakoff's reports) is frightened into hobbling after the Western Powers? Shall we hobble with her, or shall we join England and France in the chorus against Russia, or shall we alone take Russia's part, a course that would require more courage and skill than can be expected of our deaf and invalid envoy in Vienna. I consider it more dignified, effective, and successful for us to take up an entirely independent attitude towards Austria and the Western Powers. We have met with a rebuff in Paris and London. (The *züffliche*[1] Usedom and his Radical wife ought never to have been sent there; but that has now been done, however.) Austria has treated us with consistent perfidy. We are, therefore, released from all ties. France, with 300,000 men beyond her frontiers, and England, without an army, will not begin war with us. I do not fear Austria in the least, first because she fears us, while, in addition to that, she has

---

[1] The word "züfflich" is given in the original letter. Dr. Busch himself has never met with it before, and does not know what it signifies.—THE TRANSLATOR.

not a man to spare. It would be mere madness
to irritate us, should she really want to pick a
quarrel with Russia. She now demands with her usual
impudence and recklessness that 100,000 men be
raised as soon as possible, under the military convention which Hesse has concluded with her. (I
shudder at the thought of the foolish and puerile proceedings of April of last year.) To this the reply is
curt and bold; there is a firm conviction, based on assurances as well as information received, that the
Emperor of Russia has no idea of attacking Austria,
either on her own territories or in the Principalities, so
that no *casus fœderis* arises either for Prussia or for
the Germanic Confederation. The Prussian army is
ready for war, and can be brought into a still greater
state of readiness. It is true that Austria has provoked
Russia by the treaty concluded on the 2nd of December
without the concurrence of Prussia and the Bund, but
one is convinced that Russia nevertheless contemplates
no attack. I certainly believed that, in face of this
declaration on the part of Prussia, Austria would hardly
secure her two-thirds majority, and, indeed, that she
would probably not even try to force the matter through.
Unquestionably, nothing can be done very speedily
now. If, however, the negotiations in Vienna take such
a turn that their success may be anticipated, they will come
to us, and not ignore our 300,000 men. That would be
impossible, even now, if all confidence, as well as all
sense of fear, had not been destroyed by swaying, not
merely to and fro, as frequently happens, but in three
different directions, which is of rarer occurrence. I am
very anxious that you should come here, if only for
a few days, in order to discuss matters. . . . Do, please,
write soon, and criticise this my letter. Write also, if it

can possibly be managed, that you are coming. . . . I yearn for political death. A man who has grown old and blunt and peevish is no longer the right man to wriggle his way through between such a singular master (for whom, all the same, I have an affection of forty years' standing) and such a premier. Indeed, my bodily conformation is a symbolic warning against doing anything of the kind." [1]

Seventh Envelope. Documents of the period extending from the 7th of November, 1858, to the 21st of June, 1861, chiefly letters from Minister Schleinitz to Bismarck, and from the latter to the former from St. Petersburg, including a very long one of the 12th of May, 1859, in which B. deals with the improvement of Prussia's position in Germany as opposed to Austria, indicating ways and means of bringing it about. . . . Then a very interesting communication, dated the 14th of May, from Bismarck to Alvensleben, which was accompanied by a copy of the letter of the 12th. According to this, the latter was really intended for the then Minister President, the Prince of Hohenzollern, yet the writer is "in the end in a state of doubt as to how his Highness is in his heart likely to regard this matter." The letter to Alvensleben then goes on to say : " I believe too that Schleinitz will not withhold my letter from H.R.H. the Regent, although I scarcely hope that it will be received with favour there. If you are so disposed and have an opportunity of kindling in the Prince a spark of royal ambition in this sense, I beg of you to make use of the contents of the enclosure, as if I had written to you privately on the same subjects upon which I wrote to Schleinitz. Of course, the only difference is in the head and tail of it, and to whether in your case the title of Excellency

[1] Gerlach was very stout.

already connotes externally the excellences of the inward man. There is almost always an element of mistrust and discontent when I write to Schleinitz, sending you at the same time a copy of my letter, and the Prince allows it to leak out." On the 29th of May, 1859, Bismarck gives his Minister a serio-comic description of the petty proceedings of the envoys of the German Middle States at St. Petersburg, with whom Gortschakoff has little intercourse, and who worry the more fortunate Prussian representative in their efforts to obtain some material to satisfy their love of gossip. The Hanoverian, Münster, is particularly active and importunate. The Saxon, Könneritz, manifests the warmest enthusiasm for Prussia, abuses Beust and Austria, and "speaks as if he were serving under a Carlowitz Ministry; but we have an old and good proverb[1] that teaches us never to trust a Saxon from Meissen. Montgelas is most profoundly depressed at the fall in the value of Austrian securities, and seems to think, strangely enough, that the remedy to this evil lies in bringing about a general war." Schleinitz's letters are almost always full of praise and thanks for Bismarck's excellent reports. Yet on one occasion (June 24) he acknowledges that many insinuations against him personally, and against his official conduct have reached Berlin. But he adds: "With your reports in my hand I have, however, succeeded in effectually repelling them;" and continues: "if, nevertheless, I take the liberty of requesting you to conform as far as possible to the views of your Government in your non-official conversations and relations, that request is perhaps entirely superfluous, but I am induced to make it by a desire to prevent your laying yourself open in any direction to the attacks of opponents."

[1] "Meissner sind Gleissner." The people of Meissen are double-dealers.

Eighth Envelope. Undated letters and other documents, as well as some of uncertain date.

On Friday, the 12th of October, we were joined first at lunch and then again at dinner by a plump lady in black silk, a Frau von Patkowski from East Prussia, a daughter of Kaiserlingk, an old friend of the Chief's. I begged the Prince's permission to absent myself for three days, and took leave of him and of the ladies of the house.

I started for Berlin at 12.45 P.M. on Saturday, the 13th. On my going down to his bureau to see Rottenburg, who wished to accompany me to the train, I met the Chief in the antechamber. He said, smiling, " It is lucky that I have met you before you leave. Frau von Patkowski is travelling with you, so please take care not to lay siege to the pretty plump little lady on the way!" " Those times are over, Serene Highness, and besides, she travels first class and I second." " Well, in that case she will no doubt be safe." I expressed a hope that during my absence he would have good weather, as it is necessary for his health, so that he may get his walks and rides. " I do what I can," he said, " to keep illness at a distance, but it will come all the same, and probably soon. It will be a sudden break down, just as I stand." Thanks be to God, his appearance in no way justified such a foreboding, as he proceeded to the station with the lady on his arm, walking erect and the very picture of health.

On Wednesday, the 17th October, at 8.30 A.M., I again left Berlin for Friedrichsruh.

I had previously been accustomed every evening after dinner to spend some time romping in the next room with the three little Rantzaus. When I asked their mother at lunch how the boys were, she asked me not to let them have their usual game to-day as a punishment, the two elder lads having been rude and insolent to their governess in the morning. The Prince said they must be whipped for that. The Countess replied that she had deprived them of their bath and slapped them on the cheek for it. He rejoined, however, "That is not enough for such naughtiness. They ought to be well whipped." He then related how he had chastised Herbert and Bill on one occasion, when they took some hazel nuts and then ran away from the ranger. "It was not on account of the nuts, but because they had obliged the old man to run after them through bush and briar until I caught them and gave them a good trouncing, at which the ranger seemed to be greatly surprised." I inquired of him whether governesses and other persons entrusted with the education of princes were at liberty to chastise them when they were naughty, or whether they had to tell the parents, who decided as to their punishment. He answered the first part of my question in the affirmative, and went on to say that the governess of the Emperor William II. said as she was administering physical chastisement to him on one occasion : "Believe me, Royal Highness, that it hurts me as much as it does you to do this." "Ah!" exclaimed the little Prince, "and does it hurt you in the same place?" Everybody laughed heartily at the queer form taken by the boy's curiosity. As we rose from table and Lindau was taking leave before returning home, the Prince asked me: "Are you going to your room now?" "Yes, Serene Highness." "I will send for you there. I have something I should like to show you." In about a quarter of an hour I was summoned to the Prince's study, where the Chief handed me a large packet of letters. "These are from the old Emperor," he said, and then read me some passages from them. He wished to have them arranged like the former papers. "Again in mere chronological order, according to the dates." He asked: "But will not that be too much for you?" I replied with an emphatic negative. I was there for that purpose, and it was a pleasure to me to serve him, and at the same time to have something to read and take with me for my information. He continued: "And here, too, is one from old Bodelschwingh-Schwindelbod. And there are others (pointing to a second packet), the correspondence with Andrassy, for instance, in the summer of 1879. You will find information enough there." He took up the third pile. "These are from the Emperor Frederick when he was Crown Prince, and also one from *her* from the villa Zivio." He was about to return them to the drawer of his writing table, but I begged him to let me have them also. He said smiling, "But, Büschlein, haven't you already enough?"—"It will be better for me to have everything there is at once, so that I may have a general idea of all the documents and arrange them more rapidly."—" But there are still plenty more, and that pile is already heavy enough to carry!" I took all he had by him, however, and carried them upstairs in order to begin my inspection of them next morning. But I could not rest until I had read through some of them as specimens in the afternoon. For example, a long letter from the Crown Princess, dated San Remo, the 22nd of November, 1887, giving the Chancellor particulars of her consort's illness and of the doctors; and also Bodelschwingh's communication, on the top of which the Chief had written in pencil "Old hypocrite." Then before dinner a further walk with Rottenburg in the wood where it is cut through by the road leading to

Mohnsen. Lively conversation on a variety of matters serious and amusing, as for instance on Darwin and the high esteem in which he is held by the Chief.

Early on the morning of Thursday, October 18th, I began to assort the papers. The numbering and packing away in envelopes was to follow later, after a thorough inspection of the whole lot. Out of doors a beautiful autumn day, the sun, in a blue sky, casting high lights on the stems and branches of the trees in the wood. During lunch, at which Schweninger again joined us, I handed the Chief the Crown Prince's letter introducing Geffcken to him and his answer justifying his refusal by a description of Geffcken's character. I had found this among the papers on the previous day. He was pleased at the discovery, and the letters were handed to Rottenburg to be copied and used. Immediately afterwards Schweinitz, our Ambassador at St. Petersburg, arrived— a grey-headed, portly gentleman with a moustache, who speaks little and in a low voice. We were joined at dinner, in addition to Schweinitz, by a big-bearded gentleman in a shooting jacket. This was Major von Goldammer of Frankfurt, the sportsman who recently— to the great regret of the head forester—shot the stag with fourteen antlers that had broken out from the Chief's preserves on to the shooting which he had rented. "If it had only been Count Herbert!" Bleichröder is to present his respects to-morrow.

On Saturday I spent the whole forenoon and two hours after lunch in arranging the papers in order of date. Bleichröder and his Jewish-looking Secretary took lunch with us. The banker related anecdotes of Amschel Rothschild and Saphir, and spoke of Lehndorff's businesses. At table I observed that since 1871 Bleichröder, whom I saw at dinner at Versailles, had hardly altered in the least. "Not in his person" rejoined the Chief, "but very considerably in his fortune."

On Sunday, the 21st of October, I began to examine and number the papers, which were now in chronological order, whereby I found that a good deal of rearrangement was necessary. Here follow some particulars.

The documents begin with a letter dated Oct. 19, 1862, from Bismarck to King William. Then follows a short letter from the Crown Prince to the Minister, dated Nov. 21, in which he says : " I trust that, as you express it to me, success may, in the present difficult phase of the constitutional life of our country, attend your efforts to bring about what you yourself describe as the urgent and necessary understanding with the representatives of the nation. I am following the course of affairs with the greatest interest," and so on. Letter from Bismarck to the King, in which Eulenburg and Selchow are proposed as Ministers. (I shall not quote unimportant letters from the King and the Crown Prince, nor in future any matters of only slight interest.) A letter from Bismarck to the King, dated 20th February, 1863, on the convention with Russia. Goltz communicated it to Napoleon, but without the secret article, with which he himself was not acquainted. (Probably the article by which Prussia was bound eventually to render assistance against the Polish rebellion.) The Minister wrote : " As matters stand in Poland we shall hardly be called upon for active co-operation there. By means of the convention we have, therefore, the advantage of securing at a cheap rate for the future the gratitude of the Emperor Alexander and the sympathies of the Russians."

Writing to Bismarck, from Stettin, on the 30th of

June, 1863, the Crown Prince says: "I see from your letter of the 10th instant that at his Majesty's command you have omitted to communicate officially to the Ministry of State my protest respecting the rescript, restricting the liberty of the press, which I sent to you from Graudenz on the 8th of June. I can easily understand that the opportunity of treating as a personal matter an incident which, as you yourself have acknowledged, might, in its consequences, acquire widespread significance, was not unwelcome to you. It would serve no purpose for me to insist upon that communication being made, as I am justified in inferring from your own words that it will have been done unofficially. It is necessary for me, however, to speak plainly to you respecting the alternative which you place before me, namely, to lighten or to render more difficult the task which the Ministry has undertaken. I cannot lighten that task, as I find myself opposed to it in principle. A loyal administration of the laws and of the Constitution, respect and good will towards an easily led, intelligent and capable people—these are the principles which, in my opinion, should guide every Government in the treatment of the country. I cannot bring the policy which finds expression in the ordinance of the first of June into harmony with these principles. It is true you seek to prove to me the constitutional character of that rescript, and you assure me that you and your colleagues remember your oath. I think, however, that the Government requires a stronger basis than very dubious interpretations which do not appeal to the sound common sense of the people. You yourself call attention to the circumstance that even your opponents respect the honesty of your convictions. I will not inquire into that assertion" (Bismarck's comment in pencil : " Not over courteous,") " but if you attach any importance to the opinions of your opponents, the circumstance that the great majority of the educated classes among our people deny the constitutional character of the ordinance must necessarily awaken scruples in your mind. The Ministry knew beforehand that this would be the case. It was also aware that the Diet would never have approved the provisions of that rescript beforehand, and it therefore laid no Bill before the Diet, and in a few days promulgated the ordinance under Article 63 of the Constitution. If the country does not recognise in this course of action a loyal administration of the Constitution, I would ask what has the Ministry done to bring public opinion round to its own view? It found no other means of coming to an understanding with public opinion than to impose silence upon it. It would be idle to waste a single word as to how far this ordinance harmonises with the respect and good will due to a willing and loyal people that has been condemned to silence because the Government will not hear its voice.

"And what is the success which you anticipate from this policy? The tranquillisation of the public mind and the restoration of peace? Do you believe that you can appease public sentiment by again offending its sense of justice? It seems to me contrary to human nature to expect a change when the existing feeling is being constantly confirmed and aggravated by the action of the Government. I will tell you what results I anticipate from your policy. You will go on quibbling with the Constitution until it loses all value in the eyes of the people. In that way you will on the one hand arouse anarchical movements that go beyond the bounds of the Constitution; while on the other hand, whether you intend it or not, you will pass from one venturesome interpretation to another until you are finally driven into an open breach of the Constitution." (Bismarck's comment: "Perhaps.") "I regard those who lead his Majesty the King, my most gracious father, into such courses as the most dangerous advisers for Crown and country." (Bismarck quotes in pencil: "Leicht fertig ist die Jugend mit dem Wort" = Youth is hasty in its judgments.) "P.S.—Already before the 1st of June of this year I but rarely made use of my right to attend the sittings of the Ministry of State. From the foregoing statement of my convictions you will understand my requesting his Majesty the King to allow me to abstain altogether from attending them at present. A continuous public and personal manifestation of the differences between myself and the Ministry" (Bismarck's pencil remarks on this point: "Absalom!") "would be in keeping neither with my position nor my inclination. In every other respect, however, I shall impose no restrictions upon the expression of my views; and the Ministry may rest assured that it will depend upon themselves and their own future action whether, in spite of my own strong reluctance, I find myself forced into further public steps, when duty appears to call for them." (In face of the menacing attitude assumed in these threats, Bismarck's undaunted pencil shouts out, "Come on!" "Nur zu!")

On the 3rd of September the Crown Prince writes to Bismarck: "I have to-day communicated to his Majesty the views which I set forth to you in my letter from Putbus, and which I begged you not to submit to the King until I myself had done so. A decision which will have serious consequences was yesterday taken in the Council. I did not wish to reply to his Majesty in the presence of the Ministers. I have done so to-day, and have given expression to my misgivings—my serious misgivings—for the future. The King now knows that I am a decided opponent of the Ministry." At the end of the letter Bismarck added, apparently as part of a draft reply: "I can only hope that your Royal Highness will one day find servants as faithful as I am to your father. I do not intend to be of the number."

On the 5th of June, while at Dantzig, during a tour in the performance of his military duties, the Crown Prince, speaking in public to the Chief Burgomaster Von Winter, declared himself to be opposed to the policy of his father. The latter wrote demanding a recantation, and stating that otherwise the Prince would be deprived of his dignity and position. The Crown Prince declined to retract anything, offered to lay down his command and other offices, and begged to be allowed to retire with his family to some place where he would be under no suspicion of interfering in State affairs. Intimations as to the contents of this correspondence were published (of course, first of all) in *The Times*, then in the *Grenzboten* (through Gustav Freytag) and in the *Süddeutsche Zeitung* (through me, at Freytag's instance). A memorandum, dated Gastein, the 2nd of August, in Zitelmann's handwriting, and probably dictated by Bismarck, expresses the belief that the publication was due to the Crown Princess, "whether it be that she has herself attained to definite views of her own as to the form of government most advantageous for Prussia, or that she has succumbed to the concerted influences of the Anglo-Coburg combination. However this may be, it is asserted that she has decided upon a course of opposition to the present Government, and has taken advantage of the Dantzig incident and the excitement to which it has given rise in the highest circles, in order to bring her consort more and more into prominence by these revelations, and to acquaint public opinion with the Crown Prince's way of thinking. All this out of anxiety for the future of her consort." It is then stated that the Crown Princess's most powerful supporter is Queen Augusta, who is extremely anxious as to her own position towards the country. They have had a memorandum drawn up by President Camphausen on the internal situation in Prussia, attacking the present Government, which was laid before the King. In a marginal note the King observes that the principles therein recommended would lead to revolution. Meyer, the Councillor of Embassy, is Augusta's instrument, and it is beyond question that he is associated with the Anglo-Coburg party. The participation of Professor Duncker [1] as also of Baron Stockmar, would appear to be less certain. The memorandum dictated to Zitelmann is accompanied by comments in the Chief's handwriting—either a long letter or a *pro memoriâ* for the King—in which the views expressed by the Crown Prince are refuted point by point. In the course of his criticism the writer says, *inter alia* : "The pretension that a warning from his Royal Highness should outweigh royal decisions, come to after serious and careful consideration, attributes undue importance to his own position and experience as compared to those of his sovereign and father. No one could believe that H.R.H. had any share in these acts of personal authority, as everybody knows that the Prince has no vote in the Ministry. . . . The *démenti* at Dantzig was

[1] As a matter of fact, he was not concerned in it. See Haym's work, *Das Leben Max Dunckers*, pp. 294, 295.

therefore superfluous. The liberty of H.R.H. to form his own conclusions was not affected by his attendance at the sittings, where he can keep himself in touch with the affairs of State and hear the views of others and express his own, which we hold to be the duty of the heir to the throne. The performance of this duty, when it becomes known through the newspapers, can only elicit on all sides approval of the diligence and conscientiousness with which the Crown Prince prepares himself for his high and serious vocation. The words 'with my hands tied' have no meaning. It is utterly impossible that the country should identify H.R.H. with the Ministry, as the country knows that the Crown Prince is not called upon to take any official part in its decisions.

"Unfortunately, the attitude which H.R.H. has adopted towards the Crown is sufficiently known in the country, and is condemned by every father of a family, to whatever path he may belong, as a disavowal of that paternal authority which it is an offence to our feelings and traditions to ignore. Even now clergymen are preaching from the text 2 Samuel, ch. xv., verses 3 and 4. H.R.H. could not be more seriously damaged in the eyes of public opinion than by the publication of this answer." (That of the Prince to his father's letter.)

Page 2 (of the answer). "It is true that H.R.H.'s situation is a thoroughly false one, because it is not the business of the heir to the throne to raise the banner of opposition to his King and father. He can only fulfil his 'duty' by retiring from that position and again adopting a proper attitude."

Page 3. "There is no conflict of duties, as the first of these duties is self-imposed. It rests with the King, and not with the Crown Prince, to provide for the future of Prussia, and the future will show whether 'mistakes' have been made, and on which side. In cases where the 'judgment' of his Majesty is opposed to that of the Crown Prince, the former must always be preponderant, and there is therefore no conflict. H.R.H. himself recognises that in our Constitution there is 'no place for the opposition of the heir to the throne.' Opposition within the Council does not exclude obedience to his Majesty once a matter has been decided. Ministers also oppose when they hold different views, but they nevertheless obey" (The last three words are underlined in pencil by the King, who added on the margin: 'When it is not opposed to their consciences,') "the will of the King, although it may be part of their duty to carry into execution the measures they opposed."

Page 4. "If H.R.H. knows that the Ministers act in accordance with the will of the King, he cannot fail to see that the opposition of the heir to the throne is directed against the reigning King himself."

Page 5. "The Crown Prince has no call and no justification to enter upon a 'struggle' (Kampf) against the will of the King, for the precise reason that his Royal Highness has no official status. Each Prince of the Royal House would be equally justified in 'laying claim' to the duty of offering public opposition to the King, where his views differed from those of the sovereign, and thus defending the eventual rights of 'himself and his children' against the effects of alleged mistakes by the Government of the King, that is to say, in order to secure the succession, after the manner of Louis Philippe, if the King were to be deposed by a revolution."

Page 6. "The Minister President is to give a more

detailed explanation of the words used by him at Gastein."

Page 7. "His Majesty has not caused the Crown Prince to attend the sittings as one of the King's advisers, but only for the Prince's own information, and as a means of preparing him for his future calling. The attempt to 'neutralise' the measures of the Government would mean a struggle and rebellion against the Crown. More dangerous than all the attacks of the democracy and all 'gnawing' at the roots of the monarchy is the loosening of the bonds that still unite the people with the dynasty through the example of open and avowed opposition on the part of the heir to the throne, through the intentional disclosure of discord in the Royal House itself. If the son and heir to the throne revolts against the authority of the father and King, to whom can that authority still remain sacred? If a premium is set by ambition for the *future* upon present desertion from the Sovereign, every bond will be loosened, to the detriment of the future King, and the damage done to the authority of the present Government will bear evil fruit for its successors. Any Government is better than one which is divided against itself and paralysed. The shocks which the Crown Prince may provoke affect the foundations of the structure over which he himself will hereafter have to preside as King.

"According to the constitutional law hitherto in force, it is the King who *governs* in Prussia and not the Ministers. Legislative and not governmental power is alone shared with the Chambers, and before them the Ministers represent the King. Therefore now, as *before* the Constitution, the Ministers are legally the servants of the King, and his Majesty's authorised advisers, but they are not the regents of the Prussian State. Even since the Constitution, the Prussian monarchy does not stand on the same level as the Belgian or English monarchy. On the contrary, in Prussia the King still governs personally, and *commands* according to his own discretion, in so far as the Constitution has not otherwise provided, and it has only so provided in matters of legislation."

Page 8. " The publication of State secrets is an offence against the criminal law. What is to be treated as a State secret depends upon the King's command respecting official secrecy. Why is so much importance attached to giving ' outside ' publicity to these matters ? If his Royal Highness, as in duty bound, gives expression to his opinions in Council, he has satisfied his conscience. The Crown Prince has no official position whatever in State affairs, and no call to express himself publicly upon them. No one who has even a superficial knowledge of the system under which our State affairs are conducted would conclude that the Crown Prince agreed with the decisions of the Government merely because he (without a vote, and therefore without the possibility of effectual opposition) had listened to the discussions in Council.

" 'Not appear better.' The mistake lies in the exaggerated importance attached to ' appearances.' The important point is what a man is and what he can do, and that is only the fruit of serious and well-directed labour.

" The participation of his Royal Highness in the Council is not ' active,' and no ' votes ' are cast by the Crown Prince. The communication to ' responsible ' (?) persons without the authorisation of his Majesty would be an offence against the criminal law. Of course, there is no limitation of his Royal Highness's right to express his views ; on the contrary, it is desirable that he should do so, but only in the Council, where, as a matter of fact, they can alone have any influence on the decisions that are about to be taken. The contrary course, ' to express them openly before the country,' can only be adopted as a means of gratifying his Royal Highness's *amour propre*, and must result in promoting discontent and disaffection, and thereby paving the way for revolution."

Page 10. "Unquestionably H.R.H. will render their work more difficult for the Ministers, and their task would be lighter if he did not attend the sittings. But can his Majesty shirk the duty of doing everything that is humanly possible to enable the Crown Prince to learn the business of State, and to become acquainted with the laws of the country? Is it not a dangerous experiment to leave the future King a stranger to the affairs of State, while the welfare of millions is dependent upon his familiarity with them? H.R.H. shows himself in the present memorandum unacquainted with the fact that the participation of the Crown Prince never involves any responsibility, and is only for the purpose of information, and that H.R.H. can never be asked to give a vote. The whole argument is based upon a misconception of this fact. If the Crown Prince had been more familiar with State affairs H.R.H. could not have thought of publishing the proceedings of the Council in case the King did not accede to his wishes, *i.e.*, of committing an offence against the law, and what is more, the criminal law, and that too a few weeks after H.R.H. had himself severely censured the publication of the correspondence with his Majesty."

Page 11. "Certainly the reproach mentioned may naturally occur to every one in the country. No one charges H.R.H. with such an intention, but it is said that *others*, who do entertain such an intention, hope to see it realised through the unconscious co-operation of the Crown Prince ; and that such wicked attempts now afford those who originated them a better prospect than formerly of a change of system."

Page 12. "The demand to have timely information of the business to be transacted at the sittings is perfectly legitimate, has always been recognised, and shall continue to be so. Indeed a desire has been expressed that H.R.H. should do his part in keeping himself more *au courant* than was hitherto possible. For this purpose H.R.H.'s whereabouts must always be known and within reach, the Ministers must have access to the Crown Prince, and discretion must be secured. But it is necessary that the *Vortragende Räthe* (Councillors who have the privilege of direct audience), with whom alone H.R.H. can be authorised to transact current State affairs, should be not opponents but friends of the Government, or at least impartial critics having no *intimate* relations with the Opposition in the Diet and the press. The most difficult point of all is *discretion*, particularly towards foreign countries, so long as H.R.H. and the Crown Princess are not thoroughly conscious that in reigning houses the nearest relations are not always fellow countrymen, but, on the contrary, must necessarily, and as in duty bound, represent other than Prussian interests. It is hard that a frontier should create a division of interest between mother and daughter, brother and sister, but to forget this fact is always a danger for the State. The 'last sitting of the Council' (on the 3rd) was not a regular sitting but only a meeting of the Ministers who had been summoned by his Majesty without their own previous knowledge."

Page 13. "Communication to the Ministers would give

the memorandum an official character which the Prince's effusions do not in themselves possess."

On Monday, the 22nd of October, Count Herbert was present at lunch and dinner, returning to Berlin on the Tuesday. On Monday, after we had had our coffee, I told the Chief that the sorting of the papers was now well advanced. There was a great deal more to do, however, than had appeared at first, and it might take eight or ten days more before I could hand them over to him in good order like the previous set. He replied: "Take plenty of time. But the Emperor will be here in a few days and you must not let yourself be seen then; or, better still, go to Hamburg while he is here, as otherwise he will ask who you are and what you are doing. I should then be obliged to tell him, and as he is curious he would eventually seize the whole lot, which would not suit me at all."

On Tuesday and Wednesday I was very busy sorting, numbering and taking extracts. In the evening I took a walk with the Privy Councillor until an hour before dinner. We were joined at dinner on Wednesday by the Hamburg merchant, Merik, and his wife—she very pretty, twenty-seven years of age, and he between forty and fifty. On Thursday I was again hard at work on the Chief's treasury of letters. At lunch the Chief said that formerly the rich and influential Hamburgers were strongly Austrian in their sympathies, and he referred to the millions advanced to the politicians of Vienna in 1857, and also condemned the unamiable and stupid policy of Prussia in those days. The Princess observed that even now these circles do not care much for Prussia, but are impressed, and indeed very strongly, by Bismarck. She then explained to me that the Meriks were neighbours of theirs, and occupied a country house with forty acres of ground on the edge of the forest, the remainder of an estate which a Saxon officer had acquired by marriage, and of which the Prince afterwards bought six hundred acres. In reply to my question, the Chief informed me that the Emperor would arrive on Monday evening and leave after lunch on Tuesday. I must therefore make myself scarce for thirty hours. To-day, however, we shall return to our anthology, and continue it to-morrow. Here follow some further specimens of the selection.

Letter from Bismarck to the King on the 1st of December, 1863 : " Your Majesty has been gracious enough to send me Herr von Gruner's communication of the 28th ultimo, and to observe that it reproduces the views adopted by your Majesty. Herr von Gruner's opinions are based on the same general principles as those of Herr von Vincke and Herr von Roggenbach, and the latter have found expression in the letter of H.R.H. the Grand Duke of Baden. These gentlemen, in addressing their proposals to your Majesty, doubtless proceed on the assumption that if your Majesty were to accept their advice another Ministry would be summoned to office. Other influences are also being set in motion for this purpose even outside *public* life, to which Herr von Schleinitz and other persons closely connected with the Court have either voluntarily or involuntarily devoted their services. When I entered into the Ministry I ventured to explain to your Majesty that I did not regard my position as that of a Constitutional Minister in the usual sense of the word, but considered myself rather as your Majesty's servant, and that in the last resort I would obey your Majesty's commands even if contrary to my own views. I still maintain that standpoint, but this should not deter me from explaining my views with the candour I owe to your Majesty and to the interests of the country. Speaking in this sense, I must first declare that I consider it would be of advantage for your Majesty's service, in carrying out a policy consonant with the views of Herr von Gruner, to select another Ministry, or at least another Minister for Foreign Affairs, who would enjoy in a higher degree the confidence of those upon whose support such a policy must mainly rely. Count Goltz has as yet had no occasion to come into conflict with those elements, and owing to his other qualifications may be regarded as best suited to take over the conduct of affairs."

From a letter of the Crown Prince to Bismarck, dated Headquarters, Flensburg, April 17th, 1864: "I thank you heartily for your two letters of the 11th and 12th of April. I found the communication of the 11th very interesting; but I could not gather from it such a view of the objects of our policy as would enable me, from my standpoint, to support any particular measure with conviction. I do not agree that it is too early to come forward openly with a positive programme, and I fear that we shall gain *nothing* by protracting the solution of the question, but, on the contrary, thereby increase European complications. However that may be, we should at least have a positive programme *for ourselves*, the realisation of which it is true would still remain dependent upon circumstances. Instead of this, however, I find in your communication only the programme 'to act according to circumstances,' unless I am to infer from some isolated suggestions certain secret views which are ascribed to you, and which certainly appear to tally with many of your former utterances, particularly at the last Council which I attended before my departure for the army. With regard to any such *arrière-pensées* of

Prussian aggrandisement, I may state briefly my opinion, namely, that to pursue them would entirely falsify our whole German policy, and would probably lead to our defeat by Europe. It would not be the first time that Prussia sought to outwit the world, with the result that she ultimately fell between two stools."

A letter from Bismarck to the King, dated April 3rd, 1866 : "Your Majesty has deigned to command me, through Abeken, to express my opinion whether the letter from the Duke of Coburg, which I respectfully return herewith, should be answered.

"I take the liberty to recall the fact that the Duke of Coburg has during the past four years shared in every intrigue against your Majesty's internal and foreign policy. His Highness has largely contributed to the return of democratic representatives in Prussia through his money and influence; he has associated himself with societies for arming the people (Büchsen-Groschen Vereine), and has adopted such an attitude towards the monarchy that your Majesty made strong representations to him on the subject in a long letter, and declined a visit from him on account of the bad impression it would make on the army. The Duke, together with his officials, Samwer and Francke, is the leader of the anti-Prussian Augustenburg movement; and but for him the hereditary Prince would have listened to reason. The Duke brought about the recall of Lord Napier, a diplomatist who was regarded as too Prussophil. I respectfully take the liberty of indicating the influence of the Duke upon H.R.H. the Crown Prince. I certainly do not go too far when I describe his Highness as one of the most irreconcilable opponents of your Majesty's policy, and state that no devotion to your Majesty's honour and interest is to be expected from him. The present letter from the Duke, and that from Count Mensdorff, which was obviously ordered for the special purpose of being communicated to your Majesty, and which is utterly untrue, betray their connection with the communications from Queen Victoria which have reached your Majesty through H.R.H. the Crown Prince; and it is certain that similar insinuations will have been made to your Majesty in other quarters. There can be no doubt that all these steps are based upon a well-laid plan, according to which the open and secret opponents of your Majesty endeavour to persuade your Majesty to yield to Austria, and thus to pave the way for another policy, your Majesty's present Ministry and myself in particular being for this purpose represented in the first place as the root of all evil. Your Majesty is certainly convinced without any assurance from me that even if my health had remained unaffected during the past few years, I would at any moment willingly, and with life-long gratitude to your Majesty for the many favours which I have enjoyed, retire into private life even if my continuance in office involved *no* detriment to your Majesty. How much more willingly would I do so, therefore, if my retirement could be of any benefit to my King and country. I see, however, no possibility of another Minister of your Majesty being able honestly to recommend a policy different to that which has hitherto been followed, and which was sanctioned in the Council of the 28th of February; for this policy is independent of all partisan tendencies, is enjoined solely by the interests of Prussia, and is rendered inevitable by the situation. If the Duke of Coburg recommends another policy, such as would be in agreement with what Vienna prescribes, I beg respectfully to point out that the same gentleman has for the last four years recommended *everything* that was opposed to monarchial interests, and in particular to those of the Prussian Monarchy. Notwithstanding this your Majesty has done him the honour of answering his letter of the 22nd. If your Majesty were to answer the present letter, with its offensive and untruthful enclosure, that would be an encouragement to your opponents and a discouragement to your servants. My most humble advice is that your Majesty should leave the letter of the Duke unanswered, and not conceal from his aide-de-camp that you have been disagreeably affected by the enclosure. If the aide-de-camp is a person to whom such a communication might be properly made, it would perhaps be well to signify to him verbally that your Majesty has clearly seen through the intention underlying the whole manœuvre with the Mensdorff letter, and that the tone of the latter is not to your liking."

Letter from the King to Bismarck, dated April 8th, 1866 : " Numbers 78 and 79 of the *Kreuzzeitung* have just been laid before me by an unknown hand (as I have not taken in this paper since 1861—Coronation article in June) on account of the abusive article against the Duke of Coburg. It is most unpleasant to me, as only you, the Queen and the Crown Prince had a knowledge of the Duke's letters to me, and therefore the source of the article is immediately betrayed. Although you have always told me that the Government has no influence upon the *Kreuzzeitung*, this appears to be an instance which contradicts that statement. The manner in which I replied to the Duke, and the fact that on the second occasion I sent no reply, showed him that I did not desire to continue the correspondence. But articles like that in question must render him still more hostile to us. From a political point of view this is not right, and on that account I request you to put a stop to these improper proceedings of the *Kreuzzeitung* towards the Duke.

"WILLIAM."

In reply to this Bismarck wrote as follows: "I humbly beg your Majesty's pardon if I have called down upon myself your Majesty's dissatisfaction through the article on the intervention of the Duke of Coburg, which was based, not on his letter, but upon a number of other newspaper reports on this intervention. I would never venture to deceive your Majesty, and I frankly confess that the main part of this article was written at my instance, as I—like every one of my colleagues— while having indeed no influence over the *Kreuzzeitung* to prevent the insertion of matters to which I object, have yet enough to secure the insertion of what is not directly opposed to its own tendencies. The same connection exists with the *Spenersche*, the *National Zeitung* and many others, and I believe I have never denied the existence of influence of this description.

"It appeared to me as if your Majesty were yourself indignant at the insincerity of the Duke and of Count Mensdorff; but your Majesty generously pardons the disrespect manifested in such conduct, as also the former hostility of the Duke, who has done more harm to your Majesty and the Prussian State through the favour which he has shown to the democracy, and the disturbance of the relations with England, than he can ever make good through a military convention, and who gave evidence of his real sentiments towards your Majesty at the time of the Congress of Princes. Your Majesty, while entertaining no doubt as to my devotion and obedience, will not expect me to be superior to every human weakness and to preserve my composure at all times when I see how my heavy, and I may fairly say exhausting, duties are intentionally rendered more difficult by the displeasure of such highly placed personages, in whose hearts the success of Prussian policy and the renown of your Majesty and of the Royal House should naturally be expected to hold a first place. And why am I subjected to this implacable displeasure and forced into this struggle with powerful influences which I have to meet at every step I take? Merely because I will not consent to serve two masters, nor carry out another policy than your Majesty's, nor reckon with other influences than your Majesty's commands. My offence is that I was ready to serve your Majesty according to your own will when others declined to do so, and that I did not hesitate to obey your Majesty at the risk of drawing down upon myself the displeasure of those who stand nearest to your Majesty. I could have peace if, like many of my predecessors, I were prepared to submit to your Majesty as my own convictions what was suggested to me in other quarters; and if, in particular, I were to advise you to give way in matters of internal policy and military organisation, as of course nothing is really being done in foreign affairs except what was formerly desired by those who now oppose me. I beg your Majesty to forgive me if in this struggle, owing to the feeling that I have been unjustly attacked for the sole reason that I have tried to do my duty towards your Majesty without looking to the right or to the left, I have lost that composure which I myself am desirous of preserving."

A letter from Bismarck to the King on the 1st of May, 1866: "I submit the enclosure to your Majesty in support of my urgent and respectful plea that your

Majesty's kingdom be no longer left exposed to the danger which, in my most humble opinion, at present threatens it from the warlike preparations of Austria, whose forces are already superior to ours and are being daily increased notwithstanding all pacific assurances. The Minister of War will to-morrow submit to your Majesty a report of the Ministry of State and proposals for further precautionary measures. If your Majesty will give me credit for not being easily accessible to unfounded apprehensions I may venture to hope that your Majesty will graciously consider my request that the measures to be taken as a result of my legitimate anxiety may be speedily carried out."

Letter from Bismarck to the King, dated 2nd May, 1866 : " I respectfully submit to your Majesty the communication which has just been received from Vienna. It vouchsafes no prospect that Austria will disarm, but seems to indicate that she merely wants to put us off for a few days in order to complete her armaments before adopting another tone towards your Majesty, in the belief that she will then have secured a start of us which we could no longer make up. Information reaches me from the Bourse that it is intended to adopt financial measures of a ruinous character (forced loans ?) and that the trading community here, including its representative bodies, regard the inactivity of the Royal House in presence of the superior armaments of Austria, as inconceivable, and in the highest degree alarming and detrimental to the country. This feeling, which has prevailed among your Majesty's Ministers before to-day, has now become general in the city since the facts which were previously known to the Government have found their way into publicity. This feeling would certainly find violent expression should the event show, which

God forbid, that there had been any actual negligence in providing for the protection of the country."

On Friday at lunch the Chief asked me: "What is your opinion, Busch, of Goethe's tragedies, and of his dramas altogether?" I replied that he was less of a dramatist than a lyric poet, but that "Faust," setting aside the second part, was after all a most wonderful production. "Yes, certainly," he said, "and 'Götz' too, but 'Egmont,' the man in 'Stella,' Tasso, and the leading characters in the others, are all Weislingens—weak soft, sentimental creatures—not men as in Shakespeare, always repetitions of himself, for he too had something feminine in him, and could only realise and portray the feelings of women." I finally recommended Victor Hehn's "Gedanken über Goethe," and referred him in particular to the first and second chapters. Towards evening another long walk with Rottenburg, while the Prince went to Schwarzenbeck and the Princess to Hamburg, probably to make purchases in view of the Emperor's visit. Both were back for dinner, at which the Ranger or Chief Ranger of Schleswig-Holstein, and the Head Forester Lange were also present. The conversation at table turned chiefly on forestry, the various species of trees, and other wooden subjects. A further selection from the Chief's papers, the arrangement of which will be complete in four or five days. A letter of the 5th of January, 1876, from the Crown Prince introduces Professor Geffcken, who has been to see him, and with whom he has been speaking about his book, *Staat und Kirche* (State and Church), as a man "of ripe thought and great experience." The Chief replied on the 8th: "Dr. Geffcken belongs to that party in the Evangelical Church which, like President von Gerlach and some other Protestants, is in alliance with the

Centre party and the Jesuits, and which has been and still is hostile to every phase of the German Empire's development." The letter goes on to say that his book is a superficial compilation; that his criticism of the Falk laws gives evidence of audacious presumption rather than of impartial consideration; and that his Augustenburg and Hanseatic Particularism has not been overcome by the restoration of the Empire, whose interests he opposes in Alsace. "If I were to see him without the presence of witnesses (which the Crown Prince seemed from his letter to desire) I should have reason to apprehend that my intercourse with such a tool of sectarian intrigue would arouse the mistrust of my colleagues and of public opinion."

The Crown Prince thinks otherwise. He replied on the 12th of January: "During the many years of my acquaintance with Dr. Geffcken I have never seen any leaning on his part to Catholicism, nor any opposition to Prussia as a matter of principle. On the contrary I could see from his whole attitude, as well as from the statements frequently made by him, that there is as little reason to doubt his ardent Protestantism as there is to question his patriotism."

In a letter of the 12th of May, 1876, H.R.H. cannot too strongly urge the Chancellor to give Friedberg the Imperial Secretaryship of State for Justice, which it was proposed to establish. He at the same time tried to meet the objections which Bismarck supposed the Emperor to entertain. According to a letter of the 30th of June from the Crown Prince to Bismarck Friedberg had acquired a claim upon his gratitude by his long service, which frequently involved difficulties and sacrifices, but was always marked with the same devotion.

On the 13th of June, 1878, the Crown Prince

writing to the Chief on the death of King George of Hanover, says *inter alia*: "I am of opinion that now, the unfortunate Prince being dead, we must above all things adopt a generous attitude towards his relatives."

The Crown Prince now writes to the Chancellor more frequently than before. From the 6th of July, 1879, onwards, the project of marrying Prince William to the daughter of the Augustenburger was repeatedly mentioned, Bismarck being asked to promote it. Bismarck submitted his opinion of the scheme. (Professor Schulz prepared a similar statement, in which he proved the Augustenburger's equality of birth, which had been strongly questioned.) In this opinion the Chief recommends as indispensable a previous renunciation by Duke Frederick.

CORRESPONDENCE IN CONNECTION WITH THE NEGOTIATIONS RESPECTING THE GERMAN ALLIANCE WITH AUSTRIA.

Andrassy writes to Bismarck (neat handwriting in Latin characters): "Schönbrunn, 1st September, 1879. Honoured Prince! Before leaving Gastein I communicated *in nuce* by telegraph to my most gracious master, who went direct from Prague to Bruck, the tendency and the result so far of our conferences. I laid special stress on the fact that in view of the warlike preparations and the threatening language which was heard alternately, both in Vienna and in Germany, the question we had to deal with was that of a defensive understanding, a sort of guarantee of insurance, between our two sovereigns, in the sense that any attack upon either of the two empires should be repelled by their united forces, and that the *casus fœderis* should also arise in the event of an attack upon either by a third Power with the co-operation of Russia. I afterwards emphasised the circumstance that I was strongly in favour of this combination, but nevertheless had not in any way pledged his Majesty. Hereupon I received on my arrival a telegram from Prague, in which the Emperor declares that he approves of the tendency and present results of our meeting from the *fullest conviction*, and invites me to go to see him in camp at Brück. I was at Brück yesterday, and had an opportunity of submitting a detailed report on the subject. I found the Emperor so fully convinced of the usefulness and, indeed, necessity of such an arrangement, that further argument in its favour proved to be superfluous. His Majesty sees therein not only no departure from the determination to maintain peace between the three empires, but the only possible way at the present moment of removing the sword of Damocles which constantly hangs over our relations, and of securing peace for the benefit of both States, and, indeed, for the welfare of the *third*. As a matter of course, my Emperor is always glad to see you here, and will be particularly glad to do so on the present occasion. In the meantime, I am authorised as soon as you are in a position to inform me that you have obtained the approval in principle of the Emperor William to receive your draft text and to prepare one myself. I am to remain in office until this matter is completed, my successor only taking over the conduct of affairs after the understanding has been concluded. Besides, I have initiated him into the question, and he is in perfect agreement.

"Thus far as to what concerns his Majesty. The following is personal and quite confidential. I have not ceased to think over the matter for myself from all points of view, and my conviction has thereby been strengthened. If immediately after a war for which no one in Russia will to-day accept the responsibility and which has weakened the Empire both from a financial and military standpoint, and at a time when the Nihilist movement is momentarily suppressed and there is nothing to force the Government to seek a diversion abroad, Germany is to be threatened with France, and ourselves with an increase of the army, and that in connection with such questions as Merkovitch and the post offices of Eastern Rumelia, what is to be expected when the wounds of war are healed, when internal difficulties again make themselves felt, and when a foreign diversion may seem the only means of escape?

"I must confess that I can have no ease of mind so long as I do not see the torch extinguished which the Emperor Alexander half unconsciously swings about over the European powder barrel, and while I know the peace of Europe to rest in the hands of a Milutin, a Jomini, and doubtless presently of an Ignatieff. I believe that to-day every State (although our own less than others) has enough to do to protect its authority against the subversive elements in its midst. How is that to be done, however, and who will be able to do it if the State is constantly obliged to devote half its power and attention to dangers which are not of an internal but of a foreign character, and which come not from below but from above? I entertain no doubt as to the personal intentions of the Emperor Alexander. I am convinced that he does not wish for war at present. But as the Minister of a neighbouring State I cannot forget that he had also no desire for the war just concluded, and that from the beginning to the end of it he was trying to master the movement which had originated in his immediate *entourage*. I consider it a European necessity to provide in some way against this danger, and however difficult I find it now to postpone my retirement which is already widely known to be impending, it would be an immense gratification to me, as a servant of my Emperor and country, to be able to join with you, honoured Prince, in signing this guarantee for the future of our two realms. Austria once committed the mistake of declining the overtures of Germany which would have secured our mutual interests. It is a satisfaction to me to be able to state that the same mistake will not be committed by us this time.

"In sincere friendship and genuine respect,
"Your most devoted,
"ANDRASSY."

To this Bismarck replied on the 3rd of September: "HONOURED COUNT,—Yesterday evening I received your letter of the 1st instant, which is a source of much pleasure and satisfaction to me. I hasten to send you a provisional answer. And, first, I beg you to convey to his Majesty the Emperor my respectful thanks for the gracious manner in which he has referred to my intention to come to Vienna. I am pleased to see from your letter that his Majesty (unser Herr) has one foot in the stirrup, and do not doubt that our united efforts will succeed in placing him firmly in the saddle. Unfortunately, from the nature of things, geographical and political, my task cannot be so speedily completed as yours. A verbal report has not only the advantage of saving time, but also that of confining the replies to such questions as are actually raised in the most exalted quarter. In a written report I must, as a measure of precaution, discuss all the misunderstandings of which I may apprehend the possibility. It has, therefore, come to pass that I have been obliged to dictate to my son (who, with your kind permission, also writes this letter) sixty pages, the contents of which I was further obliged to expand in detail by telegraphic and other additions. Nevertheless, I have not succeeded, in spite of all my pains, in entirely removing the apprehension that our peaceful scheme may conceal some secret views of an aggressive character. This idea is unwelcome to a gentleman of over eighty-two years of age, but I hope I may be able to dispel it altogether, even if it costs me a somewhat lengthy postcript to those sixty pages. My master's disinclination to a speedy acceptance of new situations, which is a feature of his character, offers less scope for my activity. For his Majesty, the attitude recently adopted by the Emperor Alexander has for the first time illuminated, as with a lightning flash, a situation which I have been repeatedly obliged to recognise during the past few years. It will be a matter of extreme difficulty for his Majesty to find himself forced into making a choice between the two neighbouring empires, and he will therefore close his mind as long as possible to the conviction that the moment has come for such a course. In our Royal House habit exercises an enormous power, and the instinct of persistence grows stronger with age, and resists the recognition of undoubted changes in the outer world. Besides, the Emperor Alexander (I do not know whether it be due to the influence of others, or to his own determination) now endeavours to force the Jupiter Tonans into the background by a rapid transition to sunshine. In this sense the last threatening utterances were followed within a week by a friendly invitation to send a Prussian officer to Warsaw. This was accepted by my Emperor, who announced the despatch of Field-Marshal Manteuffel and suite, without my previous knowledge of this step, as a military measure. Baron Manteuffel met at Warsaw with very considerable readiness to make advances, in the sincerity and permanence of which however, after all that has passed, I cannot place any confidence. I am not as yet aware whether the meeting which is to take place to-day at Alexandrowo, was suggested by him or by the Russians. The objections on this side against a meeting on Russian soil have been disposed of by a reference to the difficulty of taking with equal promptitude outside of Russia the necessary precautions for the safety of the Emperor Alexander. So far as I know this meeting takes place to-day, our Emperor being accompanied by an aide-de-camp. According to a report of Minister von Bülow it is mainly inspired by a desire to obtain from the Emperor Alexander an explanation of his threatening attitude. Before this has taken place I cannot expect an answer to my report, which was first communicated to the Emperor on the 2nd, and to which I have up to the present only received a telegraphic reply through Bülow. From Bülow's telegram, however, it appears that even now the Emperor approves of my re-opening at Vienna the conferences with you, upon which I have already reported to him (—At first he was opposed even to Bismarck's returning home by way of Vienna—), but that nothing must be settled without his approval. Of course that goes without saying and you will not be impatient if my master requires before coming to a decision the time which his years, his habits, and the novelty of the outlook demand. There is also a further circumstance which indeed is favourable to our plans, namely that H.R.H the Crown Prince was consulted, and therefore that an exchange of ideas must have taken place between the exalted gentlemen. From my experience of my Sovereign for years past I had hardly hoped that, within twenty-four hours after taking cognisance for the first time of such a comprehensive and novel statement of the situation, he would without more ado agree to the continuation of our conferences. As I shall not remain inactive in the meantime I hope before I leave Gastein to obtain fuller powers. Like you, every day's further consideration confirms my conviction of the usefulness and necessity of the work which we have undertaken, and I trust God will grant us to secure for our two great States the guarantee of external and internal peace towards which our efforts are directed. I have considered it my duty to inform you of the stage at which I have arrived in my work, and I shall continue to do so as soon as I receive the more detailed expression of my master's views which has been promised. Should his Majesty commit this to paper at Königsberg on the 4th it would come to my hands on the 7th or at latest the 8th instant. I was greatly tempted after your departure to go personally to Berlin in order to plead our cause verbally, but the state of my health and strength was too indifferent to permit of such a strain. Moreover, experience has taught me that in explaining important and difficult matters to my master I attain my object, not more rapidly, it is true, but more certainly, by writing than in verbal intercourse, as, in the latter, difficulties occasionally arise which have no real connection with the matter under consideration. I hope to complete my cure here by the 15th or 16th, and to be then once more equal to the demands of the coming winter. Trusting that we shall soon meet again, I remain, with friendly and cordial respect,

"Your most devoted,

"BISMARCK."

Stolberg writes to Bismarck from Berlin on the 17th of September: "In continuation of my official communication of to-day, I have the honour dutifully to inform your Serene Highness of the following. As the Emperor was almost on the point of giving his approval he suddenly became embarrassed, and said there was still another obstacle, which he had mentioned to you in his last letter, and which obliged him to attach importance to the exclusion of every possibility of our being placed under an obligation to support Austria in a war of aggression against Russia. After some hesitation his Majesty made me pledge my word that, with the exception of your Serene Highness, I would speak to no one on the subject, and then referred to an understanding entered into by the two Emperors at St. Petersburg in 1873 (with your previous knowledge, but without your counter signature), by which each was bound to render assistance to the other in certain circumstances. This has obviously been the chief stumbling-block, and has given rise to the notion of treachery towards the Emperor Alexander to which Herr von Bülow alluded from Stettin. Although this statement was too vague for me, in ignorance of the matter in question, to thoroughly appreciate the weight of the objection, I considered it my duty, in view of the approaching decision, to seize hold of the statement made by the Emperor, namely, that if the possibility above mentioned were excluded, his objection would cease, and therefore to propose the addition.

"Although this objection would be thus obviated, his Majesty nevertheless wishes to hear what your Serene Highness has to say upon that point, and desires me to inform you to that effect. After giving his sanction the Emperor was somewhat affected, and told me that this decision had cost him a great effort. He believed, however, that he ought to follow the advice of a tried counsellor like your Serene Highness.—I am, with the profoundest respect, &c."

Stolberg's suggested addition ran as follows :—

"The sanction of the Emperor William to the signature of the treaty with Austria would be obtained on condition that the Emperor might write to the Emperor Alexander : 'His Majesty is satisfied with the assurances given in Berlin by Saburoff as to Russia's love of peace, and desires, as an evidence of his loyalty and frankness, to communicate the fact that he *was on the point* (underlined in pencil by Bismarck) of concluding a treaty with Austria, in which the careful cultivation of good relations was promised, and mutual assistance was only provided for in cases of attack.'"

The letter from the Emperor to Bismarck, which Stolberg refers to in the above communication, is dated Stettin, September 15th, and runs as follows : "After I had completed my last letter to you, which you will have received to-day, Field Marshal Manteuffel forwarded to me your telegram to him of the 7th instant, with which I am greatly pleased, as I can see from it that it will be possible to bring about an understanding between us. Fortunately this opinion is confirmed by your fourth report, which reached me yesterday. But an important point has occurred to me in connection with the pourparlers which you will hold in Vienna. That is the Convention dated St. Petersburg, 1873, which was only signed by the two Field Marshals, Moltke and Barjatinsky, and was ratified by the Emperor Alexander and myself, while you declined to sign. A circumstance which goes to confirm the —— (illegible) which you then and so often raised against *binding* Conventions, in circumstances where there was as yet no positive object in view, for which reason I found much difficulty in making up my mind to sign the St. Petersburg Convention. How can you now desire to enter into a convention without giving notice of withdrawal from that concluded at St. Petersburg? Both are intended to be defensive conventions. Now, that of St. Petersburg binds Prussia and Russia to render each other *assistance* in case either should be attacked. The projected Convention is to contain the same stipulation, but against Russia. How are these two to be reconciled? It therefore appears to me that Bülow's idea (?) of leaving out the 'against Russia' would afford us an opportunity of drawing Russia into the new Convention, and thereby fulfilling that of St. Petersburg. As I do not believe Bülow junior to be initiated into the secret of the St. Petersburg Convention, I have not been able to speak of it to him, all the more so as from his silence on the subject when stating his views he seemed to have no knowledge of it.

"WILLIAM."

To this was added a postscript of no particular importance: review of troops, inspection of fleet, patriotic reception, &c.

Bismarck to Andrassy from Gastein, on the 20th of September: "Honoured Count,—In continuation of my humble communication of the 3rd instant, I have the honour now to complete the answer therein begun to your Excellency's kind letter of the 1st instant. I have, in accordance with our conferences here, sent repeated and detailed reports on the situation to the Emperor, my most gracious master. The conformity between my views, which are known to your Excellency, and those of my colleagues who represent me, have made it possible for me to overcome the difficulties which were created by distance and opposing influences from other quarters in so far that I am now in a position to state that the Emperor agrees in principle with the views by which I was guided at our recent conferences. According to an official communication from my substitute, Count Stolberg-Wernigerode, the Emperor is prepared to sanction an agreement under which both Powers mutually undertake to continue to promote the maintenance of peace, and in particular to cultivate peaceful relations between both States and Russia, but, in the event of either of them being attacked by one or more Powers, to jointly repel such attack with their entire united strength. According to this I am empowered by my most gracious master to propose an unconditional defensive alliance between Austria-Hungary and the German Empire, either with or without a limit of time. I humbly beg your Excellency to enter upon a verbal discussion of this proposal. I shall have to submit the result of our negotiations to my most gracious master for approval. I entertain no doubt as to my being able to obtain this sanction, if your Excellency be in a position to agree in the name of the Emperor Francis Joseph to the proposal made on our side, in the same simple and general terms in which it is submitted. In any case I shall consider myself fortunate if our conferences lead to this or other results calculated to promote the mutual interests of both Empires and the peace of Europe.

"With friendly and cordial respect,
"I remain your most devoted,
"v. BISMARCK."

Letter from the King to Bismarck, dated Baden-Baden, October 2nd, 1879: "I regret to see from your letter of the 24th ultimo, as also from the memorandum enclosed therewith, from the protocols of your negotiations in Vienna, and from the draft treaty which has been based upon them, that my views with regard to the latter have not found acceptance on any side. As I expressed these views in my letters from Dantzig and Stettin of the 10th and 12th ultimo as clearly as it was possible for me to do, you can see for yourself how far they differ from the results arrived at, so that there is no necessity for me to repeat them. Notwithstanding this circumstance, however, I return herewith your letter of the 24th in order that you may form an idea from my marginal notes (which, I regret to say, are only in pencil) of the impression which it has made upon me.

"Germany and Austria are desirous of attaining the same end—security against unprovoked attacks by foreign foes. But owing to the special mention of Russia as the foe in question, I cannot agree to the present proposals nor to the immediate conclusion of a treaty. After again extending the hand in friendship to the Emperor Alexander after the removal of misunderstandings (at Alexandrowo), am I now to conclude an alliance against him, even of a defensive character, in which he alone is referred to as the presumable aggressor, and keep this intention a secret from him? I cannot be guilty of such an act of disloyalty. In mitigation of this objection it has been urged that, *le cas échéant*, Russia would be informed of the existence of an alliance, if indications of a war against us became evident. This very uncertain expression is so elastic that the notice would either come too late or would only cause still greater irritation. It was further argued that in the state of ferment now prevailing in the internal affairs of Russia the knowledge of the alliance in question would give her the leverage and self-command necessary to master that ferment. But surely for that purpose official knowledge of that honourable intention is necessary. And yet it is of course impossible to give official knowledge of the fact that Russia is regarded as the sole enemy. Therefore in order that it may be possible to communicate the treaty to Russia, the reference to her must be omitted from it, and the enemy be only described in general terms, while it must be incidentally mentioned that in entering upon it the parties have this honourable intention in view. That is what I desire. I am opposed to an immediate ratification of the treaty, because there is at the present moment absolutely nothing which could lead to a war against Germany and Austria, and it is notorious that binding treaties entered into without urgent necessity are double-edged weapons. Austria urges the immediate ratification on the ground that the favourable situation which for the moment exists in France may be endangered, and that the intimacy between Austria and England may cool down. I cannot conceive how such far-reaching political combinations can possibly be made to depend upon the hazard of a Minister of the French Republic who is on the point of being overthrown. The Anglo-Austrian intimacy must after all be very shaky if it depends upon the date of the ratification of a treaty. In view of the consideration shown by Austria for the susceptibilities of France and her apprehensions as to a coolness with England, Milutin's opinion as to the possibility of a Triple Alliance may after all not be entirely unfounded.

"Now, another circumstance has arisen which may

open a way out of the dilemma in which I find myself between my conscience and honour so far as Russia is concerned, and the objections raised to my views on the Austrian side. In reply to my telegraphic inquiry, you have informed me by wire of what Saburoff told you under instructions from the Emperor. You infer from these communications that Russia has already got wind of our Austrian negotiations (as is quite natural), and you wish to conclude from the defensive attitude, which, according to Saburoff's assurance, Russia intends in future to maintain that this assurance must have been a consequence of the knowledge obtained respecting our negotiations. In these circumstances it might be possible to immediately carry out the suggestion made by me on page 3 as to the manner of communicating our proposed arrangement with Austria, and to give the treaty a general character, not only by omitting the name of Russia, but by inviting her to join in the treaty. You yourself have said to Saburoff that you are thoroughly in favour of the maintenance of the Three Emperors' Alliance; and the same idea occurs in the memorandum, the protocol, and the treaty. What, then, could be simpler than to confirm in a real written treaty the Drei Kaiser Bündniss which has hitherto been merely verbal, or, at most, only had a written basis in the St. Petersburg-Vienna arrangement? You yourself have further told Saburoff that you would not be able to co-operate in any policy by which Austria would be endangered. It is as right as it is important that Russia should thus receive the first official intimation of that of which it has already got wind. Inasmuch as our Ambassador at St. Petersburg will have informed Minister Giers of your interview with Saburoff, I would ask whether his assurance that Russia would henceforth only pursue a defensive policy based on the Treaty of Berlin is authentic, and whether it signifies a defensive policy as against Germany and Austria. If a satisfactory answer were received, and this were immediately communicated to Austria, there would be no further obstacle in the way of ourselves and Austria acquainting the Emperor Alexander in the manner above-mentioned (page 3) with the projected treaty, and inviting his adhesion.

"This would render necessary a modification of section 1; section 2 would drop out entirely; section 4 would be redrafted in accordance with my marginal notes, should it be considered desirable that the draft itself should constitute the first invitation to Russia to join in the treaty, as the whole treaty would be submitted as an instrument affecting so far only Germany and Austria. I consider the omission of section 2 to be necessary, because it is directed exclusively against Russia; and furthermore because it is specially stated in your letter of the 24th ultimo that in case of an attack by France upon Germany, Austria would be dispensed from supporting the latter, and only bound to observe a benevolent neutrality. That is as much as to say that we should support Austria against Russia with our whole power (section 1), while Austria is dispensed from rendering a like service if France should attack us. But the latter eventuality is unquestionably more possible and indeed more probable than a Russian attack, at least up to the present, since there the desire for the *revanche* is only slumbering, has never been abandoned, and will show itself again directly a suitable opportunity arises. With regard to our—Germany's—position in a war with France I differ from Field Marshal Moltke, inasmuch as I cannot endorse his view that our forces are sufficient to enable us to carry on such a war without allies. In that event we should find ourselves in presence of an army entirely different to that of 1870, as the progress which it has made is undeniable. Besides, there is a further consideration, namely, the almost hermetically sealed French frontier, extending from the Swiss to the Belgian frontiers, a continuous line of fortresses and forts, which—even if broken through—would render it impossible to send reinforcements to the front, and would, moreover, enormously hamper the strategic advance of our forces. It is on this restricted field that, according to Field Marshal Moltke, we are to deliver battle. If we are victorious we cannot pursue the defeated enemy as we did in 1870, being stopped by this girdle of fortresses, to which, instead of engaging in a pursuit, we should immediately have to lay siege. Months might pass before we could capture any of them, and this would give the defeated army time to refit at its leisure behind this line and to meet us well prepared in the event of our breaking through it at the risk of our communications with our base. But if the German army is defeated in the first battle then the left bank of the Rhine is immediately lost and we must withdraw across the river.

"For this reason Austria ought not to remain neutral in such a war, but, on the contrary, must be bound by treaty to support us with her whole power, in the same way as the treaty binds us to do with regard to Russia."

Continuation of this Imperial communication to the Chancellor, dated Baden, October 4th: "I had not finished the enclosed letter to you yesterday when your long telegram arrived, so that I had still to add the last three-quarters of a page. The standpoint taken by me in this letter has not been affected by my resolve to approve *conditionally* of the Vienna proposal. But I again ask you what are we to reply if, in reference to the Memorandum to be communicated to him, the Emperor Alexander should ask: 'What, then, have you decided to do in connection with this Memorandum? most probably concluded an agreement? Until I am acquainted with it, I can come to no decision, therefore show me this agreement.' But as the agreement in its present form cannot be shown to Russia, we must decline to produce it; and what impression must this refusal make upon the Emperor Alexander? Certainly the very worst. The wording of section 2 is, to my mind, so very strange that I merely wanted to sum up the enclosure by proposing that the neutrality of Austria in case of our being attacked by France be struck out, and Austria be called upon to assume the same obligation to stand by us with her entire strength that we undertake towards Austria in section 1, in case of a Russian attack. Otherwise the conditions are not equal. Strongly impress this upon Andrassy once more.

"WILLIAM."

Letter from Andrassy to Bismarck, dated 3rd October, 1879: "I have received your much esteemed letter of the 29th of September, for which I return my warmest thanks. I have since then received through Prince Reuss some communications referring to the position of the negotiations. I enclose them herewith in the form in which they were written down by Prince Reuss himself. I am in a position to declare myself in agreement with the intention manifested in this proposal, but I have nevertheless some scruples as to two points. The first is that a treaty is spoken of, and the second that the conclusion of the treaty is described as

impending *in the future*. My objection to the first is
that, if the intention to conclude a treaty is expressly
emphasised in the letter of his Majesty the Emperor
William, it follows necessarily that they will ask for the
text at St. Petersburg, and this will afford the Russian
Cabinet, before things are settled between us, an opportunity to commence negotiations *à trois* from which I
do not anticipate a satisfactory result for any of the
parties. For this reason I venture to submit a counter,
or, more correctly, a parallel proposal, the adoption of
which would, it seems to me, be of advantage to both
sides. This is :—

"*After having sanctioned the signature of the
Treaty* (underlined by Bismarck in pencil) his Majesty
the Emperor William can *communicate the entire contents* (underlined in pencil by Bismarck) of the Memorandum agreed upon and signed by us, which, of course,
implies an agreement, adding on his own part the
explanation that this agreement at the same time involves a tacit understanding by both Governments that
an attack upon either Empire will be regarded as
directed against both, and will also be construed by his
Majesty in that sense. His Majesty, satisfied with the
statement made by Saburoff, respecting Russia's love of
peace, makes this communication as a proof of his
loyalty and frankness. His Majesty may, perhaps, add
that this understanding is of an entirely defensive
character, and that there is nothing to prevent Russia
from removing any antagonistic tendency by herself
adhering to the principles laid down in the Memorandum.
(Pencil-marked in the margin by Bismarck.) By
this means the object of the Emperor William would be
fully attained, namely, to communicate the significance
of our understanding, while, on the other hand, no

mention would be made of the existence of a more precise agreement, and, therefore, the necessity of communicating it would be avoided.

"Such a communication of the text would have among other things the disadvantage, first, that the adhesion of Russia to this text is inconceivable; secondly, that the passage in it referring to France and Italy would become known there almost immediately, and would, at the present time, give rise to quite unnecessary combinations; and, thirdly, that the affair might transpire in Parliament, and lead to undesirable discussions. These considerations commend my proposal. Should you not be able to secure its acceptance in the competent quarter, I could agree to any other method, including the suggestion made by Stolberg, my most gracious master having before his departure declared that he would not make a *conditio sine quâ non* of preserving secrecy as to the Treaty *after signature*.

"There is, on the other hand, one point which I would regard as entirely out of the question, namely, any communication of the existence and contents of the Treaty before the sanction of his Majesty, the Emperor William, is actually given or is assured. (Bismarck added in pencil: 'Quite right.') Without desiring to forestall the decision upon this point of my most gracious master, I should prefer to *renounce altogether the conclusion of an agreement*, and in any case I should be obliged to forego for my own part any further share in the negotiations upon such basis. Pray excuse, dear Prince, the somewhat abrupt tone of this statement, but as the matter appeared to me to be pressing, I desired to let Prince Reuss have the letter to-day. Begging you to present my respects to the Princess, I remain, with unalterable and cordial respect,

"Your sincerely devoted,
"ANDRASSY."

The Crown Prince writes to Bismarck (quite confidentially) from Baden-Baden, on the 4th of October, 1879: "Count Stolberg will have already informed you prior to the receipt of these lines of the course of affairs up to the signing of the draft Treaty by the Emperor. I therefore say nothing more about this very exciting crisis, the result of which I confidently anticipate will be of far reaching importance for the position of Germany. I must point out, however, that his Majesty is quite miserable, and keeps on repeating that he has dishonoured himself by his decision, and has been disloyal to his friend the Tsar; so that one clearly sees how fearfully difficult the decision was for him, with his extreme conscientiousness."

Draft (dated Varzin, October 30th, 1879) of a verbal answer to be made to the Emperor Alexander in reply to any question which he might ultimately put: "An institution which arose under the influence of Alexander I. and which preserved the peace of central Europe for half a century, had to be sacrificed in 1866 to irresistible necessity. The German Confederation was an excessive burden to us Prussians, while it did not satisfy the aspirations of the other Germans. The discontent thus created was utilised by the revolutionary party, for the purpose of threatening every German Prince. It was necessary to deprive them of this weapon, and to satisfy the national sentiment. This was done at the expense of the security which the

Confederation afforded, almost without cost, to its weaker members.

"That the breach caused by the secession of Austria, which extended from the Carpathians to the Lake of Constance, would have to be filled up was recognised even in the *Paulskirche*. Later on, after the war of 1866, attempts were unceasingly made to bind Austria to the States, with which it had been formerly united in the German Confederation, so as to prevent her from allying herself with France against them. This object has now been attained without any obligation on our part to defend Trient, Trieste, or, indeed, Bosnia, against Italians, or Turks, or Southern Slavs. Our agreement with Austria no more involves anything in the nature of a threat to our neighbours than would do the erection of a fortress on the frontier, which, of course, has never been regarded in that light, and it is even less of a menace for instance, than the construction of strategic railways. It has, indeed, the character of a mutual assurance society, which every one having similar interests is at liberty to join."

Report of the Emperor William to Bismarck of his interview at Alexandrowo, from a copy made for the Crown Prince:—

1. *September 5th.*—"The Emperor Alexander began the conversation by an explanation of his letter to me. Nobody knew anything of it. (Marginal note by Bismarck: " Gortschakoff revised it.") (1) He had shown it to no one *before* it was despatched, and *after* it had been sent he only communicated it verbally without naming the persons. If, therefore, I had found anything offensive in the letter, as he saw from my answer, he alone was to blame, and he recognised that it was possible for me to have misunderstood him.

(2) He was *very sorry* for that, and since it had had such a serious result as to cause me personal offence, he wished it to be regarded as if it had never been written. Nothing was farther from his intention than the idea of a threat. He had only wished to call my attention to the fact, which was perfectly true, that if the press of both countries continued to rail at each other it must lead in the course of time to a feeling of hostility between the two States, and his sole object was to avoid that. (3) He considered that the preservation of the peace of Europe was only possible in the future, as it had been in the past, so long as good relations between Prussia and Russia were maintained under all circumstances. (3A) The votes given, mostly against Russia, by my Commissioners in the proceedings of the European Commissions in the East had betrayed a hostile attitude on the part of Germany towards Russia, which had caused great irritation in the latter country, and gave rise to the excited comments of the press. (4) In these Commissions Russia was pursuing the object which she had had exclusively in view during the war, namely, to improve and render more assured the fate of the Christian populations, but not to make conquests. If opposition were now offered thereto in the delimitation of the frontier, and more or more Christians were restored against his wish to Turkish sovereignty, the Commissioners must have received instructions to that effect. (5) The German votes had already produced a bad effect in Turkey also, inasmuch as the disagreement which was there seen to exist between Germany and Russia rendered the Turks more obstinate, and caused work to drag on interminably. (6) Prince Bismarck, whom he had hitherto known only as the friend of the Russo-Prussian relations, seemed unable to

forget Prince Gortschakoff's—stupid—circular of 1875. *He* had strongly advised Prince Gortschakoff *against sending this circular*, and pointed out to him the evil consequences (of his vanity, *en parenthese*) because if there actually were anything to smooth over, that was not the way to set about it. Prince Gortschakoff had his way, however. Bismarck's grudge, and his inability to forget, which began with this irritation against Gortschakoff, appeared to him to have been transferred to Russia, and it was to this that he referred in his letter to me when he said that he could not reconcile such conduct with the character of so eminent a statesman. This expression of his in the letter to me did not refer to the instructions given to the Commissioners with respect to Eastern affairs. Moreover (7), Prince Gortschakoff is a man who has outlived his usefulness, and whom he hardly ever consults now." " In reply to No. 1, I said I could not deny that I had been painfully affected by his letter, particularly because I had considered that his remarks referred only to the votes in question, and they seemed to me a matter of such slight consequence that I could not understand his irritation on that score. It was only through his declaration to the effect that his expression referred to the subject dealt with in No. 7 (doubtless No. 6 is meant) that I now for the first time understood it. I could assure him that Prince Bismarck still regards the relations between Prussia, Germany, and Russia as he always did, but that he saw a feeling gaining ground in Russia, chiefly owing to the press, which he could not understand, in view of the existing laws there, especially as semi-official organs contributed to this detrimental state of feeling. I added that I was prepared to admit that our press was also guilty of similar excesses, but, after all, these were mainly in self-defence against the Russian attacks. We are so tied by our press laws that we can only intervene in the way of personal *appeal* to the editors of the newspapers, but not legally unless a state of siege were proclaimed in certain districts. Nos. 2 and 3. If the words in question were to be understood as containing no threat I should feel reassured, as the interpretation which the Emperor gave to this passage of his letter was in perfect accord with my own convictions. As his Government had quite recently issued a serious reprimand with regard to improper articles in the newspapers, it was to be expected and hoped, from the power with which the Governor-General was invested, that energetic action would be taken. I, on my part, had caused certain *advice* to be given to the editors, the law did not *permit* any more. 3A. Our instructions to the Commissioners in question had remained the same from the very beginning: if Russia and Austria were in agreement always to vote with them; when points arose where that was not the case to vote with the majority, where the Russian proposal was not flagrantly untenable. That had been the case in the matter of Silistria, where I was entirely in favour of the Russian proposal to appoint a Commission to inquire into the question of the bridge on the spot, and also with regard to the military road through Eastern Rumelia. 4. This view was quite new to me, as nothing of the kind had previously been brought to my notice. At the same time, these little frontier details were after all so trifling that they could hardly affect the question of the Christians to any important extent. Unfortunately, the Greek frontier question had only been mentioned at the Congress as the expression of a desire, and not as a *demand*, and I foresaw, from the first, how it would be, *mais pendant le congrès je n'avais pas voix au chapitre.* I regarded in the same way the Jewish question in Rumania, the broader solution desired being, to my mind, impracticable, and therefore I wished to see the Greek modification adopted."

Continuation of this report, dated September 12th, 1879 :—

"Nos. 6 and 7. I had never noticed that Prince Bismarck was inspired by particularly hostile feelings towards Prince Gortschakoff on account of the latter's circular of 1875. My opinion and his upon that note was exactly the same as that of the Emperor Alexander himself; but at the Berlin Congress the same view with regard to Prince Gortschakoff was manifested as was expressed above by the Emperor, and I therefore understood the peculiar position which was now assigned to him. I believe that in my answer to the Emperor I adequately emphasised how little change there has been in Prince Bismarck's political views so far as Russia is concerned. He had always agreed with me that, remembering the attitude adopted by Russia towards us in 1870, we for two whole years, 1876 and 1877, tried to manifest our gratitude to the Emperor by our *neutralité bienveillante*, and actually succeeded in preventing a coalition of the Western Powers, including Austria. This seemed to me to disprove the suspicion of the Emperor that Prince Bismarck had out of spite against Prince Gortschakoff changed his political views, and on that account had adopted towards Russia an attitude to which expression had been given in such trifling questions. Up to the present Prince Bismarck's sentiments towards Russia remained unaltered.

"On the forenoon of the 4th the Emperor came to see me again in order to take leave of me after lunch. He had received a telegram from Jugenheim, from the

Empress Marie, who desired to be remembered to me, and was very pleased at our meeting at Alexandrowo. He added: 'C'est a elle que j'ai communiquée la première ma lettre a Vous dont le brouillon était par differentes correctures presque illisible. I afterwards showed my letter and your answer to Adlerberg, Milutin and Giers; they know exactly what my political opinions are concerning Prussia and Germany, and being in perfect agreement with me on this subject, they are pleased that erroneous impressions will be dispelled by our meeting.' The Emperor then read me a letter from the Russian envoy reporting a conversation which he had had at Kissingen with Prince Bismarck on the political situation; and a great deal had in particular been said about Prussia and Russia acting together. The envoy found that Prince Bismarck's former view of the Three Emperors' Alliance had remained entirely unchanged. The Emperor repeated, *en aperçu*, the views which we had exchanged, and was heartily glad the misunderstandings had been cleared up and that the old friendship would be maintained between the two States in association with Austria. As to the latter, he now added for the first time: 'Certainly I had reason to be dissatisfied with her, as her attitude towards me during the war was *louche* as usual. Without firing a shot she occupied two Turkish provinces, of course never to surrender them again, as the English will never give up Cyprus, respecting which they entered into a separate treaty during the Congress without making any communication to the Great Powers.' I interrupted him here, saying I believed there had been negotiations at Reichstadt respecting the occupation of Bosnia and the Herzegovina. 'Yes,' said the Emperor, 'but under quite different conditions, that Austria should take part in the war in some way or other. All the same, the main point is that we should hold together *à trois.*' Of course I could only confirm that view as my own conviction.

"On the same morning I spoke to General Count Adlerberg, Minister Giers, and Minister of War Milutin, one after the other. The first two spoke with equal warmth in favour of the old relations. They were aware of the Emperor's letter and of my answer, which I mentioned as *entrée de conversation,* and they were at one with the Emperor in his satisfaction at the removal of the misunderstandings which they would have thought to be impossible, knowing, as they did, exactly the views to which the Emperor desired to give expression in his letter. I have no reason to doubt the sincerity of these sentiments. I nevertheless told them quite plainly that it was the press that led to an estrangement between our countries. As a strongly worded rescript had now been issued in Russia decidedly disapproving of the hostile attitude adopted by the press towards Germany, an improvement was to be anticipated, that is, if the Governors by whom a state of siege had been proclaimed throughout almost all Russia—a measure to which I could only wish every success—made use of their power to immediately seize all newspapers, pamphlets, &c., which published inflammatory matter. If that were not done the dangerous consequences which the Emperor had foreseen would certainly follow, namely, discord between the two States. In dealing with our own free press, my hands were tied by the law and our representative Constitution, and hence the defensive attitude against the Russian press taken up in our newspaper articles. I had, however, given orders that the editors should be advised to exercise greater restraint themselves, should an improvement take place in the Russian press. The gentlemen in question agreed with me in all this, and hoped for an improvement.

"The conversation with General Milutin began with the subject described above. I then expressed my appreciation of the new organisation introduced during the war, and said I could not understand where the money was found for it. But all Europe had been alarmed at seeing the efforts and the monetary sacrifices made for carrying on the war suddenly retained on a peace footing. He replied: 'It was precisely the war which proved that the Russian army was not strong enough even to overcome the power of Turkey, its enormous forces being dispersed over the whole empire from Siberia to the Vistula. Therefore a nucleus must be maintained which shall be equal to European requirements. This cost can be met out of Russian resources that are unknown to other countries. We have war frontiers against China, against the countries on the Indian border, against Persia and against Turkey. We have received news that a coalition is being formed between Austria, England, and perhaps France. That points to a new conflict in the East. England is organising and arming Asia Minor, which is being inundated with State officials, generals, and officers in the guise of consuls, a sure indication of hostile intentions upon our position in the Caucasus. The Eastern conflict is near at hand.' I demurred to the latter statement, and asserted that if once the decisions of the Berlin Congress were carried out in their entirety, no fresh war was to be anticipated there, as Turkey required peace above everything else.

"(Signed) WILLIAM, 9/9/79."

"While the Emperor was with me on the 4th a telegram from London was brought to him, according to which England declared that, although not in favour of the appointment of a technical commission *ad hoc* for the settlement of the bridge question at Silistria, she would be pleased to see the Servian Frontier Commission entrusted with that task. The Emperor said he could agree to that, and that only technical members should be appointed to the Commission."

These papers also include the letter from the Emperor William to Bismarck, dated 10/9/79, which accompanied the foregoing report: "Herewith I send you the conclusion of the notes of my conversation with the Emperor Alexander. My letter from Berlin, which crossed your memorandum No. 1, showed you that your views, which you now repeat with more detail in No. 2, are in contradiction—first in principle, and then that an answer could not be given until I had spoken with the Emperor Alexander. Your premises in the memoranda could be transformed into truth for me only after I had spoken to the Emperor, and—as I wrote you through Minister von Bülow—after light had been thrown upon the correspondence. Up to that time I regarded your memoranda *comme non avenus*. For me my notes have brought this light. The Emperor regrets having written the letter, as it has given rise to misunderstandings; as the words 'ce qui doit avoir des suites fâcheuses et dangereuses' should absolutely not be regarded as threatening a rupture, but only as directing my attention to the fact that if some restraint were not placed upon the press, ill feeling might arise between our two countries, which neither of us desired, and therefore that measures should be taken accordingly. That being as true as anything in this world can be, I could only express my complete approval, all the more so as the Russian Government had already taken such steps, and I had ordered similar measures prior to my departure. As you will see from the notes, I corrected the view taken by the Emperor Alexander of the votes given by my Commissioners in the East, and he fully understood this, although he stated that he had already received news of the unfavourable consequences of these votes, which was quite new to me, but which explained the Emperor's dissatisfaction on that score. You will also read how I defended you against the passage in the Emperor's letter. He fully agreed that our policy during the war in the East was of the greatest benefit to Russia, which involves the highest recognition for yourself. I could assure him that *till now* you had maintained your old sentiments towards Russia, as was sufficiently proved in 1877 and 1878. On this occasion the Emperor expressed his conviction that peace could only be preserved for Europe by our holding together *à trois*, as we had done since the meeting in Berlin in 1872. Having hitherto held the same conviction myself, I could only agree with him. As the three persons, Adlerberg, Giers, and Milutin, spoke in exactly the same sense, the light which I looked for at this meeting at Alexandrowo respecting the sentiments of the Emperor and those persons who stand highest in his confidence has been forthcoming *so far as I am concerned.* None of them has the slightest wish to wage war upon us. The great additions to the Russian army which were raised as a reserve during the Turkish war, are retained as a permanent increase because they believe themselves to be threatened by a European coalition, and therefore must be in a state of preparation which would enable them to meet this *alone.*

"Since therefore, for me, the premises in your memoranda fall to the ground, namely, that owing to the danger threatened from Russia we should give up the policy we have hitherto pursued in our relations with that country and not only seek but actually conclude a European coalition of a defensive nature against Russia, I cannot lend myself to this project in its present extension. In view of the explanation given by the Emperor Alexander of his letter to me, which *I originally did not regard as a threat but only as a desire to see the existing good relations between our States maintained by means of restrictions upon the press, it could only be a source of satisfaction to me* to see the milder tone which prevailed in your answer sent by me to the Emperor, the moderate pressure and the truths which it contained being sufficiently intelligible *and also understood.* The words 'une entente séculaire, les legs de nos pères de glorieuse memoire' were written according to my own heart, and went to the heart of the Emperor, so that he repeated them to me twice. I could not therefore understand your hostility to Russia, which increases with each memorandum, nor could I see how the expressions quoted above could be interpreted as a mere empty phrase! I was just as deeply affected by the words that we should outwardly maintain a friendly attitude towards Russia while at the same time concluding a coalition against her with Austria, with England, and perhaps with France. And you have its conclusion already so fixedly in view that you have not only communicated your whole project to Count Andrassy, but have also permitted him to speak of it to his Emperor (seinem Kaiser), who also immediately accepts it. Then you invite me to send you instructions, on your way back through Vienna, to conclude a defensive alliance there with Austria against Russia, which would be followed by the larger coalition. Put yourself in my place for a moment. I am in presence of a personal friend, a near relative and an ally, in order to come to an understanding as to some hasty and indeed misunderstood passages in a letter, and our interview leads to a satisfactory result. Shall I now at the same time join a hostile coalition against this sovereign, that is to say, act behind his back in a manner contrary to that in which I spoke to him?

"I will not absolutely deny that the dangers set forth in your memoranda may arise one day, particularly on a change of rulers in St. Petersburg. I am, however, utterly unable to see that there is any imminent danger. How often have you warned me against treaties with other Powers, which tied one's hands, when there is no positive object in view, and there is only room for conjecture as to an uncertain future. My brother and Minister Manteuffel in particular burnt their fingers over the Three Years' Treaty with Austria which was concluded after Olmütz, and impatiently awaited the expiry of that term. The present case is quite similar. It is against my political convictions and my conscience to bind my hands for the sake of a *possible eventuality*.

"At the same time, I must not disavow you and the steps which you have already taken in dealing with Andrassy and his master. Therefore in Vienna, whither all the newspapers already say you are going, you may speak of the *eventuality* of disagreement with Russia developing into a possible breach, and enter into *pourparlers* respecting the joint measures to be then taken with Austria. But, following my conscience,

I do not authorise you to conclude a convention, to say nothing of a treaty.

"In this way I hope our views will again agree. If it be God's will that this should be the case, I can look forward with confidence to the future, which would otherwise for me be very dark, and anticipate a genuine continuance of the relations with Russia, which are growing more friendly. I cannot tell you how painful the episode has been to me, when it seemed, for the first time in seventeen years, as if we could not come to an understanding. I impatiently await your answer to the above authorisation, and am convinced that we shall be able to come to an agreement. God grant that it may be so!

"Your faithful and devoted,

"WILLIAM.

Finished at Stettin, 12/9/79."

"As Herr von Bülow, after taking a copy of my additions to the Alexandrowo notes, had the original immediately despatched to you, there is a corresponding change in the opening words of this letter."

Letter from Bismarck to Prince Reuss, dated Varzin, 28th January 1880 (on the left top corner, the note: "Copied a second time in the interest of history"— doubtless in Holstein's handwriting):—

"In connection with your report, No. 11 of the 10th, I take the liberty to send your Serene Highness a few words confidentially, and only for your personal information, on the relations between Austria and Italy.

"I consider it natural that Baron Haymerle should have made no official complaint respecting Urczzana, and furthermore, that he was tactically right in taking that course. I should not regard it as good policy however to adopt a purely passive attitude towards similar permanent threats. Such a course would, I fear, only encourage Italian Chauvinism, and the semi-complicity of the Government therewith. According to my political convictions a purely defensive attitude, *i.e.*, one of mere complaint, is not an effective weapon against such permanent threats or incitement. It is open to Austria to parry such attacks, by assuming the offensive, on similar lines to the Italian demonstrations. It is not the Italian Government which adopts a threatening attitude. It only suffers Italian subjects to do so. Now I am convinced that there are elements and movements in Austria that favour the restoration of the Papal States, and of the Kingdom of the Two Sicilies, just as the Irredentists work for the acquisition of the Trentino. If these elements in the press and public life of Austria were to come or to be drawn into greater prominence, that would involve a counteraction against the Irredenta, which would compel the Italians to fall back upon the defensive, without being able to make any complaint. Even the plea that Austria, in view of such threatening movements, requires a better line of defence than that which she now possesses would be quite as legitimate as a craving for the Trentino, Trieste, and Dalmatia. Italy by herself would scarcely venture to attack Austria, but her present attitude is a constant encouragement to the war party in Russia. For about twelve months I have had the impression that Italy is inclined to place herself at the disposal of a Russian policy of war if in return she were offered an accession of territory and a stretch of the Adriatic coast. The relations which it has been sought to establish between the two armies, the Italian and the Russian, and the shifting of the centre of gravity of the Italian army towards the north support this impression, not less than the indications furnished by various votes which the Great Powers have respectively given. This whole attitude shows that Italy must not be numbered to-day among the peace-loving and conservative Powers, who must reckon with this fact. I beg your Serene Highness also to think over this matter for yourself, and to kindly send me your views in an autograph private letter. Of course any initiative in opening up this subject must be carefully avoided, but Baron Haymerle, or Count Andrassy when he comes to Vienna, can hardly fail to bring it up in conversation with your Serene Highness, and thus give you an opportunity of introducing observations in the sense of the foregoing remarks, not as the expression of German policy, but as your own opinion in the character of a friendly expert. In certain circumstances the Nuncio also might afford an opportunity for an expression of opinion in this sense which would excite no suspicion. It would in any case be of interest to assure one's self of the present feelings of the Italian Prelacy with regard to strategic moves of this description.

"I cannot deny that, to my mind, the Italy of to-day offers Germany small prospect of useful co-operation with us in the possible crises of the future. On the contrary, we have much more ground to fear that Italy will join our adversaries than to hope that she will unite with us, seeing that we have no more inducements to offer her. Every encouragement to Italian policy to join the bellicose and predatory Powers in Europe is contrary to *German* interests, and in the present instance still more contrary to those of Austria. For the protection of the latter it would, I think, be useful to call the attention of the English Cabinet to the encouragement to breaches of the peace which the attitude of Italy involves. Perhaps your Serene Highness can ascertain whether anything has been done or is intended in this direction.

"BISMARCK."

The Emperor William to the Imperial Chancellor, Berlin, November 13th, 1885: "Enclosed I return you *brevi manu*, your two extremely important and interesting letters, with my observations. I beg you to excuse me for selecting this method of answering them, but you know how badly I write long explanations, and from the marginal notes you will see my complete agreement with your views, so that I believe I may adopt this shorter form of answer. I may mention to you at the same time that I consider the moment has now come to lay before my son the views with which it was all along intended to acquaint him, as to the utter inexpediency, now no less than formerly, of the marriage in question, which, of course, he himself has also always held to be impossible. Now, however, that Prince Alexander has come forward as a rebel against the peace of Paris (doubtless Berlin was meant), and the signatories thereto, whether he remains in Bulgaria or not, a marriage of this kind has become more than ever impossible. Your political explanations are quite to the point.

"Your grateful
"WILLIAM."

I left for Hamburg at 12.20 on the 29th of October, shortly after the Emperor passed through that city. On the evening of the 30th I returned to Friedrichsruh, where I arrived about 5.30 P.M. At dinner, the Prince, who was in excellent spirits, said that the most gracious Master had in all taken up five hours of his time. Afterwards, over our coffee, he observed to me: "This

afternoon he let me talk to him for three hours on end.
I stood as if in the pulpit, and I am tired out." Everybody said that the Emperor was extremely unaffected
and amiable, and the Princess noticed in particular that
he could laugh most heartily. I heard that Minister
Mittnacht would arrive next day. By 12 o'clock on the
day of my journey to Hamburg I had read through the
last of the Bismarck papers, which went as far as the
year 1887 and concluded with No. 735. Among the
most recent of the papers are three letters of the year
1880 from King Lewis of Bavaria, full of recognition
for Bismarck, the second expressing regret at his wish
to retire, and the hope that he would remain. A letter
from the Emperor William to the Chief dated May 31,
1886, on the "horrifying news from Munich," says
towards the close that there is little to be hoped from
Prince Luitpold, while King Lewis is credited with
having " shown more good will . . . . for the German
cause." Then two autograph letters from the Crown
Princess (the present Dowager Empress). One is dated
December 23, 1885, and accompanied a present of
Moselle wine which he had liked at her table; while
the other, dated from Villa Zivio, November 22, 1887,
deals with the illness of her consort, and reports the
unanimous opinion of the German doctors. Finally, a
letter of November 23, 1887, from the Emperor
William, which is very illegibly written and runs somewhat as follows: " Enclosed I send you the nomination
of your son as *Wirklicher Geheimrath* with the title of
Excellency, in order that you may hand it to him,
a pleasure which I would not deny you. I imagine that
this pleasure will be threefold, for yourself, for your son,
and for me! I take this opportunity (to explain) to
you the silence which I have observed up to the present

respecting your proposal, in view of the sad condition of health of my son the Crown Prince, to initiate my grandson, Prince William, more fully into State affairs. In principle I entirely agree with you that this must be done, but it is a very difficult matter to carry into execution. You will of course know that the very natural decision, which I took on your advice, that, in case of my being prevented, my grandson William should sign the current Cabinet rescripts in civil and military affairs with the superscription 'By Order of his Majesty' greatly irritated the Crown Prince, as if, in Berlin, a substitute were already being thought of. On considering the matter quietly my son will doubtless have reassured himself. But such reflection would be more difficult if he ascertained that his son were allowed a still greater insight into State affairs, and were even given a Civil aide-de-camp as I used to call my *Vortragende Räthe*. Things were, however, quite (different) then. As there was nothing that could induce my Royal father to appoint a substitute for the then Crown Prince (although my succession to the throne could be anticipated long beforehand), my introduction to State affairs was put off till 1 was forty-four years old, when my brother suddenly nominated me a member of the Ministry of State with the title of Prince of Prussia. It was necessary in this position that an experienced man of business should be appointed to prepare me for each sitting of the Council of Ministers. At the same time I received the diplomatic despatches every day, after they had passed through four, five, or six hands—according to the seals! A mere *conversation*, such as you propose, the appointment of a statesman in attendance on my grandson, would not have the character of a preparation, as in my case, for a *specific object*, and would certainly still further irritate my son, a thing which must absolutely be avoided. I would therefore suggest that the course of occupation hitherto followed—learning the manner of dealing with State affairs—should be continued, that is to say that (my grandson) should be attached to single Ministries or perhaps to two at a time, as during this winter, when my grandson was attached in a voluntary capacity to the Foreign Office as well as to the Ministry of Finance. This voluntary course should cease with the New Year, and perhaps (be replaced) by the Ministry of the Interior, my grandson being permitted in special cases to obtain information at the Foreign Office. This *continuation* of the course hitherto followed may cause my son less irritation, although you will remember that he was strongly opposed even to this. I therefore beg you to let me have your opinion on the matter. Wishing you all a pleasant festival,

"Your grateful
"WILLIAM."[1]

On Thursday, November 1st, I told the Prince, at lunch, that I would either immediately or next morning return him the papers, sorted and arranged. He replied, however, that he had found some more which belonged to the collection. He took me with him to his study, and handed them to me for arrangement, adding that there were very many more at Varzin, a whole box full, including private letters of historic significance. I should also go through these later on, and put them into chronological order.

On the morning of Friday, the 2nd of November, I

[1] The text of this letter is very confused as well as incomplete, and parts of the foregoing version cannot pretend to be more than an attempt to convey its probable meaning.—TRANSLATOR.

read, sorted, and numbered new documents, which were afterwards put into a fresh envelope. Among these was the announcement of March, 1877, by the Emperor William, that he had appointed Bismarck Hereditary Grand Huntsman of Pomerania, reports respecting the illness of the Crown Prince, afterwards Emperor Frederick, from San Remo, Charlottenburg, and Potsdam, a letter from the Emperor William II. to Bismarck, transferring him to the second regiment of Guards, a telegram from the same, dated October 21, 1888, expressing his satisfaction at his journey to South Germany, Vienna, and Rome, whence he had just returned, and his thanks for the Chief's counsels, which had been justified by his experience while away, and, finally, the letter already alluded to from the Empress Augusta. Nothing of importance among them.

At midday, before lunch, I personally handed over to the Chief the envelopes containing the papers. He appeared to have looked through them in the afternoon, as, when he was passing by in the evening, before dinner, as usual, with his two dogs, he gave me his hand and thanked me, expressing his surprise that I had been able to deal with such a mass of letters and papers in so short a time. I said if he wished to have those at Varzin also arranged, and could find no more suitable person to do it, I should be glad if he would let me know when he was next going to his estate in Further Pomerania, so that I might come there and complete my task. I should be delighted to serve him and learn something for myself at the same time. Rottenburg was absent from dinner. He had gone to Hamburg to meet some relatives. During dinner there was some talk of a Herr von Bülow, who had been the Chief's guest at lunch. I ascertained that in this gentleman I had had before me the famous leader of the Lauenburg nobility, to whom Bismarck had clearly explained his standpoint, first on the Ratzeburg Lake, and again on taking the oath of allegiance in the church there. He is much more harmless than I had fancied him. The Chief said: "I should have invited him to remain to dinner, and he doubtless expected it, but he is so tedious that I did not know what to do with him during the five hours before dinner." Then, after referring to the letters of the Crown Prince in 1863, which I had arranged, and to his own pencil notes, he came to speak of the Crown Prince himself. I said: "Absalom! And from what you wrote on the back you doubtless wrote him in reply that you did not intend to be ever included among his Ministers." "Yes," he rejoined, and the quotation *Leicht fertig ist die Jugend mit dem Wort!* (Youth is hasty in its judgments). He then gave a survey of the various phases of the Crown Prince's attitude towards himself in the course of his life. "First, in 1848 or 1849. At that time he was still very thin and lanky. He showed great attachment to me, and, when they forbade him to do so at Potsdam, he used to try to meet me in the dusk of the evening and shake hands with me. Then the rude letter of 1863; afterwards, since 1864, in Flensburg, better. Then again Liberal counsels, Augustenburg sympathies, the Geffcken and Friedberg introductions, and his siding with Cumberland." I said: "The Englishwoman, the Guelph." We then spoke of the latter, also over our coffee, when the Princess said she could be very amiable when she liked, as she herself had experienced; a statement which the Chief also confirmed from his own experience. (. . . .)

On Saturday I took leave of the Prince and Princess

in the dining-room, after I had fulfilled my promise to
the little Rantzaus to go with them to see a "house"
that they had begun to build on the roadside leading
to Dassendorf. I suggested some architectural im-
provements, and the eldest one, with childlike politeness, thanked me for the "good advice I had given
them," and hoped I would soon come back again. A
prospect of doing so was held out to me on my taking
leave at the house. The Chief said, as he was shaking
hands: "Adieu, Büschlein, perhaps we shall resume
our business soon at Varzin. But I must first return
to Berlin." The Princess asked me to present her
compliments to Bucher, and the Countess came down
to accompany me to the station with her children.
But first she showed me the handsome clock and
writing-table presented to her father by the German
manufacturers, and gave me a porcelain penholder
from one of the drawers as a souvenir.

On Sunday, the 10th of February, 1889, I received
through a Chancery attendant an appointment to call
upon the Chief at 3 P.M. I appeared punctually at the
hour named, in his ante-chamber. Minister Bötticher
was called into the Prince before me, and I talked
to Rottenburg until my turn came. On entering
the room I found the Prince in uniform. He asked
about my health, and I inquired as to his. He complained of insomnia, and said he could no longer get
any sleep without artificial means. On his then asking
me what I had been doing in the interval, I mentioned
the *Grenzboten* article on his attitude and that of the
Crown Prince at the Versailles negotiations with the
Bavarians, and he expressed a wish to see it, and said:
"I should like you to add something to it, and to return
to Geffcken's extracts from the diary of the Crown

Prince, or more correctly from one of the three or four diaries of the war, and of later years. A diary is a series of daily notes in which one writes down immediately afterwards what he has ascertained and experienced, just as a tourist does; and that too is the character of the first original diary. It is short, and as was natural enough in war time, it deals mainly with military affairs, and contains scarcely any political considerations. The others are interpolated later, from conversations which he had with good friends, or those whom he considered to be such—Geffcken, Roggenbach, &c. Thus he imagined that he had thought of all these things himself, as far back as 1870. English letters and influences will also have affected him. I say he imagined that and believed it, because he was a man who was very devoted to the truth. The good friends were malcontents, ambitious place hunters, and intriguers, people who felt that they had a vocation for great things, who knew more and could do better than the Government, and who would very willingly have lent a hand if they had only been allowed to do so. They were men of unappreciated talent, the wallflowers, the pettifogging attorneys and quacks of politics. He showed them the diary, and they made their observations upon it, which he then inserted. They found that in this shape it would come in usefully in the future. That accounts for the various transformations it underwent. The Crown Prince, like all mediocrities, liked copying, and other occupations of the same sort, such as sealing letters, &c. And he had time enough for it, as the King kept him apart from almost all political work, seldom or never spoke to him on such matters, and would not allow me to make any communication to him on subjects of the kind. From 1863 onward there was an uninterrupted struggle between the two, in the course of which there were several violent scenes when the Crown Prince was pulled up sharply, and he (imitating the gesture) cast up his eyes and raised his hands in despair. It was the same at Versailles in connection with the Emperor question, where the most gracious Master would not at first hear a word of our proposals, and got so angry on one occasion that he brought down his fist violently upon the table and the inkstand nearly flew out of the window. And here you may supplement the report in the diary as to this incident. Fragmentary and incomplete in every respect, it leaves out the first act in the negotiations, in which I had to wean the Crown Prince of the notion, which doubtless originated at Baden, that the Emperor idea was un-German and would damage the country. He was thinking only of the mediæval emperors, the Roman expeditions, and Charles V. For that reason he wished to have only a King of Germany or of the Germans, while the other three kings were to resume the title of Dukes—Duke of Bavaria, of Suabia and of Saxony. And to this he added the idea of coercion—they should be invited to Versailles and once we had got him there it was to be a case of needs must when the devil drives (*jetzt friss Vogel oder stirb*). I replied to him that that would be treacherous, disloyal and ungrateful, and that I would not lend myself to it, as, moreover, it would have no permanency. No friendly persuasion could possibly induce the Kings to submit to this degradation. I then pointed out to him the advantages of the Emperor idea, somewhat in the same way as I did afterwards in my letter to the King of Bavaria. The Kings would prefer to subordinate themselves to a fellow-countryman, who bore the title of German Emperor and to grant him certain rights in war and peace, than to a King of Prussia, who would only be a somewhat more powerful neighbour. Among the people, however, the Emperors had left a deeper impression than had the few princes, who, after the time of Charlemagne, called themselves, like Henry the Fowler, German Kings. In the restoration of the Empire they looked forward to the Emperor as the keystone of the arch. The Emperor still sits enthroned in Kyffhäuser in North Germany, and in the South German Untersberge. This idea should not be connected with that of a Roman Emperor, Roman expeditions or any pretensions to universal sovereignty would be against the true interests of the nation. It was, on the contrary, a purely national idea which the Emperor would represent and which we also had in view, the idea of unification after discord and decay, of new power and security through unity, of the concentration of the whole people upon the same objects. As far back as 1818 such ideas were held by the students' associations, and in 1848 they found expression in the *Paulskirche*. In 1863 Austria had something similar in view with her draft constitution to be laid before the Congress of Princes, only her first thought was for her own interests." "Later, on the foundation of the North German Confederation there was some talk of an Emperor of the Confederation, and the idea was only dropped because it would have led to a division and because in such circumstances Bavaria and Würtemburg would certainly not have joined us then, nor probably later on. For similar reasons I declined Lasker's suggestion, in February, 1870, to admit Baden into the Confederation, because that would have been an attempt to exercise pressure upon her South German neighbours. The excessive number of Kings gradually

convinced him, and he was then in favour of the
Emperor idea. In the diary he has forgotten this whole
first act. He writes as if he had discovered the
idea and had been the first to put it forward, while it
had long been kept alive, as a hope among the people,
and he himself at first would not hear of it. Then
came the second act, when it is true we acted together
at the Prefecture in order to win over the old Master
to our view. He at first vehemently rejected our
proposal, and fell into a rage when we insisted. I
asked if he wished to remain a neuter for ever. 'What
do you mean?' he said crossly, 'what sort of a neuter?'
'Why, the Presidency' (*Nun das Präsidium*), I replied.
But that also was of no avail. Then he agreed to it
up to a certain point, if he were allowed to bear the
title of Emperor of Germany. I explained to him
that this would be opposed to the treaties, and would
express territorial sovereignty over all Germany. He
said the Tsar called himself Emperor of Russia. I
denied this, and stated that his title was Russian
Emperor. (He quoted the Russian term.) He maintained his opinion, however, until he asked Schneider,
who was obliged to acknowledge that I was right."
On one occasion he mentioned in a report that Schleinitz
had been present at these negotiations. I now asked:
"What was he doing there? In what capacity was he
present, as Minister of the Household, or as former chief
of the Foreign Office, or in what other capacity?" He
smiled and said: "As confidant of the Queen, who had
sent him to oppose the bombardment and to persuade
the King against it. He had nothing to do with the
Emperor question. He had always been Augusta's
favourite, and while he was still a poor man she had on
several occasions sent him money, 300 thalers, in order

to enable him to visit her at Coblentz. It was solely through her favour that he became Minister."

We then spoke of Sybel's "Die deutsche Nation und das Kaiserreich" (The German Nation and the Empire), which he gave me; of Morier's rude letter to Count Herbert, which was quite uncalled for, as there had been no charge made against that gentleman of having given direct information to Bazaine respecting the movements of the German troops; then of the wretched attitude of the German Liberal press, which in this—as in the Mackenzie, Geffcken, and other questions—took the side of every enemy of Germany and of German interests, whose hand was against him too; and finally about Samoa, in which connection the Chief censured the arbitrary conduct of the German Consul there. The conversation had lasted for about half an hour, and the Chancellor said as I was leaving that he would now try to get a little sleep. The article desired by him was written in the course of the following week, and was to appear in No. 8 of the *Grenzboten* under the title "The Emperor Question and Geffcken's Diary Extracts." I, however, first submitted a proof to the Chancellor for revision, and he made a number of alterations which Rottenburg dictated to me in his bureau in order that I might reproduce them in my copy. Thereupon I despatched the latter to Grunow (Saturday, February 16th), but a few hours later Rottenburg, with whom I had dined at Professor Scheibler's, came back there with a message from the Chief requesting me to telegraph that the article should be returned for the present. Even after it had been toned down it was too dangerous for publication.

At noon on Sunday, the 17th of February, a Chancery attendant brought me a note from Rottenburg (begging me to call upon him at 3 o'clock at the Imperial Chancellerie. He had important instructions to give me).

On my going to see him at 3 o'clock he told me that the Chief now wished to have the article printed, but with a further slight change. We therefore telegraphed to Grunow to forward me that evening the proofs I had sent him, which I would return to him immediately. They arrived at 10 o'clock, when I at once took them to Rottenburg. We then inserted the last alterations of the Chief, and sent back the proofs to Grunow in a registered letter so that the article should appear in No. 8. *Per tot discrimina rerum.*

CHAPTER V

SIGNS OF FRICTION BETWEEN THE CHANCELLOR AND THE YOUNG EMPEROR—WITH THE CHIEF DURING THE CRISIS—HIS ANXIETY ABOUT HIS PAPERS—HOW TO GET THEM AWAY—HIS RETIREMENT A FACT—THE EMPEROR WANTS TO BE RID OF HIM IN ORDER TO GOVERN ALONE WITH HIS OWN GENIUS—COURT FLUNKEYISM—HIS RETIREMENT IS NOT DUE TO HIS HEALTH, NOR IS IT IN ANY SENSE VOLUNTARY—LETTERS FROM BISMARCK TO WILLIAM I.—THE CHIEF ON THE INITIATION OF PRINCE WILLIAM INTO PUBLIC AFFAIRS—THE GRAND DUKE OF BADEN'S ADVICE TO THE EMPEROR FREDERICK—THE CHIEF TALKS OF WRITING HIS OWN MEMOIRS—BUREAUCRATIC INGRATITUDE—FOREIGN OFFICE APOSTATES—ACCORDING TO BUCHER THE NOTES DICTATED FOR THE MEMOIRS ARE MERE FRAGMENTS, SOMETIMES ERRONEOUS—THE CHIEF'S LIFE AT FRIEDRICHSRUH—SCHWENINGER'S APPREHENSIONS.

IN February, 1890, a few days after the promulgation of the Imperial Rescript on the labour question, Bucher had already pointed out to me in conversation the difficulties in the way of an international settlement of the question, and said he imagined the Emperor was going further in this matter than the Chancellor could approve of.

Monday, February 24th, he said to me: "I have a commission for you which I must carry out before the Chancellor of State arrives. The "dragon" sent for me to-day and asked if I still had any connection with English newspapers, as he wished to get them to insert an article on the elections. I was sorry that I had no longer any such connection, but I thought perhaps you might write to the *Daily Telegraph* and get it to publish the desired article. He said: 'Busch! Why how is he getting on? I understand he has had an apoplectic attack.' I replied: 'Oh! no, he only caught a bad cold last Whitsuntide, and suffered in particular from great hoarseness, but he is quite well again now.' You will observe that the apoplectic attack comes from friend Holstein." (Probably reached the Chief's ears in quite a harmless way from Scheibler through Rottenburg.) I replied: "As a matter of fact I have not written for that paper for years, but they still send it to me daily, and Kingston, one of their editorial staff and a leader writer, has translated my book *Unser Reichskanzler* into English. I fancy, therefore, they would take an article from me on the subject suggested by the Prince." He then drew an envelope from his pocket and said: "I have here jotted down our conversation on the subject. They are for the main part his own words, pointing out the chief cause of the way in which the elections turned out, the result of which he attributes chiefly to the Rescript. Work them up into an article and see that you get it published in London. He attaches great importance to it and would like to see a copy when it appears." I promised to write and send off the article next morning, and if it were accepted, to hand in a copy of it personally to the Chief, when I should ask him whether I could be of any further use in the matter. He then mentioned to me that the Prince was not at all satisfied with the Rescript, nor was he pleased in other respects with the intentions of the young Majesty, who had become very self-confident and arbitrary, and that he had only remained in office up to the present because he had hoped that the Emperor would appoint Herbert to be his successor. He knew already, however, that this desire would not be fulfilled, as the Emperor objects to Herbert on personal grounds. (. . .)

"By the way, when you next visit the Chief, you should speak in a loud clear voice, as his hearing in not so good as it was. You should also avoid contradicting him in any way, as, according to Rottenburg, he is now very short-tempered and irritable." Bucher's notes (the original of which I have retained) ran as follows: "Explain the influence of the Imperial Rescript on the elections. The old Social Democrats (Republicans) acted as if the Rescript were a victory for their efforts. Many malcontents—and who in this world is contented?—who were hitherto deterred from joining the Social Democracy by their monarchical sentiments (and at bottom the bulk of our people are monarchical), now believe that they can vote for them with an easy conscience. The Emperor has offended the bourgeoisie, and has actually embittered the large manufacturers who regard the Rescript as an incitement to their workmen. The lower middle classes, middlemen and shopkeepers, do not see that their own interests are directly threatened, as they know how to shift from their own shoulders any increase in the price of goods, but they see their political position threatened by the fourth estate. Many of them have therefore fallen away from the *cartel* candidates who were in favour of the Government, and for whom they had formerly voted, and took up with the Progressists, whose leaders are double faced. The experience obtained during the period of conflict showed the importance of the sentiments entertained by the bourgeoisie. At that time they wished to seize the reins of power, *à la* Louis Philippe. The masses did not care, or did not see, yet repeated elections always yielded the same results. The Emperor does not understand that, he has had no experience of it; and it is difficult to make him recognise it as he is surrounded by too many servile flatterers (*Byzantinern*) who confirm his self-confidence. Among the 'Sunday' polling cards in the eastern provinces there were a great number with the name of the Emperor William. Conclusion: Had it not been for the Rescript the elections would have turned out much as they did three years ago." I worked this up into an article for the *Daily Telegraph*, and forwarded it to the office in Fleet Street on the 26th of February.

It was not accepted, however, probably because they considered themselves to be better informed by their regular correspondent, or did not think themselves justified in taking sides against the Emperor.

On reaching home on the evening of the 15th of March I found waiting for me an invitation to do Prince Bismarck the honour of visiting him on the following morning at 11.30. (Original retained.) I went to the palace, No. 77 Wilhelmstrasse, at the time appointed, and was speedily shown in. The Chief, who was in undress uniform, was sitting in the front study. He shook hands with me: "Good morning, Büschlein," and added with a smile, "you still keep your fine beard." Proceeding to the large back room he called me in to him. There were several boxes and also a big trunk with papers, while a large cupboard containing documents was half emptied. He drew out one drawer of the writing table and took out a dark green portfolio in which the correspondence with Andrassy had been kept at Friedrichsruh, as also the envelopes containing the papers which I had sorted for him, and said: "I wish you would look through these for me, first glance through those from Friedrichsruh once more, and then those from Varzin and other new ones; there is still a great number of them. I said to you at the time that we would resume the business. Do you still care to do so?"

I: "Most certainly, Serene Highness; I am only too happy to have the opportunity. I thought several times of reminding you, but I did not like to appear importunate and so preferred to wait for your invitation."

He: "Well, there are others (pointing to the trunk) and here in the green portfolio are more recent ones. You should look through these from Friedrichsruh once more and make a note of those that are of importance from an historical standpoint, then number all the rest in chronological order and add a list of the important ones. I now want to write my memoirs, and you can help me with them. That means I am going to retire. You see I am already packing. My papers are going to be sent off immediately, for if they remain here much longer, it will end in his seizing them." I expressed my amazement.

He: "Yes, I cannot remain here any longer and the sooner I go the better."

I: "But surely not immediately, Serene Highness?"

He: "It is a question of three days, perhaps of three weeks, but I am going for certain. I cannot stand him any longer. He wants even to know whom I see, and has spies set to watch those who come in and go out. For that reason, too, I do not well see how I am to get the papers away. They might be sent to you, but how?" I replied: "I could not take the more important ones away with me, a few small packets at a time, carrying them in the first place to Hehn's and then perhaps to Leipzig."

He: "Hehn? Who is he?"

I told him, and that he was perfectly trustworthy.

He: "I could also have sent them to Schönhausen, and you could go there from Friedrichsruh to fetch them. I want you to have the most important of them copied and to keep the copies for the present."

I: "But if a stranger were to copy them he might betray the contents to others."

He: "Ah, I am not afraid of that. Of course he might, but I have no secrets among them—none whatever. Come to Friedrichsruh when I am there and we will work together. But I should like you first to get a letter from Frederick William IV. into the press. I saw it at the end of a new book, of which I do not remember the title, but it was a fabricated version, inaccurate in form and full of impossibilities and absurdities. I have a correct copy of the original, but I cannot find it in your envelopes. (Searched in that for 1852.) Ah, yes, here it is. Take it with you, copy it, and then return me the original."

I suggested that it should be printed in the *Grenzboten*.

He: "All right, but it must be given as coming from Vienna, and the publication of the false version must serve as a reason for publishing it."

While I was helping him to pack the papers in one of the boxes he came to speak about the Rescript, and said: "It comes of an over-estimate of himself, and of his inexperience of affairs, and that can lead to no good. He is much too conceited, however, to believe me that it will merely cause confusion and do harm."

I: "It is the disgusting —— of the press and of the Court menials that are to blame for his self-deception." He laughed. I told him that the article on the influence exercised by the Rescript on the elections had been written and sent off, but was not published by the *Daily Telegraph*.

He: "It was quite correct, however, as reports reached us from all sides as to the bad effect which the Rescript produced on the electors." He then asked how old I was.

I: "Sixty-nine, but my father was eighty-six and my mother eighty-four."

He: "Well, I should not mind living till I am eighty, out in the country." He promised when I left to send me the latest papers (those in the green portfolio) to look through, arrange in chronological order, and copy. I thanked him for his great confidence in me, which was justified, for as I had already said to him on one occasion in 1870, he was my Master, and my Messiah.

He: "Blasphemy! But you have deserved my confidence."

At 11 A.M. on the 17th of March a Chancery attendant arrived in a cab with a message that the Prince requested me to come to him immediately. On my entering the ante-chamber, Bleichröder was with him, and afterwards Herbert, and so I had to wait. At length Rottenburg, who had already declared that he, too, would retire, told me that they had gone upstairs to lunch, but that he would immediately again announce my arrival to the Prince. He returned in a few minutes with an invitation from the Chief to take lunch with him. At table upstairs I met a nephew or cousin of the Prince, to whom I was introduced as " Büschlein," and who remembered having seen me at dinner in Versailles—doubtless the then lieutenant of dragoons with the red collar. The Princess and Count Herbert came in later. The conversation first turned on a foreign diplomatist, who would have married Countess Marie if her father had not been warned against him as a spendthrift. "Besides, I am altogether against marriages with foreigners," said the Chief, " and particularly in the case of diplomatists." He then spoke of the alleged second visit of Windthorst. It had displeased the Emperor, but it was merely a newspaper invention and ought to be contradicted. " Such intercourse, however, is useful," he said. " It is well that I should in that way keep in touch with the parties, and for that reason I have always been accessible to them. Every member of Parliament could come to me at any time, day or night, and be received immediately. But they have taken little advantage of this. They do not want to be considered by their party as having Government sympathies, and prefer to be able to abuse me for having no relations with them. It is only the Ultramontanes who come sometimes, such as Windthorst, Schorlemer and Hüne, also Frankenstein, who is now dead. The *cartel* parties hardly ever put in an appearance." He recommended me to try the caviar. "It has been sent to me by the Minister of the Imperial Household at St. Petersburg, and I take it that it is the same as that which is served to the Emperor Alexander. It is the best I have ever had." He also praised the Moselle and Yquem. On Herbert coming in he laid before the Chief a portfolio connected with the negotiations in progress respecting a partition of East Africa, and the latter gave his opinion as to the frontiers. I accompanied him downstairs, and he handed me out of the green portfolio on the table in the large room nine or ten copies in his own handwriting of letters addressed by him to the Emperor William I., during the years 1872 to 1887. "Copy these and keep the copies by you, and bring me back the originals, as well as that of the letter of introduction of 1852."

He also gave me a large envelope containing more recent letters and reports to be arranged in chronological order, with dockets on the more important ones for the purpose of the memoirs. "Return me these to-morrow or the day after," he said; and I promised to bring them back on Thursday. We then went into the other study, and I said that even now I could not bring myself to realise that he was retiring; it seemed to me utterly impossible. He: "Impossible? It is now a fact. Things have gone more rapidly than I imagined they would. I thought he would be thankful if I were to remain with him for a few years, but I find that, on the contrary, he is simply longing with his whole heart to be rid of me in order that he may govern alone—with his own genius—and be able to cover himself with glory. He does not want the old mentor any longer, but only docile tools. But I cannot make genuflexions (Ich aber kann nicht mit Proskynesis dienen), nor crouch under the table like a dog. He wants to break with Russia, and yet he has not the courage to demand the increase of the army from the Liberals in the Reichstag. I have succeeded in winning their confidence at St. Petersburg, and obtain proofs of it every day. Their Emperor is guided by my wishes in what he does and in what he refrains from doing. What will they think there now? And also other expectations which I cannot fulfil, together with the intrigues of Courtiers, rudeness and spying, watching with whom I hold intercourse! My retirement is certain. I cannot tack on as a tail to my career the failures of arbitrary and inexperienced self-conceit for which I should be responsible."

I: "When he falls into distress and difficulty he will himself come and fetch you back, Serene Highness! He will have to beg and implore you."

He: "No, he is too proud for that. But he would like to keep Herbert, only that would not do—that would be a sort of mixed goods train, and I should always have to bear part of the responsibility. Moreover, although Herbert would doubtless stand being lectured and censured by me, he would not stand it from Imperial Chancellor Bötticher." (He therefore seemed to think that the latter had been selected as his successor, and knew nothing as yet of the choice of Caprivi). "Besides they have treated his father badly." I said: "The Emperor William seems to have the same notion as King Frederick William IV. had, according to Sybel, namely, that Kings in virtue of their office know everything better than their best servants." He: "Yes, obedient Ministers! He has altogether a great deal in common with him." . . . I proposed to publish the letters of William I., or at least a few of them, and mentioned the *Grenzboten* as a paper from which they would be largely quoted. He seemed to like the idea. " I will see about it when you bring me back the originals. If you do not then see me, report yourself at Friedrichsruh in a short time. I shall now go out riding for a while." As I was leaving the room, he clapped me on the shoulder in a friendly way. In the antechamber, Rottenburg again said he would also retire. His nerves could no longer stand it. Very nice of him, but we shall see how the cat jumps.

On Thursday, March 20th, I took back to the Chief the originals of his letters to William I. He looked through them and sanctioned the publication in the *Grenzboten* of the first three, adding at the same time : " We shall first publish these which refer to family matters, and see what impression they make. Then we can let the others follow, and perhaps later on still more from the collection."

I : " Perhaps articles also ? "

He (smiling) : " Yes, perhaps. Hamburg newspapers would also accept something of the kind. I have recommended the *Norddeutsche Allgemeine*, which the company that owns it placed at my disposal, to the Conservatives (doubtless those belonging to the Free Conservative wing) as their organ."

On Saturday, March 22nd, I returned to him in an envelope the thirty-nine new papers chronologically arranged and numbered, the most important ones being specially docketed. The latter were: No. 14, letter written by William I. in 1884 ; on the Battenberger and his projected marriage, 16, 18, 21, 31, and 33 ; a letter to the Chief from the Crown Prince Frederick at Portofino, describing his eldest son as inexperienced, extremely boastful and self-conceited ; a letter from Crown Prince

William to Bismarck in 1888 on the "Battenberger"
business and Albedyll's plan for "nailing down" Prince
Alexander by a written declaration; a letter of the
Battenberger from Sofia to the Queen of England, sent
to the Chancellor with a letter from the Crown Princess
Victoria (two copies); a report by Professor von Bergmann on the illness of the Emperor Frederick; a letter
from the Grand Duke of Baden respecting an interview
with the sick monarch, which had taken place according
to arrangement with him alone (without the Englishwoman) when the Emperor listened with deep seriousness to the statement made to him by the Grand Duke:
"You cannot govern without Prince Bismarck (Ohne
Fürst Bismarck kannst Du nicht regieren)." The
Chief looked through the particulars of the contents
which I had written on the envelope, and observed:
"Those are really important papers, but take them back
with you and keep them at your house for the present."
He then reflected, however, and said: "I am being
watched, and you also, and if you are seen coming and
going with a large envelope—this will be better. Come
here!" He then went into the back study to a large
trunk standing in the middle of the room. I followed
him, and he raised the cover of a green portfolio which
was packed up in it under a round box. "Those are
maps," he said. "Lay these papers between them, and
remember where they are in case I should forget it,
when we proceed with the Memoirs at Friedrichsruh. I
am sending about 300 cases and other things away, and
13,000 bottles of wine. That is a great deal, but it
includes many presents. Besides, while I still had
money I bought several lots of good sherry, which will
come in for my children. Write to me a fortnight after
I reach Friedrichsruh and ask when you can come on a
long visit and help me with the Memoirs. I must have

a private secretary so that I may be able to dictate and dispose of minor affairs by letter. That is not for you, however, as I intend to employ you on something better. I have accordingly asked Schweninger to find a young doctor for this purpose, who would also be at hand in case of indisposition and accident, as, for instance, if I were to hurt myself out riding. It would be something for him, too, as it would in any case bring him in a couple of thousand marks. Keep yourself free for our business." I replied that I would arrange for the present to remain with him for six months, and if necessary for a further period later on, after a short holiday. We then returned to the front room and sat down, when he said: "There is one thing I would ask you to do now if you still have any influence in the press, that is, to correct a mistake which I have repeatedly noticed in newspaper articles within the last few days, as also in communications from exalted places, as, for instance, from England—with suppositions and reproaches—namely, that I had sent in my resignation owing to my apprehension of great crises, and left the Emperor in the lurch through fear of the increased Opposition in the new Reichstag. A glance at my past history and character ought to have discredited that notion, and a remembrance of the conflict of 1866, when the Opposition was much stronger, and more dangerous, and of my loyalty to my royal master, which I likewise showed and proved on later occasions. But, as a matter of fact, it is quite wrong. On the contrary, I did not want to retire until the summer, and, in the meantime, offered to defend the Imperial policy in the Reichstag, and to take up the struggle with the Opposition. I was not permitted to do so however. . . . He wants to do everything himself, and he fancies that he can." He then spoke once more of spying, and of the Emperor setting a watch upon him to see with whom he held intercourse. (Probably Windthorst's visit.) "That is one of the final reasons that have induced me to tender my resignation." He stood up, bent across the table, resting on his two hands, and smiling as he looked me straight in the face, said : " But, tell me, do you drink much wine ?" I replied : " During the daytime no spirituous liquors whatever, not even at table. In the evening two pints of thin, sour Moselle." "So!" he rejoined. "You certainly gave me the impression of having stowed away a bottle of Burgundy, and yet a short time ago you had some little trouble. (Apoplectic attack?) Otherwise I do not in the least disapprove of it, as I myself drink my share. But take care of yourself, for I wish to keep you with us for a long time yet." It was then arranged once more that I should write to him a fortnight after his arrival at Friedrichsruh, but in the first only to arrange for a shorter visit, during which we should talk over and settle about a longer stay later on.

On Monday, March 24th, the Chief again sent, by a Chancery attendant, to fetch me in a cab. I had to wait in the ante-chamber from 11.45 to 1 P.M. as Caprivi was taking lunch upstairs with the Prince. I then saw the new Imperial Chancellor, as he was going away. Scheibler congratulated Rottenburg on a second quality Red Eagle and oakleaf, which may possibly soothe his nerves. On being called in I found the Chief seated in a *causeuse* before his writing table. I handed him to-day's *Post*, which Rottenburg had given me for him. He read out to me the short leader of the 23rd (which I have kept), and said : "They, too, want to curry favour. That comes from gentlemen at Court, who want to hush up things. Please say something against that! Could the Liberals themselves abuse me worse? Not the worst, but, on the contrary, the best service that could be done to me would be to give a correct answer to the question whether my retirement has been voluntary or involuntary; and that answer is: involuntary. It is a patriotic duty not to maintain the utmost reserve, but, on the contrary, to tell the truth. The young man would, however, like to have it hushed up. Indeed, he has gone so far as to summon Schweninger, and to try to make him believe that it was due to considerations of health. Yes, there is a great deal of flunkeyism (*Byzantinerthum*) here, and they all crawl on their bellies before him, in order to attract one gracious look upon themselves." I asked if he would stay on much longer. He said: "No, to-morrow or the next day."

I: "Then I am to write to your Serene Highness in fourteen or fifteen days about my visit?"

He: "You can write even earlier, and come very soon."

The desired article was despatched to the *Grenzboten* as an appendix to that recently ordered. It appeared in No. 14, immediately following a longer article (probably by Kayser) which preached from the same text as the *Post*. The first three letters from Bismarck to William I. appeared at the head of No. 14. They ran as follows :—

1.

"VARZIN, *August 1st*, 1872.

"Your Majesty has given my wife and myself great pleasure by sharing in our family festival, and we beg your Majesty graciously to accept our respectful thanks. Your Majesty is right in giving the first place among the blessings for which I have to thank God to my domestic happiness, but happily in my house that happiness both for my wife and for myself includes the consciousness of your Majesty's satisfaction; and the extremely gracious and friendly words of recognition contained in your Majesty's letter do more to soothe disordered nerves than all the art of the physician. In looking back upon my life I have had such inexhaustible reasons to thank God for His unmerited mercies that I often fear I cannot remain so fortunate to the end. I regard it as a particularly happy dispensation of Providence that my vocation on earth should be the service of a master for whom I can work with pleasure and affection, as—under your Majesty's guidance—the inborn loyalty of the subject need never fear to find itself in opposition to a hearty devotion to the honour and welfare of the Fatherland. May God continue to grant me strength, as well as will, to serve your Majesty in such a manner that I may preserve your Majesty's satisfaction with my efforts, of which such a gracious evidence now lies before me in the shape of the letter of the 26th. The vase, which arrived in good time, is a truly monumental expression of royal favour, and is at the same time so substantial that I may hope that not the 'fragments' only, but the whole, will go down to my descendants as a proof of your Majesty's gracious participation in our silver wedding.

"The officers of the 54th Regiment, in a spirit of comradeship and friendliness, sent their band from Kolberg. Otherwise, as usually happens in the country, we were restricted to the more intimate family circle, with the exception that Motley, the former American Minister in London, a friend of my youth, chanced to be here on a visit. In addition to her Majesty the

Empress, his Majesty the King of Bavaria and their Royal Highnesses Prince Charles and Frederick Charles, and H.I.H. the Crown Prince have honoured me with telegraphic congratulations.

"My health is slowly improving. It is true I have done no work whatever, yet I hope to be able to report myself to your Majesty as fit for service in time for the Imperial visit.

"V. BISMARCK."

2.

"VARZIN, *November* 13, 1872.

"MOST GRACIOUS KING AND MASTER,

"I am greatly depressed at being unable, on receipt of your Majesty's gracious communication of the 9th instant, to proceed to Berlin at once and place myself at your Majesty's disposal in the present crisis, all the more so as towards the end of last month I believed I should soon be sufficiently restored to do so. Since my return from Berlin I found my strength constantly increasing, and for that reason and also through my interest in the matter, I allowed myself to be tempted, in opposition to the urgent warnings of the doctor, to yield to Count Eulenburg's frequent appeals, and endeavour to influence the course of affairs by communications to your Majesty, and correspondence with the Ministers and with Members of the Upper House. That is certainly very hazardous to proceed in such a fashion, and at such a distance, in the absence of discussions which might throw light upon the questions at issue, without knowledge of the opposing views, and also without sufficient assistance. I had hoped, however, that it would only last a few days and that things would soon again enter upon a more peaceful course.

Unfortunately, this attempt only too speedily convinced me that my doctor was right, and that my store of newly-recovered strength was very slight. I am greatly discouraged, as my intervention will have exercised rather a disturbing influence than otherwise, while the few days' work and excitement, with the nervous irritability which it involves, have sufficed once more to prove to me clearly the lassitude of my intellectual powers. I fear I am more exhausted than I should like to confess to myself. This anxiety, as well as the feeling of shame that I am unable to be at my post and at your Majesty's service at such an important moment, is a source of great depression, even when I say to myself that I must humbly submit to the will of God, who does not require my co-operation and puts limits to my strength. My uneasiness is counterbalanced by the confidence which your Majesty expresses at the close of your letter, and which I fully share, that the grace of God which has hitherto blessed your Majesty's Government will continue to assist it. The course which your Majesty has sanctioned in Council can lead to the same ends just as well as that proposed by me, provided there is no breach with the present Parliament and my colleagues remain united among themselves. They will do that for your Majesty's sake, although up to the present there have been many indications of differences. I fear that my correspondence with some of them individually, in reply to questions addressed to me, may have sometimes increased the elements of discord, and that misunderstandings may have arisen with respect to myself owing to the fact that the contents of my reports were fully known only to those to whom they were addressed. I have therefore requested Roon only to consult me at your Majesty's express command, and I have informed him that I shall no longer correspond with my colleagues individually.

"In this manner my co-operation, so long as God does not give me better strength, will rest in your Majesty's gracious and considerate hands. My hope and my prayer to God is that it may be soon granted to me once more to do my duty in person under your Majesty's eyes, and to again find that peace which lies in work.

"v. BISMARCK."

3.

"BERLIN, *December* 24, 1872.

"I thank your Majesty respectfully and heartily for the beautiful Christmas present, conferring fresh distinction upon me.

"My father entered the regiment of Carabineers of the Life Guard in 1783, and also had the honour, at the review, of being presented to Frederick the Great as a Junker, on which occasion the great king condescended in gracious recognition to hold up to him as a model his grandfather, Major von Bismarck (of the Schulenberg, afterwards Bayreuth, Dragoons), who fell at Czaslau.

"This and many other impressive reminiscences, which my father handed down to me from the time of Frederick the Great, as reproduced in the work of art now standing before me, and which I can supplement with a well-preserved series of letters from my grandfather in the field during the Seven Years' War, form the permanent impressions of my childhood. I have always regretted that, by the will of my parents, I was not allowed to prove my devotion to the Royal House and my enthusiasm for the greatness and renown of the Fatherland in the fighting ranks of the army, rather than behind the writing desk. Even to-day, after your

Majesty has raised me to the highest honours as a statesman, I cannot entirely suppress my regret at not having been able to win similar advancement as a soldier. I beg your Majesty, as it is Christmas Eve, to forgive this expression of personal feelings in a man who is accustomed on Christian festivals to look back upon his past. I might have been, perhaps, a worthless general, but I should have preferred to win battles for your Majesty, like those generals who adorn the monument, rather than diplomatic campaigns. By the will of God, and your Majesty's favour, I have a prospect of seeing my name recorded in books and in bronze when posterity immortalises the memory of your Majesty's glorious reign. But, independently of the loyalty of every honourable nobleman to his sovereign, the cordial attachment which I entertain for your Majesty's person, and the pain and anxiety which I feel at not being always able to serve your Majesty as I wish, and no longer with my whole strength, can find expression in no monument. Yet in the last resort it is only this personal feeling which makes the servant follow his monarch and the soldier his leader with uncalculating devotion on such paths as under Divine Providence Frederick II. and your Majesty have entered upon. My strength for work is no longer equal to my will, but up to my last breath the latter shall be devoted to your Majesty.

"VON BISMARCK."

The letter from Frederick William IV. was also published, in No. 13, and all were reproduced by numerous other papers.

I insert here, first the remaining letters from Bismarck to William I. which I copied at his desire, and then some of the more important papers in the new batch.

Further Letters from Bismarck to Emperor William I.

4.

"Varzin, *August* 13, 1875.

I have received with respectful thanks your Majesty's gracious letter of the 8th instant, and am pleased above all things to see that the cure has agreed with your Majesty in spite of the run of bad weather in the Alps. With respect to the letter from Queen Victoria I have the honour to add again that it would have been very interesting if her Majesty had expressed herself more fully as to the origin of the rumours of war circulated at that time. The sources must have been regarded as very trustworthy by that exalted lady, as otherwise her Majesty would not have again referred to them, and the English Government would also not have taken in connection with them measures of such an important character and such an unfriendly nature towards us. I do not know whether your Majesty considers it possible to take Queen Victoria at her word when her Majesty asserts that 'it is an easy matter for her to prove that her apprehensions were not exaggerated.' It would also be doubtless of importance to ascertain from what quarter such 'serious errors' could have been despatched to Windsor. The hints as to persons who must be regarded as 'representatives' of your Majesty's Government would appear to refer to Count Münster. He, like Count Moltke, may very well have spoken academically of the usefulness of a timely attack upon France, although I do not know that he has, and he was never instructed to do so. It may indeed be said that it is not calculated to promote the maintenance of peace for France to have the assurance that she will never

be attacked under *any* circumstances, do what she may.
Now, as in 1867 in the Luxemburg question, I would
never advise your Majesty to begin hostilities at once,
merely because it was probable that the enemy would
shortly enter upon them. One can never foresee the
ways of Providence with sufficient clearness to do that.
But it is also of no use to give the opponent the
assurance that one will wait for his attack *under all circumstances*. I should therefore not blame Münster if he
had spoken in that sense occasionally, and the English
Government would have no right to take official steps
upon non-official remarks of our Ambassador, and, *sans
vous dire gare*, to invite the other Powers to bring
pressure to bear. Such a serious and unfriendly course
of action gives reason to suspect that Queen Victoria
had yet other grounds for believing in warlike intentions
than incidental remarks by Count Münster, the
authenticity of which I do not even credit. Lord (Odo)
Russell declares he has always reported his firm belief
in our peaceful intentions. On the other hand, all the
Ultramontanes and their friends have charged us
secretly, and openly in the press, with wishing to bring
on war in a short time, and the French Ambassador,
who moves in these circles, sent these lies to Paris as
trustworthy information. But at bottom that too would
not be sufficient to inspire Queen Victoria with such
trust and confidence in falsehoods that had been denied
by *your Majesty* in person, as she still expresses in her
letter of the 20th of June. I am too little acquainted
with the idiosyncrasies of the Queen to be able to form
an opinion as to whether the phrase about its being
' easy to prove ' may possibly be intended merely to
conceal, instead of openly confessing, a hastiness of
action which could no longer be recalled. I beg your

Majesty to excuse me if my 'professional' interest has led me, after three months' forbearance, to dwell at such length upon an incident which has already been settled.

"The Turkish question can hardly assume large proportions if the three Imperial Courts remain united; and that end can be promoted most successfully by your Majesty, because we are the only Power that has now, and for a long time to come will have, no direct interests at stake. Moreover, it can only be of advantage to us if public attention and the policy of other Powers should, for a while, be directed elsewhere than to the Franco-German question.

"As your Majesty has been gracious enough to mention my health, I beg respectfully to report that the six weeks' cure at Kissingen has affected me more than that of last year. I feel very exhausted, can walk little, and cannot ride at all as yet. This is now to be remedied by a course of malt and brine baths, and, as a matter of fact, the first four have had a good effect. I therefore hope that the next six weeks will render me more fit for work, though I fear that I must rely upon your Majesty's consideration more largely than my sense of duty would fain allow. My wife and daughter thank your Majesty respectfully for your gracious remembrance of them, and commend themselves to your Majesty's favour.

"v. BISMARCK."

5.

"FRIEDRICHSRUH, *December* 3, 1878.

"I am deeply afflicted at not being in a position to offer my respectful greetings to your Majesty the day after to-morrow, in common with my colleagues. I can only lay before your Majesty's feet, in writing, the heartfelt wish that, in resuming the reins of Government your Majesty may find, in God's blessing, consolation and satisfaction for the crime and ingratitude of mankind, which must have cut as deeply into your Majesty's heart as the wound externally inflicted.

"The sudden transition from the cure at Gastein to the work in the Reichstag appears to have hindered my recovery, so that even to-day I am not as well as I was in September. But if your Majesty will be gracious enough to allow me four to six weeks' further leave of absence and forest air, I may hope, with the help of God, that in January I can, with fresh strength, place myself at your Majesty's disposal for the preparing the work in the Reichstag. This year, owing to the necessity for far-reaching financial and economic reforms, the proceedings in the Reichstag will be particularly laborious; and it is to be foreseen that they will be accompanied by severe struggles between the parties themselves, and against your Majesty's Government. I do not, however, doubt that, in the financial and economic questions, the result will ultimately be favourable, if concord can be maintained in the Ministry of State and with the more important Federal Governments, and if the Ministry preserves that firmness and decision which your Majesty's leadership has secured to us in all difficult situations, and to which, next to God, we owe all our great success.

"v. BISMARCK."

6.

"FRIEDRICHSRUH, *December* 25, 1883.

"I thank your Majesty respectfully and cordially for the gracious Christmas present, and in particular for the gracious wishes that accompanied it. They afford me that full gratification which I should have felt in the Niederwald, had I been able to attend the festival.

For me your Majesty's satisfaction has a higher value than the approval of *all* others. I thank God that He has so disposed my heart that I have been able to secure your Majesty's commendation, while I seldom obtain the approval of others, and then only temporarily. I also thank your Majesty for the immutable confidence always reposed in me for the long period of over twenty years, and for your Majesty's constant graciousness to me as a master, in spite of the attacks of my opponents and my own well-known failings, in the most arduous as well as in quiet times. I require nothing more in this world, in addition to peace with my own conscience before God. God's blessing has rested upon your Majesty's rule, and has favoured your Majesty above other monarchs who have achieved great things, in so far as your Majesty's servants can look back on their service with gratitude to your Majesty. The loyalty of the ruler generates and maintains the loyalty of his servants.[1]

"My wife returns her respectful thanks for your Majesty's gracious greetings in the gracious letter of the 21st instant, to which I send a separate reply. She is slowly improving in health after a few weeks during which I was very anxious as to her condition. She requests me to lay her most humble respects and good wishes for the new year at your Majesty's feet. At the present moment I myself am physically stronger than I have been for many years, and yesterday was able to take a ride of several hours in the woods with my two sons, who are staying here on a holiday. Although I may not as yet strain my nerves in intellectual work to the extent demanded by my position, I hope for a further

---

[1] On the 20th of March, the Chief called my attention to this sentence in particular, in view of the present situation.

improvement in this direction also if your Majesty will graciously permit me to remain here until the end of next month. God grant your Majesty a happy Christmas, health, and contentment.

" v. BISMARCK."

7.

"VARZIN, *September* 2, 1884.

"Your Majesty has made the anniversary of Sedan a day of exceptional joy and honour to me by graciously investing me with the Order *Pour le Mérite*, at the same time increasing the significance of the distinction by the exceedingly gracious words which accompanied it yesterday. I am happy to see from this, and to realise on looking backwards over a long series of years, that your Majesty's favour and confidence have been my constant and unalterable support, and that your Majesty's consideration also compensates for my failing strength. Your Majesty's recognition and good will is in itself the highest satisfaction to which I aspire in this world, but it is also a pleasure to me when the world ascertains that I have always been, and still am, in possession of the boon for which I have ever striven, viz., the favour of my earthly master. I will always faithfully and zealously endeavour to deserve it, so that your Majesty, as the highest and most competent authority, may recognise in me the heart and sentiments of a Prussian soldier. I desire no higher praise than that contained in those words, when they bear your Majesty's signature.

"On the 11th I hope to lay my renewed thanks personally at your Majesty's feet, and to see your Majesty in good health.

" v. BISMARCK."

8.

"BERLIN, *December* 25, 1884.

"I respectfully thank your Majesty for the beautiful Christmas present. The work of art reminds me to some extent of my own position. While the centaur has both hands engaged in lifting the huge horn to his shoulder, the woman hangs on to his beard with her whole weight. So it is with me! While I have my hands full in the service of your Majesty and the country, the Opposition in Parliament pulls and drags at me, at the risk of overthrowing me while bearing the burden of affairs. Moreover, the Opposition is unfortunately much uglier than the female form that clings to the centaur's beard. I will not, however, allow this to prevent me from gladly and firmly carrying the burden on my shoulders, so long as God gives me strength to do so, and I enjoy your Majesty's favour. With the heartiest and most respectful wishes for your Majesty's Christmas, I unite those for the coming year, reserving to myself the pleasure of reiterating them verbally.

"v. BISMARCK."

9.

"FRIEDRICHSRUH, *September* 26, 1887.

"I thank your Majesty respectfully for the gracious letter of the 23rd instant, and for the gracious present of the picture of the palace, in which I had the honour for so many years to make my reports to, and to receive my orders from, your Majesty. For me the day received a special consecration, through the greeting with which I was honoured at your Majesty's bidding, by their Royal Highnesses Prince William and Prince Henry. But even without this further evidence of favour, the feeling with which I greeted the twenty-fifth aniversary of my appointment as Minister was one of the heartiest and most respectful gratitude towards your Majesty. Every monarch appoints Ministers, but there is scarcely an instance in recent times of a monarch retaining and protecting his Prime Minister, against every kind of hostility and intrigue, during twenty-five long years of vicissitudes, when not every measure succeeds. During this lapse of time, I have seen many former friends change into opponents, but your Majesty's favour and confidence in me has remained immutably the same. In this thought I find a rich reward for all my work and consolation in sickness and solitude. I love my Fatherland, the German as well as the Prussian, but I could not have served it joyfully if it had not been granted to me to do so to the satisfaction of my King. The foundation and the indestructible core of the high position which I owe to the favour of your Majesty is the Brandenburg liegeman and the Prussian officer, and therefore your Majesty's satisfaction is a source of happiness to me, without which every form of popularity would be worthless and distressing. In addition to numerous telegrams and letters received by me on the 23rd, from Germany and abroad, I have had very gracious greetings and congratulations from their Majesties of Saxony and Würtemberg, H.R.H. the Regent of Bavaria, the Grand Dukes of Weimar, Baden and Oldenburg, and other reigning personages, as also from his Majesty the King of Italy, and Minister Crispi. The two latter communications touched on politics, and were difficult to answer. As your Majesty may perhaps be interested in the text, I have instructed the Foreign Office to submit them.

"I pray God to grant me the pleasure of continuing my service to your Majesty's satisfaction.

"v. BISMARCK."

10.

"FRIEDRICHSRUH, *December* 30, 1887."

"I thank your Majesty respectfully for the gracious letter of the 23rd, and for the evidence of favour with which it was accompanied, and first for the drinking horn with the hunting trophies, which I regard as intended for your Majesty's Grand Huntsman of Pomerania, and shall keep at Varzin. But my chief happiness arises from the recognition accorded to my son by his official promotion, which shows me that your Majesty is satisfied with his work, and therefore that he fulfils the end for which I have educated him. I crave your Majesty's further indulgence towards him, feeling certain that he will deserve it by his attachment even in those matters in which he still lacks experience.

"With reference to my most humble suggestion respecting the further preparation of H.R.H. Prince William for State affairs, I appreciate and share the anxiety with which your Majesty is inspired by your solicitude for the health of his Imperial Highness (the Crown Prince). I considered it my duty to raise the question, but I do not venture to urge it any further, not wishing to make myself responsible for the consequences upon the health of H.I.H. which any irritation might produce. Perhaps the object which it is sought to attain in the interests of the State may be approached in a manner less calculated to attract attention; and this would not be difficult if the Prince resided in Berlin instead of at Potsdam. I therefore respectfully beg your Majesty's permission to submit my views on the subject when I return to Berlin, which I hope to do next month. In the meantime, I humbly beg your

Majesty to allow me to try and move H.I.H. to submit to your Majesty, on his own initiative, the proposed scheme for a Civil Adlatus to be attached to the Prince. Count Radolinski, who called upon me to-day, thinks there is some prospect of this attempt being successful, as the Crown Prince's irritation in the matter was connected with the question whether his parental authority would be taken into consideration or not. If H.I.H. could be moved himself to propose the object in view, which would be of advantage to the State, the entire difficulty would be at an end. Should the attempt fail, no great harm would be done, as the Crown Prince could easily give *me* a negative answer, which he could not give to your Majesty. Meanwhile, the present system of giving the Prince occupation at some of the Ministries may be continued as heretofore, in accordance with your Majesty's intention.

"I have ascertained through Count Stolberg that H.I.H. has suggested the promotion of Count Radolinski to the title of Excellency. I beg respectfully to recommend this proposal of the Crown Prince, in the first place because granting it would have a favourable, and refusing it an unfavourable, effect upon the sentiments and health of H.I.H. ; and then furthermore because Count Radolinski is worthy of such a distinction. With a large fortune and very considerable private interests, he has given up an easy position in the diplomatic service, and, solely in obedience to your Majesty's wishes, has willingly undertaken his present duties, which, often very onerous, are rendered specially difficult by the rivalries to which they expose him ; and it is desirable that a nobleman of his prestige and uprightness should continue to discharge them. Moreover, he is one of the few Polish noblemen who, like the deceased Count Raczinski, may be relied upon with perfect safety by your Majesty and the Prussian State, and in my opinion this attribute alone deserves to be recognised by a distinction. Indeed, custom alone would have secured him such a distinction even if, without being a Court official, he had lived on his estates in Posen as a magnate loyal to the Government.

"I beg your Majesty graciously to accept my hearty and respectful good wishes for the New Year. I hope to renew them verbally in the course of January, and to be permitted to report myself to your Majesty, at the same time as the Reichstag, in as good health as I have any prospect of enjoying in this life.

"v. BISMARCK."

Specimens of the New (Berlin) Series of Papers.

. . . . No. 31.—Letter from Prince William to the Imperial Chancellor, dated Berlin, April 2nd, 1888 :—

"Albedyll has been to see me and talked over the whole Battenberg affair (die ganze Battenbergerei) once more. On this occasion a letter was also mentioned, which the Empress is understood to have received yesterday, in which the Battenberger informs her that he would only marry with my consent—a point deserving mention. In this connection Albedyll was of opinion that a positive acknowledgment, repeating this phrase, should be demanded from the Battenberger in order to have a more certain hold over him. Would your Serene Highness approve of my sending a cipher telegram ordering Henry to go to him and demand from him for me a note containing the above declaration ? If that were in my hands, and the Battenberger were nevertheless to take any steps or to enter into any intrigues, we could prove by documentary evidence that he had been guilty of a direct breach of his word.

"Awaiting your Serene Highness's kind decision, and hoping that you enjoyed your birthday celebration, I remain always,
"Your faithful and devoted,
"WILLIAM,
"Crown Prince."

No. 33.—The Grand Duke of Baden to the Imperial Chancellor :—

"Serene Highness,—I hasten to let you know in this inadequate form that I had occasion to-day to speak to the Emperor Frederick *alone*. In the manner arranged yesterday I explained to him how I came to know your sentiments and state of health. My explanation greatly impressed the Emperor, and I took advantage of this to proceed to the general situation of political affairs in Europe, and—referring to the firmly established position of Germany during the reign of the Emperor William, as compared to the troubles and confusion in the rest of the world—emphasised the necessity for us and for Europe of perseverance in the course adopted.

"The Emperor manifested a friendly disposition, and warmly approved of my statement. He is anxiously expecting your visit. His features wore an expression of deep seriousness when I said to him : 'You cannot possibly govern without Prince Bismarck.'

"This, in bare outline, is the result of my weak endeavours.
"Your cordially devoted,
"FRIEDRICH GR. V. BADEN.

"CHARLOTTENBURG, *March 31st*, 1888."

A few days after our last interview, the Chief left for Friedrichsruh. On the 11th of April I wrote him (respecting my proposed stay there). I received no answer for a week. The newspapers, however, published a report that the Prince had selected as his private secretary a Dr. Chrysander, who had hitherto been Professor Schweninger's assistant, and who would help him in preparing his memoirs. According to a second press notice, he was also to be assisted by a member of the editorial staff of the *Hamburger Nachrichten*. Bucher ultimately wrote me that he was going to Friedrichsruh, and hoped we "should be harnessed together." (. . . .)

I called upon him the same day to congratulate him, and mentioned to him my fear that nothing would now come of my proposed visit to Friedrichsruh. Perhaps my letter of the 11th had not reached the Chief's hands; or perhaps he had been turned against me by an article on his retirement, published in the *Grenzboten*, which was, however, written by Kayser, and reached Grunow just before mine. Bucher reassured me as to this supposition, but said that Kayser, like Lindau and Holstein, had actually gone over into the other camp. (. . . .) Although he considered it quite impossible that the Prince could now give up the idea of employing me in connection with the papers, I did not feel sure of this, and so a few days afterwards I wrote again to the Prince, and registered my letter. Count Herbert replied that "the Prince intends to invite you here in order to sort some papers. In the meantime, however, he is too much occupied by visits and the arrangements rendered necessary by his removal to take these papers in hand immediately."

A fortnight later, after I had received a post card

from Bucher informing me that he had started for Friedrichsruh, I wrote to him there (as to the proposed visit, and giving him an account of my future movements). This crossed the following letter, which Bucher sent to me under cover to Frau Hedwig Hämmerling :—

"FRIEDRICHSRUH, *May* 15, 1890.

"I have two reasons for sending you this letter under cover to another person; first, because you have not informed me of your whereabouts, and secondly, because there is some reason to suspect the existence of a Dark Cabinet. Therefore be prudent when you write to me here. I have had a large bundle to sort and register, and in doing so have satisfied myself that you have exhausted the materials. What came into my hands was very unimportant,—congratulations, letters of thanks, telegrams, reports from aides-de-camp and such like. (. . . .) I am expected to remain until H. returns from England, probably towards the end of this month. He (the Chief) is physically well, and is gradually quieting down."

I immediately acknowledged the receipt of Bucher's note, and reminded him of the concluding request in my former letter. He replied on the 17th of May, 1890, again under cover to Hedwig Hämmerling : "To enable me to answer your questions I should be obliged to ask him, and up to the present I have had no opportunity of doing so. (. . . .) After your registered letter and the reply thereto, it seems to me not to be in your interest that I should also press the matter. Besides, he talks of presently starting on a lengthy tour to countries [1]

---

[1] To the United States—according to what Rottenburg told me at lunch at Scheibler's on Sunday, the 18th of May. He added: "In that case you should accompany him."

which he has not yet visited—certainly a very happy idea. I take it that he will not begin work before his return in the autumn; and then he will doubtless remember his arrangement with you. I will write you as soon as the departure is approximately settled."

On the 20th of May I had an attack of apoplexy combined with paralysis, from which it took me six months to make an almost complete recovery; that is to say, with the exception that my handwriting had changed and my voice remained hoarse.

On the 10th of July, Frau Hämmerling received a note from Friedrichsruh (from Bucher, inquiring as to my illness). On Frau Hämmerling informing him of the truth he wrote me as follows:—

"DEAR BUSCH,—"I need not tell you how heartily I sympathise with you. I now write to put your mind at rest on one point, to tell you that you have missed nothing here, and will not miss anything during the next few weeks. I have had five or six thousand letters, extending from the fifties to the present day, to arrange in chronological order. They were all mixed up anyhow, both as regards dates and matter. They contain little on politics, and of that little again but a small portion refers to foreign affairs. He was not prepared to accept my suggestion that it would be well to put the begging letters, medical counsels, schemes for the improvement of the world at large, thundering hurrahs and fiery 'salamanders' into the fire. Therefore, when the preliminary work begins you will have to wander through a desert from which I have only removed tradesmen's bills, &c. It is as yet impossible to say when that will be. He complains, with that humorous self-mocking air of desperation which you know, that he has now no time to set about anything. His excuse for the present is that of course the whole material must first be chronologically arranged, which will doubtless take a fortnight longer, although I am keeping hard at it. And then he will certainly be obliged to make some change in his way of living and in the apportionment of his time. The projected journeys will hardly come to anything; but even if he remains here he will not begin work before you are recovered—according to what F. H. (Frau Hämmerling) writes me. There is no idea of calling in Poschinger. He knows that the man is incapable of giving shape or form to anything of the kind.

"He himself and Herbert desire me to express their sympathy to you. With good wishes for your improvement,

"Truly yours (in English),
"BUCHER."

In the days immediately preceding and following this letter, the newspapers published many things from Friedrichsruh which were anything but pleasant reading to me, or were at least at variance with my conception of the greatness and distinguished character of the Prince, and also to some extent with the opinions which he had himself formerly expressed. He allowed it to be seen too often and too plainly, for the benefit of the Court and to the delight of the Radical Thersites, how mortified he felt at his base dismissal; he expressed himself, as I thought, too confidentially, and indeed it would appear sometimes with conscious untruth, in speaking to importunate Jew press spies and other eavesdroppers and talebearers from the newspaper factories. The most inexplicable of all to me was what he was represented as having said to Kingston, of the *Daily Telegraph*, concerning the excellence of the late Emperor Frederick—which was diametrically the opposite of what he had said to me in Berlin and at Friedrichsruh. The principal passage in the Englishman's report runs as follows : " Finally, the conversation turned on the Emperor Frederick, of whom Prince Bismarck spoke with the profoundest admiration. He was in truth a man of rare and most estimable character, thoroughly amiable, exceptionally good-hearted, and at the same time intelligent, clear-sighted and determined. He knew exactly what he wanted, and when once he had come to a decision he held to it immutably. If he had only lived he would, as German Emperor, have amazed the world." (Retranslation—translator's note.) Really ! That would then be a case of a farthing candle developing into a first-class lighthouse ! Was it Bismarck or Kingston who said that? If the former he must have had some particular object in view. But what could it be? To elevate Frederick III. at the expense of William II. ? (. . . .)

I afterwards received from Bucher the following letter from Berlin :—

"I must send you another short contribution to your Memorabilia. When Count Herbert gave a farewell dinner to the officials, four of them—Holstein, Lindau, Kayser and Raschdau—declined the invitation. All four owed everything to the Prince. Not a word has been heard from Keudell since the 20th of March. Lehndorff, Stirum, Krupp, Stumm and Kardorf have defied the royal displeasure by visiting Friedrichsruh. After Bötticher, who owes his promotion to the Prince, had told the Emperor that Bismarck was a slave to morphia, his Majesty sent for Schweninger, and questioned him on the subject. Schweninger answered: 'Your Majesty, that is a wretched calumny, and I know the curs with whom it originated.' (. . . .)

"As a contrast to this pretty set! Shortly before my departure from Friedrichsruh, Bismarck, while out driving, dropped into conversation with an old peasant on the bad weather. 'Yes,' the latter remarked, in Low German, 'the good God has forgotten us altogether. He gives us no summer, and takes away our Chancellor.'"

On the 5th of September I had a visit from Bucher, who had returned from Laubbach on the 3rd or 4th, and on the 6th I called upon him. Of his communications the most noteworthy is that at Friedrichsruh he found a letter from Hermann Wagener to the Prince, from which it appeared that, as far back as 1876, W. was instructed to draw up a memorandum on working class insurance. At that time, when Bismarck doubtless first seriously took up the labour question and thought of positive measures for opposing the Social Democracy, it was the old *Kreuzzeitung* man who was his assistant and counsellor, and not Bucher, who belonged to the school of Lassalle and Rodbertus, as alleged by Poschinger. Bucher expressly denied that the Chancellor had ever discussed this question with him. On the 20th of September Bucher wrote to me that he had received an invitation to visit Bismarck at Varzin.

Shortly afterwards I received the following letter:—

"Varzin, *October 3rd.*

"Dear Busch,—" I have delivered your message. He is glad you are better, and wishes you permanent recovery. Here the condition of affairs is the same as at Friedrichsruh. Nothing is being done and much time is spent over the newspapers. Owing to the articles in Nos. 431 and 433 of the *Boersen Zeitung*, referred to in No. 459, a desire has been expressed to see the numbers of the *Grenzboten* which started the controversy—reproaching the bourgeoisie with opposing the paternal intentions of the Sovereign. Can you lend us the numbers in question from your file, or, if you have not got them, procure copies from Grunow? Lord Rosebery, who ran across from Scotland, was here for a few days, and is now visiting Dantzig and Marienburg. With lots of good wishes,

"Bucher."

. . . In another letter from Bucher of October 14th, the following passage occurs : " The Chief still occupies himself far too much with the press. In the meantime he has begun to dictate during the past few days, but without any real coherence, alternately from various years. It is, therefore, for the present, only raw material. Now and again news reaches here from the Foreign Office. Holstein, who for ten years was taken seriously by nobody, now does everything. He not only slanders the Prince, which he did twelve months since, but also abuses Herbert, who, with inconceivable blindness, had supported him up to the last. Paul Hatzfeldt too, Sardanapalus as his cousin Landsberg christened him, has proclaimed his apostacy in London. But I will also mention a decent man, Count Arco, Minister at Washington, who is here on a visit for a few days. *Rara avis !*"

I sent him a long jocular epistle congratulating him on his birthday on the 25th of October. But I received no answer for over seven weeks, and was already worrying myself with all sorts of fancies, when on the morning of the 22nd of December he himself called upon me. He told me that physically the Prince was in excellent health, and, as it appeared, took exercise, had a good appetite, and at table drank rather too much than too little, and besides he no longer complained of insomnia. Mentally, however, and in particular so far as his memory is concerned, " he is falling to pieces." By this Bucher meant that he could no longer concentrate his thoughts sufficiently, had no longer a firm hold of the details in a narrative, and was easily turned aside from his subject. He also tells a story one way to-day, and quite differently to-morrow. "He wished me to go to Friedrichsruh for Christmas, but they gave me to understand—and indeed very plainly—that that would not be agreeable to them ; and so I am my own master for a couple of weeks." "Urged by Schweninger he has at length decided to dictate his reminiscences to me for an hour daily, when I take them down in shorthand. But they are merely disconnected fragments, and contain many errors, particularly in the matter of dates. For instance, there were some very interesting particulars respecting 1848, but they must first be compared with Wolf's 'Chronik' and corrected. Chrysander is making himself very useful, also in his capacity of doctor, and has, for instance, done me good service with my gout. The Prince has ascertained on good authority that Lindau has been to the *Korrespondenten* (or the *Nachrichten*) in Hamburg, and the *Allgemeine Zeitung* in Munich, setting them against his old Chief and patron, and 'threatening' the latter paper with disciplinary measures if it continued to take the Chancellor's part. The Princess's 'dear Rüdchen,' who for other people is a shameless Judas ! Kayser, his countryman from the East, who is indeed less of a stock jobber and less worthless for official purposes, was recommended to the Foreign Office by Herbert, while Rashdau, also one of the children of Israel, who has married a millionairess of his tribe, was—if I understood Bucher rightly—introduced by Bill. (. . . .) I asked what the Prince thought of Caprivi. He only knew that the Chief had had an interview with his successor (doubtless while he was still in Berlin—at lunch), when Caprivi said that if the Emperor sent him with an army corps into a position where its destruction might be anticipated, he would remonstrate; if the order were then repeated, he would remain at his post and await events. Bucher feared that nothing would come of the projected autobiography. 'He has indeed dictated quite a pile of notes, which of course include a great deal of new and valuable matter; but his account is not always reliable, and in particular he often believes that he said or did something which he ought to have said or done but omitted to do, or at least could not have said or done in the manner alleged by him. And in the most important matters he sometimes stops, like a well that runs dry, and does not return to the subject. In that way he recently began to speak of his relations with Napoleon previous to 1870, but then let the subject drop, and since then I have never been able to bring him to give a coherent account of it. There is yet another drawback. In these notes he might think of history, of a legacy for the future, and that would certainly be most praiseworthy and useful, as there are many things of which he alone has a complete and accurate knowledge. But he seems to be thinking rather of something else. His thoughts are still with the e sent, which he desires to influence. He wishes to warn and to teach, and for that reason he often selects a subject that has nothing whatever to do with his own life, and sometimes one of which he has not a thorough knowledge, but which seems to him to offer a suitable opportunity for introducing his own reflections. For instance, he is afraid that the Emperor will not be careful and thoughtful enough in tacking between Vienna and St. Petersburg, and may, perhaps, on some occasion forget himself and draw too near to the Austrians; all the more, as of course he is aware that the gentleman in Berlin cannot endure the other in St. Petersburg, because the latter had treated him somewhat *de haut en bas*. Now Bismarck does not want to say that straight out and give a plain warning, but tries to work it into a survey of the treaty of Reichenbach, as the relations were then somewhat similar, the people in Berlin not rightly knowing what they wanted or with whom they really had to deal. The idea was merely to show that one was also a power—(in English) a mere show of power! I have now read it up in Ranke, however, and according to him the situation was not all as the Chief represented it. At that time, Herzberg still had charge of the conduct of affairs, and he knew exactly what he wanted, namely, Dantzig and other towns on the Vistula, in order to round off West Prussia.'"

Bucher continued: "What I have done up to the present could be done equally well by any shorthand writer, the only difference being that yet another stranger would have to be taken into his confidence. But I have no taste for criticising and editing, however much Schweninger may beg and urge me to do so. That would be too much trouble and responsibility. Besides, there are not the necessary books for reference and comparison. It is true that for twenty-five years hardly a historical or political book has been published of which a copy has not been sent to him, but she has acted as librarian and has divided them between the different rooms, putting some of them in the cellar, where they rot and fall to pieces, and others in the visitors' apartments, so that nothing can be found when it is wanted."

Bucher agreed with me that the Chief was not prudent in his dealings with the eavesdroppers of the press; that his attitude towards the Court was not sufficiently dignified, and that he let his anger be too easily seen. At the same time, Bucher, speaking of those who came to question the Prince, observed, not inaptly: "Whoever wants to know much learns a great deal, even though it be not always unadulterated truth, and that applies with particular force to the commercial travellers for newspaper firms, who, of course, do not deal in truth." As to the Prince's state of feeling, Bucher said: "He diligently reads the newspapers, but on the whole he is indifferent to politics. 'I am no longer so very much interested even in the management of my own estate.' There is no longer the old devil-may-care spirit arising from that high sense of easy superiority and ready power of mastery—no longer the unconcerned glance cast down as from a great height, but only apathetic indifference, weary satiety."

January 2nd, 1891.—Called on Bucher this morning. Schweninger is trying to provide the Prince with occupation on hygienic grounds. He fears that otherwise he would become still more sulky, cross-grained, and peevish, and, indeed, might in the end become mentally affected. (. . . .)

In the course of conversation on the Prince's notes, Bucher, in speaking of their didactic aim, referred to Nicoll's "Recollections and Reflections" as a model for that kind of writing. He believes he must soon return to Friedrichsruh, "although it will probably lead to nothing." "God grant that there may be an improvement!" he sighed on our parting at the door. I heartily joined in that prayer.

It was not until the 21st of February that I again received a sign of life from Bucher, and then in the form of an unsigned note enclosed in an envelope to Hedwig. It ran: "You will probably soon receive an invitation to the place from which I write. The enclosure is for publication, with an introduction or note to the effect that the letter was read to the guests on the 28/7/72, and that several of them took copies of it. Do not forget to write to G. to impress upon the sub-editorial ass and on the proof-readers that not a single letter is to be omitted, and that the abbreviations, &c., and the Latin characters in 'Borussia' and 'Material' are to be retained. The Chief will have it so. If you happen to write to me, remember the Dark Cabinet."

The "enclosure," a letter from the Emperor William I., ran as follows:—

"COBLENZ, *July* 26, 1872.

"On the 28th instant you will celebrate a beautiful family festival which God in His mercy has granted to you. I may not, and cannot, withhold my sympathy on this occasion, and therefore you and the Princess, your consort, will accept my heartiest and warmest congratulations on this elevating festival. That your domestic happiness should always have held the first place among the numerous blessings which Providence has elected to bestow upon you both—it is for this that your prayers of thanksgiving should rise to Heaven! But our and my prayers of thanksgiving go further, inasmuch as they include thanks to God for having placed you at my side at a decisive moment, and thereby opened up a path for my Government far beyond imagination and understanding. But you will return thanks to Heaven for this also—that God granted you to achieve such great things. And in and after all your labours you have constantly found recreation and peace in your home. It is that which sustains you in your difficult vocation. My constant anxiety for you is that you should preserve and strengthen yourself for this vocation, and I am pleased to learn from your letter, through Count Lehndorff, and personally from the Count, that you now think more of *yourself* than of the documents.

"As a souvenir of your silver wedding you will receive a vase representing a grateful Borussia, of which —however fragile its material may be—every fragment will nevertheless express what Prussia owes to you for her elevation to the pinnacle on which she now stands.

"Your faithful, devoted and grateful King,
"WILLIAM.

CHAPTER VI

I AM INVITED TO FRIEDRICHSRUH—BUCHER AND THE PROPOSED "MEMOIRS"—HE DOUBTS WHETHER THE LATTER WILL BE COMPLETED—THE CHIEF—"BÜSCHLEIN" AS BEFORE—THE ANGLO-GERMAN AGREEMENT—THE EMPEROR AND RUSSIA—THREE KINGS IN THEIR NAKEDNESS—BUSCHLEIN WILL WRITE THE SECRET HISTORY OF OUR TIMES—THE PRINCE GIVES ME IMPORTANT PAPERS TO EXAMINE IN MY ROOM: HIS RESIGNATION IN 1890, A DRAFT OF A CONFIDENTIAL STATEMENT OF THE MOTIVES OF HIS RETIREMENT AND NOTES ON THE ATTITUDE OF THE INDIVIDUAL MINISTERS ON THAT OCCASION—STILL ANOTHER BOOK ON BISMARCK IN VIEW; CORRESPONDENCE ON THE SUBJECT WITH BUCHER AND THE CHIEF HIMSELF; THE PLAN DROPPED—LAST VISIT TO BUCHER IN JANUARY, 1892—HIS DEATH—LAST STAY AT FRIEDRICHSRUH IN MAY, 1893—GOOD-BYE, DEAR OLD FRIEND.

ON the 23rd of February I again received a letter from Bucher, also under cover to Frau Hedwig Hämmerling: "23/2/91. He says he would like to see you once more, and requests you to visit him. You may choose the time most convenient to yourself, but give two days' notice in advance, so as to avoid clashing with an invitation to Hamburg. Be sure to bring your sleeping garments with you, if you are as little in favour with the lady of the house as I am."

I replied that I should have preferred to go the day after to-morrow, but that as I was at liberty to name my own time, and was now engaged in reading over papers, arranging and packing for my removal on the 16th of March, I would come on the 18th. I further requested him to say by what train I should come, and called attention to the fine cartoon and verses, " Dropping the Pilot," in *Punch*, of the 29th of March, 1890, which an acquaintance had sent me the previous day, and which I should bring with me if they had not already seen it.

Bucher replied that they had the "Pilot" from *Punch* at Friedrichsruh; and that he himself had travelled by the slow train. I arrived at Friedrichsruh at 3 P.M. on the 18th of March. The Prince had gone out for a drive with Buhl, the member of Parliament, who had come on a visit. A servant showed me upstairs to No. 4 as my room, where Grant, Bancroft, and the busts of Washington and Hamilton kept me company. I immediately visited Bucher, whose room was opposite mine. He complained that the work of the "Memoirs" stood exactly where it did before. In dictating, the Prince wandered from one point to another, told many things several times, and almost always differently, &c. A huge pile of dictated notes had already been transcribed, he calculated some sixty printed sheets. It would, however, have to be sifted and worked up, and the Chief had not as yet looked through a line of it. Hardly anything would come of it, and, in any case, he had not as yet decided whether it

should be published during his lifetime or after his
death. Bucher intends to leave again for a time at the
end of the month, and is very dissatisfied with his
occupation hitherto. He showed me in the pile on the
chair a thick packet, endorsed, "Nicolsburg," and
observed that it dealt less with the important events that
took place there than with a variety of other matters.
He had seen few of the papers arranged by me in 1888,
none at all of those relating to the alliance with
Austria, only two or three letters from the Gerlach
correspondence, and he had also seen nothing of
the correspondence with Manteuffel and Schleinitz.
He believes that the Chief has sent all those that
are missing to a bank in England for safety. But a
few days later he modified this surmise, and said he
thought the papers were in the keeping of some trusty
friend.

Downstairs before dinner, Buhl, a lean old gentleman with a grey beard, introduced himself to me. I
now made the acquaintance also of Dr. Chrysander, a
slight young man. The Chief appeared shortly afterwards with the Princess. He greeted me with the
customary "Büschlein," was pleased to see from my
appearance that I was well again, and said I must sit
next to him at table on his right, while President Buhl
sat on his left between himself and his consort. The
Prince looked very well, was most good-humoured and
talkative during dinner, was surprised that I still had so
much hair, told amusing stories and expatiated with
knowledge on various fine wines and judges thereof.
(. . . .)

Dinner was followed by some more serious conversation in the coffee room. In reply to a question by Buhl
the Prince disapproved of Caprivi's East African policy :

"Zanzibar ought not to have been left to the English. It would have been better to maintain the old arrangement. We could then have had it at some later time when England required our good offices against France or Russia. In the meantime our merchants, who are cleverer, and, like the Jews, are satisfied with smaller profits, would have kept the upper hand in business. To regard Heligoland as an equivalent shows more imagination than sound calculation. In the event of war it would be better for us that it should be in the hands of a neutral Power. It is difficult and most expensive to fortify"—a point which he then explained in detail. "That does not make one an 'extender of the realm,' not even to the extent that I was in the old days when I travelled back to Berlin with the cession of a strip of land on the Jahde in my pocket, thinking not a little of my achievement!" The Prince is also opposed to building any more large ships: "rather two small vessels than one big one; the North Sea and Baltic Canal doubles our naval strength." (. . . .)

On Friday, March 20th, after lunch, at which the Chief was again very bright and communicative, Bucher at my request allowed me to read the chapter on Nicolsburg from the material dictated for the "Memoirs," in the first place that I should note the numerous digressions from the real subject. These excursions included, among other things, references to the anti-German Queen of Holland, intended annexations, Frederick the Great, an intrigue during the Regency, the indemnity, the impression made in Russia by the events of the summer of 1866, the Dantzig Pronunciamento, the German question in 1848, dynastic sentiments, a lost opportunity in 1848, factions, the *Wochenblatt* party, Augusta, the removal to St. Petersburg and the Italian war. In doing this I ran through the greater part of the manuscript, and found some new and interesting matter respecting the King's desire for annexation, Bismarck's reasons for moderation, and a speedy conclusion of peace; Moltke's strategic plans; a visit of the Crown Prince, who comes to Bismarck and promises to support him at a time when he was almost despairing of carrying through his scheme; and the final consent of the King, who complains, however, that it is an "ignominious peace." Further matters of interest are: Augusta's influence on the Regent, Bismarck's audience before his transfer to St. Petersburg, his condemnation of the Ministers of the new era, as for instance of Schwerin, and afterwards of Usedom and his English wife; the remarkable allegation that Frederick the Great was also vain, supported by references to the King's own judgment of a poem written by himself immediately after the battle ("*n'est pas trop mal après une battaille*"), and to his flute playing. In conclusion, the views expressed as to our relations with Austria and Russia, and the policy which they impose upon us, well deserve to be taken to heart. Irritation against the Russians has arisen (this doubtless refers to the Emperor William) out of personal impressions (due to inadequate appreciation); yet we cannot be quite certain of Austria, as the possibility of a breach with her depends upon one person. Bucher says that the Chief would doubtless speak to me about Windthorst, as to whom there were still many things to be said, and suggested that I should start the subject when opportunity offered. This was done indirectly over our coffee after dinner, but the Prince did not take it up. Later on, however, it was suggested that such excessive honours would never have been paid to the old Guelph advocate at his death if the Emperor had not set the example.

To-day the Chief dictated to Bucher on "questions of State rights," but was unable to get properly under way and could not verify or complete what he had to say, as he had not got his books, "his tools." (. . . .)

At noon on Saturday, the 21st of March, the Chief sent Bucher, to whom he had again been dictating in the morning on questions of State rights, to ask if I would go for a walk with him. (. . . .)

I took an opportunity of inquiring how his "Memoirs" were getting on, mentioning that I knew he had begun to dictate his reminiscences and views. "That is so," he rejoined; "but it is probable that in the end it will come to nothing. I have no documents, and even if I remember the main points—quite clearly—one cannot after all carry in his head every detail of what has happened in the course of thirty years. Then as to the publication during my lifetime. Ever since 1847 I have constantly represented the monarchical principle, and held it aloft like a banner. Now I have seen three Kings in a state of nakedness, and frequently these three exalted gentlemen did not make altogether a very good show. Still it would not do to say that openly before the world—it would be inconsistent—opposed to principle. And yet I can just as little keep silent when once I come to deal with that point, to say nothing of asserting the contrary. And if it (the publication) takes place after my death, then they will say: 'There you have it! Even from his grave! What a detestable old wretch!'" I could only reply that one has duties towards himself, and his own honour,—duties towards that which one has created; that one ought as a man of experience and judgment to warn the country against wrong courses into which it may be led through the impetuousness or thoughtlessness and excessive self-confidence of new

politicians; and furthermore that one has duties towards
history, to dispel misunderstandings and chimeras, and
the falsehoods of flattering courtiers; and that truth,
which stands above all things, must have its rights—
truth of which Jesus said that it will make us free. He
listened in silence to this eager and audacious outburst;
and I then spoke of another subject—namely, Kingston's
report in the *Daily Telegraph* of an interview with him,
and in particular of the very favourable opinion of the
Emperor Frederick, therein ascribed to him, which could
not be reconciled with the views I had heard him express.
He replied: " I know nothing of any Kingston, or of any
interview in an English newspaper. The report must be
an invention (*Schwindel*)." He then mentioned the
picture (in *Punch*), " Dropping the Pilot," and said:
" The Emperor was delighted with it. He saw in it a recognition of his right to smash the pot—you know as in the
witches' kitchen: ' *Entzwei, entzwei, da liegt der Brei.*' "

At lunch among other things the Prince related the
history of some excellent old Jamaica rum, of which a
bottle stood on the table. The conversation then led to
a few corrections. It was Kayser and not Rudchen
Lindau who had warned and threatened the *Allgemeine
Zeitung* in Munich; and Bötticher had not told the lie
about the morphiomania of the Chancellor direct to the
Emperor, but to the Grand Duke of Baden, who then
related it to his Majesty. The statement that the latter
questioned Schweninger is true, as also the rough answer
given by the doctor. "And as a matter of fact," said
the Chief, "I have only taken morphia when in great
pain, and it has never done me any harm; although
Bötticher asserted that he found me quite deranged
mentally and irresponsible for my actions."

After dinner while reading the papers the Chief

remarked, I now forget in what connection : " One day, long after my death, Büschlein will write the secret history of our times from good sources." " Yes, Serene Highness," I replied, " but not a real history—I cannot do that—rather a compilation of good materials, conscientiously collected and placed in a proper light. Nor shall it be long after your death, which of course we pray may be as remote as possible, but immediately, without delay, as in these corrupt times one cannot too soon vindicate the rights of truth." He then came to speak of the newspaper reports to the effect that more friendly relations were gradually growing up between himself and the Emperor, a statement which he denied as something obviously impossible. He referred to the new communal regulations, which he disapproved of. He said they had offended the farmers, whom they put on a level with the small traders and artisans in communal affairs. He then spoke at some length of Minister Herrfurth, addressing himself for the most part to me, much to the following effect (Bucher afterwards recapitulated his statement to me upstairs) : while the Emperor was still Prince and lived at Potsdam, he, Bismarck, desired to prepare him for the government, and to provide him, so to say, with tuition in the various branches of the art of governing. Up to that time he knew little, and indeed did not trouble himself much about it, but preferred to enjoy himself in the society of young officers and suchlike. The plan was to get him to remove to Berlin, somewhere near Bellevue. But the financial authorities at Court were of opinion that that would be too expensive. The Prince was then to hear lectures at Potsdam, and Bismarck proposed Herrfurth, the Under Secretary of State,—who was reputed to be well informed, particularly in statistics—as his tutor on internal questions. The Prince agreed and invited Herrfurth to lunch with him, and then told the Chancellor he could not stand him, with his bristly beard, his dryness and tediousness, and asked whether the Prince could not suggest some one else. Yes, he would send him *Regierungsrath* von Brandenstein. The Prince had nothing to say against that, so Brandenstein was written to. But H.R.H., although it is true he lunched with him several times, paid so little attention to his explanations that Herr von Brandenstein lost patience, and begged to be given some other employment. In the meantime, shortly before the death of the Emperor Frederick, Minister Puttkammer was dismissed. When Prince William ascended the throne Bismarck spoke to him on the subject, and he said he would of course make Puttkammer Minister again, but a certain interval must be allowed to elapse—for appearance sake. Bismarck proposed that Herrfurth should hold the post in the interval, and told him that he must carry on the policy which Puttkammer had adopted, and resign his place to the latter after a certain time, receiving in return a post of Chief President. Would he agree to that? Yes, he would; he had always followed the course laid down by his superior, Puttkammer, and would willingly make way for him when the time came. But when Bismarck, after a few weeks or months, observed to his Majesty that the time had come to reinstate Puttkammer, the Emperor replied, no, he did not think of doing so any longer, as he had in the meantime grown accustomed to Herrfurth, and was now quite satisfied with him. The change had come about in this way. Herrfurth had, without previous consultation with the Prime Minister, put himself in direct communication with the Emperor, and taking advantage of the

Sovereign's wishes, recommended a liberal reform of the Communal Regulations, as a measure by which he could gain numerous friends and secure imperishable fame. "After a few days," concluded the Prince, "my Schönhausen people came to me and asked, 'What does this mean?' They had received papers, and were, it would seem, to report whether they desired to have all the old arrangements upset, and every one put on the same level. And this was done throughout the seven old provinces, much to the surprise and dissatisfaction of the peasantry. That too was one of the causes of my retirement." The Chief afterwards said that when I left he wished to give me some papers to take with me and keep for him. I was to make copies of them, which I could publish at a future day. I promised to remind him, and also offered my services for other purposes in the future; "I had always regarded myself as his little archer, who at his call would even shoot my bolt at the sun himself." He smiled, and said: "Many thanks, perhaps."

Sunday, March 22nd.—During the forenoon the Chief dictated to Bucher some notes on the question as to how the German Constitution might be altered in case it should no longer work. He also told him that he wished to give me certain important documents to take with me. (. . . .)

Monday, March 23rd.—(. . . .) I had waited yesterday in vain to see the Chief on his return from lunch to his study, in order to remind him of the documents which I was to take with me. To-day, after lunch, I called upon him in his own room for this purpose. I apologised for disturbing him, but, as I intended to leave to-morrow, I thought it was of importance to him that I should take the papers with me. "So it is," he rejoined, "and it is well that you have reminded me of it while I am alone. But why are you going away so soon?" "I do not wish to be any longer a burden to you, Serene Highness." "But you are nothing of the kind. On the contrary, I am glad to see such a faithful old comrade of the war time; and, moreover, you are so quiet that you disturb no one." We then agreed that I should remain for a few days longer, and remind him of the papers once more later on. (. . . .)

During the day workmen were engaged unpacking large cases of silver plate—a valuable treasure which German manufacturers had presented to the Prince as a token of their esteem. At dinner the old gentleman, who still remains the same lover of nature and of animals, had a great deal to tell about the starlings, for whom he had had a few dozen small wooden shelters put up in the trees behind the house. "They held a public meeting to-day," he said, "probably in connection with the approach of spring. As I was going for my walk I first saw seven of them sitting together in one place and making music. Shortly after their numbers increased, and finally there were thirty of them sitting together, wing to wing." He then cast a glance at the grey bull-dog waltzing round the room, and observed, "That reminds me of the funeral honours paid to Windthorst. I should never have thought of getting him (the dog), but the Emperor presented him to me. If it had not been for the Emperor's intervention at the beginning, they would never have made such a fuss about Windthorst." After dinner the conversation turned on newspaper tattle, as, for instance, that he had sent twelve cases full of important papers to an English bank to keep for him. "Twelve!" he exclaimed, smiling, "I wish I had even one such case full." The gossips of the press also reported that he had recently purchased a house in Berlin, such and such a number in the Königgrätzerstrasse—better informed authorities had it that it was two houses—at a very high price. From this he went on to say that they once assessed the rent of his palace (the Palais Radziwill) in the Wilhelmstrasse (for the inhabited house duty) at 50,000 marks. On his remonstrating, they replied that the English Ambassador had assessed his own house, which was not so large, at as high a figure.

In the forenoon of Tuesday, March 24th, the Chief sent upstairs for me and handed me, first, three metallographic copies of documents, with two letters and a memorandum. All these were from the year 1885, and referred to the protection of municipalities against arbitrary school rates. "They are metallographs," he said, "and as such I dare say I may publish them at some future time. You can take them with you for that purpose, but they should be returned to me afterwards." "Then I will copy them." "Yes, but that means a great deal of work, twenty or more pages, in parts closely written." "That does not matter, it shall be done." "And then here is my resignation, and this is the statement of my motives. You may read that through—" (and, as I boldly assume, with tacit permission to take a copy away with me, at present merely for my own information). "This is about Herbert—you can read that also, and then bring them all back to me." I went immediately to my room and began to copy the resignation and the statement of motives, as well as the answer of the Chief to the Imperial acceptance thereof, which he had given me instead of the paper referring to Herbert. The metallographic documents will be dealt with later on.

Resignation.

"B(erlin) 18.3.90.—On the occasion of my respectful report of the 15th instant, your Majesty commanded me to submit the draft of an Order which should revoke the Royal Order of the 8th of September, 1852, by which the relations between the Minister President and his colleagues have hitherto been regulated.

"I take the liberty most humbly to submit the following statement of the origin and significance of this Order. Under the absolute Monarchy the office of a President of the Ministry of State was not required; and it was in 1847, in the United Diet, that the Liberal members of that time (Mevissen) first pointed to the necessity of paving the way for constitutional arrangements by the appointment of a 'Prime Minister' ('Premier Minister'), whose task it should be to take charge of and provide for the maintenance of a uniform policy by the responsible Ministry, and to undertake responsibility for the entire results of the policy of the Cabinet. This constitutional arrangement came into force with us in 1848, and the 'President of the Ministry of State,'—in succession Count Arnim, Camphausen, Count Brandenburg, Baron von Manteuffel, and the Prince of Hohenzollern,—was responsible in the first place not for any single department, but for the entire policy of the Cabinet, and, therefore, for the departments, as a whole. Most of these gentlemen had no separate department but only the Presidency, as for instance, prior to my entrance into office, the Prince of Hohenzollern, Minister von Auerswald and Prince von Hohenlohe. It was their duty, however, to maintain that unity and continuity in the Ministry of State itself and in the relations between the latter and the monarchy without which Ministerial responsibility, such as arises under a constitutional system, would be an impossibility. The relations of the Ministry of State and its individual members to their newly instituted Minister President, however, soon required to be regulated in more strict accordance with the Constitution. This was done, in concurrence with the Ministry of State, in the Order of the 8th of September, 1852. Since that time this Order had governed the relations of the Minister President to the Ministry of State, and through it alone the Minister President was invested with the authority which enabled him to assume that degree of responsibility for the policy of the Cabinet as a whole which was attributed to him in the Diet and by public opinion. If each individual Minister can receive commands from the Sovereign without previous arrangement with his colleagues, a coherent policy in the Cabinet, for which some one is to be responsible, is an impossibility. It would be impossible for any of the Ministers, and especially for the Minister President, to bear the constitutional responsibility for the Cabinet as a whole. Such a provision as that contained in the Order of 1852 could be dispensed with under the absolute monarchy, and could also be dispensed with to-day if we returned to absolutism without Ministerial responsibility. But according to the constitutional arrangements now legally in force, the control of the Cabinet by a President under the Order of 1852 is indispensable. All my colleagues agree with me upon this point, as is shown by yesterday's sitting of the Ministry of State, and also that no one who succeeds me as Minister President can assume responsibility for his office if he lacks the authority vested in him by the Order of 1852. This necessity will be felt even more strongly by any succeeding Minister than by me, as he will not be immediately sustained by that authority which I have hitherto enjoyed, owing to my long tenure of the Presidency and to the confidence reposed in me by the two late Emperors. Up to the present it has never been necessary for me, in dealing with my colleagues, to expressly appeal to the Order of 1852. Its existence and the certainty that I possessed the confidence of the two late Emperors, William and Frederick, was sufficient to secure my authority in the Cabinet. To-day, however, this certainty exists neither for my colleagues nor myself. I have therefore been obliged to fall back upon that Order for the purpose of securing the necessary unity in your Majesty's service. For the reasons stated above, I am not in a position to carry out your Majesty's command in accordance with which I should myself introduce and countersign the revocation of the Order of 1852 (to which I myself recently called attention), and nevertheless continue to hold the Presidency of the Ministry of State.

"According to the communications made to me yesterday by Lieutenant-General Hahnke and *Geheimer Kabinetsrath* von Lucanus, I can entertain no doubt that your Majesty knows and believes that it is not possible for me to revoke the Order and yet remain Minister President. Notwithstanding that fact your Majesty has maintained the command given on the 15th instant and indicated that my resignation, which is thereby rendered necessary, would be accepted. From previous conferences which I had with your Majesty on the question whether your Majesty desired my continuance in office, I gathered that it would be agreeable to your Majesty that I should resign my position in the service of Prussia, but continue in that of the Empire.

After considering this matter more closely I took the liberty to call attention to some critical consequences of such a division of my offices, particularly so far as the future action of the Chancellor in the Imperial Diet is concerned, and therefore refrain from repeating here all the consequences which would attend such a divorce between Prussia and the Imperial Chancellor. Thereupon your Majesty deigned to agree that for the present everything should remain as it was.

"As I have had the honour to explain, however, it is not possible for me to retain the post of Minister President after your Majesty has repeatedly ordered it to be subjected to the *capitis diminutio* involved in the revocation of the fundamental Order of 1852.

"On the occasion of my respectful report of the 15th instant your Majesty was pleased to confine me, as regards the extent of my official authority, within limits which do not allow me that degree of participation in the affairs of State, that supervision of the latter, and that freedom in my Ministerial decisions and in my intercourse with the Imperial Diet and its members, which I require if I am to accept constitutional responsibility for my official acts.

"But even if it were possible to carry on our foreign policy so independently of our home policy, and our Imperial policy so independently of Prussian policy, as would be the case if the Imperial Chancellor had as little share in the policy of Prussia as in that of Bavaria and Saxony, and had nothing to do in the Imperial Diet with the decision as to the Prussian vote in the Federal Council, it would nevertheless— after your Majesty's recent decisions on the direction of our foreign policy, as laid down in the confidential letter with which your Majesty yesterday accompanied the report of the Consul at Kieff—be impossible for me to undertake to carry out the instructions respecting foreign affairs contained therein. I should thereby endanger all the important results for the German Empire, which our foreign policy, in agreement with the views of your Majesty's two predecessors, has for decades past under difficult circumstances secured in our relations with Russia, results that have attained a significance beyond all expectations great for the present and for the future, a circumstance which was confirmed by Count Schuvaloff after his return from St. Petersburg.

"Attached as I am to the service of the Royal House and of your Majesty, and accustomed for many years to conditions which I have hitherto regarded as permanent, it is very painful to me to sever my wonted relations with your Majesty, and to break off my connection with the entire policy of the Empire of Prussia. Nevertheless, after conscientiously weighing your Majesty's intentions, which I should have to be prepared to carry out if I were to remain in office, I have no alternative but most humbly to beg your Majesty graciously to relieve me of the offices of Imperial Chancellor and of Minister President, and Prussian Minister for Foreign Affairs, under the usual regulations as to pension.

"From my impressions of the last few weeks and the communications made to me yesterday by your Majesty's Civil and Military Cabinet, I may respectfully take it for granted that I meet your Majesty's views in thus tendering my resignation, and therefore that I may reckon with certainty upon its being graciously accepted.

"I would have submitted to your Majesty the petition to be relieved of my offices a year ago if I had not been under the impression that your Majesty desired to take advantage of the experience and capacity of a faithful servant of your predecessors. Now that I am assured your Majesty does not require them, I may retire from political life without fearing that public opinion will condemn my decision as untimely.

(Signed) " VON BISMARCK."

At the present stage of international affairs I consider it hazardous to publish the "Draft of confidential statement as to the motives of my retirement from office." The interest of Germany in keeping it secret for the immediate future seems to me to be greater than the interest of history in its publication now.

" NOTES ON MY RETIREMENT.

"The Vice-President of the Ministry of State (von Bötticher) declared that he and his colleagues were deeply grieved at my retirement. He had hitherto hoped that the only differences of opinion between his Majesty and myself were connected with home domestic policy, and therefore that the arrangement indicated by me, namely, that I should confine myself to the control of foreign affairs, would prove a satisfactory solution. My withdrawal from all my offices involved incalculable difficulties ;] and although he could understand my displeasure, he could only beg me urgently to come to a compromise.

"I replied: The expedient of withdrawing from the Prussian service and confining myself to the position of Imperial Chancellor had met with objections from the Federal Governments and the Imperial Diet. It is felt to be desirable that the Chancellor should have an

official position in which he can control the casting of
the Prussian vote; and I, too, could not accept a position
in which I should be obliged to take from the
Prussian Ministers instructions in the preparation of
which I had had no part. Therefore this expedient also
would not be free from difficulties.

"The Minister of Finance declared that the Order
of the 8th of September, 1852, by no means went beyond
what was necessary, and could not form an insurmountable
difficulty. And also so far as the difficulties
in the matter of foreign affairs were concerned, he could
only agree with the Minister of State, von Bötticher,
that a compromise ought to be sought. Besides, if the
retirement took place not for reasons of health, but on
political grounds, and from all offices, then the Ministry
of State itself would have to consider whether it should
not take part in this step. Perhaps that would contribute
to avert the fatal event.

"The Ministers of Public Worship and of Justice
considered that the differences referred to were due
solely to a misunderstanding, which it might be possible
to clear up for his Majesty. The Minister of War
added, that for a long time past his Majesty had not
let fall a single word that had any reference to warlike
complications with Russia.

"The Minister of Public Works (Maybach) described
my retirement as a misfortune for the security of the
country and the peace of Europe. Every possible effort
should be made to avert it. In these circumstances he
considered that the Ministers should place their offices
at the disposal of his Majesty, and he at least was
determined to do so.

"The Minister for Agriculture declared that if I
were convinced that my retirement was desired in the

highest quarter I could not be dissuaded from this step. But in any case the Ministry would then have to consider what course it should adopt."

ANSWER TO THE ACCEPTANCE OF THE RESIGNATION.
(From Bismarck's autograph pencil draft.)

"MOST AUGUST EMPEROR, KING AND MASTER,

"I thank your Majesty respectfully for the gracious words with which your Majesty has accompanied my discharge; and I am highly gratified at the bestowal of the likeness, which —— (illegible) will remain an honourable souvenir of the time during which your Majesty permitted me to devote my strength to your Majesty's service.

"Your Majesty has at the same time graciously invested me with the dignity of Duke of Lauenburg. I have respectfully taken the liberty to explain verbally to *Geheimer Kabinetsrath* von Lucanus the reasons which render it difficult for me to use such a title, and at the same time requested him not to make public this second act of grace. The fulfilment of this request was not possible, as at the time when I expressed my scruples on the subject the publication had already taken place —on the 17th of March. I venture, however, most humbly to beg your Majesty graciously to allow me in future to bear the name and title which I have hitherto borne. I beg to be allowed to lay at your Majesty's feet my most respectful thanks for the high honour bestowed upon me by my military promotion as soon as I am able to report myself, which at the present moment I am prevented from doing through indisposition.

"With the most profound respect, &c."

Wednesday, March 25th.—The Chief started for Hamburg to-day, first to pay a return visit to Waldersee at Altona, and afterwards to make a few calls in Hamburg. He had not left, however, before lunch, at which he joined us, in undress uniform and wearing an order. He was back again in time for dinner. He had not found Waldersee at home, and at the other houses also had only met the ladies. At table there was a great deal of talk about the torchlight procession with which the Prince's Hamburg admirers wished to celebrate his birthday here on the 1st of April. It was anticipated that 3,000 to 4,000 persons would come to Friedrichsruh by special trains to take part in the procession. They could marshal their torches and go through their evolutions with tolerable ease in the meadows on the right bank of the Aue.

At lunch the Chief said that after all it was not necessary that I should copy the metallographic documents here. I could do that at my leisure in Leipzig—a blessing, as it would, otherwise, take me three days to do it, and the Princess expects some visitors on the 28th, for whom she wants my room. Therefore off and away at noon to-morrow! Baron Merck and his wife, whom I have known since 1888, were with us at dinner to-day. Among other things the Prince spoke of his new silverplate. It was very rich and beautiful, but his household was not at all prepared for it, and silver-plate and dishes had never been used at his table. He would, perhaps, have the chandeliers hung up, but the other things would doubtless be sent to the bank for safe keeping.

Friday, March 27th.—Took lunch alone, and somewhat earlier than usual on account of my departure. After a while the Princess, who was on this occasion particularly good-humoured and communicative, came.

Among other things she related that Schweninger's predecessor, a celebrated doctor recommended by Bleichröder, had once treated the Prince for cancer of the stomach; and that it is Versen and the "detestable Hinzpeter" who have most influence with the Emperor and who stimulate the high opinion he has of his own capacity and encourage his arbitrary tendencies. Finally the Prince also came in to say good-by, and invited me to report myself again shortly at Friedrichsruh. Then back to Berlin, and a few days later, on the 2nd of April, to Leipzig, my new home. (. . . .)

I had hoped that at length I might rest, but it was not to be. The mill must still grind on! Indeed, there is no alternative, as people would not otherwise know how I came to the extraordinary notion of writing yet another book on Bismarck, and how that scheme fared. On the 23rd of June *Kommerzienrath* Kröner, of Stuttgart, previously only known to me by name, called upon me and proposed that I should write for him a biography of the Prince. I agreed to do so in case the latter approved. With this object I next wrote the following letter to Bucher, who was again at Friedrichsruh with the old gentleman:—

"DEAR FRIEND,

"I yesterday had a visit from a Stuttgart gentleman, hitherto unknown to me, who asked if I would write a biography of the Prince, three or four volumes; I could speak out exactly as I liked, and also lay down such other conditions as were convenient to me. As he came direct from Friedrichsruh, and had there spoken to the Prince and also to you, his intention in putting this question to me was possibly known and approved of at Friedrichsruh. If that be the case, and if the

Prince gives his permission, I am disposed to make the attempt, particularly as I may then hope also to be assisted with contributions on doubtful points. I would take time and provide for complete freedom from interference on the part of the publisher and would serve the truth so far as it is known to me.

"Please, therefore, inquire to-day or to-morrow whether he gives his blessing to the affair or not, and let me know the result." (. . . .)

The following answer came from Bucher :—

"FR. 26/7/91.

"DR. FR,—Your letter of the 24th, which curiously enough bears the Leipzig postmark of the 26th, reached me last evening, and I have this morning communicated its contents. The reply ran literally : 'I have nothing whatever against it. I have sometimes a feeling that the end will come suddenly for me one day. I should like to have the opportunity of correcting many errors *viva voce*, as Busch has a great deal of material. Things are going badly with me. I have pains in my hand, and other pains which I cannot write about. When I have pushed the stone a little way uphill it rolls back again to the bottom. I wish you better luck."

On receipt of this information I finally agreed with Kröner to write the book, and entered into a contract with him. A few weeks later, however, in thinking over the prospect, I was half sorry that I had done so, and wrote to Bucher (pointing out certain objections in the event of the Prince's "Memoirs" being published, and competing with the book : and suggesting that in case they were not to appear until after Bismarck's death, judicious extracts from them might be included in the biography, &c.)

Bucher's reply:

"LAUBBACH BEI COBLENZ, *September* 1, 1891.

"DEAR FRIEND,—" Nothing will ever come of the 'Memoirs,' even if He[1] and I were to live for ten years to come. The chief hindrance is laziness, as He himself expresses it. My work can only consist in dividing up the chaos of dictated material, and uniting the pieces into mosaics, as also in correcting his chronology, which is quite untrustworthy, and of course falsifies the casual relations of things. What He has to do is to read over the chapters which I have put together, and at the same time the letters referring to the subject, which I put with them. He cannot, however, be brought to do that. Of the fourteen chapters which I have submitted to him since last September he had on my departure from Kissingen read one through, and a portion of another! In correcting his chronology in four important instances I have forced him to acknowledge that the affair cannot really have happened in the way in which he had dictated it; but it was impossible for me to squeeze out of him any statement as to what actually had occurred. I am well nigh desperate, and should be very pleased if my work were stopped and the whole thing handed over to you. I do not know what he will think, but in any case make the attempt.

"Schweninger, who is very anxious to get him to take up some serious, continuous occupation, persuaded me to go to Kissingen, assuring me that he would keep the two disturbing elements, the Princess and Herbert,

[1] "He" is given with a capital letter in original.—THE TRANSLATOR.

at a distance; we two should have him to ourselves, and he would therefore begin a new life. Nothing of the kind has occurred. It was the old lazy life in the Castle of Indolence (Schlaraffenleben) — guests and drinking every day. And, as I had suspected, the baths did me no good whatever. My right hand is greatly swollen, and it is only since I repeated my former cure here that a slight improvement is perceptible. In any case I shall be back in Berlin at the beginning of October, although He has expressed a wish that I should go direct from here to Varzin. For months together last year there was a temperature of 12 degrees in my room there, and that has ruined me.

"Ever yours (in English),

"B."

I wrote in reply from Leipzig, on September 2nd, 1891, *inter alia*: that if the "Memoirs" were never to be completed but remain mere materials, there was all the more reason for rescuing at least a portion from destruction. . . . . I would do nothing in the matter before consulting him, but I was not without hope that the Chief would allow himself to be persuaded by my arguments, and would assist me with the dictated matter in my otherwise desperate undertaking. (. . . .)

After some consideration, however, I addressed my request to the Prince direct, ... and in the course of a week, on the 17th of September, the following answer came by post:—

"Varzin, *September* 14, 1891.

"I have received your letter, and will willingly accede to your wish that I should—before its publication—look through the work which you have arranged to write. I cannot, however, as yet place what I have myself written and dictated at your disposal. It is not possible for the present to publish any part of it either directly or indirectly. Even if made public in an indirect way its accuracy would be questioned, and I should be challenged to produce my proofs.

"I should be glad to receive a short provisional communication, either written or verbal, as to the plan and contents of the work.

"v. BISMARCK."

(Probably written by Chrysander, but signed by the Prince in his own hand. Not the most favourable answer, still the "as yet" and "for the present" leaves room for hope.) (. . . .)

On the 5th of October I paid Bucher a visit in Berlin in connection with this matter. I showed him the draft of a reply I had sent within the course of a week to the Chief, and he told me he had already been informed by Schweninger. He said I ought first to have arranged with him before writing to the Prince, and mentioning his name. As it was, Bismarck would believe that he had suggested my plan respecting the "Memoirs." I was mistaken in thinking that Kröner had come to me about the biography with the knowledge and at the instance of the Prince. Kröner (who hoped to secure the publication of the "Memoirs") probably thought I would enter into competition with him, and therefore decided to come to me, and thus become his own competitor. Not very clear! As publisher of the "Memoirs" that will never be completed, and which according to Bismarck's verbal and written assurances are never to be published? It did not tally either with Bucher's present statement that the Prince was thinking of leaving two copies of the "Memoirs," one for the Emperor and one for his own sons.

Moreover, the text of these two could not be the same. One of them would have to be first trimmed and Bowdlerised, *in usum Delphini*, as—according to Bucher's own assertion—it contained a variety of things calculated to give offence. Referring to the differences between the Prince and the Emperor, Bucher stated that their origin was to be sought in the following incident, as well as in the demand with regard to the Order of 1852, and the steps which—according to Bismarck's statement—had been taken in connection with Windthorst's visit. (The Prince's account of the Windthorst incident appeared to him, Bucher, not to be credible, at least so far as the date was concerned.) On the 15th of March, as the Emperor was returning home from a drive with Bismarck, he told the latter that he wished to inform the Tsar that he intended paying him a visit of some days' duration at his estate—(I have forgotten the name of it). Bismarck dissuaded him on the ground that the Tsar liked to be alone there, and because the Emperor had not made a very favourable impression in St. Petersburg. His Majesty asked how he came to know that. B. replied through a private letter; whereupon the Emperor desired to see it. B. at first did not wish to show it; but finally, yielding to further pressure, drew it out of his pocket. The Emperor, after he had read it, ordered the carriage to stop, and set down the Chancellor at his residence.

It was evident from the foregoing that in my affair the Prince wanted to know—and in certain circumstances to alter, and probably to a great extent—whether I was in a position, and what I might perhaps be inclined to say about himself, and indeed generally. Hence Kröner's proposition. In that case, however, I could not, as I had hoped, do a service to the truth and to history, and

therefore could only write an empty book. I therefore
informed Bucher I would tell Kröner that an alteration
in my health would prevent me from carrying out our
contract, and beg him to cancel it. This was done in a
letter from Leipzig on the 11th of October; and I was
relieved from that burden and anxiety.

On the morning of the 5th of January, 1892, I again
spent an hour with Bucher at his place in Berlin, and
found him the same dear old friend. His hopeless feeling
with regard to the "Memoirs" had only grown deeper since
I saw him last. In the interval he had paid a further
long visit to Friedrichsruh, where he remained till shortly
before Christmas. He was to return again soon on the
Prince's invitation, although the gout in his hands had
begun again on the previous Sunday to give him great
trouble, and the outlook and condition of affairs in the
Sachsenwald pleased him less than ever. "Thank your
stars that you are not in my place with these 'Memoirs,'"
he said. "One's work is in every respect void of profit
and pleasure. One exhausts himself on an utterly
hopeless task, which will yield nothing for history. It is
not alone that his memory is defective, and he has little
interest in what we have done—up to the present he has
looked through very few of my packets—but he begins
also intentionally to misrepresent even plain and well-
established matters of fact and occurrences. He will
not admit his own share in anything that has failed, and
he will acknowledge no one to be of any consequence
compared to himself, except perhaps the old Emperor
(to whom he now, as a foil to the young Emperor, gives
a much higher place than he is fairly entitled to) and
General Alvensleben—I cannot say why—who concluded
the treaty with Russia and commanded at Vionville.
Falk also is now praised, perhaps because he fears he

might otherwise retort with disclosures. (But of course these "Memoirs" are not to be published at all.) He insists that he is in no way responsible for the Kulturkampf, that he did nothing to oppose Pio Nono's views respecting the Infallibility, and just as little against Arnim's mischievous ambition—although everybody knows the contrary to be the fact. As if he and his work did not shed enough light to enable men to overlook such shadows! Even in cases where his policy was brilliantly successful he will not hear of acknowledging anything, as for instance the trap which he set for Napoleon in the Spanish affair. He denied the letter to Prim until I reminded him that I myself handed it to the general in Madrid, and that the world is now well aware of it through Rothan." (So I understood the name, but perhaps he meant Grammont.) On this occasion Bucher also referred once more to his zigzag journey with Salazar and his audience with King Wilhelm at Ems. "The whole candidature of the Prince of Hohenzollern," said Bucher, "is now represented by Bismarck as having been a purely private affair of the Court, a mere family matter, although he was obliged to confess that it was discussed at a sitting of the entire Ministry."—I also added some reminiscences, but observed in conclusion that in spite of all that, the Chief remained the great political genius and saviour of the Germans. But he was not qualified to be a historian. He was to such a large extent the author of the history of the past decades that it might be called his history, but he did not understand how to relate it. Bucher, of course, agreed with me, and then continued his account of the last few weeks. Bismarck wanted to attend the Reichstag at all costs, in order to speak against the Commercial Treaties. It was in vain to point out to

him the danger of malicious and coarse attacks from the Richter and Bebel corners of the House, and to warn him that the President would now be at liberty to call him also to order. 'In that case I would answer him ironically' was the laughing reply. It was only Schweninger who succeeded in dissuading him on medical grounds.—Hoffmann, of the *Hamburger Nachrichten*, comes every week, and prints whatever the Prince says to him, quite indifferent to the fact whether it is a well-considered statement, or the contrary."
"An old copying clerk has now been set to work on the 'Memoirs,' as Chrysander, to whom I dictate my notes, is over-burdened with other things, and can no longer manage all the copying." "They are to be left as a bequest to the sons, but will hardly be published by them,"—because they know that they contain too many misrepresentations of a kind which people could detect and easily disprove, and because they are full of unjust judgments on prominent personages, as, for instance, on most of the Prince's former colleagues. At the very most, a last chapter might ultimately be published on the preliminary stages of his disgrace, and ultimate retirement. Herbert has made copious and reliable notes on this subject, in which, however, the old gentleman has made all sorts of inaccurate and false corrections. The Princess is still the same." .... On my asking after the daughter, Bucher fetched a bottle of old Hungarian wine from behind the green curtain of a bookcase. Countess Rantzau had brought it with her from Hamburg for him, and we drank a glass of it to the health of the honest and excellent lady who had always been a friend to him. "And not forgetting our old master," I added. "How is he getting on?" "Our old lion is well," he replied, "and is always in

good humour at table; eats and drinks heartily, cracks a joke, and is equal to the youngest of them in paying court to the fair ones."

In the course of his remarks Bucher mentioned as "not inconceivable" that the Prince might return one day to his old place in Berlin.—He did not give his reasons for thinking so. In the absence of such reasons, and they would have to be very good ones, I cannot believe in such a possibility, so far as he personally is concerned. It is not impossible, after the ill-success of the present *régime*, that the spirit of his policy may return to the palace in the Wilhelmstrasse.

We were not destined to meet again. Bucher died on the 12th of October, 1892, after he had lived away from the Prince for a few months. I gave a sketch of his life and character in the *Illustrirte Zeitung* of the 29th of October, which was accompanied by a good portrait.

Next spring I could find no rest until I greeted the Prince once more; and I was permitted to do so. I arrived at Friedrichsruh at 1.30 P.M. on the 1st of May. Chrysander and a servant waited for me at the station, and conducted me to the house where I was lodged in room No. 4. After a snack, which took the place of lunch, I went for a walk with Chrysander, who then showed me in one of the ground floor rooms a number of presents and beautiful addresses from Costa Rica and California, which had come to the Prince on his birthday a month previously. Before dinner I met the old gentleman in the coffee-room, where hung the portraits of his ancestors. He has changed very little. I must sit down with him on the sofa, and am "Büschlein" as before. Had I written anything lately, and what about? Complained of faceache, "which, however, comes no doubt from the sharp atmosphere out of doors during my walk this morning."—At dinner, at which we were joined by the Princess, Countess Rantzau, Dr. Schweninger, Count Herbert and von Kardorff, member of the Reichstag, my place is again next the Prince on his right. As is almost invariably the case on such occasions, he is amiable, lively and good-humoured. (. . . .)

May 2nd, at 11 *a.m.*—Schweninger called at my room as he was going away. We spoke once more about Bucher, whom he praised highly. Long before the 15th of March the doctor had known, "through his connections at Court" of the Emperor's intention to get rid of Bismarck, and had informed the latter. At 12 o'clock Chrysander summoned me to the Prince, whom I met alone in the dining-room, where he was waiting for me. I first handed him back the three metallographic copies, which I should get published in some weekly paper as they were still of interest. After I had turned the conversation on Bucher I mentioned his mission to Madrid and the letter to Prim, giving him clearly to understand that I had been fully informed by my deceased friend of every detail of his Spanish journey, and also knew that at one time he wished to deny the letter to Prim and the trap set for Napoleon, which he had baited afresh by condensing the Ems despatch. But to repudiate that would be to remove the finest leaf from his wreath of laurels, and so on. These details recalled to him the whole circumstances, and he no longer denied anything. He brought the conversation to a close with the words : " We will talk it over some other time. Of course you will remain for a while yet, and I must now speak to Kardorff." No opportunity however occurred of returning to the subject. (. . . .)

After dinner in the evening, *Commerzienrath* Kröner,

over our coffee, recommended the Prince to pay an early visit to Leipzig. The Chief Burgomaster Georgi had told him that they longed to see the Prince there, and that he would be received with universal enthusiasm. I considered it right to tone down the effect of this statement by pointing out that, in addition to sincere but silent veneration for the Prince, there was also a great deal of loud and obtrusive fustian and party self-seeking, whose sole object was its own advancement; that, together with a certain understanding for Bismarck's methods and aims, there was also a great deal of unreason; and that the great lights of the National Liberal persuasion, who held the upper hand at Leipzig, would think less of manifesting their gratitude to him than of once more giving prominence to themselves and their party, and gaining popularity for future elections to the Municipal Council or the Reichstag. Our *Geheimer Commenzienrath* was obviously unable to appreciate such an unbusinesslike argument. What I said was, however, perfectly true.

May 3rd.—Took a walk in the morning. In the garden, near the road leading to the station, was a block of sandstone with the inscription: "From Grotenburg, near the site of the monument to Arminius in the Teutoburger Wald," which was recently presented to Bismarck "by a German," a bookbinder of Detmold. He doubtless knows no more than the learned themselves where the Teutoburger Wald was really situated, but he certainly knows better than many of the learned that Bismarck is the founder of the German Empire. In addition to the Chief and his wife and daughter, only Chrysander and myself were present at lunch. Conversation: On the newspaper report that Rottenburg was about to pay the Prince a visit, of which, however, the latter knew nothing, and which is all the more improbable, as Rottenburg is just engaged to Miss Phelps, the daughter of the American Minister. The Chief mentioned that Mr. Phelps wrote to him recently, and asked for an expression of opinion on the World's Fair at Chicago—of course a favourable one. The Prince, however, does not seem inclined to do this. He said: "If I were to give an honest expression of my view it would not be what he requires. These exhibitions are of little value for industry and art, and are more for the benefit of hotel keepers and such people. They are good for those who feel bored, who want a new sensation, new amusements, and who have money enough to gratify their inclinations and afford themselves such pleasures." The most gracious and his intimates were then discussed—a General von Versen is one of the favourites. The conversation then turned on the diplomatic world, and first on Marschall, who has little capacity, but has been recommended by his Grand Duke and a relative (or an official); on von Schweinitz, who has nine children, and also on "Sardanapaul" Hatzfeldt. The Chief afterwards referred to Maximilian Harden (Witkowski), whom he praised as "a quiet unpretentious man of great tact; not at all like a Jew—and also not like my intimate friend Blum," he added, laughingly, as he looked towards the Princess. On the mention of the Grand Duke of Baden I reminded him of his letter with the words, "You cannot govern without Bismarck," and of the letter written by the Crown Prince Frederick from Portofino in which he described his son. The Chief said that he no longer had the original, and asked me to send him a copy of it. "But not direct through the post, and also not to Dr. Chrysander," suggested Countess Rantzau. "No, he will also be watched. Send it to Baron Merck, Sachsenwald bei Reinbeck; I shall then get it safely." I further referred to the King of Saxony and his regard for Bismarck, and I mentioned that a doctor, who at the time acted as Physician in Ordinary to the King at Pillnitz, told me how, immediately after the Prince's dismissal, the King travelled alone by night from Pillnitz to Berlin, probably for the purpose of a conference with the Emperor or Caprivi.

On Bötticher's name coming up after the diplomatists, the Prince placed him even below Caprivi, and concluded as follows: "Moreover, he is under petticoat government." Of Marschall he said: "He writes bad French, even in official documents, speaking for instance in a recent communication to Italy of '*l'empereur et l'empereuse.*'"

May 4th.—At lunch we were joined by Baroness Merck and a professor from Giessen, who plied the Prince with all sorts of questions, and whom we shall here entitle Herr Y. In the course of this inquisition we ascertained, among other things, that "Dutken Sommer" (in Hesekiel's book), whom I had hitherto taken to be a countrywoman, is in reality of the masculine gender, and the son of the Pastor at Reinfeld. The Prince said he was blind, and somewhat of a simpleton, while the Princess described him as musical. Y. hastily jotted that and other facts down in his pocket book while discussing his cutlet and omelette. Phelps, Chicago, and the Prince's opinion of these "World Fairs" once more. The Chief then spoke of Prince and Princess Reuss at Vienna, and of the position she took up towards the notorious rescript. ("The Uriah Letters.") She said: "My husband is a (public) servant. I am not." Somebody brought up Ahlwardt's name, and the Prince said: "He too has one merit. He brings a change into the commonplace tediousness of the Reichstag." He observed with regard to the good reception accorded to the Emperor by the Swiss : " They do nothing gratis. We shall be made to pay for it with a higher customs duty." The professor informed us that he was a vegetarian, and that it was an illness which had converted him. I mentioned the approaching advent of the editor of the *Kladderadatsch* and his friend Jacobsen, praising both of them highly. After a glance at his pocket book, Y. inquired about the attitude of France in 1866, mentioning Moustier. The Prince corrected his pronunciation of the name, and then went on to say : " Once in the course of conversation he reminded me in a threatening way of Jena. I said to him, ' If you talk to me of Jena I will talk to you of Leipzig.' I might also have mentioned Waterloo. Moustier then complained to Manteuffel, and he reported the matter to the King, who, however, said that I had acted rightly." Coming in the further course of the conversation to speak of the policy which was at that time pursued by the Italians, he said : " La Marmora was a scoundrel, and was paid by France, but Govone was a respectable man." He gave his reasons for both opinions in detail. The Prince then added, having perhaps noticed the eavesdropping publicist : " I would not have said that to Sybel if I had had any idea that he would publish it—a remark which applies to other matters mentioned to other good people, such as my worthy friend Blum, whose statements are very indiscreet and mostly false."

At 4 P.M. the professor came to my room, " in order to become better acquainted with his neighbour" ; that is, thought I to myself, to pump me too for his own purposes, *de omnibus rebus et quibusdam aliis*, according to all the rules of the art. And so it proved. He suggested a walk, and I proposed that we should go to the mill on the Aue. We had not gone a hundred yards before he set to work as I had anticipated, with a hardihood which was only equalled by its many-sidedness. Truly a thirst for knowledge of the most naïve kind, as if it were the most natural thing in the world, although it was only two hours since he set eyes on me for the first time. As at lunch, the result was in each instance immediately committed to his pocket book. What a lingual pumping apparatus that was! Now here, now there, sounding and boring, screwing and sucking! First about myself, then as to Bucher, his character as an official and in social life, &c. The Prince's turn came next, and after him the Princess, the sons, the daughter and the grandchildren. What did I think of Schweninger? How did I like Lange, who, by the way, also took lunch with us; in short, his inquiries, conducted with a peculiar thoroughness and charm, extended to everything upstairs and downstairs, chick and child, *ad infinitum*. I was even expected to give information respecting Baroness Merck. Had I observed at table that her eyes looked as if she had been crying, and that she sobbed a couple of times? And whether I knew or suspected why? In return he spontaneously revealed his own inner man unasked, and as a reward for my patience I ascertained a variety of things about himself, and also obtained some information which appeared to me to be of importance. He is to write an obituary of the Prince for the *Kölnische Zeitung*—now? He will publish an account of his visit to him—where? He had been to see him last year, if I rightly understood, at Varzin, and had been for a walk with him for nearly two hours. He is an intimate friend of Aegidi, whom, doubtless as a congenial soul, he praises to the skies, and who, he says, once gave him a document from the archives of the Foreign Office for perusal. He is a vocalist, and intends to sing something to the Princess, &c. I answered his questions, for the most part with an expression of regret at my ignorance, and where this was not possible with that description of truth which is alone expedient in the presence of embarrassing or dangerous curiosity : *Sanheden ved modification*, truth with modifications, as the Danes jestingly define lies. I took an opportunity before dinner to speak to Chrysander about this odd fish. He was, however, just on the point of fetching him to see the Prince. I thought to myself that Bucher ought to have postponed his death for a while. At dinner Y., who again diligently pumped the Prince for the benefit of his note-book, strongly urged him soon to pay a visit to South Germany and the Rhine, and held out a very tempting prospect there. The Chief, however, replied that, like Parson Primrose, he now preferred the journey from the brown bed into the blue to all others. " Were I to go, however," he continued, " I should prepare a speech once for all and learn it by heart." He added an experience of his at the time of the Erfurt Parliament : " There was one of them there who spoke often and well, and who, on one occasion, delivered a speech which I heard and liked. On my mentioning it to an acquaintance, however, he said : 'Yes, but you should have heard it last year; it was much finer then !' "

May 5th.—In the morning a letter from my little Gretchen, with greetings to the dear Prince and the whole princely family. Y. called for me again and we took a walk through the wood along the road leading to Möhnsen. The octopus again applies a new sucker : he wants to know about the " Memoirs." Had formerly on one occasion (I believe he said in 1891) seen the Prince over a pile of folio sheets. Could these have been the " Memoirs ?" I did not know, but doubted it. " I did not wish to ask him," observed the good creature. At lunch he cheerfully proceeded with the work of extracting information from the Chief. He had evidently turned a deaf ear to the indirect warning as to "indiscreet friends," or considered that full-blown professors formed an exception.

I delivered Gretchen's greetings, and was instructed to thank her very kindly. In the afternoon Chrysander came to my room and begged me to send him from Leipzig my opinion of the professor and the "intimate friend." "It is my duty," he said, "to protect his Serene Highness against tactlessness."

After dinner, when the Mercks, who had also been present, had withdrawn, there was a scene in the coffee room. The indefatigable Y. once more addressed a series of questions to the Prince, whose newspaper hour had arrived, but who nevertheless listened to him politely, until suddenly—I did not notice to what special point the sucker had been applied, but it must have been an exceptionally tender spot—he exclaimed angrily: "You should not put such questions, professor. I cannot imagine how any one can put such idiotic questions." Tableau! A thunderbolt! Silence for a moment, and then the conversation is resumed with the ladies on matters of no importance, while the Chief studies his paper. On Y. rising to leave, the Countess makes a sign to me to remain, and I talk for some time to her and the Princess. On taking leave I kiss the Chief's hand for the first time, and doubtless also for the last. He says: "Good-bye, dear old friend, but come back again soon."

In the meantime may God protect our dear old master from his new friends—his business friends! Amen!

INDEX

INDEX TO PROPER NAMES.

William I.—Prince Bismarck—Busch, the Author—France—Germany and smaller German States occur so frequently that they have not been indexed. The prefixes " von " and " de " have been generally omitted.

A.

Aali Pasha, vol. i. 417
Abeken, vol. i. 21, 26, 70, 71, 74, 75, 83, 91, 94, 104, 116 to 118, 157, 171, 211, 226, 229, 252, 296, 323, 337, 342, 344, 358, 377, 386, 388, 389, 404, 405, 409, 412, 415, 416, 419, 421, 425, 427, 428, 447, 453, 456, 458, 486, 488, 490, 515, 519, 533; vol. ii. 24, 25, 26, 28, 44, 72, 79, 80, 81, 113, 124, 126, 143, 147, 162, 165, 170, 244, 340, 445; vol. iii. 13, 42, 43, 121, 249
Abel, vol. ii. 432
Abzac, d', vol. ii, 299, 300.
Adalbert, Prince, vol. i. 402, 561; vol. ii. 226
Adelebsen, vol. ii. 110
Adlerberg, vol. i. 411; vol. iii. 282, 283, 286
Aegidi, vol. ii. 13, 78, 79, 105, 106, 115, 116, 119, 123, 148, 149, 161, 173, 183, 188, 189, 194, 195, 197, 202, 203, 205, 220, 223, 224, 233, 239 to 241, 247, 250, 252, 254, 256, 257, 281; vol iii. 386
AFGHANISTAN, vol. ii. 456; vol. iii. 119, 121, 124, 133, 135, 150
Aftonblad, vol. ii, 155
Agence Havas, vol. i. 43
Ahlwardt, vol. iii. 384
Albedinski, vol. ii. 43
Albedyll, vol. iii. 316, 335
Albert, Prince Consort of England, vol. iii. 43, 45, 177

Albrecht, Archduke, vol. i. 16, 17, 178, 179, 232, 272; vol. ii. 411
Alençon, Duc d', vol. i. 365
Alexander II., Emperor. See Russia, Tsar of
Alexander III., Emperor. See Russia, Tsar of
Alexandrine, Princess, vol. ii. 404, 405, 418
Allgemeine Zeitung, vol. i. 308; vol. ii. 172; vol. iii. 356
Alopaeus, vol. ii. 4, 32
Alphonso, vol. i. 41.
Alten, Major v., vol. i. 148, 291, 311, 318, 319, 350, 352
Altvater, vol. i. 442
Alvensleben, Count, vol. i. 106, 107, 195; vol. ii. 143, 164, 402; vol. iii. 125, 206, 225, 228, 378
Amelia, Queen of Greece, 135
AMERICA, vol. i. 9, 176, 238, 241, 242, 250 to 252, 265, 283, 354, 386, 429, 465, 472, 526, 558; vol. ii. 46, 76, 205, 378, 383, 386, 397, 450, 473; vol. iii. 82, 85, 213
Andrae-Roman, vol. iii. 116 to 118, 126, 208
Andrassy, vol. i. 463; vol. ii. 83, 122, 128, 129, 132, 181, 182, 190, 191, 197, 198, 202, 410, 411, 423; vol. iii. 143, 257 to 260, 266, 273 to 276, 287, 288, 291, 309
Anethan, d', vol. ii. 81, 85
Angelis, vol. ii. 212; vol. iii. 155
Angoulême, Duc d', vol. i. 36

INDEX

Antonelli, Cardinal, vol. i. 17, 417; vol. ii. 103, 204, 212
Aosta, Duke of, vol. i. 313
Apponyi, vol. ii. 181
Arabi Pasha, vol. iii. 52
Archbishop of Reims, vol. i. 167
Arco, vol. iii. 343
Armand le Chevalier, vol. i. 540
Arnim, Harry, vol. i. 136 to 215, 307, 416, 417, 431, 457, 506; vol. ii. 29, 30, 74, 117, 127, 133, 147, 163, 166, 222, 235, 236, [237, 260 to 266, 279, 286, 332, 476, 477, 478; vol. iii. 9, 44, 218, 362, 378
Arnim, Boitzenburg, vol. i. 306
Arnim, Heinrich, vol. ii. 25
Arnim, Krochlendorff, vol. i. 402
Ascher, vol. iii. 5
Auber, vol. i. 60
Auersberg, Adolph, vol. iii. 2
Auerswald, vol. ii. 333; vol. iii. 22
Augsburger Allgemeine Zeitung, 6; vol. ii. 197, 308, 423
Augustenburger. See Frederick VIII of Schleswig-Holstein
Aumale, Duc d', vol. ii. 199, 207
Aunay, d', vol. i. 560
AUSTRIA-HUNGARY, vol. i. 21, 24, 30, 31, 32, 41, 136, 174, 179, 180, 207, 220, 257, 270, 278, 279, 288, 299, 310, 329, 334, 335, 339, 341, 351, 363, 366, 373, 374, 382, 410, 431, 432, 434, 452, 544; vol. ii. 42, 52, 57, 82, 89, 102, 110, 112, 114, 119, 123, 127, 128, 137, 142, 147, 148, 158, 172, 180 to 182, 190, 191, 197, 200, 201, 210, 213, 248, 250, 304, 318, 326, 337, 343, 348, 386, 392, 393, 395, 404 to 406, 408, 409, 411, 412, 431, 479 to 481; vol. iii. 21 to 26, 43, 44, 52, 62, 76, 79, 81, 83 to 85, 87, 119, 130, 148, 149, 160, 170, 182, 216, 218, 224, 226, 227, 246, 250, 254, 258 to 292, 301, 352, 354
Austria, Emperor of, vol. i. 178; vol. ii. 85, 113 to 115, 119, 122, 216 to 219, 265, 266, 326, 407, 412; vol. iii. 87, 216, 219
    Archduchess Gisela of, vol. ii. 194
    Archduchess Sophia of, vol. ii. 115
Avenir de Loire et Cher, vol. ii. 46

B.

Bach, vol. ii. 179; vol. iii. 218
Back, vol. ii. 97
Baden, Grand Duchess of, vol. i. 175; vol. ii. 273, 274; vol. iii. 140
Baden, Grand Duke of, vol. i. 292, 305, 403, 501; vol. ii. 273; vol. iii. 183, 198, 204, 247, 316, 332, 336, 356
Balan, vol. ii. 27, 73, 80, 124, 175, 216, 224, 245, 251, 252, 256
Bamber, vol. i. 84
Bamberger, vol. i. 103, 168, 222, 223, 233, 255, 286, 350, 361, 362, 484, 493; vol. ii. 86, 87, 187, 200, 385, 388, 436, 453, 454, 458, 473, 484; vol. iii. 36
Bancroft, vol. ii. 401
Banneville, vol. i. 18
Bargatinsky, vol. iii. 265
Barral, vol. i. 400
Barrot, vol. i. 440
Bastide, vol. ii. 76
Battenberg, Alex., vol. iii. 149, 171 to 174, 180 to 182, 292, 315, 316, 335
Baude, vol. ii. 81
Baudelot, Widow, vol. i. 140, 141
Bauer, vol. ii. 119
Bauer, Caroline, vol. ii. 421
Bauffremont, Duc de, vol. i. 288
Bavaria, King of, vol. i. 178, 246, 256, 319, 323, 348, 357, 359, 400, 431, 463, 464, 465, 523, 561; vol. ii. 50, 138, 142, 169, 217, 226, 325, 332; vol. iii. 198, 293, 300, 321, 332
    Prince Luitpold of, vol. i. 98, 127, 165, 168, 178, 179, 180, 329, 360, 464, 562; vol. ii. 126, 194; vol. iii. 87, 213, 293
    Prince Otto of, vol. i. 331, 562; vol. ii. 126, 143
    Prince Charles of, vol. i. 410, 431
    Queen of, vol. ii. 296; vol. iii. 140
Bazaine, Marshal, vol. i. 95, 126, 131, 271, 319; vol. iii. 303
Beaconsfield, Lord, vol. ii. 423, 430, 456
Beatrice, Princess of England vol. iii. 174
Beaufort, d'Hautpoule, vol. i. 507, 508
Bebel, vol. ii. 57, 81; vol. iii. 379

INDEX

Bechtoldsheim, vol. ii. 190
Beckedorff, vol. i. 422
Becker, vol. iii. 106
Beckmann, vol. ii. 237
Beckx, vol. iii. 67
Belgians, King of the, vol. i. 430; vol. iii. 138, 178
BELGIUM, vol. i. 60, 63, 142, 176, 177, 295, 430, 501; vol. ii. 54, 57, 81, 82, 85, 124, 126, 166, 192; vol. iii. 272
Below, vol. iii. 128
Benda, vol. ii. 473
Benedetti, vol. i. 22, 60, 61 to 63, 193, 288, 544; vol. ii. 33, 117, 118, 154, 340
Bennigsen, vol. i. 7, 30, 233, 270, 272, 274; vol. ii. 281, 388, 437, 453; vol. iii. 28, 30, 31, 34 to 37, 142
Berg, vol. ii. 44
Berghen, vol. i. 485; vol. iii. 146
Bergmann, vol. iii. 175, 316
Berlichingen, vol. iii. 164
Bernhardi, vol. i. 493
Bernhardt, vol. ii. 304
Bernstorff, Count, vol. i. 135, 198, 203, 213, 319, 342, 345, 386, 417, 428, 443, 455, 458, 469, 489, 509, 512, 517, 554, 559; vol. ii. 43, 83, 90, 138
Bernus, vol. ii. 52
Bernuth, vol. ii. 457, 461, 473
Beseler, vol. ii. 473
Besseda, vol. ii. 214
Beust, vol. i. 17, 18, 20, 30, 175, 176, 179, 188, 253, 277 to 279, 286, 314, 339, 434, 453, 463, 553; vol. ii. 42, 52, 83 to 85, 88, 117, 120 to 122, 126, 129, 131 to 133, 137, 138; vol. iii. 170, 171, 186, 187
Beuthner, vol. ii. 164
Beyer, vol. i. 501
Biedermann, vol. ii. 172
Biegeleben, vol. i. 314; vol. ii. 89
Biron, vol. i. 193; vol. ii. 256
Bismarck, Princess (Countess Johanna), vol. i. 251, 273, 289, 384, 387, 411; vol. ii. 32, 205, 221, 246, 281 to 283, 324, 332, 335, 359, 420; vol. iii. 14, 66, 106, 107, 109, 110, 112, 131, 199, 206, 208, 231, 246, 255, 293, 297, 298, 312, 320, 329, 344, 348, 352, 370, 374, 379, 381 to 384, 386, 388

Bismarck, Herbert, vol. i. 89, 102, 108, 289, 537, 543, 550, 551; vol. ii. 219, 283, 312, 315, 317, 319, 363, 365, 416, 424, 449, 483; vol. iii. 5, 10, 13 to 15, 42, 58, 60, 73, 101, 118 to 120, 125, 131, 135, 137, 143, 146, 231, 233, 246, 293, 303, 307, 312 to 314, 333, 337 to 341, 343, 344, 361, 374, 379, 381
 William, vol. i. 95, 129, 291, 389, 444, 447, 448, 453, 454; vol. ii. 281, 282, 381; vol. iii. 10, 16, 33, 34, 42, 89, 97 to 99, 109, 145, 231, 345
 Heinrich, vol. iii. 92
 Philip, vol. i. 189
 -Bohlen, vol. i. 34, 69, 70, 71, 74, 83, 91, 98, 113, 131, 141, 148, 149, 163, 165, 168, 169, 171, 183, 190, 195, 205, 213, 229, 254, 258, 280, 284, 305 to 307, 314, 318, 321, 322, 330, 349, 351, 354, 358 to 360, 396, 425, 435, 483, 487 to 489, 495, 498, 499, 501, 503, 504, 515, 516, 518, 519, 543; vol. ii. 27, 123, 162, 372; vol. iii. 205
 Marie. See Rantzau, Countess.
Bissinger, vol. i. 387
Bitter, vol. ii. 453
Blankenburg, vol. i. 233, 270, 272, 274; vol. ii. 261, 317. 318, 328; vol. iii. 126, 128, 129
Bleibtreu, vol. i. 321
Bleichröder, vol. i. 271, 518, 532, 554; vol. ii. 317, 318, 432, 454; vol. iii. 62, 63, 67, 68, 74, 75, 79, 80, 161, 188, 198, 233, 312, 371
Blind, vol. i. 541
Blome, vol. i. 451
Bloomfield (Lady), vol. iii. 94
Blowitz, vol. ii. 394, 395, 441, 442
Blum, vol. iii. 383, 385
Blumenthal, Gen., vol. i. 151, 181, 203, 354, 477; vol. ii. 337, 345
Bock, Dr., vol. i. 6
Bockh, vol. ii. 19
Bodelschwingh, vol. ii. 462; vol. iii. 232
Boersen Zeitung, vol. i. 13, 44; vol. ii. 375; vol. iii. 161, 188, 198, 343

BOHEMIA, vol. i. 34, 270; vol. ii. 112, 114, 120, 122, 147, 176, 177, 178, 179, 180, 326, 405
Bohmen, vol. iii. 127
Bojanowski, vol. iii. 137
Bölsing, [Sec., vol. i. 71, 174, 213, 229; vol. ii. 12, 164
"Bonbonnière," vol. ii. 274 to 279; 284, 287, 296
Bonnechose, vol. i. 417, 424, 428, 439; vol. iii. 213
Borck, vol. i. 135, 303, 483
Borel, vol. ii. 76, 77, 79
Bose, vol. ii. 117
BOSNIA, vol. iii. 277
Bothmer, Gen. v., vol. i, 146, 207, 293
Bötticher, vol. ii. 476; vol. iii. 93, 151, 210, 214, 298, 314, 341, 356, 367, 368
Bourbaki, vol. i. 383, 447, 482
Böuterweck, vol. ii. 111
Boyen, Gen. v., vol. i. 161, 171
Boyer, Gen., vol. i. 252, 253, 265
Brandenburg, vol. iii. 362
Brandenstein, vol. iii, 358
Brandt, vol. ii. 15; vol. iii. 9
Brass, vol. i. 16, 17, 33, 55, 213, 308; vol. ii. 48, 86 to 88, 101, 103, 105, 173, 191, 217, 339
Brater, vol. iii. 195
Bratiano, vol. ii. 129
Brauer, vol. iii. 203, 208
Braun, vol. ii. 52, 127
Bray, vol. i. 23, 190, 220, 221, 233, 360, 410, 428, 431, 523, 534; vol. ii. 53, 117, 221; vol. iii. 198
Breintz, v., vol. i. 113
Bright II. 435
Brincourt, vol. ii. 43
Bronsart, vol. i. 349
Brühl, Count, vol. i. 169; vol. ii. 462
Brunnow, vol. i. 418; vol. ii. 90
Buch, L. v. vol. i. 415
Buchanan, Sir A. vol. i. 343
Bucher, Lothar, vol. i. 4, 16, 18, 34 to 37, 39, 43, 45, 60, 62, 71, 225, 226, 230, 241 to 243, 257, 319, 328, 335, 340, 349, 366, 371, 377, 383, 388, 391, 422, 431, 440, 448, 460, 483, 484, 499, 519, 520, 532, 561; vol. ii. 12, 13, 15 to 23, 25, 28, 41, 44, 48, 71, 72, 78, 79, 82, 105, 108, 117, 123, 137, 138, 144, 151, 162 to 164, 166, 167, 170, 172 to 176, 183, 191, 193, 199, 202 to 206, 209 to 211, 217, 219, 220, 221, 223, 224, 233 to 235, 239, 241, 245, 251 to 253, 255 to 258, 260, 263 to 266, 272 to 275, 279, 281, 288, 294, 296, 301, 302, 305, 311, 312, 328, 342, 354, 357, 372, 395, 399, 400, 433, 444, 445, 448, 449, 467; vol. iii. 1, 3 to 6, 9 to 13, 15, 16, 41 to 43, 45 to 48, 60 to 68, 70 to 75, 80, 93, 112 to 116, 118, 119, 121, 123 to 125, 130 to 137, 142 to 146, 154 to 156, 169, 171, 184, 185, 187, 189, 198, 298, 306, 307, 337 to 348, 350 to 355, 357, 359, 372 to 381, 386, 387
Buchner, vol. ii. 96
Budberg, vol. i. 510
Buhl, vol. iii. 352
BULGARIA, vol. ii. 165; vol. iii. 148, 149, 171
Bülow, vol. ii. 11, 21, 22, 219, 240, 255, 356, 357, 372, 399, 400, 402, 403, 406, 424, 453, 467; vol. iii. 4, 18, 262, 264, 266, 285, 289, 296
Bülow of Mecklenburg, vol. ii. 27, 273
Bunsen, George, vol. iii. 46, 138
Bunsen, Josias, vol. ii. 24; vol. iii. 4, 42 to 46, 53, 110, 178, 225
Bunsen, Theodore, vol. iii. 44, 46, 224
Buol, vol. ii. 318, 334, 339; vol. iii. 218, 224
Burgomaster of Apolda, vol. i. 138
Burnaki, vol. ii. 57
Burnside, Gen., vol. i. 215, 216, 219, 237, 246, 250, 269
Busch (Under Sec.), vol. ii. 445, 449; vol. iii. 13, 59, 68, 93, 124, 137, 144, 306
Byglewski, vol. ii. 126

C

Cahn, vol. ii. 68, 69
Calonne, vol. ii. 130, 131
Calvel, vol. i. 507
Cambriel, vol. i. 400

INDEX

Camphausen, vol. i. 14, 33, 505 ; vol. ii. 164, 267, 279, 288, 289, 290, 457, 458, 459, 461, 462 ; vol. iii. 239, 362
Canrobert, vol. i. 271
Canstein, Gen., vol. i. 106
Capalti, Cardinal, vol. i. 27
Caprivi, vol. ii. 22 ; vol. iii. 214, 318, 345, 352, 384
Carlyle, Thomas, vol. i. 378
Casimir-Perier. *See* Perier
Castelneau, Gen., vol. i. 153, 161
CENTRAL ASIA, vol. iii. 131
Chamberlain, J., vol. iii. 58
Chambord, Comte de, vol. i. 267, 269, 484 ; vol. ii. 74, 81, 90, 162, 207
Chancy, Gen., vol. i. 383
Charette, vol. i. 295
Chaudory, vol. i. 278, 392, 393, 395, 399, 467, 468, 469, 518
Chauvin, Gen., vol. i. 292
CHINA, vol. iii. 153, 284
Chrysander, vol. iii. 337, 344, 352, 375, 379 to 383, 387, 388
Cissey, vol. ii. 208
Clam-Martinitz, vol. ii. 121
Clary, vol. ii. 43
Cluseret, vol. ii. 58, 59, 60, 61, 69
Cobden, vol. ii. 18 ; vol. iii. 2, 3, 7, 8
Coburg, Duke Ernest of, vol. iii. 178, 184, 186
Coburg, Grand Duke of, 143, 146, 147, 238, 259, 280, 293, 294, 296, 397, 403, 428, 486, 564 ; vol. ii. 162, 306, 368, 390 ; vol. iii. 198, 249 to 252
Cochery, 38, 296
Cockerell, 454, 455
Coffin, vol. iii. 207
Cogalniceano, vol. ii. 129
Constitutionnel, vol. i. 32, 45, 83
Coppet, vol. i. 269
Costenoble, vol. ii. 338
Courier, vol. ii. 260
Courier de la Champagne, vol i. 172
Cousa, vol. ii. 129
Cremieux, vol. i. 382, 553
Crimean War, vol. i. 59, 203, 407 ; vol. ii. 248 ; vol. iii. 132, 179
Crispi, vol. iii. 332
Crown Prince. *See* German Emperors
Crown Princess. *See* German Empress

Cumberland, Duke of. *See* Hanover, King of
Curia. *See* Pope.
Czartoryski, vol. ii. 128, 147, 222, 297
Czas, vol. ii. 297
Czechs. *See* Bohemia
Czernicki, vol. i. 157

D

Daily News, vol. i. 285, 308 ; vol. iii. 124
Daily Telegraph, vol. i. 238, 379, 519 ; vol. ii. 418, 433, 446, 448, 449, 476, 477 ; vol. iii. 4, 5, 15, 132, 134, 136, 137, 188, 306, 308, 310, 341, 356
Dalwigk, vol. i. 430, 443
Danton, vol. i. 383
Darboy, vol. ii. 145
Darenthal, vol. iii. 145
Darmstadt, Grand Duchess Mathilde of, vol. i. 484
Grand Duke of, vol. ii. 174
Daru, 22, 23 ; vol. ii. 144, 145
Darwin, vol. iii. 233
Dauphinot, vol. i. 167
Daxenberger, vol. ii. 221
Decker, vol. ii. 244
Deichmann, vol. i. 66, 68
Delacroix, vol. i. 213
Delbrück, vol. i. 14, 171, 233, 246, 256, 257, 267, 276, 284, 287, 289, 292, 302, 307, 325, 339, 383, 390, 391, 415, 430, 450, 451, 494, 507, 512, 523 ; vol. ii. 6, 75, 130, 230, 265, 267, 279, 307, 385, 386, 397, 422, 435 ; vol. iii. 29 to 31
DENMARK, vol. i. 30, 31, 54, 477, 526 ; vol. ii. 214, 215, 343, 389, 392 ; vol. iii. 205
Denmark, King of, vol. i. 174 ; vol. ii. 69, 329, 337
Derosne, vol. ii. 396
Dessau, Duke of, vol. i. 414
Deutsche Presse, vol. ii. 223, 251
Deutsche Reichszeitung, vol. ii. 147
Deutsche Revue, vol. ii. 467 ; vol. iii. 20, 21, 32, 44
Deutsche Rundschau, vol. iii. 191 to 193, 196, 199, 203, 204, 212, 214
Deutsche Zeitung (Vienna), vol. ii. 252

Dewitz, vol i. 388
Dhuleep-Singh, vol. iii. 169
Diest, vol. ii. 284, 304, 317, 318, 453; vol. iii. 39, 83, 126, 168
Dietze, vol. i. 337; vol. ii. 294, 322, 382
Dilke, Sir C., vol. iii. 58
Dixon, Hepworth, vol. ii. 214, 215, 216
Doerr, vol. i. 30; vol. ii. 124, 164
Döllinger, vol. ii. 51, 52; vol. iii. 214
Dombrowsky, vol. ii. 54, 55, 57
Dönhoff, Count, vol. i. 165, 478, 550; vol. ii. 117
Drei-Kaiser Bund, vol. i. 178; vol. ii. 393
Droits de l'Homme, vol. i. 381
Ducrot, Gen., vol. i. 189, 219, 252, 270, 276, 289, 352, 383, 397, 400, 443
Dufferin, Lord, vol. ii. 391, 395; vol. iii. 132, 133
Duncker, vol. iii. 239
Dupanloup, Bishop, vol. i. 332; vol. ii. 276, 382
Duparc, vol. i. 526
Düring, vol. ii. 109
Dürrbach, vol. i. 507, 510, 511
Dusch, vol. ii. 119
Duval, vol. i. 166
Duvernois, vol. i. 417, 455, 512; vol. ii. 125
Dziennik Poznanski, vol. ii. 163

E

Ebers, vol. ii. 110
Eckart, vol. ii. 137, 214, 233; vol. iii. 62
Edwards, vol. iii. 216
Egloffstein, vol. ii. 227
Baroness v., vol. ii. 227
EGYPT, vol. iii. 51 to 53, 62, 131, 133 142
Eichmann, vol. i. 440; vol. ii. 117
Eisenhart, vol. i. 431; vol. ii. 51, 142, 143
Engel, vol. i. 142, 148, 149, 182, 274, 287, 389
Engelmann, vol. ii. 251
ENGLAND, vol. i. 24, 42, 54 to 57, 140, 174, 199, 241, 242, 252, 278, 312, 317, 319, 323, 329, 330, 334, 343, 358, 371, 376, 384, 385, 416, 419, 432, 438, 452, 454, 458, 467 to 469, 471 to 474, 477, 481, 499, 500, 526, 538, 550, 552, 554; vol. ii. 18, 47, 49, 54, 82, 84, 85, 126, 139, 148, 157, 158, 205, 260, 291, 292, 297 to 299, 308, 309, 337, 339, 348, 383, 386, 393, 396, 397, 405. 410, 418, 431, 450, 456; vol. iii. 5, 45, 51 to 53, 57, 58, 62, 83, 95, 110, 115, 116, 119 to 125, 131 to 136, 140, 142 to 146, 149, 150, 152, 154, 171, 174, 175, 177, 179, 180, 183 to 186, 205, 206, 213, 218, 226, 252, 269, 282, 284, 285, 287, 291, 317, 325 to 327, 352, 353
Queen Victoria, vol. i. 69, 315, 338, 354; vol. ii. 139, 158, 277, 297, 298, 306, 413; vol. iii. 53, 95, 140, 169, 171, 174, 178, 180 to 183, 185 to 191, 196, 198, 213, 250, 316, 325, 326
Prince of Wales, vol. ii. 116, 413
Princess of Wales, vol. ii. 116
Princess Beatrice, vol. iii. 174
Erkert, vol. ii. 281, 315, 317
Ernsthausen, vol. i. 458
Esquiros, vol. i. 267, 268
Ester, d', vol. iii. 21
Esterhazy, vol. i. 363, 364, 544
Eugénie, Empress, vol. i. 33, 36, 45, 135, 169, 204, 283, 417, 428, 490, 535; vol. ii. 90, 142, 144 to 146, 186, 276, 288, 295
Eulenburg, vol. i. 16, 203, 481; vol. ii. 228 to 231, 371, 468 to 470; vol. iii. 30, 35, 234, 321

F

Fabrice, vol. ii. 45, 53, 59, 60, 61, 65, 66, 74, 75, 79, 80, 90, 91, 92, 93; vol. iii. 107
Faidherbe, vol. i. 383; vol. ii. 208
Falk, vol. ii. 309, 369, 402, 422, 423
Falkenstein, Vogel v. vol. i. 77, 277, 324, 525; vol. ii. 186
Fatio, Miss Jenny, vol. ii. 315, 328, 335
Favre, Jules, vol. i. 169, 174, 182, 188, 190, 191 to 193 196, 197, 204, 208, 211 to 214, 229, 231

269, 282, 285, 288, 290, 356, 362, 400, 421, 443, 460, 467 to 469, 471 to 473, 477, 483, 484, 486 to 490, 495 to 497, 498, 502, 507 to 509, 511 to 513, 516, 518, 519, 521, 525, 526, 531, 533, 534, 537, 541 to 545, 547, 548, 550, 551, 553, 563; vol. ii. 56, 57, 61, 63, 65, 68, 71, 73 to 75, 84, 88, 90, 93 to 95, 97 to 99, 208
Fersen vol. iii. 371
Figaro, vol. i. 326, 560
Figaro (Berlin), vol. ii. 254
Finkenstein, vol. i. 94, 97, 101
FitzJames, Duc de, vol. i. 198 to 200
Fleming, vol. iii. 203
Fleury, vol. ii. 125, 126, 165
Forbes, Archibald, vol. i. 308
Forchhammar, vol. ii. 462
Forckenbeck, vol. i. 7, 505 to 507; vol. ii. 462, 470; vol. iii. 30, 56, 138, 163
Forsythe, vol. i. 90, 96, 132
Fourichon, vol. i. 382
Fouriere, vol. i. 118
Franchi, vol. i. 417
Francke, vol iii. 249
Franco-German War (Declaration), vol. i. 49
  Battle of Wörth, vol. i. 65
  Gravelotte, vol. i. 85, 102
  Beaumont, vol. i. 132, 138
  Sedan, vol. i. 141 to 162
  Bombardment of Paris, vol. i. 427
  Prelim. Treaty Peace, vol. ii. 40
Frankenberg, Count, vol. i. 320, 389, 390
Frankenstein, vol. iii. 312
Frankfurter Zeitung, vol. ii. 115, 116, 122; vol. iii. 184
Frederick VIII. of Schleswig-Holstein, vol. i. 110, 113, 140, 174, 293, 354; vol. ii. 33, 306, 307, 390; vol. iii. 205, 213, 257
Frederick the Great, vol. i. 73, 203, 293, 338, 412; vol. ii., 3
Frederick William III., vol. i., 370; vol. ii., 261
Frederick William IV., vol. i. 304; vol. ii. 186, 261, 262, 334; vol. iii. 44, 210, 215, 225, 310, 314, 324
Frederick, Crown Prince and Emperor; see Germany

Freiberg, Maj., vol. i. 113, 165
Fremden-Blatt, vol. ii. 249, 250
Frese, vol. ii. 52, 113, 481
Freycinet, vol. iii. 53
Freydorf, v., vol. i. 9
Freytag, vol. ii. 306; vol. iii. 65, 195, 205, 238
Friedberg, vol. iii. 173, 256, 297
Friedenthal, vol. i. 7, 233, 270, 272; vol. ii. 422, 423, 424, 457, 461, 462
Friederich, vol. ii. 141
Friedländer, vol. ii. 353
Fries, v., vol. i. 115
Friesen, vol. ii. 117
Fröbel, vol. ii. 123
Fuchs-Nordhof, vol, i. 121
Fürstenstein, vol. i. 217

G

Gablentz, vol. ii. 85; vol. iii. 87, 88, 115
Gabriac, vol. i. 413; vol. ii. 70, 127
Gagern, vol. i. 314; vol. ii. 89, 381; vol. iii. 224
Galiffet, vol. i. 196
Gambetta, vol. i. 169, 253, 268, 271, 290, 380, 400, 408, 409, 413, 414, 415, 417, 433, 459, 468, 506, 516, 521, 526, 531, 536, 537, 538, 540, 541, 545, 548, 550, 551, 553, 556; vol. ii. 55, 199, 207, 208, 222, 235, 236, 249, 423, 468; vol. iii. 11, 12, 32, 53
Gans, vol. ii. 14
Garibaldi, vol. i. 53, 245, 267, 294, 304, 311, 330, 380, 399, 526, 532, 533; vol. ii. 49, 55, 79, 118; vol. iii. 46
Gartenlaube, vol. ii. 268, 280, 311, 320, 362, 366
Gasser, vol. ii. 217, 221, 227
  Fr. v., vol. i. 524
Gaulois, vol. i. 371
Gauthier, vol. i. 268, 276
Gazette du Midi, vol. i. 267; 268
Geffcken, vol. ii. 273, 306; vol. iii. 43, 204, 233, 255, 256, 297 to 299, 303
Gegenwart, vol. ii. 206
Georgi, vol. iii. 382
Gerlach, vol. i. 368; vol. ii. 187, 334; vol. iii. 60, 129, 130, 210, 211, 215, 216, 218 to 225, 352

Germania, vol. ii. 173, 192, 294, 367, 419
German Emperor, Frederick, vol. i. 101, 109, 110, 113, 139, 146, 147, 164, 181, 185, 198, 203, 227, 231, 232, 238, 244, 246, 257, 291, 292, 315, 328, 330, 332, 333, 338, 344, 354, 356, 360, 399, 402, 403, 408 to 413, 459, 477, 484, 551; vol. ii. 116, 253, 319, 336, 337, 367, 368, 389, 405, 413, 421; vol. iii. 56, 65, 84, 90, 93, 110, 115, 133, 136, 138, 140, 150, 151, 161, 163, 167, 172, 175 to 177, 181, 185, 187 to 192, 194 to 198, 203 to 206, 212 to 214, 232, 234 to 245, 248 to 251, 255 to 257, 262 to 276, 292 to 301, 315 to 321, 334, 341, 354, 358, 364, 383
German Emperor William II., vol. iii. 56, 61, 171, 172, 184, 188, 201, 202, 231, 257, 294 to 296, 310, 314, 315, 318, 331, 333 to 336, 346, 356 to 358, 362 to 367, 376, 377, 383 to 385
German Empress Augusta, vol. i. 138, 164, 175, 187, 293, 320, 332, 335, 338, 367, 368, 422, 448, 458, 499, 529; vol. ii. 162, 183 to 187, 269, 274, 275, 277, 278, 284, 287, 319, 368, 369, 416, 479; vol. iii. 59, 67, 68, 94, 141, 180, 203, 239, 251, 296, 302, 321, 353, 354
German Empress Frederick (Victoria), vol. i. 139, 293, 315, 325, 354, 397, 422, 458, 500; vol. ii. 116, 253, 269, 289, 336, 337, 368, 389; vol. iii. 95, 111, 132, 138, 139, 151, 171, 172, 177, 183, 185, 188, 194 to 196, 198, 232, 238, 239, 245, 293, 297, 316
Gerstäcker, vol. ii, 423
Ghika, vol. ii. 129
Gichtel, vol. iii. 128
Giers, vol. iii. 108 to 110, 150, 159, 181, 282, 283, 286
Giskra, vol. i. 544
Gladstone, vol. i. 559; vol. ii. 18, 418, 442, 456, 468; vol. iii. 47, 52, 58, 61, 111, 115, 119, 123, 143, 145, 156, 163
Glais-Bizoins, vol. i. 382
Glasbrenner, vol. ii. 223

Glaser, vol. iii. 2
Gletty, vol. i. 327
Gneist, vol. ii. 422; vol. iii. 14
Gobineau, vol. i. 561
Goeben, Gen., vol. i. 132
Goëthe, vol. i. 138, 337; vol. ii. 185
Goldammer, vol. iii. 233
Golos, vol. ii. 215, 391, 394
Goltz, vol. i. 135, 136, 416, 489; vol. ii. 255, 263, 278, 446, 447; vol. iii. 49, 50, 134, 248
Gontaut-Biron, vol. ii. 302
Gortschakoff, vol. i. 312, 325, 350, 358, 384, 413, 510, 515, 559; vol. ii. 70, 122, 135, 136, 148, 187, 201, 204, 391, 393 to 395; vol. iii. 277, 279, 281
Goulard, vol. ii. 73, 74
Govone, vol. iii. 385
Graham, Sir G., vol. iii. 133
Grammont, Duc de, vol. i. 34, 38, 39, 43, 45, 47, 58, 60, 61, 82, 343, 353, 371; vol. ii. 80, 81; vol. iii. 170, 378
Granville, Lord, vol. i. 55, 56, 57, 174, 269, 279, 312, 350, 430, 468, 471, 473, 519, 559; vol. iii. 120
Grävenitz, vol. i. 402
Grenzboten, vol. i. 3; vol. ii. 148, 151, 172, 176, 258, 270, 275, 289, 294, 297, 302, 305, 316, 366, 369, 371, 372, 380, 390, 391, 396, 400, 407, 416, 418, 425, 426, 432, 433, 434, 445, 450, 454, 468, 475, 476; vol. iii. 3, 6, 7, 33, 36, 42, 43, 46, 47, 71, 76, 77, 81, 84, 85, 92, 94, 119, 121, 123 to 125, 134, 135, 151, 156, 157, 165. 169, 170, 187, 188, 195, 205, 238, 298, 303, 311, 315, 319, 337, 343
Greppi, vol. ii. 138.
Grevy, vol. ii. 199, 207
Grimm, vol. i. 366
Gruner, vol. ii. 274, 277, 305; vol. iii. 247, 248
Grunow, vol. iii. 97, 99, 102 to 104, 107, 191, 303, 304, 343
Guisolphe, vol. ii, 43
Guizot, vol. i. 26
Gundlach, vol. ii. 27, 28

H

Haber, vol. i. 440
Hagen, vol. ii. 403

Hahn, vol. i. 15, 16 ; vol. ii. 124,
  399, 434 ; vol. iii. 71
Hahn's Literary Bureau, vol. i. 41
Hähnke, vol. iii. 364
Haldy, vol. i. 69
Halifax, Bishop of, vol. i. 27
Hallberger, vol. ii. 188, 189
Hamburger Correspondenten, vol. ii.
  196, 374 ; vol. iii. 344
Hamburger Nachrichten, vol. iii.
  337, 344, 379
Hammerling, vol. iii. 338 to 340,
  350
Hammerstein, vol. iii. 166, 167
Häuel, vol. ii. 281, 413, 454, 480 ;
  vol. iii. 40
Hannoverscher Courier, vol. ii. 224,
  241, 251, 252, 258, 388
Hanover, King of, vol. i. 50 ; vol. ii.
  109, 110, 390 ; vol. iii. 297
Hansemann, vol. ii. 22
Hapsburgs, vol. i. 365, 461
Harcourt, vol. ii. 127
Harden, vol. iii. 383
Hardenberg, vol. i. 3
Harper's Monthly, vol. iii. 81, 83
Hartmann, Gen. v., vol. i. 111
Hartrott, Gen. v., vol. i. 336
Hatzfeldt, Count, vol. i. 70, 74, 82,
  83, 91, 94, 110, 114, 143, 144
  147, 157, 160, 192, 230, 239,
  240, 263, 274 to 277, 294, 296,
  308, 322, 349, 366, 371, 383,
  396, 413, 424, 487, 488, 497,
  498, 503, 510, 518, 561 ; vol.
  ii. 21, 23, 71, 282, 415, 424, 447,
  449 ; vol. iii. 4, 13, 15, 49, 58,
  59, 62, 67, 68, 82, 90, 93, 94,
  112, 118, 124, 125, 130, 136,
  141, 343, 383
Hauke, Fr., vol. iii. 180
Hausmann, vol. i. 414 ; vol. ii. 58,
  59
Haussonville, d', vol. i. 406 to 408
Hauterive, vol. ii. 154
Havas, vol. i. 43
Haye, de la, vol. ii. 65
Haymerle, vol. iii. 289, 296
Hedwig, vol. iii, 191, 348
Heffter, vol. i. 55
Hegel, vol. ii. 14, 19
Hegenberg, vol. ii. 142
Hehn, vol. ii. 22 ; vol. iii. 155, 169,
  310
Heide, vol. i. 6, 60
Heise, vol. ii. 381

Held, vol. iii. 41
Hélène, Grand Duchess, see Russia
Hell, vol. i. 193
Helmholtz, vol. iii. 165, 186
Henckel, Count, vol. i. 84, 103, 513,
  522, 554 to 556, 564 ; vol. iii.
  69
Hengst, vol. iii. 195
Hepke, vol. i. 65 ; vol. ii. 22, 23,
  253 ; vol. iii. 13, 43
Hérisson de Saulnier, vol. i. 511,
  513, 547
Hermieux, vol. i. 276
Herrfuth, vol. iii. 357, 358
Herring, vol. i. 544
Herzberg, vol. iii. 346
Herzen, vol. ii. 17
Herzog, vol. iii. 20
Hesekiel, vol. ii. 244, 331 ; vol. iii.
  29, 71, 72, 126, 384
Hesse, vol. ii. 12
Hesse, Grand Duke of, vol. i. 109,
  430
Heyking, vol. iii. 69
Hietzing, vol. ii. 110
Hill, Major, vol. i. 324
Hindersin, Gen., vol. i. 146, 315
Hinzpeter, vol. iii. 371
Hirsch, vol. iii. 62, 80
Hobrecht, vol. ii. 403
Hochschild, vol. ii. 159
Hoff, 327
Hoffmann, vol. ii. 273 ; vol. iii. 379
Hohenlohe, Cardinal, vol. ii. 195,
  196 ; vol. iii. 106
Hohenlohe, Prince, vol. i. 183, 490 ;
  vol. ii. 415, 422, 445 ; vol. iii.
  67
Hohenwart, vol. ii. 52, 112, 119, 127
Hohenzollern, Prince of, vol. i. 34,
  37, 38, 40, 43 to 47, 52, 60, 155,
  226, 313, 483 ; vol. iii. 112 to
  114, 117, 228, 362, 378
HOLLAND, vol. i. 57, 63, 257, 413,
  477, 496 ; vol. ii. 192, 397
Holland, King of, vol. i. 384
Holland, Queen of, vol. i. 151
Holstein, Count, vol. i. 71, 328,
  329, 354, 359, 360, 374, 387,
  396, 431, 561 ; vol. ii. 350
Holstein, Baron v., vol. i. 437, 445,
  454, 467, 477, 478, 517 ; vol. ii.
  59, 92, 117, 317, 319, 328, 333,
  336, 337, 341, 365, 463 ; vol.
  iii. 9, 13, 49, 60, 112, 118, 126,
  146, 289, 306, 337, 341, 343

Holtz, vol. iii. 117, 128, 208
Home, vol. i. 330
Horn, vol. i. 260
Horsitz, vol. ii. 360
Hory, vol. ii. 139
Hour, vol. ii. 262
Hoverbeck, vol. i. 28, 30; vol. ii. 87
Howard, Sir. H., vol. i. 28; vol. ii. 138, 139
Hoyos, vol. i. 304
Hubbe, vol. iii. 221
Hubener, vol. iii. 221
Hudtwalker, vol. iii. 215
Humboldt, vol. i. 368, 369; vol. ii. 185, 381
Hune, vol. iii. 312
Huster, vol. ii. 120
Hyacinth, vol. iii. 214

I

Ignatieff, vol. ii. 165; vol. iii. 259
Illustrirte Zeitung, vol. i. 454; vol. ii. 267; vol. iii. 380
Im Neuen Reich, vol. ii. 169
Imparcial, vol. i. 18, 45, 483
Indépendance Belge, vol. i. 252, 311, 365, 399, 415
Indépendant Remois, vol. i. 172
Italie, vol. ii. 197
Italy, vol. i. 41, 51, 54, 63, 178, 294, 329, 330, 340, 382, 416, 419, 457, 477, 527, 544; vol. ii. 82, 84, 102, 123, 142, 144, 167, 172, 180, 187, 192, 204, 213, 237, 419, 431; vol. iii. 165, 182, 275, 277, 289 to 291, 385
  King of, vol. i. 51, 97, 251, 429, 457; vol. ii. 103, 265, 325; vol. iii. 332
  Crown Princess of, vol. ii. 159, 160
Itzenplitz, vol. ii. 183

J.

Jacobson, vol. iii. 385
Jacoby, vol. i. 15, 185, 219, 235, 258, 259, 260, 262, 284, 324
Jahn, vol. ii. 14
Jeanjot, vol. i. 148
Jelowicki, vol. ii. 222

Jerald, Col., vol. i. 433
Jesse, Mme., vol. i. 228, 230, 233, 350, 563; vol. ii. 46, 282, 396
Joinville, Duc de, vol. i. 365
Jolivar, vol. iii. 3
Jomini, vol. ii. 391; vol. iii. 259
Journal des Débats, vol. i. 480; vol. ii. 28
Journal Officiel, vol. i. 462

K

Kaiserlingk, vol. iii. 230
Kallay, vol. ii. 197, 198
Kameke, vol. i. 557
Kapnist, vol. ii. 196, 197
Kardorff, vol. iii. 341, 381
Karlstadt, vol. i. 241
Katt, vol. i. 216, 218
Kaunitz, vol. i. 366
Kayser, vol. iii. 319, 337, 341, 344, 356
Keil, vol. ii. 268, 269
Keller, vol. i. 247, 249
Kerartry, vol. i. 264
Kerl, vol. i. 414
Kern, vol. i. 479, 483, 484
Kernitz, vol. ii. 402
Ketteler, v., vol. ii. 172, 174
Kendell, vol. i. 1, 4, 53, 54, 70, 74, 83, 91, 94, 104, 167, 176, 191 to 193, 195, 208, 211, 228, 230, 237, 258, 263, 344, 366, 369, 376, 383, 396, 408, 440, 480, 503, 509, 512, 532; vol. ii. 11, 79, 104 to 108, 110, 117, 183, 189, 190, 206, 219, 220, 223, 240, 245, 247 to 257, 260, 265, 266, 401, 415; vol. iii. 8, 13, 14, 50, 93, 131, 136, 145, 156, 165, 211, 341
Khevenhüller, vol. iii. 148
Kieler Zeitung, vol. i. 173; vol. ii. 454
Kielmansegg, vol. i. 55
Kingston, vol. iii. 306, 341, 356
Kirke, Sir J., vol. iii. 145
Klaczko, vol. i. 20, 33, 179, 544
Kladderadatsch, vol. i. 428, 501; vol. iii. 6, 385
Klapka, vol. i. 311
Kleist-Retzon. See Retzon.
Klerhalm, vol. ii. 52
Klotz, vol. iii. 10, 168
Knak, vol. iii. 126

Knobelsdorff, vol. i. 169, 214, 483
Köller, v. vol. i. 505, 506
Kölnische Zeitung, vol. i. 5, 10, 11,
   17, 20, 29, 30, 32, 34, 41, 43, 51,
   57, 99, 223, 238, 356, 399, 432,
   434, 435, 485, 546, 547 ; vol. ii.
   46, 54, 58, 66, 70, 88, 115, 133,
   138, 139, 141, 144, 148, 149, 163,
   166, 167, 170, 173, 206, 207,
   212, 214, 219, 221, 223, 224, 228,
   232 to 234, 288, 290, 292, 339,
   388 ; vol. iii. 41, 61, 76, 77, 80,
   84, 172, 184, 386
Könneritz, vol. i. 486
Kotze, vol. i. 553
Kozmian, vol. ii. 172, 173, 187, 222
Kraj, vol. i. 256
Krausshaar, vol. i. 122
Krauthofer, vol. ii. 177
Kreiss, vol. ii. 110
Krell, Chancellor, vol. i. 241
Kreuzzeitung, vol. i. 21, 48, 50, 65 ;
   vol. ii. 47, 147, 150, 160, 161,
   164, 169, 170, 187, 275, 278,
   279, 286, 287, 453 ; vol. iii. 96,
   117, 166, 251, 252, 342
Krohn, Col., vol. i. 324, 418
Kröner, vol. iii. 371, 372, 375 to
   377, 381
Krüger, vol. i. 191
Krupp, vol. ii. 209 ; vol. iii. 341
Kruse, vol. i. 223 ; vol. ii. 234, 339 ;
   vol. iii. 81
Kuehlwetter, vol. i. 103
Kühnel, vol. i. 563
Kusseroff, vol. ii. 22
Kutusoff, vol. i. 143, 240, 287

L.

Laity, vol. i. 76
Lamarmora, vol. iii. 385
Landsberg, vol. iii. 343
Landuski, vol. ii. 57
Lange, vol. ii. 353 ; vol. iii. 106,
   210, 255, 386
Lanterne, La, vol. i. 169
Lasker, vol. i. 7, 10, 12, 14, 28, 29,
   30, 33, 383 ; vol. ii. 86, 256,
   398, 424, 436, 454, 474 ; vol.
   iii. 3, 30, 35, 37, 38, 40, 301
Lassalle, vol. ii. 19 ; vol. iii. 342
Lauer, vol. i. 172, 243, 306, 371, 378,
   483 ; vol. iii. 56, 141

Laurier, vol. i. 409
Lavino, vol. ii. 432, 433
Lebœuf, vol. i. 271
Lecky, vol. iii. 121
Ledochowski, Archbishop, vol. i.
   292 ; vol. ii. 187, 200, 204, 278,
   287, 478
Leflô, vol. i. 550
Lehndorff, Count, vol. i. 106, 108,
   203, 328, 350, 367, 389, 420,
   444, 460, 492, 502, 541 ; vol. ii.
   367 ; vol. iii. 79, 233, 341, 349
Leibnitz, vol. i. 26
Leipsiger Zeitung, vol. ii. 375
Lemberg, Archbishop of, vol. ii. 200
Lemwitz, vol. ii. 147
Lenbach, vol. ii. 437, 440 ; vol. iii.
   155
Leonhard, vol. i. 14
Leopold, King of Belgians. See
   Belgium
Lepsius, vol. ii. 24
Lescinsky ; vol. iii. 207
Le Sourd, vol. i. 49
Lessing, vol. ii. 48
Leverström, vol. i. 149 ; vol. ii. 5,
   275
Lewascheff, vol. ii. 165, 169
Leyden, vol. ii. 387
Liberté, vol. i. 51, 252
Lindau, vol. ii. 206, 236, 237, 455,
   467 ; vol. iii. 9, 10, 41, 68, 145,
   231, 337, 341, 344, 356
Lindelhof, vol. ii. 89
Linstedt, vol. ii. 5
Lippe, vol. i. 28, 29, 400 ; vol. ii.
   187, 457, 461, 462
Lobanoff, vol. ii. 394
Lobkowitz, vol. ii. 221
Loewe, vol. i. 7, 388 ; vol. iii. 81
Loftus, vol. i. 343, 430, 454, 455,
   550 ; vol. ii. 43
Lonyay, vol. ii. 265
Löper, vol. i. 482, 486
Lorenz, vol. i. 65
Louis Philippe, vol. i. 37
Lowe, vol. ii. 432 ; vol. iii. 28
Löwenfeld, Gen., vol. i. 106
Löwensohn, vol. i. 266, 350, 398,
   399, 415
Löwenstein, vol. ii. 103, 318, 339
Lucanus, vol. iii. 364, 369
Ludolf, vol. ii. 197
Luitpold, Prince. See Bavaria
Lumsden, Sir P., vol. iii. 124
Lundy, vol. i. 319

Lutz, vol. i. 233, 431 ; vol. ii. 51, 121, 148, 221
Luxburg, Count, vol. i. 176
Luxemburg, Grand Duke of, vol. i. 515
   Prince Henry of, vol. ii. 151
Lynar, Prince, vol. i. 161
Lyons, Lord, vol. i. 182, 469

M.

M. L., vol. i. 198 to 202
Mackenzie, vol. iii. 303
MacLean, vol. i. 90, 96, 171
MacMahon, Marshal, vol. i. 126, 127, 151, 195 ; vol. ii. 76, 77, 94, 207, 258, 299, 300
Macore de Gaucourt, vol. i. 104
Magdeburger Zeitung, vol. i. 6 ; vol. ii. 196, 205, 293, 294
Magnin, vol. i. 526, 553, 555
Mailinger, Gen., vol. i. 146
Maire of Rheims, vol. i. 167
Maire of Versailles, vol. i. 265
Malet, Sir E., vol. i. 182, 238
Malinkrott, vol. i. 295
Malortie, vol. ii. 110
Maltzahn, Count, vol. i. 330, 466, 522
Manteuffel, vol. i. 256, 314, 315, 326, 334, 417, 428, 447, 448, 450, 461, 482 ; vol. ii. 115, 318, 334, 338, 339, 457, 462 ; vol. iii. 23, 24, 25, 83, 86, 200, 201, 211, 215, 218 to 225, 262, 265, 288, 352, 362, 385
Mantey, vol. i. 497, 498 ; vol. ii. 240, 381
Marquart, vol. iii. 129
Marschall, vol. iii. 383, 384
Martin, vol. ii. 478
Marx, vol. i. 448
Massenbach, Baroness, vol. ii. 227
Matin, vol. iii. 191
Matthiote, vol. i. 84
Mauder, vol. ii. 133
May, vol. ii. 113
Maybach, vol. ii. 435, 471 ; vol. iii. 32, 93, 368
Mayer, vol. ii. 480
Mazzini, vol. i. 380 ; vol. ii. 17
Mecklenburg, G. Duke of, vol. i. 106, 127, 131, 143, 158, 170, 183, 495 ; vol. ii. 369
Mecklenburg-Strelitz, G. Duchess of, vol. ii. 115

Meding, vol. ii. 109, 110, 189, 190 ; vol. iii. 136
Meidam, Col., vol. i. 292
Meiningen, Duke of, vol. i. 272, 294, 403, 548
Melchers, vol. ii. 478
Mémorial Diplomatique, vol. i. 18 ; vol. ii. 378
Mendelssohn, vol. i. 404
Mengerssen, vol. ii. 111
Mensdorff, vol. iii. 88, 250 to 252
Merck, vol. iii. 246, 370, 383, 384, 386, 388
Mermillod, vol. ii. 166, 269, 276
Metternich, vol. i. 32, 225, 304, 366, 370, 518 ; vol. ii. 132, 180
Metzler, vol. i. 1, 2, 238 ; vol. iii. 43, 164
Meulan, vol. ii. 43
Mexico, vol. i. 59, 187, 283
Meyendorff, vol. i. 420
Meyer, vol. iii. 112, 239
Meyerbeim, vol. i. 404 ; vol. ii. 382
Michaelis, vol. ii. 193, 386
Miguel, vol. i. 7 ; vol. ii. 437
Milutin, vol. iii. 259, 282, 283, 284, 286
Mirbach v., vol. ii. 75
Mittnacht, vol. i. 233, 524, 562, 563 ; vol. ii. 148, 227 ; vol. iii. 33, 37, 293
Mohl, vol. i. 220 ; vol. iii. 203
Möllendort, Gen., vol. i. 315, 316
Müller, vol. iii. 82, 89
Moltke, vol. i. 87, 97, 103, 104, 141, 143, 146, 147, 148, 150, 151, 153, 155, 156, 164, 181, 195, 196, 226, 254, 255, 270, 287, 349, 350, 371, 405, 458, 466, 505, 506, 533 ; vol. ii. 74, 75, 136, 162, 292, 326, 340, 381 ; vol. iii. 56, 207, 265, 271, 272, 325, 325, 354
Mommsen, vol. ii. 481 ; vol. iii. 65
Monbrisson, vol. i. 326
Moniteur, vol. i. 371, 379, 383, 414, 419, 433, 462, 483, 484, 486, 548, 553, 557, 560
Moniteur Official de Seine et Oise, vol. i. 271
Montagszeitung, vol. ii. 223, 224
Monteglas, vol. iii. 229
Montholon, vol. ii. 154
Montpensier, Duc de, vol. i. 18, 37, 41, 80, 483

Morier, Sir R., vol. ii. 138; vol. iii. 303
Morning Post, vol. i. 283; vol. iii. 7
Morny, vol. i. 503
Moscowa, Prince de la, vol. i. 153, 161
Motley, vol. iii. 320
Mouchy, vol. i. 561
Moustier, vol. i. 353; vol. iii. 385
Muffling, vol. ii. 392
Mühler, vol. ii. 226
Müller, Max, vol. ii. 273, 308; vol. iii. 43
Munch-Bellinghausen, vol. i. 208
Münchener Nachrichten, vol. iii. 43
Münchener Volksboten, vol. i. 248
Münster, vol. ii. 422; vol. iii. 118, 120, 133, 154, 325, 326
Munzer, vol. i. 241
Murat, vol. i. 46
Musurus, vol. i. 512

N.

Nanczonowski, vol. ii. 231
Napier, vol. i. 343; vol. iii. 249
Napoleon I., vol. i. 36, 42, 43, 420
Napoleon III., vol. i. 33, 45 to 47, 52, 58, 59, 61 to 63, 70, 103, 104, 133, 146, 147, 149, 150, 153, 154, 156, 159, 161, 164, 165, 169, 172, 184, 187, 189, 244, 252, 253, 256, 265, 271, 272, 285, 311, 313, 321, 322, 331, 341, 343, 407, 420, 490, 501, 503, 512, 535, 543, 554, 556, 557, 558; vol. ii. 43, 81, 90, 101, 103, 105, 116, 125, 138, 140, 141, 142, 156, 158, 337; vol. iii. 134, 381
Jerome, Prince, vol. i. 107, 439, 443; vol. ii. 33, 159, 216
Louis, Prince Imperial, vol. i. 107, 169, 283
Nathusius, vol. ii. 278
National Zeitung, vol. i., 8, 15, 16, 54, 65, 186, 187, 356, 436, 544, 546; vol. ii. 1, 17, 19, 20, 47, 86, 97, 155, 158, 161, 195, 234, 292, 379, 388, 484; vol. iii. 11, 31, 43, 115, 252
Nazione, vol. ii. 213
Neininger, vol. i. 350
Nemours, Duc de, vol. i. 37
Nesselrode, vol. ii. 278; vol. iii. 49, 218

Neue Freie Presse, vol. i. 83, 326; vol. iii. 188, 189
Neue Preussische Zeitung, vol. i. 5
New York Tribune, vol. ii. 354
New York World, vol. i. 90
Nicholas, Tsar. See Russia
Niethammer, vol. i. 355; vol. ii. 217
Nippold, vol. iii. 43
Nobling, vol. iii. 32, 56
Noeldeke, vol. i. 113
Norddeutsche Allgemeine Zeitung, vol. i. 5, 16, 17, 29, 31 to 34, 38, 48, 55, 60, 243, 244, 266, 334; vol. ii. 48, 50, 74, 86, 88, 99, 104, 106, 124, 137, 164, 175, 176, 195, 198, 202, 211, 232, 234, 251, 252, 374, 414, 477; vol. iii. 4, 6, 7, 35, 42, 46, 61, 73, 74, 115, 122, 124, 188, 315
North American Review, vol. ii. 441
North German Gazette, vol. i. 6
Nostitz-Wallwitz, vol. i. 207, 475, 476, 477
Nouvelliste, vol. i. 266, 269, 271

O.

Obermueller, vol. ii. 120
Obernitz, vol. iii. 112
Obrutscheff, vol. ii. 409
Obstfelder, vol. i. 209
O'Donovan, vol. iii. 119, 121, 125, 130
Oertzen, vol. i. 206
Ohlen, vol. iii. 106, 109
Okolowitch, vol. ii. 55, 57.
Oldberg, vol. i. 85
Oldenburg, G. Duke of, vol. i. 403; vol. iii. 332
Oldenburg, Peter, Prince of, vol. ii. 72
Ollivier, vol. i. 343, 372, 383, vol. ii. 144
Oppenheim, vol. ii. 339
Orloff, vol. ii. 43, 159, 165
Orloff, Princess, vol. i. 244
Orlowski, vol. ii. 222
Oubril, vol. ii. 43

P.

Paine, Thomas, vol. i. 241
Palikao, vol. i. 428, 513
Pall Mall Gazette, vol. i. 121; vol. iii. 6

Palmerston, Lord, vol. ii. 18, 339 ; vol. iii. 177
Pape, v. vol. ii. 75, 333
Paris, Archbishop of, vol. ii. 60, 69
Paris, Comte de, vol. i. 269 ; vol. ii. 207
Patkowski, vol. iii. 230
Patow, vol. ii. 457
Patrizzi, vol. ii. 212
Pays, vol. i. 268
Perglas, Pergler v., vol. i. 281
Perier, vol. ii. 130, 131, 165, 199
Pernay, vol. i. 110
Perponcher, vol. i. 110, 224, 303, 495 ; vol. ii. 369
Perseveranza, vol. ii. 380
PERSIA, vol. iii. 284
Persigny, vol. i. 283, 417, 424, 428, 439
Pester Lloyd, vol. ii. 106, 107, 183
Petersburger Zeitung, vol. ii. 391
Phelps, vol. iii. 383, 384
Phelps (Miss), vol. iii. 383
Philippsborn, vol. ii. 219, 401, 416
Picard, vol. i. 290, 553
Pietri, vol. ii. 59
Pindter, vol. ii. 414
Platen, vol. ii. 154
Plater, vol. ii. 49, 163
Pless, Prince, vol. i. 116, 318, 319, 330, 389, 390, 396, 397, 466
Princess, vol. ii. 367
Pobedonoszeff, vol. iii. 149
Podbielski, vol. i. 315, 508 ; vol. ii. 384
Podlewski, vol. ii. 126
POLAND, vol. i. 34, 257, 382, 411, 412; vol. ii. 49, 55, 57, 126, 128, 136, 147, 150, 157, 163 to 165, 173, 192, 200, 201, 348, 371 ; vol. iii. 37, 44, 160, 205, 224
Archd. Karl Ludwig, vol. ii. 200
Politz, vol. iii. 156
Pope, the, vol. i. 12, 18, 19, to 23, 26, 213, 214, 215, 251, 293, 294, 295, 296, 303, 336, 417, 431, 457 ; vol. ii. 88, 102, 127, 141, 142, 144, 146, 166, 167, 171, 172, 180, 183, 191, 192, 193, 195, 196, 204, 205, 212, 213, 214, 219, 270, 271, 272, 273, 301, 304, 305, 309, 310, 369, 383, 419, 424, 425, 437, 439, 476, 477 ; vol. iii. 6, 41, 49, 91, 95, 97, 153, 162, 163, 167, 198, 291, 378
PORTUGAL, vol. ii. 122, 192, 213

Poschinger, vol. iii. 11, 60, 64, 71, 86, 105, 340, 342
Post, vol. ii. 289, 290, 296, 376, 463 ; vol. iii. 12, 61, 81, 319
Pourtales, vol. i. 256 ; vol. iii. 45
Pouyer-Quertier, vol. ii. 73, 94, 95
Précurseur, vol. ii. 162
Presse, vol. i. 436
Preussische Jahrbücher, vol. i. 3 ; vol. ii. 123, 481
Price, vol. iii. 3, 5
Prim, vol. i. 38, 43, 44, 45, 52, 264, 265 ; vol. iii. 378, 381
Primker, vol. iii. 63, 73 to 75
Prokesch, vol. i. 373, 374, 542 ; vol. iii. 223
Provincial-Correspondenz, vol. i. 15, 413 ; vol. ii. 124
Prussia, Charles, Prince of, vol. i. 127, 143, 165, 249, 287, 338, 402 ; vol. ii. 279, 369, 404, 405, 418 ; vol. iii. 321
Queen of. See German Empress.
Frederick Charles, Prince of, vol. i. 61, 181, 265, 300, 414 ; vol. ii. 75, 125 ; vol. iii. 321
Henry, Prince of, vol. iii. 331, 335
Victoria, Princess of, vol. iii. 171 to 174, 184, 185
Przemysl, vol. ii. 200
Pückler, Count, vol. i. 110, 143, 272
Puffka, vol. ii. 120
Punch, vol. iii. 351, 356
Putbus, Prince, vol. i. 233, 320, 341, 374, 376, 377, 396, 397, 398, 422, 485, 541 ; vol. ii. 256
Puttkammer, vol. iii. 65, 173, 358

Q

Quadt, vol. ii. 80
Quehl, vol. iii. 215, 219, 223, 225

R

Rabe, vol. ii. 457
Raczunski, vol. iii. 335
Radolinski, vol. iii. 334
Radowitz, vol. i. 136, 367, 535 ; vol. ii. 165, 197, 198, 254, 296, 342, 402, 415, 416, 445, 446, 448 ; vol. iii. 44, 94, 211

INDEX

Radziwill, Prince, vol. i. 214, 215, 233, 311, 352; vol. ii. 4, 170, 244, 269, 278, 299
Rahden, vol. i. 94
Rameau, vol. i. 240, 497, 498
Rantzau, Count, vol. ii. 371, 457, 458, 459, 463; vol. iii. 9, 13, 15, 60, 61, 64, 92, 103, 104, 106, 109, 112, 157, 192, 193, 199
— Countess, vol. i. 64; vol. ii. 281 to 283, 335, 359; vol. iii. 112, 202, 298, 312, 379, 381, 382, 383, 388
Rasch, vol. i. 53, 54; vol. ii. 79, 118
Raschdau, vol. iii. 341, 344
Ratibor, Duke of, vol. i. 233, 553
Rauch, vol. iii. 110
Rechberg, Count, vol. i. 205, 206, 207, 373; vol. ii. 367; vol. iii. 34, 221
Rechenberg, vol. i. 20
Reichsanzeiger, vol. ii. 22, 124; vol. iii. 193
Reichscorrespondenz, vol. ii. 247
Reichsglocke, vol. ii. 288, 304, 479; vol. iii. 96, 117
Reille, Gen., vol. i. 147, 148, 153, 321, 331
Reinhard, vol. i. 208, 542
Reitlinger, vol. i. 443
Remusat, vol. ii. 134
Renard, Count, vol. i. 103
République Française, vol. ii. 249, 254
Retzow, vol. ii. 186, 187
Reuss, vol. i. 21, 94, 97, 386, 413, 444; vol. ii. 216, 218; vol. iii. 143, 273, 275, 289, 384
Reute, vol. iii. 144
Reuter, vol. i. 447
Revue des deux Mondes, vol. i. 376, 414; vol. ii. 46, 189
Reymond, vol. iii. 165
Reynier, vol. i. 219
Rheinbaben, vol. iii. 145
Ribeaupierre, vol. i. 491
Rice, vol. ii. 441
Richter, vol. ii. 385, 471, 474, 483; vol. iii. 40, 132, 162, 379
Rickert, vol. ii. 422, 423, 424, 436, 453, 454
Rilvas, vol. ii. 122
Rimsky-Korsakow, Mme., vol. i. 32
Rink, vol. i. 193
Rio, del, vol. i. 487, 488, 497
Rios Rosas, vol. i. 80

Rittberg, vol. ii, 457
Robespierre, vol. i. 383
Rochefort, vol. i. 169
Rochow, vol. i. 207, 502; vol. ii. 462
Rodbertus, vol. ii. 19; vol. iii. 342
Roemer, vol. ii. 387
Roessler, Prof., vol. i. 6, 65; vol. ii. 188, 189
Rogge, vol. i. 404
Roggenbach, vol. i. 233, 355, 356, 359; vol. iii. 196, 247, 299
Rohlfs, vol. iii. 144, 145
Rohrschuetz, vol. ii. 139
Roland, vol. i. 63, 213; vol. ii. 11, 143, 407
Rollin, vol. ii, 17
Roncière, vol. i. 513
Roon, Gen., vol. i. 66, 69, 130, 143, 146, 196, 226, 255, 302, 306, 345, 390, 405; vol. ii. 162, 229, 231, 340; vol. iii. 322
Rosebery, Lord, vol. iii. 135, 136, 144, 343
Rosen, vol. ii. 181, 197, 198
Rosenberg-Grudcinski, vol. i. 496
Rossel, vol. ii. 69
Rössler, vol. ii. 172, 376
Rothlan, vol. i. 55; vol. iii. 378
Rothschild, vol. i. 104, 183, 193, 194, 195, 224, 225, 271, 341, 445, 446, 514, 518; vol. iii. 39, 62, 68, 233
Rottenburg, vol. ii. 360, 361; vol. iii. 7, 136, 157, 166, 169, 170, 173, 184, 186, 191 to 193 205, 206, 208, 209, 212, 230 to 232, 255, 296, 303, 304, 306, 307, 312, 315, 318, 338, 382
Rudchen, vol. iii. 344, 356
Rudhard, vol. ii. 134
Ruestow, vol. ii. 135
RUMANIA, vol. i. 439, 452, 453; vol. ii. 129, 395; vol. iii. 58, 80, 181, 281
— Charles, Prince, afterwards King of, vol. i. 439, 452, 453, 550, 555; vol. ii. 4, 129
Rumbold, Sir H., vol. ii. 43
RUMELIA, vol. iii. 148, 149, 181, 259, 280
Russell, Odo, vol. i. 233, 327, 337, 341, 342, 343, 353, 371, 384, 420, 500, 534, 535; vol. iii. 120, 213, 326
Russell, W. H., vol. i. 244, 245

INDEX

RUSSIA, vol. i. 22, 31, 112, 179, 185, 203, 224, 252, 272, 312, 317, 328, 329, 334, 358, 386, 413, 415, 417, 440, 457, 463, 468, 477, 495, 503, 504, 510, 512, 515 ; vol. ii. 136, 137, 148, 157, 159, 165, 166, 173, 174, 181, 182, 187, 190, 196, 201, 204, 214, 215, 237, 248, 250, 297 to 299, 318, 333, 386, 392, 393, 396, 397, 404, 405, 408, 411, 430, 431, 450, 476, 482 ; vol. iii. 5, 45, 48, 52, 53, 76, 77, 84, 85, 119, 121, 124, 133, 138, 149, 150, 159, 160, 161, 170, 179, 180, 182, 206, 213, 217, 226, 227, 234, 258 to 292, 302, 354, 366, 367

Grand Duchess Hélène of, vol. i. 112, 560 ; vol. ii., 43, 69, 70 ; vol. iii. 9, 10

Grand Duke Nicholas of, vol. ii. 218

Prince Alexander of, vol. ii. 218

Prince Wladimir of, vol. ii. 218

Tsar, The, vol. i. 99, 112, 178, 180, 316, 317, 327, 331, 340, 358, 385, 453, 560 ; vol. ii. 42, 43, 69, 70, 72, 82, 95, 125, 135, 141, 148, 169, 190, 216, 217, 219, 333, 392, 393, 395 ; vol. iii. 49, 138, 139, 149, 159, 175, 180 to 184, 219, 234, 313, 314, 376

S

Saburoff, vol. iii. 265, 270, 274
Sachse, vol. ii. 365, 430, 434, 457 ; vol. iii. 16, 33, 50, 75, 89
Saeshsische Zeitung, vol. ii. 120
St. Blanquart, vol. i. 71, 87, 511
St. Simon, vol. ii. 83
St. Vallier, vol. ii. 120, 168
Salazar, vol. iii. 114
Saldern, von, vol. i. 344
Salisbury, Lord, vol. iii. 143
Samuel, vol. ii. 222
Samwer, vol. i. 140 ; vol. ii. 306 ; vol. iii. 249
Saphir, vol. iii. 233
Sapieha, vol. ii. 147
Sauer, vol. i. 431
Savigny, vol. i. 170, 243, 547 ; vol. ii. 14, 44, 45, 326 ; vol. iii. 39, 96, 156, 225

Saxony, Crown Prince of, vol. i. 477 ; vol. ii. 326
Saxony, Dowager Queen of, vol. i. 440
Saxony, King of, vol. i. 109, 175, 528 ; vol. ii. 324 ; vol. iii. 225, 332, 384
Saxony, Prince George of, vol. ii. 455
Schaeffle, vol. ii. 113
Schapira, vol. iii. 68
Scheibler, vol. iii. 303, 306, 318, 338
Scheidtmann, vol. i. 532, 554
Schelling, vol. iii. 192
Schiller, vol. i. 138 ; vol. ii. 185
Schleinitz, vol. i. 256 ; vol. ii. 269, 274, 277, 289, 302 to 304, 318, 339 ; vol. iii. 22, 25, 59, 83, 164, 213, 228, 229, 247, 302, 352
Schlesische Hans Blätter, vol. i. 246
Schlesische Zeitung, vol. ii. 261 ; vol. iii. 7
SCHLESWIG-HOLSTEIN, vol. i. 83 ; vol. ii. 33, 152, 337 ; vol. iii. 40
Schloetzer, vol. ii. 22
Schlotheim, vol. ii. 76
Schlözer, vol. ii. 402
Schmidt, vol. i. 340
Schneider, vol. ii. 421 ; vol. iii. 205, 302
Scholz, vol. iii. 93
Schorlemer, vol. iii. 312
Schrader, vol. iii. 186
Schraps, vol. ii. 57
Schrenkh, vol. i. 207
Schuckmann, 370, 490
Schulenberg, vol. i. 28 ; vol. iii. 225
Schulte, vol. ii. 119
Schulze, vol. ii. 281 ; vol. iii. 257
Schuster, vol. i. 350
Schuvaloff, vol. ii. 201, 203, 204, 209, 216, 395 ; vol. iii. 366
Schwäbische Merkur, vol. i. 166; vol. ii. 224
Schwarzburg, Prince, vol. i. 104
Schwarzenberg, vol. ii. 179, 180 ; vol. iii. 19, 218
Schwarzkoppen, vol. i. 561
Schweinitz, vol. ii. 81, 83, 173, 182 ; vol. iii. 49, 233, 383
Schweninger, vol. iii. 106, 108, 109, 139, 148, 173, 200, 210, 233, 317, 319, 337, 341, 342, 344, 346, 347, 356, 371, 373, 375, 379, 381, 386.
Schwerin, vol. iii. 354

INDEX

Seckendorf, Count, vol. i. 113; vol. iii. 224
Seidal, vol. iii. 23
Selchow, vol. iii. 234
Senfft-Pilsach, vol. ii. 187, 332; vol. iii. 19. 128
SERVIA, vol. ii. 197, 198; vol. iii. 148
Sheridan, Gen., vol. i. 90, 91, 96, 98, 103, 121, 131, 132, 143, 171, 223, 250
Sick, vol. ii. 149
Siemens, vol. ii. 22
Simon, vol. i. 553; vol. ii. 302
Simson, vol. i. 233, 387, 400, 403, 446
Situation, La, vol. i. 197; vol. ii. 109
Skobeleff, vol. iii. 49
Smolka, vol. ii. 147
Solms, Count, vol. i. 38, 159, 428; vol. ii. 28, 123, 415; vol. iii. 193, 194, 199
Sonnemann, vol. ii. 480
SOUTH AFRICA, vol. iii. 120, 124, 125, 132, 144, 145, 153, 154, 313
SPAIN, vol. i. 22, 34 to 48, 80, 155, 178, 226, 249, 264, 313, 382, 477, 527; vol. ii. 182, 192, 213; vol. iii. 153, 381
  Hohenzollern candidature, 35 to 52, 63, 483; vol. ii. 76, 122
  King of, 518, 534
  Queen Isabella of, vol. i. 36, 37, 41
Spenersche Zeitung, vol. i. 5, 10, 32, 41, 42, 43, 48, 58, 60, 363, 432; vol. ii. 106, 161, 256; vol. iii. 252
Staatsanzeiger, vol. i. 6, 277; vol. ii. 197
Staatsbuergerzeitung, vol. i. 426
Stampf, Anastasia, vol. i. 94
Standard, The, vol. i. 198; vol. ii. 47, 448
Stauffenberg, vol. iii. 30
Stein, vol. i. 294
Steinmetz, Gen., vol. i. 77, 85, 95, 98, 394, 420
Stephan, vol. i. 170; vol. ii. 425, 432
Stepki, vol. i. 502
Sternsche Correspondenz, vol. ii. 124
Stieber, vol. i. 103, 118, 119, 269, 487, 498, 519; vol. ii. 27, 120, 121

Stieglitz, vol. i. 411
Stiehle, vol. i. 518
Stillfried, vol. i. 359; vol. ii. 278
Stirum, vol. ii. 22, 402; vol. iii. 128, 341
Stocker, vol. iii. 16
Stockmar, vol. iii. 42, 43, 178, 186, 239
Stoffel, Col., vol. i. 51, 53
Stofflet, vol. i. 295
Stolberg, Count, vol. i. 318; vol. ii. 273, 412; vol. iii. 164, 264, 265, 267, 275, 276, 334
Stolle, vol. ii. 121
Stosch, vol. i. 315, 486, 516, 551; vol. ii. 230, 270, 413, 421
Strantz, Capt. von, vol. i. 444
Strenavoukoff, vol. ii. 147
Strossmayer, vol. i. 26, 27
Strousberg, vol. i. 502, 553
Stumm, vol. ii. 117; vol. iii. 341
Stupny, vol. ii. 57
Suckow, vol. i. 190, 524; vol. ii. 168
Süddeutsche Post, vol. iii. 68
  Presse, vol. ii. 123
  Zeitung, vol. iii. 238
Sulzer, vol. ii. 457
SWEDEN, vol. i. 54, 477, 552; vol. ii. 43, 153 to 155
  Charles, King of, vol. i. 257, 439, 525; vol. ii. 43, 151, 152, 153, 155, 156, 158, 159, 164
  Oscar, Prince of, vol. ii. 154, 159
SWITZERLAND, vol. i. 9, 62, 177, 479; vol. ii. 51, 69, 110, 139, 272; vol. iii. 5, 214, 272
Sybel, vol. iii. 10, 11, 64, 303, 314, 385

T

Tageblatt, Berliner, vol. ii. 477; vol. iii. 7, 9, 15
  Deutsches, vol. ii. 484; vol. iii. 42, 62, 68, 74, 184
  Leipziger, vol. i. 444
  Wiener, vol. i. 432
Taglioni, Councillor, vol. i. 85, 192, 563; vol. iii. 14, 93
Taine, vol. iii. 41, 42, 47
Tann, vol. i. 111, 332, 334
Tarnassi, vol. iii. 49
Tarnau, vol. ii. 200
Tauffkirchen, vol. ii. 102, 103, 127, 212

Tettau, vol. ii. 462
Thadden, vol. i. 224, 350 ; vol. iii. 105, 128
Theiss, vol. i. 308, 427 ; vol. ii. 280, 381, 399, 425 ; vol. iii. 32, 75, 173, 183
The Times, vol. i. 17, 244, 350, 378, 379, 447, 550 ; vol. ii. 28, 84, 159, 298, 378, 380, 383, 394, 395, 432, 433, 442 ; vol. iii. 120, 122, 132, 134, 180, 184, 238
Thibaudin, vol. iii. 92
Thiers, vol. i. 103, 231, 252, 269, 271, 275, 276, 281, 282, 283, 284, 285, 286, 287, 288, 289, 290, 292, 299, 301, 477, 488, 556, 557, 558, 561 ; vol. ii. 56, 57, 63, 65, 67, 71, 90, 94, 95, 103, 104, 129, 130, 132, 159, 165, 166, 181, 187, 199, 207, 208, 222, 235, 236, 250, 414
Thile, vol. i. 38, 61, 243, 457 ; vol. ii. 75, 111, 113, 219, 252, 253, 266, 284, 400, 401, 406 ; vol. iii. 12, 13, 38, 39, 43, 46, 49, 50, 134
Thuengen, vol. i. 396
Thun, vol. i. 370 ; vol. ii. 112, 120
Tiedemann, vol. ii. 315, 316, 333, 407, 429, 431, 440, 477 ; vol. iii. 7
Tilly, Col., vol. i. 324
Tims, vol. ii. 369
Tissier, Col., vol. i. 433
Tissot, vol. i. 469
Tolstoi, vol. ii. 204
Topete, vol. i. 80
Tornau, V., vol. ii. 190
Torre, de la, vol. ii. 162
Trautmansdort, vol. i. 18, 30
Treitschke, H., vol. i. 182, 340, 386, 466
Treskow, vol. i. 97, 204, 315, 557
Tribune (Berlin), vol. ii. 302, 304
Trochu, vol. i. 265, 285, 290, 326, 356, 365, 371, 383, 408, 414, 415, 429, 466, 484, 488; vol. ii. 101
Tsar. *See* Russia.
TURKEY, vol. i. 329, 386, 417, 512; vol. ii. 46, 124, 165, 197, 248, 250, 297, 333, 339, 456; vol. iii. 45, 51, 52, 53, 62, 68, 74, 75, 80, 133, 160, 277, 278, 282, 284, 327

U.

Ujest, vol. iii. 79
Ungarn-Sternberg, vol. i. 65
Unger, Gen. von, vol. i. 418
Union, The, vol. i. 247, 249
UNITED STATES, the. *See* America.
Unruh, 459 ; vol. iii. 20 to 31, 33, 34
Urezzana, vol. iii. 289
Urquhart, vol. ii. 17
Usedom, vol. iii. 226, 354
Uslar, vol. i. 486

V

Valden, vol. i. 511, 512
Vallon, vol. ii. 97, 98
Van Zuylen, vol. i. 86, 413
Varennes, vol. ii. 250
Varnbüler, vol. ii. 148, 149
Varnhagen, vol. i. 369
Vaterland, vol. ii. 120, 121
Vatican. *See* Pope
Vaubert, vol. i. 153
Verdy, Major, vol. i. 97, 340, 349
Verrier, Comm., vol. i. 439
Versen, vol. iii. 383
Victor Emmanuel. *See* Italy
Victoria, Queen. *See* England
Viereck, vol. iii. 68
Villiard, vol. i. 394, 395
Vincent, vol. ii. 76
Vincke, vol. i. 29 ; vol. iii. 247
Vincy, vol. i. 271
Vinoy, vol. i. 383, 443, 488, 513
Virchow, vol. ii. 471 ; vol. iii. 13, 56, 65, 164, 165
Visconti-Venosta, vol. iii. 156
Vogt, vol. iii. 92
Voigt-Rhetz, vol. i. 216, 264, 418, 485
Volkszeitung, vol. i. 168, 173, 361, 505 ; vol. ii. 96 ; vol. iii. 61, 68, 213, 214
Vossische Zeitung, vol. i. 14, 282, 335 ; vol. ii. 379 ; vol. iii. 7, 9

W

Wächter, vol. i. 233, 562 ; vol. ii. 80
Wagener, vol. i. 428, 437, 442, 477 ; vol. iii. 342

Wagner, vol. i. 71 ; vol. ii. 206, 256 ; vol. iii. 220, 221
Wagner, Richard, vol. ii. 169
Waldeck, vol. i. 525, 535 ; vol. ii. 15 ; vol. iii. 141
Waldersee, Count, vol. i. 106, 107, 257, 258, 310, 425, 432 ; vol. ii. 84, 93, 94, 95, 103, 116, 117 ; vol. iii. 207, 370
Walker, Col., vol. i. 143, 330
Wallenberg, vol. iii. 112
Walujeff, vol. ii. 43
Warren, Sir C., vol. iii. 124, 145
Wartensleben, Count, vol. i. 71 ; vol. ii. 28, 71, 73, 211 ; vol. iii. 14
Wartsdorf, vol. i. 259
Washburne, vol. i. 413, 526 ; vol. ii. 46, 92
Weber, vol. ii. 473
Wedell, vol. i. 94, 344
Wedemeyer, vol. iii. 117
Wehrenpfenig, vol. ii. 473
Wehrmann, vol. i. 34
Weimar, Grand Duke of, vol. i. 143, 146, 158, 159, 168, 181, 217, 219, 257, 258, 282, 327, 331, 332, 397, 403, 562 ; vol. ii. 44 ; vol. iii. 332
  Grand Duchess of, vol. i. 181
  Princess of, vol. ii. 185
Weimar Zeitung, vol. ii. 295
Welti, vol. ii. 139.
Werder, Gen., vol. i. 313, 316, 317, 482
Werle, vol. i. 173
Werther, vol. i. 360, 465, 490, 561 ; vol. ii. 123, 142, 143 ; vol. iii. 225
Wesdehlen, vol. i. 94
Weser Zeitung, vol. i. 259, 260, 335, 356 ; vol. ii. 196, 205, 206 ; vol. iii. 374
Widell-Malchoff, vol. iii. 79
Wiehr, vol. i. 71, 225
Wiersbycki (Corvin), vol. iii. 68
William II. *See* German Emperor
Willisch, vol. i. 71, 120, 165, 183, 511 ; vol. ii. 37

Wilmowski, vol. ii. 432
Wimpffen, Gen, vol. i. 151, 152, 153, 157, 163
Wimpffen, vol. i. 278
Windthorst, vol. i. 390 ; vol. ii. 160, 172, 173 ; vol. iii. 37, 91, 156, 162, 163, 312, 318, 354, 360, 376
Winter, vol. i. 475, 476
Winterfeldt, vol. i. 274
Witkowski, vol. ii. 222 ; vol. iii. 383
Wittgenstein, vol. i. 240, 352
Wolf's Telegraphic Agency, vol. i, 48, 56, 557 ; vol. ii. 22
Wolfssohn, vol. ii. 436
Wollmann, Sec., vol. i. 45, 71, 324, 326, 400, 403, 463, 478, 480, 481, 563; vol. ii. 1, 2, 45, 72, 111, 123, 162, 233, 255
Wolseley, Lord, vol. iii. 131.
Wolzoger, vol. iii. 225
Wrangel, vol. i. 183
Wurmb, 203
Würtemberg, King of, 524 ; vol. ii 80, 119, 133, 168, 227 ; vol. iii. 332
  Prince W. of, 403
  Queen of, vol. i. 168, 227
Wuttke, vol. ii. 96

Y.

York, Count, vol. i. 169 ; vol. ii. 244
Yussupoff, vol. i. 224

Z

Zabel, vol. ii. 195
ZANZIBAR, vol. iii. 144, 154, 353
Zichy, vol. iii. 83
Ziemialkowski, vol. ii. 2·0
Zitelmann, vol. i. 27 ; vol. iii. 238, 239
Zur Geschichte der Internationale, vol. ii. 86

THE END.

www.ingramcontent.com/pod-product-compliance
Lightning Source LLC
Chambersburg PA
CBHW030604300426
44111CB00009B/1099